T0003798

SCARS
AND
STRIPES

SCARS
AND
STRIPES

AN UNAPOLOGETICALLY
AMERICAN STORY OF FIGHTING THE
TALIBAN, UFC WARRIORS, AND MYSELF

TIM KENNEDY
AND NICK PALMISCIANO

ATRIA PAPERBACK
New York   London   Toronto   Sydney   New Delhi

An Imprint of Simon & Schuster, Inc.
1230 Avenue of the Americas
New York, NY 10020

First Atria Paperback edition January 2024

ATRIA PAPERBACK and colophon are trademarks of Simon & Schuster, Inc.

Simon & Schuster: Celebrating 100 Years of Publishing in 2024

For information about special discounts for bulk purchases, please contact Simon & Schuster Special Sales at 1-866-506-1949 or business@simonandschuster.com.

The Simon & Schuster Speakers Bureau can bring authors to your live event. For more information, or to book an event, contact the Simon & Schuster Speakers Bureau at 1-866-248-3049 or visit our website at www.simonspeakers.com.

Interior design by Jill Putorti

Manufactured in the United States of America

1 3 5 7 9 10 8 6 4 2

Library of Congress Cataloging-in-Publication Data

Names: Kennedy, Tim, 1979– author. | Palmisciano, Nick, author.
Title: Scars and stripes : an unapologetically American story of fighting the Taliban, UFC warriors, and myself / Tim Kennedy with Nick Palmisciano.
Other titles: Unapologetically American story of fighting the Taliban, UFC warriors, and myself
Description: First Atria Books hardcover edition. | New York : Atria Books, 2022.
Identifiers: LCCN 2022001567 (print) | LCCN 2022001568 (ebook) | ISBN 9781982190910 (hardcover) | ISBN 9781982190927 (paperback) | ISBN 9781982190934 (ebook)
Subjects: LCSH: Kennedy, Tim, 1979– | Afghan War, 2001—Personal narratives, American. | Afghan War, 2001—Commando operations—United States. | United States. Army. Special Forces—Biography. | Mixed martial arts—United States—Biography. | Television personalities—United States—Biography. | Afghan War, 2001—Veterans—United States—Biography.
Classification: LCC DS371.413 .K455 2022 (print) | LCC DS371.413 (ebook) | DDC 958.104/742092 [B]—dc23/eng/20220218
LC record available at https://lccn.loc.gov/2022001567
LC ebook record available at https://lccn.loc.gov/2022001568

ISBN 978-1-9821-9091-0
ISBN 978-1-9821-9092-7 (pbk)
ISBN 978-1-9821-9093-4 (ebook)

This book is dedicated to the men and women we have lost in the Twenty Years War.

In particular, I would like to dedicate it to the 660 Special Operations personnel we lost, and the last thirteen U.S. military personnel we lost at Hamid Karzai International Airport on 26 August 2021.

I will spend the rest of my days trying to be worthy of your sacrifice.

CONTENTS

INTRODUCTION

My name is Tim Kennedy, and I have a problem: I only feel alive when I'm about to die.

I've killed evil men on multiple continents, fought in main-event bouts in the UFC, served as a Green Beret, an EMT, a firefighter, and a cop. I've hunted Nazis, drug runners, Abu Musab al-Zarqawi, human traffickers, rhino poachers, Al Qaeda, the Taliban, wildebeests, elk, bears, and have the recipe for the perfect soufflé. I fly helicopters, jump out of airplanes, dive mixed gas to the ocean depths, wrestle bulls with my bare hands, lift heavy weights, blow things up, and am proficient in just about every weapon under the sun. I train warriors, own companies, serve my country—and I'm just getting warmed up.

But life hasn't been easy, and it sure as shit hasn't been perfect. On the surface, I make a pretty good Rambo, but the truth is for everything I've accomplished, I've screwed up a whole lot more. I don't mean that in the self-serving "my biggest fault is I work too hard" style. When I say I've hit rock bottom, I need you to understand I went for it *so hard* that if I were a car, I'd have no windows, doors, or fenders, and I'd be on fire . . . at the bottom of a ravine.

But as bad as it got (and it got really bad), *I've never quit.* I've been called a lot of things: the most dangerous man in the world, an elite fighter, a businessman, a dad, a husband, a hero, a villain, an SOB, and an arrogant asshole. There's probably truth to all of those things. But at the heart of it all, *I am a survivor.*

And that's what this book is about. It's about learning how to weather the storms, no matter how bad they are, and start making decisions to improve the situation and get yourself to a better place. And when I say "weather the storm," I don't mean that in a passive way. Sure, there's something to be said for enduring pain, but enduring that pain and not making any changes in your life until the pain subsides is pretty dumb.

You don't want to be dumb.

Your life only gets better when you do a few things:

1. Take accountability for it. It's your fault.
2. Failure is going to happen. When it does, see number 1. If you want to fail less, see numbers 3–7.
3. An ounce of prevention prevents a pound of cure. The best time to start preparing is right now.
4. You cannot mass-produce elite people. They need to be forged from hard experiences. If you want to be one of them, you need to seek these challenges consistently.
5. Take care of yourself physically, mentally, emotionally, and spiritually. For some people that means therapy. For some people that means yoga and a cup of tea or fishing with the family. For me that means embracing a constant struggle. Rejecting comfort makes me . . . well . . . comfortable.
6. Surround yourself with good people striving to also improve themselves.
7. Build goals and pursue them to the end of the earth.

No matter where you are in life, putting yourself on this path will change everything.

There are enough "guru" books out there already. I want to take you on a wild ride that literally zero other human beings have ever experienced.

I just turned forty-two. I've been selfish. I've been an asshole. I've made mistakes and I've been all too human. Twelve years ago this book would have been about how spectacular I am. That book would have sucked ass. Yeah it would have had its moments, but the last dozen years have been marred with failure and loss and gifted with growth, reflection, and hopefully, a little wisdom.

So why am I writing this book?

1. First and foremost, to tell you a hell of a story. And I won't sugarcoat it. I'm not out to make myself a hero, because I'm not one. I want to write nothing but the unvarnished truth. You'll get the good, the bad, and the ugly, and if you've ever seen my face, there's a lot of ugly.

2. To elevate all the people who have made a meaningful impact on my life. My rise to celebrity has a lot to do with being a fighter, which I don't rank very high on my list of accomplishments. Tim Kennedy the UFC star doesn't exist without all the men and women who have invested time in me along the way. And this isn't about giving shout-outs to my bros. Some of these people hate me because of the way I was when I knew them, but they made a profound impact.

3. To let you know there is always a path forward. There were many times in my life that if you just took a snapshot and read the bullet points of who I was and what was happening to me, you would have said, "What a loser!" And I was. But everyone is straight trash on their worst days. Life is about digging yourself out of those holes and doing something worthwhile, and serving something bigger than yourself. I wasn't born getting that. I had to suffer, and have it beat into my head over and over again, and even then, I had to almost die to finally understand. And I want people who are reading this thing, who feel like total losers with no way out, to see a path forward and get the fuck after it. I want them to start LIVING.

In these pages, I've gone out of my way to tell you the unfiltered truth. A lot of it was embarrassing to write. A lot of it doesn't paint me in the best light. Sometimes, I'm simply not the good guy. And as painful as it was to put on paper, it needed to happen this way. My public life tells a story of great, inspiring success. No one's public life is real. Life's messy. It's hard. And sometimes, even the best of us are total pieces of shit. I need to show it all to you in order for you to value any of it. I want you to know, to understand, to feel it in your bones, that no matter where you are in life right now, there is a pathway to get better. You can be more than you ever thought possible, but it will not be easy, and the pathway to success is not a straight line.

As I tell this story, please understand I have done so to the best of my recollection. Many of these stories happened a long time ago, under significant circumstances, and I have suffered a lot of head trauma. I did my absolute best to corroborate every single story in here, but the "fog of war" is a real phenomenon. As those of you who have been in combat or other traumatic situations know, four guys can be on the same ground at the same moment in time fighting the same enemy and remember very different things. Throughout the whole research process, I am thankful to report that all the important pieces of the story have been corroborated. Nevertheless, I'm certain my telling isn't perfect, and if there are people I have forgotten to include, or details I have omitted or changed, I apologize.

There are some names and details that I have changed. These do not affect the meat of any of the stories in this book, but they do protect critical aspects of national security and the lives of several people still doing good work.

Finally, I'm going to tell the story a little differently than most memoirs. I decided to write the whole thing in the first-person present tense. I don't want to tell you what *happened* to me. I want to immerse you in the crazy journey I have lived so you can *feel* each moment and each decision as I felt them. I want you to feel all the fear, failure, sadness, happiness, and success right along with me. That's the only way you can truly understand my journey and apply it to your own

I hope my story inspires you. I hope it changes your life.

It's been one wild ride thus far.

Hop in and let me show what I've seen.

CHAPTER ONE

THE CREEK GANG

I move quietly through the woods in standard fire team wedge formation. It's a balmy day, to say the least. The trees above us nearly block out
the sun, save for a few streaks of light that illuminate tiny pockets of the
forest floor, but the heat is relentless anyway, rolling in underneath the
leaves and hanging in the air like a thick blanket. It feels like I am sitting in a sauna. The only things missing are the old naked dudes and the
ability to leave. My skin feels dry, even though I can feel myself sweating
through my clothes. Nature is baking us and there is nothing I can do
about it. I push my discomfort to the back of my mind.

I have to stay focused.

People are counting on me.

I am the point man, meaning I am at the front of the movement.
Nick is behind me to my near left. Andrew Hackleman is behind me to
my near right. Both are set about five to ten meters away, depending on
how the terrain spreads us out. To my far left some twenty meters away
is Chad Koenig. David Gaddis is behind me in the team leader position,
controlling our movement as we parallel the creek that will bring us to
our objective.

This mission came down the pipe only twenty-four hours ago. This was the big one. High-value target. Dangerous man. Every unit, team, and agency in the region was looking for him, thus far to no avail. Now it was on us. We scoured the maps of the region as well as his last known location and, as we had been taught, developed several courses of action. All the other units were looking for him in the city or in the nearby towns.

That's not where we now hunted. We determined that he most likely would have moved from the city into the woodline at its outskirts, which was almost a jungle this time of year, and hidden himself in the deep bramble, walking the creek bed until he could disappear entirely or link up with someone who could help him escape.

We had spent the early morning making our last-minute preparations. We choked down our food, checked our packs, and readied our weapons. When we were satisfied with our pre-combat checks, we stepped off into the unknown as we had hundreds of times before. This was different, though—he was our biggest prey yet. There was a tinge of excitement (and yes a little fear), but as I looked to my right and left, there was no group I'd rather have with me as we once again crossed the Rubicon.

It was the second or third hour of our painstakingly quiet movement along the creek bed when I felt an uncanny change. The foliage transformed dramatically. Something wasn't right. It looked . . . planned. The natural brush had broken up and our walk was easier. The plants were now tall, lush, and green, and shaped like . . . marijuana.

Holy shit, we are walking through someone's secret pot field.

As I scan the horizon there is pot as far as the eye can see. Our crew seemed to register this all at the same time as we exchanged glances. Where there are drugs, there are drug dealers, and drug dealers tend to not like their product being messed with.

Now don't get me wrong. It isn't that I am necessarily worried. After all, I am with a badass group of pipe hitters who can handle anything that comes our way. The issue is that this giant field of weed added another problem. We don't care about the weed. We just don't want to have to deal with drug dealers *thinking* we care about their weed at the same time we're chasing our dangerous high-value target.

That thought leaves me as I hear a twig break in front of me. The hair on the back of my neck stands up. I give the hand signal to the team to freeze. My hands are clammy as I double-check the grip on my weapon. I hear another snap. Then another. Now I can see some movement twenty meters away in the field of weed. I can feel my adrenaline spiking. That fight-or-flight response is starting to set in. It washes over me as it has so many times before.

I motion to the team to follow me to the target and begin to cover the last twenty meters as quietly as possible. My heart is beating so hard I can see it moving through my shirt. I worry he will hear it and it will give away our position.

The boys are right behind me. They've moved into a tight wedge and we're almost shoulder to shoulder.

Suddenly a man seems to explode out of the weed field. He's unshaven, wearing a weird T-shirt, and is about two feet taller than I am. Honest to God, he's like if André the Giant and Charles Manson had a kid. He's the scariest goddamn thing I have ever seen in my entire life.

I scream out loud and drop my weapon. Before it hits the ground, I am already ten feet away from him at a full sprint. My team is right alongside me, also weaponless and scared shitless.

This is a good time to mention I am eleven years old. My brother Nick is thirteen. And the rest of our elite team, that my dad affectionately called the "Creek Gang," were also tweeners. The "weapon" I dropped ten feet back was a stick I had sharpened into a point. The giant dude who had just scared the ever-loving shit out of us was a guy who had just escaped a mental institution a few days ago and was considered dangerous. He was all over the news. The police had been looking for him nonstop. We found him.

We just weren't ready to find him.

We thought we were. Our CONOP (concept of operations) to find him had been perfect. Our analysis of the operational environment was spot on. Our tracking tactics were solid and our movement disciplined. We had even practiced how we would fight him when we found him.

But when the rubber hit the road, we learned the threat of real violence is a whole lot different than our imagined violence. The plan had been to subdue him with our spears. We practiced hitting each other's arms and legs and parrying potential fist or knife attacks. Then once we got him down, we were going to tie his hands up and march him back through the woods where we would deliver him to the police, winning acclaim for our heroics. To my eleven-year-old brain, that plan seemed not only reasonable but foolproof. But as Mike Tyson says, "Everyone has a plan until they get punched in the mouth."

But now, as I was seeing a green blur whizzing past my head on either side and getting hit with the occasional tree branch, the reality was that there was a little piss dribbling down my leg, and I was running faster than I had ever run in my entire life.

I learned right then and there that I had no mastery over violence or fear. I was pissed (no pun intended) and a little ashamed. I didn't want that kind of weakness in me.

In case you haven't figured this out yet, I'm an atypical dude, with atypical parents, and an atypical childhood. I don't exactly know how I ended up like this, but here's my closest guess as to the recipe that made me: To start, add three cups of "I grew up in the '80s." So, like many of you Gen X types, every day was an adventure. There were no cell phones. No helicopter parents. We left in the morning and came home when the streetlights came on. Then add two teaspoons of my mom, a highly educated, classically liberal woman who valued books, art, and dance. She'd probably fit best teaching at an elite East or West Coast college than anywhere else on the planet. Now, add three heaping tablespoons of my dad, an elite counternarcotics officer who literally was going up against Pablo Escobar on the daily at the peak of the War on Drugs. He had seen the worst in life and wanted his children to be tough, quick-thinking, and able to survive in any condition. He valued martial arts, gun work, and more risk taking than most parents would feel comfortable allowing. Finally, add one bucket of my insurmountable drive to prove I can do anything and you now have an idea of what makes me "me."

Where did that drive come from? My parents have a theory.

I was born with a bad heart. Specifically, I had a ventricular septal defect. Just in case everyone reading this book isn't a cardiologist, a ventricular septal defect is when you have a giant hole in the middle of your heart between the chamber that pumps out the good oxygenated blood and the chamber that pumps in the crappy unoxygenated blood that just ran through your entire body. So my good blood and my bad blood were always mixing, leaving my newborn body without enough oxygen. Basically, from zero to three I always had a bluish hue and did not look healthy. I had low energy. None of it was good. My mom and dad were faced with every parent's worst nightmare as the doctors floated the idea that I might not make it. The doctors expected to have to perform open-heart surgery to keep me alive, which is still dangerous now but in the '80s was a total crapshoot.

My parents had a choice. They could do the surgery now, and if all went well I'd live, albeit in a weaker state than the average person, or they could wait to see if I would heal on my own, knowing I might grow too weak to survive the delayed surgery and die.

My parents have tremendous faith. They wanted me to have a chance at a normal life. They postponed the surgery and asked their friends to take part in a prayer circle. Simultaneously, I was given a steroid that was meant to strengthen my heart (which I stayed on for years).

While Little Timmy remained blue and had 25 percent of the aerobic capacity of other kids his age, he apparently did not give a shit. I remember none of this, but I am told I was a force to be reckoned with. I started to walk at eight months. I began climbing out of my crib, unfazed by the fall to the floor after getting my stubby legs over the top. At eighteen months, when I saw my older brother swimming in our pool, I just jumped in, also wanting to swim. When I sank and was pulled out by my father, I grew angry and jumped in again. In fact, my first memory is of being underwater, sinking, looking up at my father through the blurry lens of the pool water. He let me stay in the drink . . . for a bit.

For most people that memory alone is probably something to be unpacked in therapy, but it's gonna have to get in line. I've got a lifetime of near-death, traumatic, and generally absurd experiences that have shaped me into who I am today . . . but it all started with that bad ticker.

An airplane needs air resistance to gain lift. A sword needs to be beaten and shaped to be made sharp and hard. I needed to be held back in order to move forward.

And, since then, I've never stopped moving forward.

Recess. Thank God. My favorite part of the day.

I have mixed feelings about kindergarten. I love being around all the kids. I love learning new things. I really like my teachers. But I absolutely despise having to sit down all day. I can handle a few minutes at a time, but hour after hour of just sitting and listening to people is painful. The last ten minutes before recess are the worst. I just stare at the clock and it seems like that glorious moment will never come.

Now I'm here. Thirty minutes of freedom. The air is fresh. The sun is shining. And I'm going to run around on my little stubby legs and have a blast!

Then I see her.

Laura LaCuri walks across the playground, and I can't stop looking at her. She has the prettiest eyes, the cutest nose, and she is just so sweet. It doesn't matter if you're an athlete, a nerd, smart, or slow, she is sweet to you every time. I never get nervous around girls, but there is something about her that always gives me butterflies.

She looks different today, though. Her mom just cut her hair, and as much as I like Laura, her mom kind of did her dirty. She looks like someone put a bowl around her head and just cut in a circle. It doesn't matter to me, though. She's still adorable.

As I run around playing tag, red rover, and anything else we dream up, I see a group of boys walk up to her. I know bad when I see it, and these guys look like they have bad intentions. I start walking toward them.

As I get close, I hear their ringleader. "You've got boy's hair! Are you a boy now?" he mocked. "Boys don't wear dresses!" another buffoon chimed in.

THE CREEK GANG   11

Laura starts to cry. I am filled with rage. As the bullies take off laughing, I follow them. They climb onto the giant wooden jungle gym everyone alive in the '80s knows and loves. I walk right up to the ringleader, and I punch him in the face. And then, to add injury to injury, while he's crying and holding his face, I push him off the jungle gym.

Moments later, I find myself in the principal's office. My parents are on their way and they are not happy. They arrive and we are told that I will not be invited back for the first grade.

This doesn't bother me: It was worth it.

I hate bullies.

———

The wind whips through my hair as the horizontal rain bites through my shirt. My cheeks are red with cold, and my white T-shirt is stuck to my body like a second skin. There's so much water coming at me that I find myself having to clear my nose and throat every few minutes by hocking a lugey. Store signs have blown down and tree branches are everywhere; the roads are littered with them, and there is not a car to be seen. I squint through the rain at the crew moving quietly with me: my brother Nick, Chad, David, and the brothers Cunningham, Jared and Jordan.

While most people are hunkered down in their homes during this El Niño tropical storm, the Creek Gang is busy thinking up ways to take advantage of this exciting opportunity. As soon as we saw the creek start to swell, we drew up our plan. The Salinas River, in my native San Luis Obispo, California, is usually a long and lazy river until it leaves my neighborhood. Then shortly thereafter, it turns into a Class IV rapids, meaning it gets faster, steeper, and meaner pretty quickly. Today, with the gift of this tropical storm, the river is trucking! And, those Class IV rapids are now Class V or VI, meaning they are pretty much a guarantee of sudden death to anyone who falls in the water.

For the Creek Gang it was mission impossible, and it was too good to pass up.

Our plan, should we choose to accept it, and we all did, was to steal some inner tubes, go a few miles away from my house to a bridge that crossed the river, jump off the bridge with the inner tubes, and ride this water highway all the way to the mouth of the rapids. That morning, we had slung a rope with handholds across the river. The plan was simple. As we hit the mouth of the rapids, we were going to grab the rope, bail on the tubes, and pull ourselves to shore. Was it a perfect plan? We thought so.

I feel exhilaration as we descend on the tire store in a sprint from the woods. We each grab an inner tube and sprint back even harder, disappearing back into the tree line. Adrenaline tickles my skin and pushes energy out of my eyeballs as we run as fast as we can away from the scene of the crime and toward the bridge. (To be super honest, it was easy. No one was really manning the store because of the storm, the inner tubes were outside unwatched because they had little value, and even if someone did see a group of kids grabbing inner tubes, it's doubtful they would have thought much of it. But in our minds, we were on the verge of capture.)

When we finally arrive, a little out of breath from our imagined race from authorities who didn't exist, hunting for inner tubes that no one cared about, we are shocked at the water levels rushing past the bridge. Typically, the drop from the road to the water is about twenty feet. Today it is ten feet, and it is absolutely roaring! That of course makes this mission all the more exciting.

We find the largest truss under the bridge and line up, one by one, inspired by the Army commercials where paratroopers run out of the plane in a perfectly disciplined line as they plunge into the abyss. Once lined up, one of us, I think my brother Nick, yells "Go!" and we all drop into the river.

My feet hit harder than I expected, and because of the size of the tube, I fly through the hole slapping my face on the surface as the water shoots up my nose. My hands, attached to arms that are now in a "V" above my head, clamor to find something to hold on to so that I don't get separated from the tube. They find a home on the inner edge, and I manage to pull my head up a little more. My ears ring with the rush of the water around me, echoing through the tube. I feel like I'm in a tunnel. I pop my hands up a little more and finally feel I have a solid grip. I pull myself up and get my feet onto the tube so that the only thing still in the water is my butt.

I start counting. *One . . . two . . . three . . . four . . . five . . . plus me makes six!* We're all here.

Looking around, it seems like all of us had some version of the same struggle I just had, but our young minds quickly forget our previous peril, and we are all grinning ear to ear. If anyone was hot on our tails, they'll never be able to get to us now. Even though we've been in this river a hundred times, right now it feels like I'm a Navy SEAL on some secret mission in South America or Africa evading capture after getting the bad guys. The Creek Gang has completed phase two!

The river seems to flow faster and faster and the bumpiness of the ride increases as we get closer to our extraction point. Earlier we discussed the best way to make sure we hit the rope. There's no room for missing it by trying to grab it with our wet and cold hands, so the plan is to hook our elbow over it and then lock hands on the other side; that way, even if we slip we're still on.

I start to see trees I recognize, then the last bend before the river opens up to my backyard. Finally, the rope. My heart is racing. This is the moment of truth. I keep my eyes focused on it as it approaches . . . hook! The rope bites into my elbow, and I grip my hand on the other side, letting the inner tube go. I throw my leg over and pull myself to shore. My brother is already there, and by the time I shake the water off my body, the other guys are out and Jared and Jordan are on the rope. We watch the last of the inner tubes crash into rapids. The last of the evidence is gone.

Mission complete.

I hear the phone ringing through the closet door. I look at my dad, and he tells me to say, "Dad is out running errands and he should be back at the house by 6:00."

I open the closet door, and there is the red phone, ringing. I pick it up and answer using our family pseudonym for these occasions. A man with a Colombian accent who I have spoken to many times answers on the other end. "Hey buddy, is your dad home?" "Sorry, he isn't. Dad is out running errands and he should be back at the house by 6:00. Do you want to leave a message?" "No, that's okay. I'll call back then," he responds.

I hang up, grab some Kool-Aid, and run outside to play with the Creek Gang. Today, we're running missions out of our tree fort. By the end of the day, the fort will be on fire because I will try to build a bonfire in it for us to sit around. It will work for a little while, until it doesn't.

That phone call is everyday life for the kid of a narcotics officer. It is probably a lot of responsibility for a thirteen-year-old but it's just what we have always known so I never really think much about it. In order to keep my dad's cover safe, we have to be available all the time, just like a real family. If my dad or my dad's family only answered the phone between 9:00 to 5:00, then they'd know he's a cop, and they'd kill him. So the police installed a special untraceable phone in our closet, and our family joined in on the cover identity to add depth to his story. It is our mission to keep my dad safe so he can keep the country safe. We take this mission very seriously.

And dad has an enormous mission right now. He just stole a plane full of cocaine from Pablo Escobar. More precisely, he just stole the largest cache of cocaine that, up to this point, had ever been stolen.

Dad's part of an interagency counternarcotics task force. It's extremely dangerous because if the Colombians figure out who he is, he's dead. In addition, the local police are not allowed to know about it, so there's always the added danger of unwanted police interaction as he's running around town with drugs. U.S. Customs, the FBI, and the San Luis Obispo (SLO) and Santa Barbara Counternarcotics Task Forces are in the know; every other agency has to be in the dark.

The drugs fly from Colombia to Puerto Rico or Guantánamo Bay. There, they get packed onto another plane and fly to Port Hueneme, outside of Ventura. Once there, my dad and his fellow officers, dressed in '80s suits or Hawaiian shirts and carrying Uzis, load the coke into vans, trucks, and Cadillacs with secret compartments and bring them to their office to prepare for distribution.

Dad's "consulting firm" has two offices. One is in Marina del Rey. It's a pimped-out '80s-style office building that is completely bugged. There is a big conference room and a bunch of actual employees that make real wages for just sitting around. When a client comes in, they all pretend to work. Thinking back, it was probably a good gig. Dad goes there for meetings and deals with new clients but doesn't spend a lot of his time there.

The other office is in downtown SLO, and it's the one I frequent. It's situated in a building that would now be described as flex-space, in a classic '80s strip mall. There is a tire store two doors down, a great café-style restaurant, and a coffee shop. I don't drink coffee, but they make decent hot chocolate. Those are the mainstays here. The other stores change a lot, as strip mall stores tend to.

And that's where I am visiting my dad today. My mom is delivering a bunch of apple pies from the world-famous Madonna Inn to the team. (My dad was part of the hostage rescue team that saved the owner of the Madonna Inn's daughter when she was kidnapped, but that's a story for another time.) We do this once a week to show our appreciation and to break the monotony for the guys. For me, as a newly minted teenager, it is super exciting because I get to be part of the op. I'm around all these larger-than-life badasses, leaning against pallets of cocaine, sporting MP5s, and fighting bad guys. I sit down, grab a slice of apple pie, and listen to story after story of these men dancing the fine line between life and death. *I'm gonna be like them when I grow up.*

My dad is gearing up to move the 980 kilos. The quantity is way too big for even the largest of local dealers, so they are going to sell the drugs to multiple organizations. They've arranged secondary transportation unaffiliated with their office for the delivery to these dealers. Then once the drugs arrive at the dealers and are paid for, they will all get hit by completely different police officers with no knowledge of my dad's crew. It is critical that there is no way to tie my dad's team to the takedowns, so everyone had to be in the dark.

In his entire career my dad never lost a gram.

Sitting there, watching my dad gear up for this massive sting operation across the entire West Coast, I am so proud of how chill he is. *My dad fights with drug dealers the way most dads deal with paperwork. It doesn't even seem like a big deal. Danger and the possibility of violence are just . . . natural.*

———————

When dad was on his crazy missions, mom brought us to my grandparents' house.

Grandma and Grandpa Sumpter's place in Cambria, sitting off the coast of Morro Bay, is my favorite place on earth. Their house sits on top of a cliff overlooking the bay and the clean salt air washes over you the second you step foot on the property, filling your lungs, heightening your senses, and making you feel alive. You can carefully climb down the side of the cliff and hit the ocean shoreline. At low tide, there are pools of saltwater left behind full of small fish, crabs, and jellyfish. At high tide, you can take a few steps and cast into the abyss, catching rockfish, lingcod, halibut, and mackerel. The sunsets and sunrises here are an incredible mix of oranges, and reds, and purples. The only way to describe the view is "majestic." I always felt it's right out of a *Lord of the Rings* book. If you were approaching from a distance, and you saw the little cottage on top of the cliff, with billowing white smoke coming out of the fireplace, you would absolutely think this is the place the old wizard or the retired knight lives. It is beautiful, but also a little foreboding, like the grounds themselves have some deep, secret knowledge the rest of the world isn't privy to. It is absolutely perfect.

In the mornings, the sun would rise, sending sunbeams shooting through the windows letting us know it was time to get up. As my brother Nick, my little sister Katie, and I stirred, our nostrils would immediately get hit with the smells of breakfast: sausages roasting, bacon sizzling, and eggs scrambling. They'd get up right away, but I'd lie there a little longer than my brother and sister, trying to sink into the mattress and get just a few more minutes of rest. I'd be tired from a night of staying up with my grandpa and my grandma watching old movies. Grandpa always made me watch movies where the hero had to make hard decisions, sometimes the wrong decisions, and then we'd talk about them when the movie was over.

The Big Country, starring Gregory Peck is his favorite. Peck plays a sailor who travels west to marry his fiancée, Patricia, at her father's ranch. Her father, "the Major," is in a rivalry with another ranch. Those rivals set upon Peck, and even though he has the opportunity to best or kill them several times, he always makes the honorable decision, even if it means losing the support of his future father-in-law and eventually his fiancée as well. *Do the right thing, even when there's negative consequences for your actions.*

There are many others: *The Searchers, The Man Who Shot Liberty Valance, Patton, Friendly Persuasion, To Kill a Mockingbird,* and *The Long, Hot Summer,* just to name a few. Each one comes with lessons and discussions deep into the night. By today's standards, it is probably a lot for a little kid to ponder, but I revel in it. Grandpa treats me like an adult. He treats me like a man and trusts me to look at examples of good and flawed men and decide for myself what right looks like. He's giving me the road map to success, one movie at a time. *I can be like these men.*

The remnants of those thoughts are still floating around in my brain as the smells of cooking food overpower me, and my feet finally find their way to the floor. I throw some clothes on, brush my teeth, and head into the kitchen. My mom is laughing at something Grandma Sumpter just said and her amazing laugh rocks the room. Katie is halfway through her first and only plate, and Nick is filling up his second. I grab a plate and fill it with bacon, sausages, eggs, and pancakes. I'm going to need the energy because we're heading to the breakers!

If Cambria is my favorite place on earth, and Morro Bay is my favorite part of Cambria, then the breakers are my favorite part of Morro Bay. Morro Bay is one of the most dangerous bays in America because it has a massive tidal shift of over six feet, which occurs in only a few hours. The effects of that fast-rising tide on boats, property, and swimmer safety, especially during inclement weather, are significant, so to lessen the threat of property damage and loss of life, they built a massive jetty of boulders, rocks, and concrete stretching out across the bay.

To the average person, that jetty was an unapproachable, insurmountable wall of rock. To me it was an adventure. As you enter the base of the jetty there is a huge sign painted yellow that says "Do Not Climb Inside Caves." The reason for that sign is pretty obvious: The tides change so fast that you can get lost exploring the catacombs during low tide, and before you know it, the entrance is underwater and you die. Well, if you leave cavities and caves full of creatures and lost treasures in a super tidal shifting quagmire of death, then post a sign specifically prohibiting its exploration, there you shall find Tim Kennedy.

On this particular day, as I leap from boulder to boulder like a tweener parkour athlete, feeling the spray of the ocean against my face, I catch something out of the corner of my left eye. *What is this? Is that a cave I have yet to explore?*

Nestled between two rocks I have climbed hundreds of times, I notice a small opening. Normally, the opening is completely filled with sand, but the waves have opened up a little pocket. I crouch down, feeling the bite of the rock on my left knee as I peer into the hole. *It's a cave! And it's big. I just have to get in.*

I immediately start to dig the sand away with my hands, throwing it behind me until the opening looks large enough for me to fit. Then I crawl in. My shoulders won't quite fit. I wiggle myself and break more of the sand loose while I work my way deeper and deeper into the crevice. Finally, I break through and drop into the cave.

The temperature inside is at least 10 degrees cooler, and even though I am only a few feet from the surface of the rocks, that added an aura of foreboding that I enjoy. Seaweed drips from the walls and ceiling. Barnacles and mollusks are everywhere. I cut my finger on one as I climb down and suck the blood off of my finger so it would stop. A large pool of water inside is full of crabs. I go deeper into the cave to explore the pool and see if there are any big ones worth keeping for dinner.

The crabs aren't great, but I am not anxious to return to the surface yet. After all, I am probably the first kid ever to discover this place. So I take a handful of pebbles and throw them at the crabs to annoy them and make them move while I just enjoy the quiet. Then I hear something. Or rather a lack of something. The sound of the wind is suddenly far less prevalent. I turn around to look back at the way that I had come.

The cave is filling up with water!

My stomach drops. My mouth goes dry. My heart races. *Holy shit. I have no way out.* I sprint up toward where the water is coming in. *Maybe I can hold my breath and squeeze back in there?* But I know I cannot. I had barely fit on the way in. There was no way to do it against the current.

I am going to die.

"Hey, Tim," a familiar voice shouts.

I look up. There, above me, is the nonplussed face of my grandfather. He has been watching me the entire time from a distance, and the second I crawled into this damn cave, he made sure there was another way out and that I was safe. "Time to get out of here now," he continues with no visible emotion. All of my fear slips away in an instant. I almost want to cry in relief. I'm safe.

He reaches down and helps me out.

———

"If you want to eat, you're going to have to catch and kill one of those chickens," the tall, wiry man in front of me states plainly. His name is Woody Shoemaker. He is my pastor.

It had been a very long day, and I am starving. There is no way I am not going to eat. I stand up and start walking down the chickens, eyes fixated on one plump one with a patch of black against her brown body. I walk it down into a corner and then lunge for it. Miss.

I repeat this process, honing my technique. On the fourth attempt, I catch it. As they had shown us, I twist its neck, breaking it and killing it instantly. Then I set up on a rock and begin gutting and de-feathering my dinner.

The other fourteen-year-old kids are now following my example, try-ing to catch and kill their own chickens.

I am a Royal Ranger undergoing survival camp. The Royal Rangers, if you've never heard of them, are a lot like the Boy Scouts used to be in the 1940s, 1950s, and 1960s, in that they teach you pretty hardcore survival skills and don't really worry about the emotional impact of that training. So they take the old Boy Scout recipe for men-making and add a few heaping tablespoons of Jesus to the mix.

The chicken killing is quite an emotional event for a lot of these kids. Some of them are crying. Others have a thousand-yard stare going. Some seem to feel like they have accomplished something adult and manly and are showing signs of pride. For me, it's a Friday. The Creek Gang has hunted for years, either with the supervision of my dad, or on our own using snares and traps we made ourselves. I had never done it with my bare hands before, so that added a certain primal element to it, but this made the experience nuanced, not new.

While the other kids were wrestling with their emotions, I was gear-ing up for the final phase of this survival school so I could go home, get away from these neophyte tough guys, and get back to my friends.

Our final mission is a thirty-six-hour, self-correcting land navigation course. You start with a full canteen, a map, and two partners. Every time you find a point, you can refill your canteen, but the only food you have is what you can forage on the way, which is scarce to say the least.

We begin at dawn, full of piss and vinegar. This is our final test, and everyone is anxious to prove their worth.

We quickly expel all the piss onto random trees as we take breaks that we don't need to disassociate our minds from this miserable long walk through the blaring California heat. And while there is no actual vinegar, we quickly start to smell like we're doused in it as the ammonia from our sweat settles into our clothing and evaporates into the air.

Twenty-eight hours into this thing, my two partners have become worthless. To be honest, they were worthless the entire time, but for the first twelve hours or so, they kept the whining, moaning, and constant fear of dying to a minimum. Now, they were quite comfortable letting the complaints fly. I was fucking sick of it. After over a day of walking through the woods, doing all the map work, all the navigating, and walking point while cutting through all the bramble, my patience is shot. I briefly consider eating them, as it would make me less hungry and the journey more pleasant, but instead I let them know that if they can just push on a little longer, I think we are getting close to the final point.

There were seven points thus far, labeled A through G. As promised, each one had a jug for us to refill our canteens, and each one had a little clue to help us find the next point. For a kid that lived in the woods and along rivers, the navigation is easy. The hard part is putting one foot in front of the other for this long. I'd done a lot of walking at this point in my life, but never this long without food or rest. This definitely sucks. But by far, the hardest part is dealing with these two guys that didn't have my level of training. I don't know it yet, but my intolerance of weakness will be an Achilles' heel for years to come.

Nevertheless, I catch my second wind. I am 99 percent sure we're approaching the final point. The last clue basically said as much, and while all the other points had us running around out in the middle of nowhere, we're now heading back toward the camp. "Not another damn hill," one of my partners in crime complains, but now I know where we are and I think I know exactly where we are going. I can't help myself. I pick up the pace.

By the time I see the hill with the large tree on it, I'm 100–150 meters ahead of my team. I look back and make sure they can at least see me because the last thing I want to do is lose them and have to go find them after all this walking, but I don't want to slow down. That tree has to be the final point. As I move forward, something unnatural catches my eye. Something is on the tree. I squint.

It's a bag of oranges.

I pick up the pace even more and find myself running by the time I get to the top of the hill. I arrive at the tree. *I did it. I made it.* I was at the final point.

"This is it, guys!" I yell back to my partners as I'm already ripping the giant bag of oranges apart. My fingernails cut through the orange mesh and pull out the plumpest, juiciest California orange I can find. I barely remember peeling it as I bite right into the entire orange. There's no time to break it into slices.

I have never tasted anything sweeter. No food, not at any fancy restaurant, not on any hunt, not even in mom's or grandma's kitchen, has ever tasted as good as that bite of orange did. It is impossible to describe. If you've ever cut weight for wrestling or boxing and then finally had that first bite of watermelon or first drink of Pedialyte, that comes close, but not quite to the level of satisfaction that orange brought me.

My two compatriots caught up and ripped open their oranges. The three of us sat there, eating all we could, sticky juices running down our face, coating our hands, and seeping into our shirts in puddles where it was dripping from our chins. We didn't care. The moment was absolute bliss.

My pager starts beeping. I am still getting used to this new technology my parents had invested in to try to keep track of fifteen-year-old me. Then it beeps again. And again. The messages come fast and furious from lots of different people.

"Where are you?"

"Are you home?"

"Call home, right now."

Something is going on.

I reluctantly find my way to a pay phone and call my parents. I assume I am in trouble for something. My mom answers the phone. "I'm so sorry, Tim," she starts. Her voice is quivering. It's clear she's in real pain. That throws me instantly. I'm not used to my parents being hurt. Upset, sure. Angry. Happy. Disappointed. Proud. These are common parental emotions. But not pain. I had only heard real pain in my mom's voice once before, when she lost her best friend CariLee in a diving accident in Morro Bay Harbor, less than a quarter mile from the breakers I explored. I had only heard it in my dad's voice when he lost his mom right in front of all of us to a heart attack, after he performed CPR until the ambulance arrived. I braced for the worst. Then she told me—and my world ended.

I don't remember much of what she said after that. I found myself sitting on the floor of the pay phone with tears streaming down my face. Then I was on a knee. Then the tears were dry and my senses had disappeared, leaving only a vast emptiness. At some point, I got up and started walking the long way home.

Jared and Jordan Cunningham, two members of the Creek Gang, and two of my best friends on planet earth, were heading to a party driven by teenagers in two separate cars. When I say "heading to a party" I mean that in the lamest, most wholesome way possible. They weren't going to some Hollywood-style teenage kegger. They were going to hang out at someone's house and play games. Maybe if things got wild, they'd wrestle in the grass. Just good wholesome fun. It was a church kid hangout.

But church kids are still kids, and as you've seen from me, and know from your own childhood, kids do dumb things. The two teenage drivers, finding themselves alone on a long country road, started racing each other, taking turns passing each other in the oncoming traffic lane.

It was Jared's car's turn to speed by, and they slid out from behind Jordan's car and started to pass. The brothers were right next to each other, their respective drivers in mid-acceleration, in that horrible moment. I know what the moment was like, as do you: boys yelling at each other through windows, laughing, swearing, feeling the invincible rush of adrenaline-filled youth.

Then the oncoming car came around the corner. They were doing nothing wrong. Just minding their own business, doing some last-minute shopping before Christmas.

Neither driver saw the other in time to hit the brakes or swerve.

Jared died.

Aged 13.

December 20, 1994.

Five days before Christmas, in front of his sixteen-year-old brother Jordan.

My parents did what they always did in a crisis. They helped. People always told us that the Kennedys were good at death. And I guess they were right. When everyone else was mourning, or didn't know what to do, we took action. It's not that we didn't hurt. It was just better to be useful. So I learned from my mom and dad to always be useful.

And there we were, in front of the Cunningham house, a place I had visited a thousand times, ready to be useful. My parents knock on the door and a lady I don't recognize answers. I know who she is, mind you, but I have never seen her before, at least not like this. Debra Cunningham, Jared and Jordan's mom, is an excellent mother and person. She is always upbeat, always put together with flawless makeup and dress, and always ready with a kind expression and a smile on her face. She's genuinely kind, friendly, compassionate, and amazing. She isn't here today. The woman in front of me wears a face that is gaunt and expressionless. Her eyes are puffy, red, and empty, and behind them sits only blankness. Her mascara has run to the base of her nose, and she doesn't seem to notice in the slightest.

She cannot look at me, but I understand. I can't look at her either.

As my parents usher her to the couch, I go down the stairs to head to Jared's room as I have so many times. I get to the doorway and look in, unable to cross the threshold. I've played in this room, slept in this room, plotted and planned in this room, talked about girls in this room. I cannot walk in.

I turn around and sit at the base of the stairs and wait a few hours for my parents to be ready to leave.

Jordan isn't here today because he is with family members.

I won't see him again in any meaningful way for five years. I simply cannot bear to be around him, and I would find out many years later that he couldn't bear to be around me.

The Creek Gang is no more.

My childhood is over.

CHAPTER TWO

DEVIANCE

The vibrations run through my sixteen-year-old spine, up my neck, and out my ears as my best friend Auggie Gaw, in the driver's seat, revs the engine of my brother Nick's burgundy 1993 V8 Camaro. I'm sitting shotgun. In the car next to us, revving his brother's "borrowed" 1969 midnight blue Mach 1 Fastback Mustang, sits my other best friend, Joe Silva.

The roars of both engines and the smells of the sweet, smoky fuel and exhaust permeates the country air at the entrance to Scalari Ranch, a beautiful little property in the heart of central California wine country.

The anticipation fills me to the brink as I wrestle with the fight between the tightness in my stomach and the fuzzies running through my face and ears. I revel in the fact we're sitting on atomic bombs of pure unadulterated American muscle!

It was time to answer the age-old question that has plagued philosophers and poets throughout the ages: Ford or Chevy?

This is the first time my brother has let me borrow his Camaro. It's only a year old and a real beauty. He worked hard to buy it (all with his own money), and to say he was proud of it would be a terrible understatement. He emphasized to me that he was trusting me with his most prized possession.

That was stupid.

But as dumb as my brother is for lending me his vehicle, stealing the Mustang from Joe Silva's dangerous drug-dealing brother Paul is a dumber move still. For clarity, this is the drug dealer that my narcotics officer dad had told me to avoid. He said Paul was "unhinged and homicidal." And yet here we are.

To get Paul's keys, we had to go into his room. No one was allowed in there, because that's where Paul kept the money, drugs, and God knows what else. To be caught in his room meant catching a beating. Paul is a mountain of a man—wide-chested with forearms like Popeye—with several years of testosterone and puberty on us. We did not want that smoke.

But you know . . . we *had* to know which car would win.

Scalari Ranch opens up onto Old Creek Road off of Highway 46. It's a super-curvy street that races back and forth between rolling hills and acts as a connector between the highway and the coast. It looks exactly like the kind of road they use for one of those commercials with a British lady voiceover and some generic European model dude with a five-o'clock shadow and racing gloves. He's careening through time and space as the drone shot hovers overhead and you can see the sprawling countryside. "Drive a JAG-UUUUUUU-AR and experience what it really means to be a predator of the road." Or whatever bullshit they say in those commercials.

The race is going to be a fifteen-minute sprint to the coast. Sure, most kids would knock out a straight-line quarter mile like they do in the movies, but we want to really test ourselves as well as the cars. To drive this course right means you need to be a highly technical driver. Although our licenses are still warm from being laminated, we have something other drivers don't have: the desire to flick death right on the forehead and dare him to do something about it.

As the only guy not driving (I still don't know how that happened), it's my job to start the race. I raise my arm out the car window. Auggie and Joe both stare at me as the engines swell in front of me and next *to* me.

"Go!" I scream as I drop my hand.

Gravel flies everywhere, fire leaves the exhaust, and rubber is burned into the ground as we lurch and fishtail forward. The guys race through the gears, living between second and fourth as we hit turn after turn.

Holy shit.

My back is pressed against the seat. Every time we hit a straightaway, the line blurs as we punch over 100 mph. Auggie found his groove and I start to anticipate his slowdowns and speed-ups. The Ford is a little faster on the straights, but we are owning the turns. It's gonna be close.

As we come up to the fifteenth turn, Auggie gets a little more aggressive. He doesn't quite slow down all the way and accelerates a little early. We fishtail and lose control.

My senses are shot as we spin around and then BAM! We fly off the road and get stopped abruptly by the creek bed. As the car comes up briefly on two wheels and then settles back down again, I hear the whole vehicle creak and groan, kind of like someone just twisted a rusted-out bolt.

Auggie and I look at each other. We're okay.

It is not lost on me that what just happened is eerily similar to what happened to Jared not that long ago.

That thought is quickly replaced by:

Fuck. My brother's gonna kill me!

I take a deep breath.

Maybe it's not that bad.

I open my car door.

It falls off.

Double fuck.

To be fair, it doesn't fall all the way off, but the hinges are damaged badly enough that it hits the ground. To close it, I need to lift it up and then push it shut. It makes a groaning, popping noise when I do that but I get it so it stays shut.

We try to push the car out. We try to pull it out. The Camaro is not moving. We call a couple of our friends who own trucks with winches and tow ropes and ask them to come help us out.

They arrive, and thankfully, our group of teenagers manage to yank this thing out and place it back on the pavement. As it leaves the creek bed, water, dirt, and moss pour out of the exhaust, tires, and every crevice I never knew existed on a vehicle.

On the road, it doesn't quite look right. I mean . . . sure the entire right side of the vehicle is scraped and bent, but something else seems off. I can't quite place it.

As I jump behind the wheel, it finally comes to me. The car is sitting at a 20 degree angle. Something deep inside of it is broken. Maybe the suspension. Maybe the frame. Maybe the whole shit.

To drive it, I have to keep the wheel angled hard to the right. As we crawl back to my house, there is a distinct wobble in the ride, and when I try to accelerate, it gets even more aggressive. But somehow, some way, Auggie and I get it home with Joe in the Mustang behind me.

I take a deep breath. There's only one sensible thing to do.

I park the car. I walk inside. I place the keys back in the bowl where my brother puts them. Then I leave and pretend like nothing happened.

Maybe my brother won't notice.

We jump in Joe's Mustang and head back to the ranch. Somehow I've convinced myself everything is fine and we got away with it. We park the car back where Paul had left it but when we close the doors, we realize for the first time that someone is there.

Not just someone. Paul.

"You fucking assholes! Who the fuck do you think you are?" he shouts.

He punches Auggie right in the face. Not once. Not twice. But over and over again. This was a man beating up a child. Paul could have been a professional athlete if he wasn't a dealer. He was that kind of specimen. We were still spindly teenagers.

The thuds as his fists carve Auggie's face and body up are sickening. Joe and I are frozen in fear and we keep begging him to stop, screaming that we are sorry. When he is done with him, he rag-dolls his brother, punching and throwing him around. By the time he gets to me, whether it is exhaustion from beating the other two, realization that he may have gone too far, or the fact that I wasn't one of the drivers, he took it easy on me. He slammed me into the wall and slapped me around, but he didn't do any real damage.

"Get the fuck out of here," Paul commands as he stares through Auggie and me.

We head home. Auggie's face is now swollen. He can't see through his eyes. His face is as bad as any professional fighter's I would see in my career. "Fuck, man," I say. "Yep," he replies. We bump fists and I head into my house.

My brother is there waiting.

Apparently, he noticed.

"I don't know what the fuck you're talking about," I tell him. "It was fine when I dropped it off. Don't try to blame me for your shit. I bet you crashed it and are trying to pin it on me!"

After dropping that gem, I indignantly marched off to my room, leaving my confused brother in the background. He's pretty sure I crashed his car, but now he doesn't *know* I did.

The next morning he is hovering over my bed when I wake up. Auggie couldn't sleep. He showed up early that morning to apologize to my brother for crashing his car.

Fucking amateur.

I stretch the water balloon launcher as far as it can go, as the blue bands grow translucent the further back I pull. Now that it is fully stretched, I aim the potato sitting within it at the optimal angle for maximum distance.

Release!

I watch it fly through the air at blistering speed, rapidly turning into a speck on the horizon as it clears the 101 freeway and heads toward the Kmart parking lot on the other side of the highway.

Score!

This potato hit its mark. I hear the impact on the car and see the tiny people in the distance trying to figure out where it came from and who did it. Absolutely hilarious.

I've launched about a dozen of these today, and it's been funnier every time. I look down at my watch. My break is over. I throw my apron and hat back on and head back inside In-N-Out Burger. *This job is the best.*

In-N-Out is my home away from home. I'm sixteen, and I have no idea why adults complain about work. This place is great. We get lots of freedom as to how we do our jobs. After being here for only a few weeks, I've moved some things around and now I am by far the fastest fry guy.

Better yet, my boss, Joe, is super cool. We hang potato sacks from the ceiling in the back and when it's slow, we practice throwing knives. I'm getting pretty good and can pretty much hit the mark nine out of ten times. Recently, to further spice up our slow periods, I've also introduced my teammates to the idea that mop and broom handles, unscrewed from their implement, make Bo staffs, which are big, long wooden fighting sticks like the one Donatello carries on the *Teenage Mutant Ninja Turtles.*

Last week we had our first Bo staff tournament, which I won. Brianna Sadothway, a beautiful, super nice girl that I have a crush on, did not partake, but pretty much everyone else did. The final came down to me and Tim Sobraske, a high school wrestler and football player. I bested him solidly, which hurt his ego, probably because Brianna was watching. This led to him talking a lot of shit about me—specifically my wrestling.

I am a very good wrestler, but because I am homeschooled, I cannot join or compete on the regular school teams. So I do all the club tournaments and freestyle tournaments. Although I win most of them, I don't get to compete at regionals and states, the tournaments that really matter to high school kids.

When he tells me, "You're not really a wrestler," Sobrowski sees that he struck a nerve and, like any good teenager, keeps poking it. Fast-forward about ten minutes and the homeschooled chip on my shoulder has prevailed and we are in a full-out wrestling match in front of God, customers, and everybody. I put him in a standing cradle, a position where I am standing up with one arm around his head and the other around his legs with my hands locked. I walk over to the dirty clothes laundry bin where we stick all of our clothes at the end of shift and stick him in it, butt down. He cannot get out and has to scream for help from the other associates.

My boss frowned upon my physical assault of another associate, and I was counseled by him as a result.

But that was last week. Sobrowski and I are cool again, as men of action always are after a scuffle. Brianna is looking adorable. I'm dropping fries like the elite chef that I am, and I just got to launch some quality potatoes. Life is good.

And that's when I hear it. The sound of creepiness.

"I didn't realize In-N-Out had girls that looked like you, or I'd be here all the time," says some dude in his late twenties to the sixteen-year-old Brianna. He has four buddies with him who are giggling along to his shitty pickup lines. I now have one eye on them as I work my fries.

I can tell Brianna is visibly uncomfortable as their conversation continues. She is desperately trying to just take his order and get him to move on, and he keeps trying to put his hands on her arm and lean in close to talk. She backs up. He reaches out to pull her in.

"What the hell!" Brianna screams.

This fucking asshole just grabbed her breast.

It is my time to be noble. Some people would say I am partially motivated by the fact that I really like Brianna, but I am 99 percent sure it is pure nobility that leads my cloth-apron-clad body to sprint from the fry area to the counter. Four feet before I get to the counter I launch myself in midair, perfectly sliding over it like a movie cop slides across the hood of a car.

I transition from counter slide to double leg takedown and dump him onto the hard floor, reveling in hearing him wheeze as his body loses air as it gets folded up. For good measure, I punch him in the face five times, then grab him by the leg and drag him into the parking lot like he's a sack of potatoes.

He screams like a little girl for his friends to help him. I look at them. They look at me. They decide they want nothing to do with the crazy teenager that just attacked their buddy like Macho Man Randy Savage coming off the top rope.

The police arrive. Sexual assaulter douche pretends he did nothing wrong and that I just attacked him out of the blue. A few of the people that didn't know how it started corroborate his story, as all they saw was the counter slide to beatdown transition. Luckily, Brianna, Sobrowski, and my boss Joe were all privy to the actual events and they back me up.

After the police have a brief discussion with the groper, everyone involved kind of decides that it is in everyone's best interest not to press charges.

I'm home free!

Brianna thanks me for looking out for her and I turn a little red. Lancelot has nothing on Tim Kennedy.

Hours later, Steve Cronk, who is Joe's boss, is at the store and asks me to come to the back office with him. Proud as can be, I walk in expecting to get a pat on the back and a thank-you for defending the store.

Wrong.

Steve hands me a termination letter and asks me to read it aloud. I begin, "Employee is being terminated for the following reasons: throwing knives, Bo staffing with employees to include minor injuries to those employees, launching potatoes from company property and doing significant property damage as a result, thereby placing the company at risk of lawsuit, assaulting a co-worker, and finally, for assaulting a customer."

Steve speaks after a long pause. "Tim, I like you as a person, but not only do I have to let you go, I have to warn you that you're lucky you're not in prison."

I look him right in the eyes and say, "You're losing your best fry guy, Steve."

Then I walk out.

My teenage brain meant every word.

I'm holding on to the ropes I stole from my youth pastor, John Bartle, as Auggie cuts through the skylight seal with a knife and a crowbar.

The night is pitch-black, which is the perfect condition for these two sixteen-year-olds to knock out our first felony operation, but there is a mugginess hanging in the air that isn't normal to SLO. It's making us both sweat, and Auggie's hands are slipping on the knife. We both have droplets running down our foreheads and noses.

We see headlights in the distance on this long and winding road. We throw ourselves onto the roof and lie perfectly still, neither of us making a sound. In my head, we've set off some alarm and that car is driving right to us. I can feel the blood pumping through my head and neck as my blood pressure shoots up.

The car arrives quietly. I can hear its tires grinding into the road. It's paved, but the gravel from the hardware store parking lot has spilled into it, causing the tires to kick up some of the tiny rocks. For a second of abject fear, I thought it was turning into our lot, but then it continued down the path, and we were once again left alone.

I glance at my watch. It's 3:12. Auggie and I have been watching this hardware store for a month, and we have reasoned that the optimal time to break in is 3:00 a.m. It's the time with the least traffic and the best chance of darkness. We chose tonight because it is a new moon, with low visibility, limiting our chances of being spotted by some random car.

We knew the store didn't have cameras. It did have an alarm on the doors and windows (as well as metal bars on both), so normal entry was a no-go. But the skylights looked old as shit. They were giant bubbles, yellowed from the sun and caked with a mixture of pollen, dirt, and bug carcasses. We figured the owner probably hadn't planned on a couple of crazy kids climbing through the ceiling to get to his tools, so we hoped there weren't any alarms up there.

Auggie is done cutting. We both slip our fingers underneath and gently lift up the skylight, half expecting an alarm. Nothing happens. We gently and quietly lay it down.

While Auggie was cutting, I had secured the rappelling ropes to the roof in a couple of places. I feel confident it will hold. I secure the line to my, or I should say Pastor Bartle's, harness and with one last look at Auggie, descend into the darkness.

My feet hit the floor. Even though I have been in this hardware store a hundred times, *tonight* it feels like uncharted territory. It is so quiet without the whine of the overhead fluorescent lights and customer chatter. The only visible light comes from a couple of glowing red exit signs and a single night-light on the wall. I look for lasers, and cameras, and motion sensors, expecting them to appear, even though they weren't here earlier. I'm half disappointed and half relieved they are not present.

I break out a red lens flashlight as Auggie hits the floor. (If you don't know, red lens flashlights are much harder for others to see at night.) Auggie does the same. We immediately get to work.

We know exactly what we need. You see, this heist is simply the initial phase of a greater robbery we have planned. We know where everything is in the store and run to grab it. We pile everything in one pot at the center of the store so we can quickly hoist it to the roof.

Wire cutters, plasma torches, industrial drill, metal saws, crowbars, and lock cutters. The pile keeps getting bigger. I throw some flashlights onto the pile, just for good measure.

I hear another car.

Oh shit, oh shit, oh shit.

Auggie and I go silent once again, but this time the fear is worse. On the rooftop, we could still leap off and make a run for it if we got found out. Here, there was nowhere to go but through whoever came through the door.

The tires hit that gravel.

Our eyes meet.

What the fuck have I gotten myself into?

The light hits the windows and dances across the inside of the store. And then the car passes and is gone.

"Fuck!" Auggie says.

"Holy shit, man," I say. (We both have a gift with words.)

Back to the mission.

Auggie climbs back up to the top of the roof, ready for me to tie off the first items and get them out of here. I grab a plasma torch and

I grab the rope. I hold them both for what feels like an eternity, but is probably ten seconds.

I look up at Auggie.

"Auggie, I don't want to steal this guy's stuff."

"Me either," he replies.

I climb up the rope. We quietly gather all of our things and, under the cover of darkness, flee into the night.

It is 3:28.

———

It is an absolutely beautiful California morning, and I am so freaking happy to be out on this boat. I'm only two days and two dives away from becoming a junior master diver, which is something I've been working toward for a while. This is day two of a three-day trip. Day one went swimmingly (pun intended), and I'm hoping for more of the same today. The dive master checks in with me before I drop into the water, because at sixteen, I am the only kid on the boat. He kind of looks like a younger Captain Quint from *Jaws* but with an extra twenty pounds. Nice enough guy. I'm a little aggravated at all the extra attention, because I am the best diver here by far, but still . . . a nice enough guy.

The master diver gives the signal for me and my dive partner to start the dive. I take one last deep breath of sea air and then place my regulator in and drop with my dive partner into the ocean. He and I check everything and then give each other the okay symbol, meaning we're good to go. We then begin our descent.

The ocean is absolutely stunning today with all kinds of marine life humming about. California really is beautiful both above and below the waterline. Colors dance everywhere, whether it's the coral, the various plants, the starfish, the octopus, or all of the various fish. There's a few rockfish, and all kinds of minnows and schoolies swimming this way, that way, and every which way. My partner points to a small leopard shark swimming by; it's always fantastic to be in the water with a shark, even a little one.

What a great start to this dive!

I'm taking it all in, doing my thing, and checking on my partner, when I see him. Those beady little eyes *are* looking right at me. Daring me. He's one of the biggest lobsters I have ever witnessed. I have to have him. And he knows, because the moment I make that decision he takes off, scampering along the bottom. *Fuck that.* I give chase, abandoning my dive partner and blasting past the depth limit for the dive.

Before, he thought I was coming for him. Now, he knows it. The lobster picks up speed and bolts into a cave. I too speed up in a flurry of bubbles and quickly arrive at the cave's entrance. I peer in. I can just barely see the reflection of those cocky little beady eyes once again. *I'm getting this bastard.*

I try to swim into the cave. I don't fit. I rotate. I don't fit. I try a different angle. I still don't fit. Suddenly realizing that I'm now at almost 150 feet, without my dive partner, past the "hard deck," trying to cram myself into a tiny cave, I realize the lunacy and danger of the situation I've placed myself in and I do the obvious right thing. I take off my buoyancy compensator and my tank and lay them next to the cave. Then I take one last, long, glorious pull from my regulator and, holding my breath, swim into the cave.

Nowhere to go now, you fuck!

I corner the lobster and shoot both hands out at once, pinning him against the rock. His tail lashes out against me trying to get free, but I quickly grab and secure him. Victory is mine! My mission now complete, I back out of the tight cave, as I don't really have room to turn around inside. When my head finally clears the entrance, I come face-to-face with fins. Specifically, the master diver's fins.

I look up. Even though I cannot see his face very well, it appears he is not happy. Apparently, when he saw the massive stream of bubbles coming up from me, he assumed the worst, as that's what a massive stream of bubbles usually means coming from a diver. He sprinted down here to save my life. He is not happy to realize I am here for a crustacean, even one this giant.

He's been holding my regulator waiting for me to exit, and when I do, pushes it aggressively toward me. I take the regulator, and try to smile through it. He signals to let the lobster go and get my gear on. I absolutely refuse, instead choosing to awkwardly get my equipment back on one-handed so as not to lose control of my prize. On a dive, the thumbs-up signal means you have to ascend. There's no real sound underwater, but if his thumbs-up signal could have been screaming, it would have been.

Finally, with my gear on and my lobster in hand, we begin to ascend. We have to stop often to adjust for our ascent and avoid the bends, and although he cannot say anything, his glare is telling me that his anger is growing.

We finally surface. One millisecond later, I am greeted with the most impressive display of vulgarity and anger that I have ever encountered up to that moment, or at any point since. I'm serious. I've now been in the military for almost twenty years, and this master diver puts any drill sergeant, Ranger Instructor, or SERE Instructor to shame.

As I climb the ladder back into the boat, he picks up again, poking me in the chest and shouting, "You'll never get back in the water with me, and if I can help it, you'll never get back in the water with anyone ever again in your life! That is the absolute dumbest shit I have ever seen, and I have seen some dumb shit. And you know what? To teach you a lesson, we're gonna enjoy that lobster you seem to love more than your own safety or that of your fellow divers."

Up until those last two sentences, I am okay with everything he is saying. It's his job to keep people safe. I broke the rules. It's his boat. It's his dive. It's his call. A normal kid would have just gone with it. But those last two sentences crossed a weird line I have inside me.

I fire back, "Hey, I'm not your fucking kid! You have every right to not let me go back into the water, but this is my lobster. The only way you're getting this lobster is if you can fucking take it from me, and I don't think you can."

It's the best lobster that I've ever eaten.

————————

I pluck an apple from the fruit bowl and step outside into the California night. The air is still warm, but a little crisp, and the waxing gibbous moon (I was a scout, remember?) is letting off plenty of light. Fifteen neighborhood teenagers, including my brother's friend Mike Turnquist, have been over the house all day for a classic Kennedy party. We are "good kids" (well, the other kids are) so there is never any booze or anything. Our house is just the hangout spot for the neighborhood—both for adults and kids. My parents love to entertain, and it has rubbed off on us.

Today isn't anything wild. We are spending the day running around the yard, being silly, watching movies, and playing video games. Everyone is having a blast, but I cannot be stuck in one place for too long or I get stir-crazy. So I head out, apple in hand, to do a quick lap around the yard.

As I turn the corner from my door to the street, I see a Chevy Blazer idling right next to Mike's car. *Who is that?* Then I see the other piece of this puzzle: two dudes are rifling through his glove box and backseat.

"Hey! Get the fuck away from that car!" I scream as I take off at a dead sprint toward them.

I'm just a skinny teenager, so there isn't really a reason for them to be afraid, but for the first time I learned that violence of action has a profound effect on the spirit of the enemy. The two dickheads startle, with one hitting his head on the roof of Mike's car, and run back to the Blazer. They burn rubber and jump way ahead of me, but I do not slow down. I know there's a 90 degree turn coming up before the bridge.

I'm running faster than I ever have, screaming for my brother at the top of my lungs. Sure enough, the bandits have to slow down to make the turn. I catch them . . . barely. My right hand hooks around the very back of their open window, and I leap onto the step on the driver's side. I try to reach in, but he elbows me, and I start to lose my balance. I only have one weapon left. Like David facing Goliath with nothing but a stone, I face four ruffians and a Chevy Blazer with my mighty apple. I whip it at the driver's head as I fall off.

The apple strikes true.

I watch as the Blazer swerves, and then flips over and rolls upside down. It's like a scene from *Bad Boys II.*

Holy shit.

In moments the whole neighborhood is outside. Almost immediately, the police arrive as well. The four bandits tell the police that they were just driving by and I assaulted them. For a moment, everyone there considered their account was plausible. None of them had records and I was known as a, well . . . "interesting" kid. Then the police found a ton of stolen goods, pot, and the icing on the cake, Mike's high school football ring with his jersey number.

Vindicated, I returned to the party with my friends, comforted with the knowledge that I had protected our home—and flipped my first car.

————

I'm on my belly in the woods next to Auggie Gaw and Chris Silva. We're here to complete phase three of the mission we started two months ago. Phase one was to steal rappelling gear from Pastor Bartle. Phase one complete. Phase two was to steal the tools necessary for phase three from the hardware store. Phase two, not complete, but we grabbed a crowbar and some bolt cutters from our parents' house and that was going to have to be good enough. So now it was time to execute phase three: break into the gun store and steal some guns.

The store is not one of the modern-day mega-deals. The building is made of tin. There are bars on the windows. It's dilapidated. The roof is sun-worn. But it's also in the middle of the country, as opposed to being downtown where we'd have a better chance of being spotted and caught, so it's ideal.

I don't know why Auggie and I want guns. I don't know why we feel like this is a good idea. I don't know why we think we'll have the stones to steal, of all things, weapons, when we didn't have the guts to take tools from a hardware store. Nevertheless, here we are, on our bellies, preparing to once again commit a "Big F" felony.

I fully admit this is insane. I know it is. But two months ago, Auggie and I had set out on this mission, and neither of us was willing to leave a mission undone. There is something in both of us that refuses to quit, even when we know the circumstances are not in our favor.

So we stealthily creep toward the gun store. As we reach the building, we hear something that has shot fear into the hearts of would-be thieves for millennia. We hear a guard dog growling. Then barking. Then we hear, "Do you hear something, boy?" Then we see the lights come on in the trailer right next to the gun store.

The owner lives on the property. Of course he does.

On the fly, Auggie pitches a new plan. We take the guy out, zip-strip him, tie up his dog, and then use his keys to get into the store the easy way. The three of us quickly talk this plan out, at first filled with youthful bravado, and then taken over by two maxims:

1. We didn't want to hurt someone who hadn't done anything to us. We didn't know this guy, and we knew we were in the wrong.
2. Deep down, we didn't really want to steal the guns. We just wanted to know we *could*. It was all about mission completion, not violence.

We hear the door of his trailer open, and we scurry away like cockroaches.

Lying in bed that night, it occurred to me for the first time that the owner of the gun store might have had a gun himself, and that trying to subdue him might have been dangerous. I consider it for a moment, and then shrug it off. *I would have taken him.*

I nod off to sleep.

———

Betsy.

That's what we'll call the girl that holds Auggie's infatuation. She is not my favorite. There's nothing wrong with her personality. She is super fun. She's pretty. When she's around, she's cool. My problem is that she is not one hundred percent on Team Auggie.

Betsy splits her time between two very different cliques. Clique one is made of fifteen-to-sixteen-year-old meathead jocks: Auggie, Aaron Graves, Matt Romo, and me. Clique two is made up of seventeen- to nineteen-year-old BMXers and dirt bikers who spend a lot of time drinking and smoking. Neither clique is very fond of the other.

It's a nice summer night and we're all at a party having a good time except for Betsy, who was invited but never showed up. The phone rings and the kid who lives at the house comes over and hands the phone to Auggie. "It's Betsy," he says, looking kind of worried.

Auggie picks up the phone and is instantly agitated. I see the veins in his neck pop out. Apparently, Betsy is at a party with the dirt bikers on the hill behind El Camino Real, and the guys are getting real douchey and handsy. She sounds really upset on the phone and begs us to get there quickly.

Normally, Auggie would have gone himself or with just me to pick someone up, but something in the back of both of our heads said these guys might start some shit and we better take backup, so we asked Aaron and Matt to come too.

The four of us pile into Auggie's car and head toward El Camino Real. When you drive south on El Camino, it dead-ends at the 101 highway on the north side of Atascadero. From there, you can either hop on the on-ramp to the 101 or you can continue driving down what becomes a dirt road. That dirt road ends on a hilltop. The back end of that hilltop is where all the kids go to party. The cops can't see them from the road or the highway, even if they have their headlights on, so unless a cop is extremely motivated, it is basically a safe place to drink or smoke or do whatever you want. It is also explicitly dirt biker and redneck turf. If you have a four-wheel-drive truck, a four-wheeler, or a dirt bike, you could drive all the way down the hill to the Salinas River and camp out. If you don't, you have to park at the back side of the hill and then walk a few hundred meters down.

We park at the top of the hill and begin our descent. A few steps down and we can already tell the party is in full swing. Kids are drinking everywhere. Other kids are having sex in the back of trucks, while their friends make jokes nearby. There are a few bonfires raging, but all of the headlights are out.

"Where's Betsy?" Auggie asks anyone who will listen. We keep getting pointed deeper and deeper into the party. I have a very uneasy feeling. This part of the camp reeks of weed.

Finally, a girl tells us she's right behind a nearby truck. We walk over and there she is. "Betsy!" Auggie calls out. She will not make eye contact with him. My feeling about this situation transitions from very uneasy to extremely bad. Headlights pop on from several of the nearby vehicles lighting up her face but blinding us.

"She doesn't want to go with you," comes a voice beyond the light.

"I think she does. She called us and asked us to come get her," I answer firmly.

"How about you guys go fuck off?" comes the not-so-subtle reply from one of the bikers, who is now visible. He and his group begin to emerge from beyond the light. We are outnumbered.

"Well, we're not leaving without her," Auggie says without a moment of hesitation, even though we are now being surrounded very quickly.

That's when a bottle breaks over Aaron Graves's head.

Bikers come from everywhere. This is not a kid fight. This is our first fight for our lives.

Violence envelops me. I don't know how many people I hit. Maybe thirty? Maybe fifty? They come at us with beer bottles, chains, and bats. I feel both my hands break for the first time in my life, but I cannot stop punching or I might just die.

Auggie gets hit with a bottle and falls to a knee for a split second but bounces back up and just fucking drops the guy to hell. Aaron is not as lucky. He catches some kind of a baton to the face, knocking him out, and then gets kicked in the face while he's down. Auggie and Matt rush near him to keep him from taking more damage. There's blood running down Matt's face, and his eye is almost swollen shut. I feel a chain whip across my back and then loop around and hit the side of my neck. I pivot and throw a wild elbow in that general direction and connect with a face. I back up toward the guys.

"We need to get the fuck out of here!" Matt yells. He's right. Pound for pound we're the better fighters. We're the fucking lions. But four lions can't beat scores of hyenas and jackals.

A small part of Auggie doesn't want to leave. He wants to keep fighting. Or at least, he doesn't want to leave unless I'm on board. "Let's go!" I shout.

With Matt and me as his shield, Auggie bends over and scoops up Aaron into a fireman's carry.

"Fucking go!" I yell when I see him waiting for me. Matt and I stay in the pocket for a minute or so, keeping the fight going to give Auggie a lead. I'll never forget the smell of that moment. My mouth is full of blood, and I can taste the iron, while my nose is full of dust, truck engine exhaust, and dry plains grass. These are scents and flavors that do not usually mix, at least not for most people. Certainly not for me. Little did I know, this smell and taste would revisit me later in far more dire circumstances.

Matt and I keep backing up, heading in Auggie's direction. Now only the bravest of the jackals are veering out. "Go!" I yell at Matt. "Catch Auggie!" With that, Matt takes off up the hill. I keep swinging. I give Matt thirty seconds, then I lunge at the closest guy and knock him on his ass. I take advantage of that brief moment of shock and turn tail and sprint up the hill. About halfway up, I look back. No one is following. They're just screaming at us and calling us pussies and laughing at our expense. Auggie is almost to the top with Aaron. *What a fucking stud.* That is a hell of a fireman's carry. Matt is walking, not far behind him, looking back at me. I don't slow down just in case they hop on their bikes or four-wheelers, looking for more action.

We load Aaron into the car and peel out.

Aaron looks really fucking bad. Something is wrong with his face. He's now conscious, but he needs a hospital. Auggie is bleeding badly from his head. Matt and I look like shit, but except for our hands, nothing seems insanely out of place.

Auggie drops Matt and me off at the party and takes Aaron and himself to the hospital. He was going to bring me too, but my teenage brain told me to go to Ann Johnson's house, because her sister was a nurse.

Aaron had a broken orbital socket and a broken jaw. Auggie had a skull fracture. We all had at least one broken hand and a lot of scrapes, cuts, black eyes, and bruises.

In the ultimate measure of teenage stupidity, Auggie forgave Betsy for her part in the debacle and kept dating her.

For the first time, I had to fight for my life. It's a fight most people will never understand. We all think we will rise to the challenge when the moment comes, but most of us go our whole lives without that belief being tested. I tested it today. I learned to fight through fear, to stay calm in a sea of chaos, and that I will not quit, even when the odds are against me. For all my cuts and bruises and breaks, I am happy it happened.

I am different because it happened.

CHAPTER THREE

I DIDN'T CHOOSE
THE FIGHT LIFE

"Fuck!" I scream out.

After beating five guys in a row with ease, a dude that has never submitted me catches me in an armbar. I am not mad at him at all. I am absolutely furious with myself for being careless. I am so consumed by my rage. I don't realize the dojo has suddenly gone quiet.

Barry, one of our head black belts and an active police officer, walks toward and behind me with purpose, unsheathes a wooden sword, and whacks me on the head as everyone—including my dad—watches.

It hurt like a motherfucker!

I look up at my father, incredulous, waiting for him to say something to my instructor in his youngest son's defense. He smirks and leans back, placing his hands over his head. He said nothing, but his face said, *"You deal with it."*

I suppose after the firing, the river fight, the car theft, and my generally bad attitude, my dad had had just about enough of sixteen-year-old Tim's shenanigans. He knew, if left unchecked, I was going to end up dead or in jail given the reckless and self-destructive pace I was keeping.

That's how I ended up at Do Kan Jiu Jitsu.

Do Kan Jiu Jitsu is a traditional Japanese Jiu Jitsu gym in Atascadero run by Terry Keller and Barry Smith. This place is nothing like what today's Jiu Jitsu players are used to, where people start from their knees without takedowns or strikes, nor does it resemble a friendly Taekwondo place of today. It is purely about unflinching, brutal self-defense; it doesn't mess around with katas and forms where everyone is lined up punching in unison in a preplanned dance. The players train hard. There is striking, knife work, takedowns, and of course, the groundwork Brazilian Jiu Jitsu is now known for. More than anything else, though, the senseis demand respect, of which teenage me is not particularly fond of doling out.

In fact, that's probably a charitable representation of my attitude. I am kind of a cocky asshole, and to make matters worse, I am really strong for sixteen with a natural gift for grappling that's been honed through years of wrestling with my friends and brother along the riverbanks near my house. Within a couple of months of joining, I am beating most of the other people there, just on raw athleticism and meanness. Unsurprisingly, this only reinforces my cockiness.

Neither Terry nor Barry care about my prowess. They care about my *character*. Still, that whack on the head hurt and is still reverberating through my skull. I consider saying something to Terry, but as I look around and absorb the judgmental energy coming from so many people I respect, for once in my life I think twice and swallow my pride. For once in my life, I keep my mouth shut. The training continues and the eyes leave me.

At the end of practice, Terry lines all of us up, placing me at the very end of the line. He calmly walks up to each person and asks, "What is respect and what is disrespect?" I listen as each person responds in turn, my face redder and redder with each answer. When he gets to me, he doesn't ask me for a long while. He just stares at me . . . long and hard so that I feel the weight of it. By the time the sound of his voice rings in my ears, I am completely consumed with shame. I have nothing to say for myself that has any meaning, so I offer him and the class an apology. He continues to stare, then slowly walks back to his place at the front of the class.

Once there, he absorbs the entire line one last time, leaves his eyes on me for just a beat, and dismisses the class. We bow and I attempt to flee as fast as is humanly possible. As I get close to the door, my dad strikes up a conversation with another student. To this day, I don't know whether that was just because he was being friendly, or whether he wanted me to wallow in my humiliation just a little bit longer.

I think that was the first time I cared what someone other than my family really thought about me.

Man, this place is a dump.

Even though I am nervous as hell walking to the front door, the underwhelming nature of this place takes me aback. It took me two months to build up the courage to come to SLO Kickboxing. The place had not been on my radar until sixteen-year-old Jake Shields visited my dojo and beat me over and over again. At seventeen, I am bigger and stronger than Jake, but he and his Carlos Gracie Jiu Jitsu got the better of me.

I always want to be the best guy in the room doing the hardest stuff, so I am unwilling to put the blinders on and ignore that a greater power than my dojo exists. In his *Allegory of the Cave* (thanks for the classical education, Mom!), Plato describes men who were perfectly happy their entire lives living in a cave and looking at the occasional shadows of the outside world reflected on the cave wall, believing that the shadows are all there is in life. When they are finally released from the cave, the blinding light of the sun hurts them, but in time they grow accustomed to the brightness and the fullness of the real world. When they are brought back to the cave, where they were once happy, they are now sad and depressed, because they now know their world is incomplete. Well, my life isn't that deep, but I am definitely living the *Allegory of the Jake Shields*. I was so happy two months ago! Fuck that guy.

Just kidding.

I love Jake. In a decade, I will be super proud of him when he wins the EliteXC, and then Strikeforce Championships. But right now, at the age of seventeen? Yeah, fuck that guy!

So here I am, at SLO Kickboxing, walking into one of the most dilapidated buildings I have ever seen. I am going to be training with a rising star in the UFC, a guy by the name of Chuck Liddell, alongside his merry band of badasses. First, we have Gan McGee, an almost 300-pound wrestler from Cal Poly who fought for the UFC world championship against Tim Sylvia. Gan lost, but Tim popped for steroids that fight. Next, we have Eric Schwartz, another Cal Poly wrestler who is undefeated in the WEC and the K-1 kickboxing circuit. He's Chuck's main training partner. Never far from him was Scott "Lights Out" Lighty, a K-1 kickboxer and mixed martial artist. Then there's Jason Von Flue . . . you know . . . the guy that the famous Jiu Jitsu choke is named after? Yeah that guy. Cruz Gomez is the one little guy in the mix, meaning he was about my size of 5'11", 170 pounds, but what he lacks in stature he makes up for in abject savagery. Finally, there is Glover Texeira, a Jiu Jitsu badass, who would go on to become the UFC Champion with the most subs at light heavyweight in UFC history.

Of course, I know none of these people; a friend of a friend set it up so I could come train with them. I walk up to the door and push it open. As sad as the outside of the building is, the inside is somehow worse. The first thing that hits me is the smell. Is that puke? Is that urine? Is that armpit sweat? I have no idea, but if you can imagine a concoction of all the possible scents that can come from a human body and mix them together and bake them in an oven, that is SLO Kickboxing. The environment is especially jarring because I'm used to Terry and Barry's place where everything is clean, bleached, and taken care of daily. But this is clearly not a dojo, and not a place to learn life lessons. This is a fight house. Welcome to the MMA world of the late '90s. There's no coaching, science, or structure. Everyone just beat each other up and the toughest guys make it.

The first thing I see is a flier on the wall for "Friday Night Fights." I don't know it yet, but these fights are where fraternities can ride the

MMA craze by getting drunk and fighting drunk dudes from other fraternities. Because they are amateur fights, there is no governing commission needed, which means they can be completely unsafe and unfair. The place fills with coeds and kegs. Beer spills everywhere. That skunkiness still hangs in the air from the last one, which apparently occurred a few days ago.

The place is dark for no good reason. It is wall-to-wall shitty industrial drop ceiling panels and flickering fluorescent lights. They are probably the same lights that were in the place when they started renting this building because many of them were out or dim. The room is warm and not in a good way. It's the suffocating, oppressive warmth of too many human bodies pushing themselves to the max. I see a continuous spray and perpetual drips coming off the heavy bags landing in puddles on the pieced-together assortment of mats; this is *not* a nice place.

"Tim!" Chuck hoarsely shouts from across the room. As I make my way toward him, I see the guys for the first time. They all look like monsters to my young eyes, especially Gan, who is literally twice the man that I am. Glover and Cruz are about my age, but the rest all have a few years on me. These are real men. It's clear everyone here has been training hard and together for some time.

Nowadays, when someone new comes to train, there are always pleasantries. You shake hands, share a few things in common, warm up a little, and build a little friendship bond before training. None of that happened to me at SLO Kickboxing. They all sort of acknowledged that I was there with little more than grunts and nods. Then I hear: "We're going to start with wrestling."

By the way, I wasn't really invited to this camp. I wanted to be here so I figured out who I knew that would get me in for a workout, but I definitely wasn't asked or recruited. It's not that they don't want me; they just don't care. I am an unknown quantity to these men who have all earned their reputations with hard training and, in the case of Chuck, Eric, and Gan, elite accolades.

I start to wrestle with Eric. I am a good wrestler for a kid but I am not an elite Division 1 wrestler. The pressure testing begins. Eric smashes me. He's quicker, stronger, and more technical. I can't get to his legs. He gets to mine easily. I eat a cross face on one of my shots and I'm already bleeding. No one tells me to go stop the bleeding. The blood just mixes with the sweat and we keep going. The timer rings and all 280 pounds of Gan jumps in. I shoot. He sprawls and the sheer power of his sprawl is so great that my face hits the mat and I feel his jockstrap hit my ear through his sweaty shorts. It's beyond gross. It's probably the same jockstrap he wore for ten years. It probably carries four different strains of the bubonic plague in whatever remains of its fabric. As he flattens me out completely, he laughs and reaches over my body and grabs my leg, then pulls me into the air upside down and throws me aside like a child. No, that's an insult to children. He throws me aside like a homemade sock puppet. I offered him no resistance. Gan didn't even wrestle me in the real sense of the word. He big-brothered me.

My reprieve (if you can call it that) is wrestling Von Flue and Gomez. They are a little smaller and my wrestling is on par or slightly better than theirs. So after getting absolutely mauled by Team Cal Poly, I at least am not embarrassing myself. But wrestling with them isn't easy. It's more like the state champ wrestling with the guys who got third and fifth. I'm winning more than I'm losing, but I'm definitely not dominating. Still, this is good, because I need something to cling to after having my world literally turned upside down by Eric and Gan, and winning some exchanges pushes my confidence back up. *I do belong here.*

As quickly as the wrestling begins, it ends. Apparently, wrestling is the warm-up. That's definitely a new one for me. The guys start slapping on shin pads and sixteen-ounce gloves, so I do the same. It's time for some kickboxing. We walk over to the ring. It's not even really a ring. It's four posts banged into the concrete with a piece of canvas kind of stretched over the floor. It's stained with blood and sweat. My rounds are going to be with Eric, Chuck, Gan, and Scott. Right before I get in the ring with Eric, Gan provides me with the only kind words I would receive that day, although I didn't realize it in the moment. "If you hit Chuck hard, he hits back hard. You should avoid that."

These guys think I'm some fucking kid. I'll hit as hard as I want. Aggravated, I am standing across from Eric. The bell sounds. I move forward and he lazily does the same.

Whack!

I eat a jab I didn't see.

Whack!

Fake jab that I bite on. Leg kick.

Whack, whack, whack!

Jab, cross, hook.

Those stung. I'm already bleeding. *How is he this fast?* Looking across the ring, Eric looks so chill, it pisses me off. He's sparring with me the way that most people do the mundane. Is Eric grilling, changing the channel in his boxers on a Sunday morning, or sparring with Tim Kennedy? I'm not sure, because apparently they take the same amount of effort. For two minutes, I chase Eric. For two minutes, I fail to catch him. Not one hit. Not one landed punch. I am a slab of meat dangling in front of Rocky Balboa. He tattoos me. The round sounds. I have thirty seconds to compose myself before I will have my first round ever with Chuck Liddell.

Chuck climbs into the ring. There's a calm about him that I haven't really seen in anyone else. He doesn't waste energy. There's no talk or fanfare. He just gets in the ring and kind of looks at the ground until the bell rings. Then he looks up and his eyes find me. I walk forward. He cannot be as fast as Eric. He just can't be. And he doesn't seem like it. He doesn't seem fast. But I still cannot hit him. Every swing misses him. They all feel like they will connect, but then he simply isn't there, and I am getting hit in return. The hits sting, but they don't sting like Eric's. *Maybe this guy has just been hyped up?* Finally, and I don't know if it was my luck and athleticism (because there was no skill at this point) or if Chuck just let me land one, but I connect. And I hit him hard. As hard as I could.

Big mistake.

Chuck hit me back. At will. And now I understand.

Now I understand what I mistook for "slowness" is actually skill. What I mistook for "softer hits" was generosity. That is gone. Every punch goes through my skin, through my flesh, through my bones, and into my soul. Chuck's punches hurt. Every fucking one. No matter where they land. Face. Body. Legs. Every strike makes me want to quit.

That one punch is the only clean hit I land the whole day. After Chuck beats the shit out of me, Scott and Gan do the same. At some point it all ends. I can barely move. I thank them for the workout. They barely acknowledge me.

I stumble outside. The world looks different. I almost forgot there was a place that existed that didn't involve pain. I walk over to my grandpa's sun-worn blue Ford Escort wagon and lean against it for a moment. Pain is splitting my head and seemingly coming out my ears. Finally, I want to move again, but as I do, I realize I have left a bloody imprint of my face against the side of the car. I look in the car mirror and see that my entire face and shirt are covered in a mist of my own blood.

My eyes are swollen, and I may have some new cauliflower ear. I throw my gear in the back. I'm sure I am concussed because it is hard to focus my eyes on anything. I sit for a moment in the driver's seat haphazardly sipping on one of those green Gatorade bottles and then start my twenty-minute drive home. I feel dejected. I thought I was gonna be the badass. Everything I thought I knew is gone.

I fucking sucked.

––––––––

Today was a good day. After an entire year of inviting myself to training at SLO Kickboxing and legendary trainer John Hackleman's "The Pit," the guys invited me to Chuck's fight camp. Chuck will be fighting Steve Heath, a Cesar Gracie guy. Eric Schwartz made it perfectly clear I am not coming in as a partner but as a meat bag: I will be one of the guys that Chuck is going full force on as he prepares for the fight. This is a very different scenario than I have ever encountered before, and I do have some trepidation. Chuck has beaten me up many times, but he has never been in it to hurt me. Eric warned me that this will be different.

Still, I am finally becoming one of the cool kids. For a dude who is eighteen on his way to nineteen, officially being part of Chuck Liddell's fight camp is a huge deal. Up until this point, I've received a lot of mixed messages from these guys and the greater Pit universe. Hackleman, the maestro of this group of violent men, doesn't seem to know what to do with me. He's always nice, always positive, but also reserved, as if there's something about me he doesn't seem to love. Lots of the veteran fighters at the gym tell me that I'm too cocky for a new guy, but I have no idea what I'm doing to make them feel that way. I'm just being me! The only clear message Hackleman gave me was to stop flirting with this brown belt from the gym, Casey. Casey is 5'5," blond hair, blue eyes, tough as nails, and more mature than any girl I have ever met. She's Chuck's ex, but since he has apparently moved on, I don't see it as a huge deal. Hackleman is obviously overreacting.

But those are problems for another day, because I am 29 hours and 59 minutes into a 30-hour drive from Paso Robles, California, to New Orleans, and yes, it is Mardi Gras. Technically, I'm not here for a good time. My dad (you remember him, the elite counternarcotics cop) got me a job doing grunt work for Knoxx Industries, an ultra-high-end gun company run by Gary Cauble and Jim Bentley. Even though I am their youngest employee, they have a lot of trust in me, because they have a lot of trust in my dad, and the apple can't fall that far from the tree, right?

In retrospect, it's possible some of that trust was misplaced.

A few weeks ago, they asked me to drive their black Lincoln Navigator down to the gun show in New Orleans. It was loaded with prototype experimental weapons they are developing for the government. They allotted me five days to get down there, enough time to allow for the trip and preparation for the gun show. While this was the amount of time a reasonable human being with good decision-making skills would require, I can certainly improve on the schedule; their way lacked efficiency. I decided that if I drove nonstop without resting, while simultaneously pissing in Gatorade bottles, I could get there in just over a day, giving me three and a half days to drink in Mardi Gras. I had never been, and as an eighteen-year-old, the idea of hanging out with a bunch of beautiful women celebrating whatever it is that Mardi Gras is supposed to celebrate is appealing. Also, I understand there will be nudity and beads. I like both of those things. Is this a perfect plan? Yes. Yes, it is.

So, I arrive in New Orleans and the pre–Mardi Gras festivities are in full swing. I haven't slept in a day and a half, but this place completely energizes me the second I arrive. This is wild. I've been to Vegas, but this puts it all to shame. It is a total commitment to fun. Alcohol is flowing freely. There is a limitless supply of beautiful women in all shapes and sizes, and apparently there is some kind of law that prevents any of them from covering more than a few square inches of their bodies in clothing. Music is blasting everywhere with such a constant fun rhythm that as a nondancer, I still find myself haphazardly swaying to the music. I need to get up close and personal with all of this Mardi Gras stuff, and I need it right now.

I park my Navigator full of experimental prototype weapons on the street, lock the doors, and start scoping for a place that looks interesting. After five to six minutes of exploration, I plop down at a little touristy bar full of coeds so I can people-watch . . . and by people, I mean girls. This is an odd situation for me. I've never been afraid to talk to women, but there are so many beautiful women here that I'm sort of overwhelmed by so many choices; I'm not sure which group to walk up to first.

So I order a cranberry and 7UP and decide to soak it all in before making a decision. Almost immediately after my first swig, two college bros start yelling at some dude that just bumped into them. I saw him walk into them. The way he bumped them caught my eye. It seemed planned. He now has my attention. Upon closer inspection, I notice he has a nice case of cauliflower ear going. *Awwww, here we go!*

Ears starts jawing at the two bros, and it looks like I am going to get to see a fight in my first fifteen minutes here. I take a nice pull off my cranberry spritzer and lean back to watch. In fact, the entire bar is now giving these three meatheads their undivided attention. But then two guys at a booth walk over, break it up, and ruin all the fun.

One of the guys, a skinny, kind-of-tall guy, wearing a gray T-shirt and dark jeans, pipes up, "We own a bar down the street. If you guys want to work this out in a ring, then we'll pay the winner. What do you say?"

The bros really like this idea, because like most men, they think they can fight. This idea is as dumb as someone who has never played the oboe thinking that in a pinch, they can pick one up and knock out Benedetto Marcello's Oboe Concerto in C Minor (again, thanks for the education, Mom!), but nevertheless, this belief persists because fighting is so interlaced with masculinity that for one to admit one cannot fight demeans a man's ego too drastically to bear. Moreover, unless you're in the fighting family, if you have gotten into a fight or two you have only fought other nonfighters, giving you a false sense of security and capability about fighting in general.

I know what the bros don't know. Ears is a fighter, and this will only end one way. They depart, I give them a quick toast, and then flip a coin, which results in me going over to talk to the table of mostly blondes, as opposed to the table of mostly brunettes. The ladies are super friendly and embrace me as one of their own. In a few minutes we are all laughing and having a good time, and I am about to order my second beer. And that's when I notice that Ears is back. It's only been about twenty minutes, maybe thirty since his departure. I watch him scout the room, find his target, and execute. Like clockwork, he bumps into the next set of bros. Now I am really intrigued. Once again, the two guys materialize. Once again, they find their next suckers. I put my drink down. I order a beer.

The third time Ears shows up, I am ready. As he finds his place at the bar, I turn around quickly and shoulder-check him, spilling the beer on him. "Watch where you're fucking going!" I say to him, mean mugging him. He pushes me back a little. I step forward into his space as if we're in a UFC weigh-in. Lo and behold, the two hustlers show up. "Maybe you'd like to settle this in our bar," they ask. "Winner gets $200."

"That sounds perfect," I say, without breaking eye contact with Ears.

When I arrive at their bar, the scene is hilarious by today's standards. The motif is clearly "The Dive Bar in Any '80s Movie." Am I in the Double Deuce from *Road House*, or is this place real? I don't know. But the floors are sticky, it reeks of mildew, and the clientele leave much to be desired. The "ring" is not a boxing ring; rather, a literal ring made with red rope on the floor. It bothers me a little that they didn't make the ring a perfect circle, but then I leave that thought as I contemplate the rest of this setup. The base of the ring is a thick cardboard coating made of cut-up boxes covering what is essentially a stone floor. There are no gloves or protective equipment. There are no corners. There is no medical support. They just put you in the ring, a fat guy announces the fighters, and a bunch of drunken assholes cheer what amounts to Ears beating the shit out of some college kids and then throwing their unconscious bodies out the back door. And when I say that I mean that literally, because that's what happened to all of my opponents that night.

Ears is up first, and I assume because he has those ears, he is a grappler. At this point in fight history, there really aren't any true MMA fighters. Almost everyone who fights knows one discipline, maybe two if he was lucky. I was lucky. I trained at the Pit. I had boxing, kickboxing, Jiu Jitsu, and wrestling, and I was used to Gan McGee and Chuck Liddell handing me my ass. Ears tries to take me down with his junior varsity Jiu Jitsu takedown attempt. I cross-face him hard, staggering him and forcing him to his feet, and then cave his face in with a basic jab, cross, hook combination. It is short and brutal. The crowd is shocked but also titillated that their champion is defeated. Their drunk cheers fill the mildewed air. I become the new "Ears."

The two shady dudes bring me four more opponents that night, all of them big college bros. I choke a couple of them out and knock a couple of them out. I only catch a few shots the entire night, but because they are bare knuckle shots, they leave a mark. Nevertheless, at $200 a win, that was the easiest thousand dollars this eighteen-year-old had ever made. Plus, the bartender is super cool (and hot) and lets me crash on her couch for the next few days until my bosses show up.

For the remaining seventy-two hours of my first Mardi Gras, I have an absolute blast. I tour the city with my new roommate, fight all day until the sun goes down, and then party all night. It is absolutely an amazing experience! Best of all, I pocket almost $5k after three days of hard work. This is crazy-good money and I am so thankful to be a Pit fighter right now.

The next day, I arrive at the convention center in my pleated kha-kis and a polo looking like a fucking blueberry. I have a black eye and marks all over my face, and I can barely use my hands because I have been bludgeoning men with them in a bar for the past few days, and my fingers are swollen like sausages. Ostensibly, I am at this gun show to show people how our attachment can convert a tube-fed shotgun into a magazine-fed one. The problem is that I cannot use my hands . . . at all.

Gary sees me and as a good and decent man, he is concerned. He asks good and wholesome questions like, "Are you okay?," "Were you in an accident?," and "What happened?" To my credit, I tell him the truth. In my entire life (and you know what kind of life I have lived), I have never seen a more shocked face. After a long pause of reflection, Gary slowly raises his shaking head, his gaze leaves the floor he is staring at, and his eyes find mine. His voice is almost cracking as he quietly asks:

"Where were the hundreds of thousands of dollars' worth of proto-type guns while you were sleeping on couches and fighting in bars?"

Gary is desperately hoping for a good answer.

"They were locked in the car, parked on the street," I answer.

I was wrong.

Now I had seen the most shocked face of my life.

Gary never asked me to drive again.

On the flip side, though, this is the first time I have ever been paid to fight, and I definitely have a taste for it. While these fights didn't count toward my official amateur record, they were the first of my thirty or so "off the books" fights that happened in dingy bars, Indian reservations, and Mexican strip joints. I like to think my path to the UFC began at Mardi Gras as an eighteen-year-old.

So, Gary: Thanks for trusting me to drive to New Orleans . . . and sorry for everything else!

I crawl out of my car and the sweltering air that hits me is somehow refreshing, even though it's already over 90 degrees outside on this Sep-tember morning. I'm parked on the outskirts of Las Vegas. I can only afford to stay in a hotel every two to three days, so most of the time I find a cheap parking deck or sit under an overpass to avoid the sun and my car doesn't become a convection oven. I still have a little bit of a dehydration headache, so I wash down some warm water out of my bottle. I stretch out, reaching for the sky, and let my body crack and pop and get ready for the day. I feel the clothes that I've had sitting on top of the car all night. They're dry. Still, I'm going to have to find a sink and some soap to wash them in and get in a shower today for sure. I walk over to the side of the road, make sure no one is watching, and let out the kind of long, exciting piss that is only possible when you know you're pissing in the wrong place. *Time to get going.*

It's about 10:30. Chuck and the boys were out all night partying with John Lewis. John is a former kickboxer that fights in the UFC. He's well connected in Vegas and can get into any party or strip club at a moment's notice. Some fighters treat MMA like a professional job and watch their weight and make sure no impurities enter their systems. My boys partied. Even the night before a fight, Chuck would be out drinking. These dudes are apex predators in every sense of the word. But I am nineteen. And I cannot get into clubs. And I do not have a hotel room.

After a year of being invited to fight camps for Chuck, the magic has worn off a little. It isn't that I'm not happy or appreciative to be part of the big boy's club, but I'm still an outsider. I'm good enough to beat up and have around, but the guys never see me as good enough for the show. This is my first trip to Vegas with them. I was excited, but then realized they got everyone but me a hotel room. It's not that they don't like me; it's that they don't care whether I'm here or not. And that's the worst feeling in the world. I almost wish they just told me they didn't want me here. That would hurt a little less. It's incredibly frustrating because it's not as if I haven't built up my own record of success.

I have a 30–1 amateur record and finished my ammy career by winning the 2001 California Cobra Championship on an Indian reservation. It was a who's-who of talent. I had four fights and defeated Scott Smith in the finals. Nick Diaz, Bo Taylor, and Jake Shields were all there and they all won their weight classes. Nate Diaz tried to get into the tourney, but he was only fifteen so no one would let him in or take an exhibition match. Other than my early loss, I had finished every single one of my fights except for that finals match against Scott Smith, which I dominated.

I throw my crispy clothes into the backseat and slide in behind the driver's seat. I look into my rearview mirror and see it, the scar that is my constant reminder of my first pro fight, a loss to Scott Smith. Yeah, the same Scott Smith that I beat in my final amateur fight. *Fuck.*

Last month, I was back on the same Indian reservation at the Gold Country Casino for my first pro fight at the IFC Warriors Fight Challenge 15. The promoter is a guy by the name of Paul Smith. Paul Smith is exactly the kind of guy that would be running a semilegal MMA fight on an Indian reservation. If you're a fighter, that picture should be easy to create. If not, then take Dana White, add some spray tan, some Drakkar Noir, a gold chain (or five), purple fucking contact lenses, and some excessive biceps and you're there.

The card is huge! There's Dennis Kang, Frank Mir, Nick Diaz, Paul Buentello, and Ivan Salaverry all on one card. I am the first fight of the night. There is no place to warm up. The place reeks of weed and bar water. I can't tape my hands because there is no one here that can do it. My only corner is my dad. They give me the gloves for the fight.

They aren't MMA gloves. They are fingerless boxing bag gloves.

I put them on, get announced, and I walk out completely cold. The crowd is shouting obscenities at me. I don't think they hate me per say, as they shouted the same things at Scott, but this is new for me. I don't feel like I'm going to a fight.

In my head, my dad's words are on repeat: "Get off first. Don't take him for granted. You just beat him, and he wants revenge. He's coming in hungry. Make sure you get off first!"

When I get in the ring, it still doesn't feel like I'm about to fight. None of it feels real. My skin is cold from the air-conditioning and words are being spoken by the announcer but I'm not really hearing them. When we are asked if we are ready, we both say yes. The bell rings and it is somehow a surprise.

Get off first.

I shoot a terrible double leg takedown with no setup and without closing the distance. Scott hits me with an uppercut that rips my head wide open. Blood is pouring onto my face as I scramble and pull him into my guard, a position where I am on my back with my legs wrapped around him to control his ability to punch me.

The referee stops the fight. *What is happening?*

He calls the doctor over, who sticks his fingers into my head wound and moves it around. "I can see bone," he says nonchalantly, adding, "We're done here."

I cannot believe it. I'm fine. It's just a cut. I'm part of the Chuck Liddell camp! I cannot lose my first fight!

But I did.

They take me in the back in what can only be described as a large broom closet. The same doctor that was in the cage came back here with me. There's a bendable light that he's using to see my wound. His black-and-gray hair is pulled back into a ponytail, and he pops a cig into his mouth and smokes while he breaks out the needle and thread to sew me up. My eyes focus on his bone necklace of an eagle claw, which bounces around every time he moves his arm. He is not using medical sutures. This is a normal needle and thread. He at least has the decency to blow the cigarette ashes to the side so they don't fall into my face.

My dad and I are silent the whole way home. I am mad at myself, but I let some of that spill onto him. I prefer to be in a calm zone before a fight, but he had me amped with the whole "get off first" thing. I decide then and there, probably unfairly, that my dad will never corner me again. Most of all, though, I'm shaken because I thought I was unstoppable.

Anyway, I've been running that fight through my head the past month. That was my chance to really become one of the guys—to be a real pro fighter. I do not want to be here. An 0–1 pro sleeping in a car on the side of the road because no one got me a room and I have no money, and no one took me out because I'm too young, heading to continue my job as a meat bag for Chuck's first workout of the day.

As I get closer to the Strip there is a billboard of Chuck and Busta-
mante. It's huge and surreal. The guy I have been training with for two
years is up on billboards, on flyers, on television. It's wild and exciting
because I feel I am a part of all of it, but it's also soul-crushing, because
I am the only one sleeping in a car. I so desperately want to feel a part
of something. There is no place else to go. (This is before the days of
Xtreme Couture, or Team Quest, or Venom. One's only choices are go
to random BJJ or boxing gyms and hunt for partners or go to a fight
house.) These guys are the only game in town, and they don't care that
I exist.

I want it not to hurt. I know I am tougher than this. But their indifference cuts so much deeper than anything Chuck is about to do to me
for the next hour.

After the brutal workout that afternoon, Gan McGee and Eric
Schwartz buy me lunch. It's a huge deal for me. Later that night, Chuck
hands out tickets to watch the fight. I quietly sit and hope that I am
going to get one. I do. It's the first time I feel like anyone thought of me.
I let that small thought fill me up.

The next night at Mandalay Bay, Chuck beats the crap out of Mu-
rilo Bustamente. I have never seen such opulence and pageantry up
close before. The announcers, the ring girls, the big screens, the giant
crowd—all of it makes the event seem enormous. It doesn't smell like
cigarettes and beer. It's clean. It's fancy. I feel like I am living part of
history.

This is what I want for myself.

I want to be the guy with the spotlights on him in the middle of a Las
Vegas arena. But I am 0–1.

It's time to fix that.

On November 9, 2001, I return to the IFC, this time for Warrior
Fight Challenge 16, and I face Jody Burke. John Hackleman, Cruz
Gomez, and Jason Von Flue corner me. It was a big deal to me that
Hackleman showed up. I didn't realize he considered me one of his guys
until that moment. Turns out, though, that I didn't really need anyone
that night. I beat Burke in forty-two seconds with a forearm choke.

I get paid for the first time as a professional fighter. $200 if you win. $0 if you lose. It's nice to be on the $200 side of things!

I will not lose a fight again for six years.

———————

Chuck Liddell is passed out in the seat next to me as we fly from San Luis Obispo to Salt Lake City. I'm stoked. After my second win, I was invited to Extreme Challenge 50 (EC 50) to take part in their middle-weight tournament. EC 50 is a significant step up in both competition and professionalism. They provide two plane tickets and offer a purse for the winner of $5,000. That probably doesn't sound like much given that I would have to win three fights in one night to earn that, but it was a lot better than most people were seeing at this point.

I'm surprised and happy that Chuck is here. Despite my best efforts, I never get the sense that we're friends, just training partners. Don't get me wrong, things have gotten a lot better lately. At the Vitor Belfort fight, he got me a hotel room . . . well, five of us had to share that one room, but still, it wasn't a car. He recently also started to include me in some of the security gigs that the boys got hired to do for concerts and events. And yet, it always feels like we are almost friends, as opposed to actual friends. In fairness to Chuck, it is possible that I did not help my cause by dating his ex-girlfriend Casey.

Nevertheless, when the opportunity came up, I did not have to ask him. He just told me he was coming with me. He was superhuman that weekend. To start, he paid for the hotel room. This was an incredible gesture because I straight up did not have the money. In fact, I traveled with $20, because that is all that I had and didn't want to ask my parents for it. For these little fights there isn't a "Fight Week" like there is nowadays; you show up the day before and make weight, then fight the next day.

The plane lands in Salt Lake City, and we grab our bags and head to the hotel room and dump off our stuff. I immediately get into my "slicks," which is a wrestler term for a plastic suit that you put on that helps you sweat your ass off, and Chuck takes me to the local YMCA.

He pays the $5 fee for each of us to get in and he sits in the sauna with me. Most people think of a sauna as a nice place to go, smell a little wood, and relax after a workout or a hard day at the office. To wrestlers and fighters, it's a very different experience. It's where one goes to suffer. If you haven't pushed a stationary bike into a sauna and pedaled it for two hours while that dry, hot air permeates your lungs and you start to lose vision because your body is overheating, you haven't really lived. Anyway, I hop on that bad boy and get to pedaling. It doesn't take long for the sweat to run off my nose and slide down my slicks into a puddle on the floor underneath me.

Chuck keeps the conversation light but does what a good corner is supposed to do and tries to keep my mind off the misery. When my legs get heavy and I hear sloshing sounds, I pause for a moment to pull the leg cuffs away from my ankles so the sweat can dump out onto the ground. I am baking.

"Let's check your weight," Chuck says finally. *Thank God.* I fall off the bike and stumble outside. That first breath of cool air is indescribable. It's the best thing that can ever happen to you short of drinking a gallon of water. I peel out of the slicks as sweat dumps all over the ground and use a plastic scraper to squeegee anything stuck to my skin off of me. Finally, I pat myself down with a towel. I get on the rickety old high school wrestling-style scale with the weights that you slide to the right. I close my eyes and breathe out as Chuck moves the weights.

"You're one pound over. That's good enough. We have time," Chuck says quietly. I take a shower, resisting the urge to open my mouth and drink some of the water, then I pat myself down once again and don some old gray sweats. We have a couple hours before we can weigh in. Weigh-ins for EC 50 are not like they are nowadays where fighters square off and there's fanfare and photographers. Weigh-in is between 5:00 a.m. and 8:00 a.m. The sooner you make it, the sooner you can eat and drink.

The waiting is the worst part. You have a headache from being dehydrated. You desperately want liquid in your body. Then there is anxiety about whether the scale will be accurate. If it isn't, there is more misery and more cutting of weight in your future.

Chuck and I are at the scale ten minutes early. I step on the scale. A half a pound under.

I start drinking water immediately. Years later I will do this scientifically with proper nutrients and timing and all healthy foods. Right now, it's water and a Snickers bar that Chuck grabbed from a candy dispenser. Let me tell you, I could have kissed him; it was so good.

We walk across the street to California Pizza Kitchen and Chuck buys me my own pizza. I was so happy. I ate every crumb. Nutritionists everywhere, you heard it here first: the optimal pre-fight meal is a Snickers and pizza. I slept like a baby that night.

———————

The fights start at around 5:00, because the tournament is supposed to culminate around 10:00 p.m. The rules at this point in MMA are savage. You can kick and knee a downed opponent, which keeps him from attempting a lot of sloppy shots for fear of getting caught underneath and getting massacred. This ruleset is great for me, because Gan, Chuck, and Eric had made me into a savage wrestler, especially for MMA. Unless someone sends an All-American wrestler out there, I get to dictate where the fight goes. It's a huge advantage. MMA rules will evolve in the future to become less brutal, more controlled, and more humane.

My first draw is Ryan Narte. He's very fast and has a career as a successful kickboxer. I close the distance and take him down, mount him, and bludgeon him, forcing a TKO from strikes at 1:22 of the very first round.

So far so good. It might be an easy day.

Next up is Jason "Mayhem" Miller. Miller is an excellent fighter and is becoming one of the first fighters to have a real fanbase. His crew is called the Mayhem Monkees, and they follow him wherever he goes. Don't get me wrong, it isn't like they are filling stadiums, but they are a presence, and they give him a certain gravitas. That makes me want to beat him more.

Our fight goes the full three rounds, but I barely get touched. I beat him in every position, significantly out-striking him on the feet, and when we get to his bailiwick, the ground, I hold top position and do damage. Chuck is calm in the corner, making one small correction in each round, but basically letting me do my thing. Right before the end of the third round, the seam of Miller's glove, which they tape nowadays, slices my face open above my eye. As the judges deliver my unanimous decision win, Chuck whisks me away before the athletic commission gets into the ring.

"What are we doing?" I ask.

"When those idiots see the blood, they will end your tournament. We need to hide you," Chuck replies commandingly. I agree and follow him to the back.

These face bleeds are a common thing for generation one MMA fighters. We all had so many fights as amateurs and we went so hard in training compared to the smarter training fighters go through nowadays that our faces are basically all scar tissue. So we bleed a lot. Doctors hate bleeding. Hence, doctors are our enemies.

Once inside the back area, Chuck keeps watch by the door. When he sees them coming, he drags me into a broom closet far removed from where the fights are occurring and hands me a cold compress to push against the wound. "I'll come get you when it's time to fight," he says, before leaving.

At some point the bleeding stops, and I just enjoy the quiet of the room. I'm in an alternate universe. Moments ago, I was being cheered on by a crowd while fighting as a prizefighter and now I'm in a closet surrounded by janitorial supplies. Except for the smell of cleaning agents, it is actually pretty Zen.

Chuck busts through the door. Whether a half hour or an hour or two hours has passed since I saw him last, I have no idea. "We have to fight now, Tim," he says. *Here we go.*

As we walk out, Chuck leans into my ear and says, "Let's try to end this quick. If you start bleeding again, they might take it from you." *Looks like I will need to end this quickly. Got it.*

Cruz "the Saint" Chacon is standing between me and $5,000 and the respect of the closest thing I have to a mentor. I will not be denied.

The bell rings and we touch gloves. He's a tough dude, but he does not like it when my fists touch him. Finally, I close the distance enough to take him down and punish him. He gets through the round, but he is tired and I have not been touched. Somehow, I am not bleeding. I get to my corner and Chuck just says, "Keep it up," in that low voice of his.

The seconds get called out and round two begins. I land a good punch combo and then take him down again, getting a dominant knee on belly to mount position. His fight fades as I rain down punches on him. At 1:21 of the second round, the ref calls the TKO due to strikes.

I did it! I am the EC 50 Middleweight Champion!

The crowd cheers, but once again, Chuck whisks me out of the ring and to the back. He finds the producer and demands the $5,000 check, which the producer provides. Chuck throws me in a taxi and we shoot over to a 24/7 pawn shop slash cash checking place. We have to give up 5 percent of the check in order to cash it. "Why don't we just wait until tomorrow and cash it at home?" I ask him. "Trust me, you need to cash it now," he replies.

Chuck takes me back to the California Pizza Kitchen, and even though I have $4,750 in my pocket, he buys me another pizza. I order the BBQ Chicken Pizza.

Whether he likes me or not, Chuck absolutely looked out for me. The guy that I aspire to be in the cage donated a week of his life to me. He's on billboards. He fights UFC main events. He doesn't need to be here. In fact, he probably shouldn't be here. But I don't know what I would have done without him. He had my back in every way, even though there was nothing in it for him at all. *He does care.* I am so thankful for this moment.

It's one of the best weekends of my life.

CHAPTER FOUR

RED, WHITE, AND BLUE

In the late '90s and early 2000s, no one is "just a fighter."

We all have grown-up jobs. The guys fighting now, in the late '90s and early 2000s—the Chuck Liddells, the Jorge Riveras, the Diaz brothers, the Nate Quarrys, the Randy Coutures, and yes, little old me too—are not trying to be famous or make money. We simply want to be the best. We love fighting.

It's impossible to even compare our crew to the crop of professional fighters who will follow; we are meaner, tougher, and dumber. Our path to success is harder and we have no expectation of making real money or achieving great fame, although both would definitely be welcome. We do it purely for the love of martial arts. At this point, MMA is not a sport. It is not a place for athletes. It is a place for people who want to test themselves to the limit—to know who would win if life and death were on the line. But when someone asked what any of us did for a living, no one was answering, "I'm a fighter."

So during this time period, while fighting consumes a huge portion of my life, it is not my professional goal. I want to be a cop. My dad is a cop. My brother is a cop. My sensei is a cop. They are my heroes. That's what I am going to do. The problem is that in California, you cannot go to the police academy until you are twenty-one. So at the age of eighteen I need to kill time until I can become a cop. What's the next best thing? Being a firefighter. In California, before you can become a firefighter, you need to become an emergency medical technician (EMT). So I develop a plan:

1. Become an EMT.
2. Become a firefighter.
3. Become a cop.
4. Be awesome for all time, like my dad, brother, and sensei.

Many before me and many after me have and will execute this exact plan. The real question is: Can I do it?

Most people know that police officers refer to themselves as the "Thin Blue Line." The Thin Blue Line represents a line of defense comprising uniformed men and women intent on keeping criminals away from civilians and protecting social order from chaos. Over time, firefighters, borrowing heavily from their blue brethren, began calling themselves the "Thin Red Line," and EMTs followed shortly thereafter calling themselves the "Thin White Line."

I'm gonna join all three of them.

WHITE

As we pull up to the accident, my nineteen-year-old brain can't help but think this is the scene of a horror movie. The lights of our fire truck cut through the night, but instead of finding any solid shapes, they just find floating brown dust. The combination of the new moon, the dust, and the flickering blue and red lights from the engine makes seeing virtually impossible. Tom Way, our senior paramedic, slows the vehicle down. Tom's expression doesn't change as we get closer. In fact, I'm not sure anything ever changes about Tom. Looking at Tom, I don't know how old he is. I've seen pictures of Tom from decades ago. He looked sixty then. He looks sixty now. He will probably look sixty twenty years from now. Anthony Stornetta and Star Harrington, the other members of our team, a man and a woman who are usually boisterous and fun, are quiet, their eyes piercing the night intently looking for victims. They sense what is coming, while I do not. Finally, the lights catch the outline of the white fifteen-person church van. It is hard to make out a lot of detail through the refracted light, but one thing is very clear: it is upside down and the windows are shattered. Its tires are still spinning, propelling it nowhere, as useless as a fish's fins are in the air. It's sitting in chest-high weeds just off of the road, and the whole thing looks like the opening to *Children of the Corn*. I'm half expecting some creature to walk out of the stalks.

"Let's go," Tom quietly but urgently tells us.

I have only been assigned to Station 2, in Atascadero, for a couple weeks. We don't get a lot of information when the call comes in, so heading in on October 22, 1999, at 11:02 p.m. we only know that there is a traffic collision on the southbound side of the California U.S. 101. We don't know the number of vehicles involved or the number of passengers. Apparently, someone called because they saw hazard lights blinking and dust in the air. Until this moment, we had no reason to believe this would be a major incident.

Like I said, I'd just turned nineteen years old, and while I've been on a few calls already, nothing up to this point would prepare me for what I am about to see.

As I step off the truck and my boots hit the ground, I can already taste the dust. Continuing the horror movie motif, the things that immediately catch my eyes are hymnals being gently blown toward me across the ground. I can smell the burning fuel of the vehicle interlaced with the dust. I also smell the burning weeds near the van, and the acrid smells of blood, urine, and feces. I now hear the wailing of people in pain, seemingly coming from everywhere. I realize quickly several people have been thrown from the vehicle. The wails are not screams. When people are screaming, they have their faculties and are generally aware of acute pain and injury. Wails are worse. They come from a deeper place inside a person. They happen when one's body is so broken that it cannot muster a scream, or even a full breath. And those wails and moans flood my senses, freezing me where I stand. Again, I am just nineteen.

I hear Tom finishing up the radio call. "Send everyone," he says. The radio operator understands and confirms. Tom places the radio back in its proper place and hops out of the truck and, as he strides past me, says, "Pick one."

That's something my teenage brain can understand. I move toward the wail that sounds closest. Tom moves elsewhere. Anthony and Star have already disappeared into the night. As I sprint into the dust storm, I suddenly realize it is a miracle we did not hit any bodies driving in. Bodies are everywhere. Blood is everywhere. Bibles lay strewn across the ground. Hymnals and evangelical pamphlets flow across the fallen and into the night beyond my vision. One man is wandering the scene, in shock. Anthony tends to him.

I arrive at the first body splayed across the road. He is a mess. His entire body is covered in so much blood I can't make out all the wounds, and I start running through my memorized checklist for trauma assessment and begin to administer care. I'm working on the body for maybe two minutes when I feel someone hovering over me. I look back over my shoulder just as Tom grabs it.

"Hey Tim, let's go find someone else, okay?"

I cannot comprehend what he is saying. I keep working. I have to save this one. He squeezes my shoulder again. "I need you to find someone else."

This time I get up and wander into the night, confused. I look back and I see that Tom has left that person as well. It didn't make sense. I have watched too many television shows, where things always work out the way they should. Tom knew what I didn't know yet—there was no way we could bring that guy back, and there are a lot more victims that needed us.

Then something snaps me out of that thought. I hear a sound that is different from the rest. It isn't a wail. It's crying. But not high-pitched crying. It's the kind of guttural, hiccupping crying that every parent knows. It probably started as a high-pitched scream, but has faded as the lungs have gotten weaker and weaker . . . *Oh my God, that's a kid.*

I run to the sound, but the rule is that you have to care for people as you find them, and as I begin to move in that direction, I come upon a dozen more bodies scattered across the pavement and in the grass of the median. This is my first mass casualty event and I freeze again. Between the sights of the wounded and dead near me, the cries piercing the night, and my desire to find this kid at all costs, I've lost the ability to process all of the information. All of these people are depending on us, and I am overwhelmed. I don't know enough. I can't partition my brain and do a real assessment. I am in lizard-brain, react-to-the-stimulus mode.

Thank God for Tom.

Tom sprints around the scene, quickly triaging victims and telling Star, Anthony, and me exactly what we need to do for each one and in which order. Up until this point in my life, I thought I understood excellence. Tom showed me I did not. Not blood, not screams, not the ticking clock reminding us that lives are hanging in the balance blur Tom's vision of what needs to be done. He is unrelenting. He also knows the skill levels of his team. He knows who can handle what. He knows I am a total newbie and to expect me to save the hardest cases is a bridge too far. The calculus this man is processing by the second in order to maximize the number of lives saved is astounding. I want to be like Tom. But I don't have anything that he has because I haven't earned it. I don't have the reps. I don't have the training. I have not sacrificed the time and effort necessary to make what he possesses mine. And I already hate that.

Satisfied that he has the situation under reasonable control, Tom gives me a task up to my skill level as an EMT. "Tim, go find the kid," he quietly commands. He doesn't need to say it twice. I run off in the direction of the crying. After what seems like a lifetime, but is probably one to two minutes, I literally stumble on her. She's beautiful. Maybe four or five years old. A tiny little thing. So perfect, but so very broken. I take a sharp breath. "It's going to be okay," I tell her, trying to convince both of us that it was true.

It needs to be okay!

My initial assessment is grim. She has a broken pelvis, four broken limbs, probably multiple ruptured organs, and massive hemorrhaging. *She is going to die.*

"She's here!" I yell, but I realize Tom Way is already here. "Find someone else. I've got her," he says. Fear grips me. He said basically the same thing when he left the first guy I found. I take a couple steps away and look back. He isn't leaving. He's working on her.

Thank God. Tom thinks she still has a chance.

The next patient I move to is a woman. Her leg looks like you gave a toddler a Gumby toy and let him just bend it the craziest way possible. Her leg is literally an S. Her arm is backwards. Smell dominates the moment. California has beautiful smells and soils. It always smells fresh. I can pick up California dirt blindfolded and know it. The smell of that soil mixed with gas, bile, blood, urine, and feces is another scar I carry that will never heal. Twenty years later, all I have to do is think about this day and that smell fills my mind again with a vengeance, even if I am halfway around the world. It's forever part of me.

We still can't see. We're using sound and feel to find the injured. Anthony runs back to the truck and shuts it off so we can at least hear better.

The night becomes a blur, challenging the boundary of every skill I possess. I plug holes. I apply tourniquets. I brace broken limbs. I put people on stretchers and apply neck braces. It's four guys trying to save fourteen lives. An ambulance arrives. Now there's seven of us. A second fire truck arrives, and with it comes a godsend, Captain Keith Aggson. He is 6'4" and 300 pounds with a booming voice and as soon as he is on the ground, everything gets better. Without any discussion whatsoever, Tom moves himself from the command role and into a pure lifesaving role. More and more vehicles arrive. Seasoned veterans take one step into the scene and I see their faces change. Each and every one bites down on his proverbial mouthpiece and gets into the fight.

What felt like an hour later because of adrenaline but was probably only fifteen-to-twenty minutes, Tom Way is loading the little girl into an ambulance, and he gets in with her. There are dozens of men here now and Aggson is running the scene with brutal efficiency and professionalism. I keep working, doing everything I can with the limited knowledge I have to help. At some point, the last body is being lifted into the last ambulance. The doors close. Our mission is over.

It is light outside now. Looking around, I have no idea how long I have been working. I have no idea how many bodies there were or how many I worked on.

Everyone pauses and looks around. We are all covered in blood and dust and bodily fluids. Everyone I see has a thousand-yard stare. The scene looks more like the beaches of *Saving Private Ryan* than it does a California highway. The Chief calls us all into a small circle. No words are really said. We stand at the tailgate of the captain's engine. We don't really know what to do. We just stand there . . . empty. Many of these hard-as-nails men start crying. I realize I am crying too. The moment is beautiful and horrible all at once.

Every patient but one could have died. Some died on the scene; several more made it to the hospital alive but died of their injuries. In the end, seven of the fourteen people lived. And those results were an absolute miracle. Whether you believe in God, divine providence, or just dumb luck, I know for certain that if three other men were on station and responded that night instead of Tom Way, Anthony Stornetta, or Keith Aggson, we would have lost a lot more patients.

As I ride back to Station 2, I feel a sense of loss, but also a sense of pride, and a passion to become better. I feel good about what I have done today, even though I feel sick about what happened. While I wasn't "the man" today (and now fully appreciate how much I have to learn), I didn't quit under the pressure. I know I can handle the chaos with more training and experience. I need to earn what Tom has earned. I don't want to be an EMT or firefighter for life, mind you. But I now know the difference between simply passing an EMT course and truly being able to handle a trauma crisis. Most of all, I don't want to be the rookie who needs guidance. I want to be the calm, experienced leader inside the storm.

When I get home, I find my dad waiting for me. Someone from the station called him before I got home. He has lived this life for a long time, and he knows how it affects a man.

"How are you, son?"

"I'm okay, Dad. I did my job. I'm gonna catch a shower," I reply.

He nods.

Then he adds, "Wipe the tears out of your eyes before you see your mom. Good job today."

I didn't realize I was crying. I didn't know I could. Now it makes sense why it was so hard to see through the windshield when I was driving home.

That week, every one of the hundred guys that worked that van wreck is forced to take convalescent leave and attend counseling. I don't think I need the counseling, but as I sit next to Tom, Anthony, and others in group therapy and they recount what happened, it is shocking that what they remember is nothing like what I remember, nor do their stories match each other. When trauma hits, you remain laser-focused on what's in front of you. You lose peripheral vision and a sense of the bigger picture. Memory, a thing I have always viewed as ironclad, becomes very malleable.

The men in therapy struggle with the same things I do. *What if I had known more? What if I moved faster? Did I do everything I could have?*

I feel emotionally sound, perhaps more so than others, but I don't like my answers to these questions. I don't want to feel that weakness again.

While everyone else talks and shares, I look at Tom Way, sitting calmly off to the side. No one did more than he did. No one saw more blood and pain. But he is comfortable; the rest of us are not.

Generally, we never hear how our patients do once they leave us and head to the hospital, but we all needed to know about just one of them: the little girl with literally everything wrong with her and no chance of survival.

She lived.

Tom. Fucking. Way.

RED

Right about the time I turn twenty, I graduate from being an EMT to a full-fledged firefighter. This is a huge step forward for me. I am no longer the low man on the totem pole. I am now the real deal.

There is one problem: I hate my boss. Unlike the amazing Captain Aggson, my Fire Chief (a Hall of Fame shitbox who I refuse to name and will simply refer to as "Fire Chief") sucks. He has anger issues, an alcohol problem, and is a womanizer. And while those attributes describe an awful lot of men of action in the '90s and early 2000s, they were often overlooked.

He also sucks at his job.

So as I begin my official firefighting career, I have a boss that lacks the requisite skill to do the job but is chock-full of formal authority. I am a guy who has always respected skill and experience, but not necessarily formal authority. It's a recipe for disaster, but since one of us is the fire chief and one of us is the rookie, a wise person would know that if push comes to shove, the disaster is going to land on the rookie.

I am not a wise person.

My Fire Chief has a "three strikes and you're out" policy. All you have to do as a rookie firefighter is not make three big mistakes in your first year and you're golden. Since he was almost always drunk or trying to bang some random woman, that made avoiding negative attention a simple goal, but young Tim Kennedy is an overachiever.

Strike One

I'm just getting back to my apartment after a workout at the Pit when my pager goes off. I'm off duty, but I look anyway. It's a medical call for a potential suicide victim. I see the address. *That's right next door.*

Given that the incident is happening inside my apartment complex, I walk over to see if there is anyone that needs help. As I walk up, I see a fire truck parked out front. I wave. Some firefighters are setting up a staging area to provide any aid once the police give the all-clear. They're going about their business, oblivious to the apparent danger that is happening inside the building.

Right after I see them, I see a police officer. She is the first officer on the scene, and she is tiny. I identify myself and ask if there is anything I can do to help. She explains there is a man inside who may be armed with a knife, threatening to kill himself. As the only officer present, she is going to go in alone.

I look at her again. 110 pounds soaking wet.

I look at myself. 220 pounds. Riddled with muscle. Trained in MMA, Jiu Jitsu, stick fighting, knife fighting, and sword fighting. I was literally just sparring with Chuck Liddell!

This is a no-brainer. It is dumb for a 110-pound woman to walk into a house alone. Frankly it would have been dumb for me to walk into the house alone, or anyone. No one should ever walk into a dynamic and dangerous situation without backup. One of the things my dad always hit home with us is that you never know what can happen, and when it happens, it happens faster and more violently than you expect.

"Hey, do you want me to go in with you until the other cops show up?" I ask.

I see her bathed in relief the second I suggest it. "If you don't mind, that would be amazing," she replies.

"Of course. I know you'd do the same for me," I say in my best team player voice.

We walk to the door of the apartment and knock.

"Go away!" comes from a man's voice inside.

The officer reaches for the door handle and it is open. "Sir, we're coming in!" she shouts.

As we enter the room, we see a thin, average-sized man with brown hair. He is holding a knife and is clearly under duress.

"How's it going, sir?" she asks.

"Hey, man, I'm Tim," I chime in.

He looks back and forth to both of us.

"I don't need you here. You need to leave me alone,"

He says this, but he says it without the gusto of a man truly committed to what he is saying. In my "expert" opinion, he doesn't want to kill himself. He's just having a bad day.

While the officer uses her soothing feminine voice to calm him down, I slowly close the distance. She does a phenomenal job, and in no time, he isn't even looking at me. I pick my moment and lunge forward, grabbing his wrist. The second I make contact, he drops the knife. He absolutely does not want to hurt me. When I am sure of this, I slowly walk him over to the police officer, who gently cuffs him.

"It's going to be okay, man," I assure him. And with that we begin to leave.

What a day! And to think I almost didn't respond to this!

As we exit the door and hand the man over to the police who have now arrived on the scene, I notice my Fire Chief is now here. In fact, there is a crowd of firefighters and police officers present. I see him walking over to me. I expect he's going to pat me on the back for a job well done.

"Why in the fuck is one of my firefighters walking out of a building with someone in handcuffs?" he barks.

I quickly begin to explain the situation to him and am cut off. I can smell the alcohol on his breath.

"Do you think I give a fuck? Firefighters do not detain people. We do not wrestle knives away. That's not our fucking job! If you want to be a cop so badly, you should go to the fucking police academy and be a fucking cop!"

Yes, dickhead, I know. I plan to go to the police academy the second I turn twenty-one, you piece of shit.

Luckily, I don't say that out loud. That would be dumb. Instead, I drop, "If we're the kind of guys that would let a 110-pound woman walk into a building with a guy holding a knife alone, then we are a bunch of cowards. We aren't cowards, are we, Chief?"

I thought this was a fucking masterful response by a rookie in front of a crowd of forty people to provide to the anger-riddled, drunken Fire Chief. Deep within my soul, I thought he would see the error of his ways and come around to my way of thinking and perhaps caution me to be more careful in the future.

Instead, he spent the next thirty minutes swearing at me like a dive captain who had just chased a teenager who took off his dive gear to chase a lobster. He then decided to convert this oral reprimand into a formal written reprimand.

Strike Two

I look over the ledge at the smashed car. It's beat up. We were first on the scene, but the second engine has since arrived and the five other firefighters are all excited, breaking out all kinds of ropes and pulleys and shit to do a technical rappel into the ravine to safely get the driver out. The ledge isn't that steep and what they are doing seems dumb and a waste of time. I climb stuff like this all the time by myself. Hell, I climbed stuff like this all the time when I was ten years old!

It's only a few months after I got yelled at the first time for violating the rules, so there is a voice in the back of my head warning me that I should just wait for these guys. That voice gets interrupted.

I hear crying down below. I look at them. They're busy laying shit out on the road and arguing the merits of different anchor points. They're discussing who will rappel down and in what order.

While they are doing that, I walk around the vehicle, grab a Halligan tool, and start climbing down the ravine. It took me less than a minute to scale down the forty feet. When I get to the bottom, I see that there is a middle-aged woman inside. I can tell she has a broken femur, and she is bleeding profusely from the leg. There is no time to wait for the other guys.

The door is busted in, so I use the Halligan to pop it open and use my gorilla strength to rip it out the rest of the way. I undo her seat belt and pull her out of the vehicle, laying her on a ledge a little away from the car. I immediately apply pressure to the wound to slow the bleeding. Luckily, she reacts well to the pressure, and there is only a trickle coming out from either side of my hands.

I look up. They are still setting up their contraption. She one hundred percent would have bled out if I hadn't come down.

"We're going to need a splint and a tourniquet!" I yell up.

They look down. They see me. At this distance I can't see their glares, but I can definitely feel them. A few minutes later, they rappel down what can only be described as part of a child's playground. One would think they were scaling K2. I kind of chuckle to myself because it all seems so ridiculous watching them.

Three of them arrive with a stretcher, a tourniquet, and a splint. In no time, they do their thing, and she is strapped down to the stretcher and ready to head back up to the top using a winch and an intricate system of pulleys. Props to the team, because as humorous as it was watching them climb down, they did a good job setting this up. I grab the bottom of the stretcher and climb up as the guys who are strapped into the lines grab the top and either side.

Up is obviously a little harder than down, but in about three minutes we're back on the road and our patient is safe! The ambulance is already here and as soon as the patient is disconnected from our line, the paramedics take over. In less than a minute she is safely in the back of the ambulance as it pulls away to take her to the hospital.

"Great job, guys," I say with a smile on my face. They aren't super smiley in return.

I ruined their dopey, ropey game fun and they are mad at me.

Who cares? If I hadn't gone down there, she would be dead.

When we return to the station, the Fire Chief is waiting for me. He is not pleased.

"Did you go down a fucking ravine without safety equipment?" he bellows.

"Well, I wouldn't call it a ravine. More like a tiny hill, but yes, I climbed down myself," I reply.

"Did someone tell you to do that, Kennedy?" he asks, knowing the answer.

"No, but she would have bled out if I hadn't gone down there! The ropes were taking forever," I fire back.

"And what if you had slipped and fell and broken your own fucking leg? Then you'd both be fucking bleeding out and you would have been a fucking liability to the team. Then what?" he asks.

I know he's not expecting an answer, but clearly I needed to respond to provide context. "First of all, I'm not drunk or fat, so I wouldn't fall down. Second, everyone is just mad because they didn't get to save the day using their fancy ropes," I retort.

How's he gonna come back from that one?

I was written up a second time.

Strike Three

I can already feel the heat of the fire raging through the house in front of me. I am on the hose. Alan Linear is right behind me. The twins are behind him. Anthony Stornetta is way back, constantly clearing the hose over obstacles as we push forward.

As soon as we are inside the archway of the front door, I feel myself baking. Even under air and with a mask on, nothing prepares you for the oppressive sweltering heat that is a house fire. Hot air moves just like ocean water. It finds the slightest crack, the most minute crevice, the tiniest imperfection, and it floods it. The heat hit my neck and ears, and I felt it dry my eyes as the seal on my mask was the slightest bit off. Adjusting the mask to fix that problem, I push forward, almost at a jog.

I can see the heart of the fire. I watch it licking the ceiling and crawling up the banister. It's beautiful and evil and it is time for it to die. I open my hose wide and revel in the hiss of the cold water hitting the wood, creating steam, but delivering the first death blow to the blaze. Excitement and adrenaline roll right through me, and I push deeper and faster into the house, dragging Anthony with me. Every once in a while, a droplet of water, now boiling, hits my neck. It hurts, but I push forward. In addition to the hiss of the wood, I also hear a strange popping sound as the water penetrates wood. There's something incredibly fulfilling about it. Every one of my senses is working overtime.

I feel Alan, my team leader, pull on my back. I ignore it. The fire is shrinking rapidly as I pour thousands of gallons of water into this home. I'm not backing out now, only to have to retake this ground again if we let the fire spread back here. The popping is coming faster and more frequently now. It must be because this wood is even hotter.

I drive forward into the final room even more aggressively. I watch pieces of wood disappear as my stream of water hits them, reducing the ash they have now become into wet soot. The popping sounds like popcorn at this point. The pulling on my back is more insistent and more urgent.

Why is Alan being such a pussy? Let's just get this done!

I stay with it until the fire in my quadrant is dead. At some point the pulling stopped. I'm happy Alan finally found his balls and let me do my job. I keep hitting the burnt-out walls and floors with water, making sure that they don't reignite. Finally, when I am certain I have done my duty, I begin to walk back. I didn't realize it at the time, but as I backtrack out, I notice we'd moved almost the entire length of the house. *I did even more than I thought!*

As I looked at all that I had conquered, I felt completely vindicated. I beat that fire.

When we hit the night air, my neck feels cold, almost frigid, but then I feel a stinging sensation. Maybe I got hit with more water droplets than I thought. It felt like a bad sunburn already.

"What the fuck was that, Tim?" Alan yells at me as he rips off his mask and helmet.

Before I can answer, I see him. He looks like shit. Any exposed skin he has is red as fuck. As his helmet comes off, his neck looks like a red ring—almost like he has a choker on. He rips his gloves and jacket off. They're soaking with near boiling water and his arms and hands are red.

He is pissed!

The other guys look equally pissed.

"When I tell you to back the fuck off, you need to back the fuck off! You were spraying us with boiling water the whole time because you pushed too hard, too fast, and we are all burned to shit. And, you also almost killed yourself. Look at your fucking mask and helmet," he yelled.

I have no idea what he is talking about, but to humor him, I pull off my helmet. As it comes off, my hand bangs against the mask that separates air from fire, life from death. It shatters and my finger goes right through it.

Only now do I see what he was trying to tell me inside. My helmet was melting. It was literally on fire and I had no idea. The edges are melted. It is now an odd shape. Worst of all, though, the quarter-inch mask shield had melted to less than a millimeter. It was like the top of a perfectly scorched crème brûlée (again, thanks, Mom). It looked perfectly fine and stable, but the slightest touch and it fell apart. It had no strength at all.

That popping sound wasn't wood. It was bubbles forming on my helmet and mask that were popping as it melted. Alan was watching my safety gear bubble and disintegrate, and he had been trying to save me.

If that mask had failed inside, I would have passed out instantly. My face would have been burned. They would have had to drag me out. I would have been a huge fucking liability.

For once, I had nothing to say. I loaded my gear into the truck and stripped down to my waist, realizing my whole body was covered in soot.

I was written up again.

Third strike!

I am out.

BLUE

You know a great way to get over failing at something? Trading that thing, that you didn't really love anyway, for the thing you always actually wanted to do. Just as I receive my third strike as a firefighter, I turn twenty-one, which means I am heading to the police academy.

As I mentioned, both my dad and brother Nick are cops. The Kennedys make great cops. It is now my time to continue that Thin Blue Line.

My police journey starts at the Santa Maria Police Academy and I am thrilled to be here. The structure is rigid and consistent. Every morning we start with physical training (PT). The training is painfully easy for me, and I expect the same for all of my classmates, but I realize on the very first day that many of these people can't even do a pull-up or a push-up. As hard as I try, I can't remember a time when I couldn't do a pull-up or a push-up. For me and my friends, a pull-up is part of the warm-up before the exercise. It isn't the exercise! How did these people think they were going to be police officers? Oh well. Not my problem. I'll leave that to the instructors to solve.

After PT, we have a classroom session. That session includes, over time, things like California state law, report writing, penal codes, traffic law, and many subjects that police officers are required to know in order to execute different aspects of their jobs. After class, there is a lunch break, then some kind of semi-physical or physical activity. The activities are varied: combatives, arrest and control, defensive tactics, getting Maced, getting Tazed, or an obstacle course. These are probably my favorite activities and my favorite part of the day. I consider these exercises of primary importance for honing the real police work.

After, we have another class similar to the first one, but on a different block of instruction. About halfway through, we also do the Emergency Vehicle Operations Course (EVOC), which lasts for about a week straight. Prior to EVOC, I thought I could drive. After all, I had held my fair share of races and could drive better than anyone I knew.

I had nothing on these instructors, however. The lead instructor could literally drive faster, cleaner, and with more accuracy backwards than I could forward. Whether it was cone work, stopping another vehicle, or using the emergency brake to cut a hard corner, my driving skills grew exponentially every time I rode with them.

In short, everything is going great and I love everything about being here.

Santa Maria is about an hour away from Atascadero, so after the first few days, I start carpooling with three of my classmates. These guys are not what I consider physical specimens. In fact, they are probably below average in fitness, but I really like them because they have the perfect hearts for police work. They are gentle, calm, soft-spoken, and maybe most important, great listeners. The physical stuff can be improved upon if they really want it, but personalities rarely change very much. To be honest, there are probably only two to three studs in the entire class. The rest of the class is roughly 50 percent average and 50 percent terribly unfit.

After my carpoolers failed the first few days at doing pull-ups, I offered to help them and they accepted. The weirdest part for me isn't that they can't do a pull-up. It's that they want to but they don't know how to get to the point where they can. I can look at any problem, especially a physical one, and develop a road map to solve that problem. Can't do push-ups? Start from your knees. Can't do a pull-up? Use bands. This concept was foreign to them, and to the class. So I built a framework. Every time we had a break, they'd do one pull-up. If they couldn't get it, they'd jump up on the bar and do a couple negative pull-ups. After a while, one became two, and two became five, and five became ten, and they could do pull-ups.

Some of the other students who were struggling with the physical requirements saw the workouts and the results, and asked me if they could join our group. Of course. I always respect people who want to improve themselves, no matter where they are starting from. So my little group of three added a person or two every week. We practiced climbing walls, running the obstacle course, and improving our physical fitness. I had my own little pack and I felt like I was leading this motherfucker.

And I was. I had the highest physical grade, the highest practical grade, and the highest academic grade. I was crushing everyone. And crushing everyone brought out a little bit of good, old-fashioned Tim Kennedy cockiness, which in turn had a tendency to get me in trouble.

"A trained person can beat any number of untrained people," I casually explain to my arrest and control cuffing class. They do not want to hear me say this. Not the students. Not the instructors. Not even my little pack of workout buddies. Everyone wants me to shut up and admit I am wrong, but do I? No, I do not back down one inch.

At this point, I am not belted in Brazilian Jiu Jitsu, only Japanese Jiu Jitsu. However, if I were to guess as to my level, I am a purple belt. A purple belt that wrestles every day with Division 1 wrestlers and kickboxes with K-1 fighters. (Guys like me do not really exist in the early 2000s.) I double down. "There is no one in this class that could get handcuffs on me. Not in a million years."

The head instructor, a little muscular Asian guy, steps in. "Three officers, using the proper technique, can stop anyone, period."

I smile.

Of course, I don't consider that he has to say that to the class. I don't consider that he needs to build confidence in these students. I only think about what I know to be true and the lesson I must teach everyone as the superior trainee. You see, after I was at Barry and Terry's for about a year, Barry would take me to his police substation for arrest and control exercises. I was sixteen or seventeen at the time with way less muscle than I have now, and actual cops would try to cuff me. They'd put the padded suit on me so they could use their batons, but their batons are basically built off the ninja weapon known as the tonfa, which I trained with often. So as a teenager, I routinely fucked up a bunch of dudes who had been cops for years, stole their batons, and then put on a baton clinic. Now I am twenty-one years old with thirty-five pounds of additional muscle, and I have been training with Chuck Liddell and Gan McGee. I know exactly how this is going to go if it goes down . . . and I need to tell them and, if necessary, show them.

"There is no way on God's green earth that three officers can get cuffs on me, and there's no way anyone in this room can get cuffs on me if I don't want to be cuffed . . . period," I add, just to be a dick. I hear groans. I see eye rolls.

My instructor bristles.

I need to bring the point home, so I continue, "You'd have to be able to catch me. Then you'd have to get me on the ground. Then you'd need to control my arms. Then you'd need to get them together. You have no chance. Period."

"Well," my instructor says, "let's find out."

It is now officially on and I couldn't be happier!

He sends in the three toughest dudes. The whole class is cheering for them. There is not a single person here who wants me to win.

They are all going to be disappointed.

When you do the three-man cuffing drill, there is a high guy, a low guy, and an arm guy. The high and low guys work together to take you down and hold you down and the arm guy controls your arms and cuffs you once you are on the ground.

The high guy comes at me and I throw him to the ground. Not a big dramatic skilled throw. That wasn't necessary. I bitch-snap him to the ground with something that would never move a wrestler or a judoka. As I finish tossing him, the low guy dives for my legs. I stuff his head, forcing him to face-plant into the ground, and then catch the arm guy as he dives in and hold him by the wrist. I take the cuffs from him and cuff him to the low guy. Absolute humiliation. They're out of the fight, but the high guy has climbed back to his feet.

Just as I am about to smoke him, the instructor calls two more people in. I crush them. Then three more. Then three more. This continues for four iterations before rage and frustration sets in and the mob decides to attack me en masse. That makes it harder, but it still isn't a real fight. When you're a fighter and you fight untrained people, they might as well be children. Training regularly is a superpower. These people cannot really hurt me unless I let them. Given that, I make the conscious decision not to knock anyone out or hurt them too badly. Instead of punching them, I use open hand slaps and not at full force. Just enough to let them know they'd be knocked the fuck out if that's what I wanted.

I fight my entire class for about fifteen minutes. Finally, the instructor shouts out, "The exercise is over."

I'm bleeding. I have bruises all over my arms from the cuffs hitting my skin. There are two sets of handcuffs partially hanging off of me. I look like a cornered rabid dog just hissing at everyone and mouth-breathing while I assess the next threat that I will need to bite.

After the exercise, everyone is mad at me. Not "kill Tim and send his limbs to the four corners of California to teach other cocky fighters a lesson" mad, but anytime you taste a slice of humble pie, it does not taste good. For the entire week, there is a palpable pall hanging over my relationship with my classmates.

The next week is boxing, with the same instructor. He leans over to me and whispers in my ear, "If you hurt anyone badly, I will consider it cause for separation."

I make the decision to let everyone get a few licks in before I beat them. I throw almost all light jabs. No crosses with any weight on them. No hooks except to touch them. Again, these people couldn't really hurt me, but I thought it best to let them regain some pride, mend fences, and of course, not get kicked out.

So for once, I opted not to crush anyone's soul. At the end of the exercise, I am the only one bloody.

———

Four months later, my family is here, proud of me. I'm in my uniform, looking sharp. I'm the Honor Graduate, and I have the highest GPA physically, academically, and tactically. All of my friends improved their physical skills enough to graduate. And yet, I am pissed. Why? Because I am watching the valedictorian receive his award.

You see, while I have the highest GPA, I am not the valedictorian. And I'm not the valedictorian because of a stupid fucking reports instructor. I had to turn in a report for a fake incident as if I were turning it in to a real police station. I looked at the way the report was set up and I thought it was inefficient, so I spent extra time making an entirely new report methodology that was far more clever than the one the instructor had provided. He didn't see it that way and told me as much. I argued with him and explained how my method was superior and would save time and reduce mistakes.

He failed me.

It was a must-do requirement.

When you fail a must-do requirement, you can retest and if you pass, your grade is replaced. I retested and did it his way, grudgingly, and received 100 percent on the report, maintaining the highest GPA.

There is only one problem: If you have any retests, you cannot be valedictorian.

That sonofabitch took it from me.

I am also aggravated at how many graduates there are here today. I know for a fact that many of these people never met the standard. And now they are going to go out and walk a beat. *How are they going to protect anyone?*

This just reaffirmed my opinion that the system rewarded the weak and punished grit and ingenuity. I know what policing is supposed to look like. My dad and his peers are extraordinary, and they do extraordinary things. These guys are pencil-pushing nerds. They don't have the mental agility to fight crime. They're bureaucrats, and they're churning out more bureaucrats.

I'm tired of bureaucrats. First, at the fire station, and now at the police academy, they've squelched my ingenuity and penalized me for solving problems with ingenuity. I've been unfairly targeted by weaker men for things that were not my fault. This is completely unacceptable and unfair.

I watch the valedictorian walk down the stairs. He's going to go work in Morro Bay. What's he going to do? Break up a ring of teenagers crabbing without a license? As a twenty-one-year-old he wants to go police a fucking retirement community.

Not me. My job offers came from Santa Barbara and Stockton.

I was finally going to be a real cop.

CHAPTER FIVE

THE FALL

I am standing naked at the edge of the ocean, halfway through my twenty-third year. The cold surf washes over my feet and the wind spreads gooseflesh across my skin. The sun will be up soon, but for now I remain wrapped in darkness. It's nice to bask in the stillness of this moment. The only sounds are the waves lapping against the shore. There is something cathartic about being alone on the beach I grew up on and stripping my clothes off and letting them hit the sand. I feel incredibly free for the first time in ages. Normally, I'd worry about my wallet and keys getting stolen, but I do not care at all.

What difference does it make?

I wade into Morro Bay, just north of "The Rock," ignoring my brain's warnings that it is too cold and too dark. There is a wall of fog closing in that will soon make it hard to see my way through the black water. I don't worry about that either. As I wade deeper, my legs start to burn from the cold water. I pay it no attention, though. Even as it covers my legs, then waist, and then chest, I barely acknowledge the surf's effects. I don't want to acknowledge it.

I don't want to think about it.

I don't want to think about anything.

When the waves start picking me up off the sandy ocean floor, I begin to swim west.

I have failed everyone I know, and there is no way to fix it. *What the fuck is wrong with me? How did I fuck everything up this quickly?*

I'm a strong swimmer and in no time the shore is a distant memory. It is so peaceful out here. My breath mists a little in the waning moonlight, but other than my own breathing and the sound of my hands and legs cutting through the surf, there is nothing.

I didn't plan on going for a long swim to nowhere in the predawn blackness, but I needed to forget all of it: my actions, the hurt they caused, and the disappointment they manifested in everyone around me. I can't hold on to all this pain anymore. I'm just not strong enough.

Casey and I, the beautiful blonde I met at the gym, had gotten a lot more serious and had been together for over a year. She was the first real relationship I was ever a part of. It felt good. It felt positive and safe. Well, we did fight over normal dumb young people stuff: Did I flirt with that other girl at the gym? Did she talk to this guy too long?

We got all emotional and melodramatic about it and broke up. I actually think it was more that I said something dumb like, "Well if you feel that way, maybe we should just fucking break up?" And she said, "Fine." I don't think either one of us really wanted this outcome, but we are both prideful and lacking in relationship skills, so that's the outcome we got.

Given that we both still really liked each other, one would have expected us to behave how other people would have under the circumstances: probably sleep on it, talk in the morning, hash things out, and work out our issues.

Not me. Being the alpha-male-twenty-nothing idiot that I am, I had to show that I was unaffected by this breakup.

There was this really hot girl named Savanna that had liked me for a long time. I wanted to feel better and she was a smokeshow, so I gave her a call. We grabbed some food, hung out, drank a little, and then we fucked. I didn't really consider the ramifications of what it would mean for her, as she had real feelings for me. She apparently thought of this as the start of a relationship. I didn't think at all.

That weekend, I had a fight in the WEC. I won in dominant fashion but still felt like shit, so I drank myself to fucking oblivion and ended up at an afterparty with some of the ring girls. I flirted with all of them, then made out with each of them, then asked them to kiss, and at some point I was having a foursome with three ring girls. This is not how I was raised. This is not how the men I respected acted. But this is one of the "perks" of being a prizefighter and I am reveling in my newfound popularity and status as a pro. Every time I hesitate and question my behavior, I bullshit myself internally saying that all of this is okay, and this is just what guys in my position do.

I stop for a moment and tread water. I'm at the edge of the Morro Rock, which marks the end of the inlet into Morro Bay and the end of any protection from the bigger surf.

I am now in the unprotected ocean; I feel the increased current. I know this is dangerous and that this water has claimed many strong swimmers over the years. Fog is starting to close in. I should go back. *Fuck it.* I keep swimming into the ocean.

Well, Casey and I did start talking again, and then she let me in on a little news. She is pregnant. *Okay,* I think, *This is scary and insane, but I can handle it.* After all, we have a long history together and, frankly, I miss her a lot. I've had my fun but it wasn't better than my time with her. Maybe this is God's way of bringing us together.

And then I began to receive call after call from Savanna. I'm ghosting her because I'm an asshole; I know she wants to continue the relationship and I do not. I'm going to be a dad and I'm going to follow in my dad's footsteps and be a family man to Casey and our future child. Finally, I answered her call.

"I'm pregnant," she says.

Casey, while understanding, had a very hard time dealing with the fact that I got another girl pregnant within twenty-four hours of our breakup.

Savanna, who thought we'd be working through this as a couple, now had to deal with the fact that not only was I not looking for a relationship despite her pregnancy, but that I was back with Casey, who is also pregnant.

Fast-forward nine months, and my two beautiful daughters, Sabrina and Julia, were born just nineteen days apart.

The girls are the only amazing thing that came out of my selfishness; I hurt everyone else.

Even though I am absolutely the asshole here, society judges women even more harshly than they judge me. It is grossly unfair and makes matters worse. Their pregnancies brought critical comments, whispers, and giggles about both of them, which created a lot of negative feelings all around. Their resulting unhappiness focused on the man who put them in this position, and I felt the full brunt of it. For my part, while I found the nerve to tell my parents about Casey, I couldn't quite bring myself to look my mom and dad in the eyes and say, "Oh, and also there's this other girl."

They are the people that raised me to be righteous, the people who are leaders in our church group, and the people that raised two other perfect kids. I didn't have the balls to tell them I had knocked up two girls. Turns out secrets and cowardice are never a good plan.

Sure enough, eight months after my one-night stand, my pastor called my dad to let my parents know I was at the hospital with Savanna. When my dad corrected him and said, "You mean Casey?" and was given a quick education on my goings-on as of late, he was not particularly impressed with his youngest son. He was even less impressed with the manner in which he found out that he was now a grandfather.

The fiery feeling in my skin is now gone and has given way to numbness. The fog has thickened significantly and very quickly. I look toward the shore and can barely see the Morro Rock, which is the best way to find your way home in that ocean. No matter, I need to keep swimming. I shiver as I keep pushing deeper out into the surf.

It's been a rough year. Regardless of how hard I tried I couldn't pull it all together; there was nothing that seemed to work. Casey and I were strained. Savanna hated me. I was giving all my money to my two baby mamas and still felt like I was coming up short. Despite working multiple jobs, ranging from sales to bouncing, it was not enough.

That might have been enough for any one person to handle, but I was only just starting to meet and suffer the consequences of my actions.

One of the ring girls I slept with during that orgy walked into my gym looking for me. When she finally found me working the heavy bag in the back, I barely recognized her, as I hadn't seen her in three months. When I did, I thought, *Oh fuck, this girl wants to get together again. I don't need that shit.*

She wasn't looking for a relationship. In fact, she didn't even remember my name, but she knew I trained where Chuck trained. I quickly realized I had left absolutely no impression on her, other than a vague memory she had bad sex with me. Once she confirmed I was, in fact, the guy she boned, she cut right to it:

"Hey, I'm really sorry to tell you this, but I have HIV. I definitely got it before we slept together. You need to get tested."

Then she just left. I stood there with my mouth wide open and my mind racing.

That notification was kind of like when you go to the grocery store and your card comes up with insufficient funds and everyone is looking at you, but instead of wondering whether to put the milk back, you wonder if you're gonna die.

The only respite I had from all of this crap and pain had been my family. One glorious day, my brother grabs me, some paintball guns, and a couple of our friends and drags me down to our creek to play a few games. Our eleven-year-old neighbor comes with us. It is the right prescription. We are having a great time, and for a few moments my mind is finally clear from everything that is happening in my life and to me.

And then some assholes pull up in a car and park over a bridge that overlooks the creek bed. They start throwing rocks at us. These things would really hurt, maim, or worse if they connected. One rock, the size of a cantaloupe, almost hits my little neighbor; it could have killed him. I don't know if it's the stress from being a new dad, the fear of HIV, or just general rage at these guys trying to hit an eleven-year-old with a rock, but I absolutely lose my shit. I cover the 200 meters to their car way faster than they expect. I get to the car just as they are slamming the door, but before they do I get the muzzle of my paintball gun into its crevice. The door slams off my muzzle with a metallic "clunk" as I pull the trigger and shoot both of these cocksuckers point-blank with about a kajillion rounds of paint.

They take off and I am extremely pleased with myself. Somewhere in my mind, I think of myself as Sherlock Holmes, Hercule Poirot, or Columbo. I figure I will be able to use the paint on their clothes and car to prove that they were the perpetrators when the police, which I am currently a junior member of, arrive.

I am wrong.

Instead, the city police chief, an even bigger cocksucker than those two kids, and a political opponent of my dad on the police force, decides to use this situation to make an example of me. He charges me with a felony. The felony doesn't stick, but the fact that I have been charged with one negates my two job offers onto the police force. I just spent the last four years of my life working to this moment. Being a cop is literally the only thing I am absolutely sure I want to do.

And now I can't be one.

The fog has closed in on me. My body is shivering. I look back to where I think the shore is and cannot see it. Even worse, I can't hear it. I probably won't be able to find my way back. *Who gives a shit?*

I keep swimming deeper into the ocean.

I have two babies with two different women, neither of which is my bride. My parents think I'm a fuckup. I've blown my dream of becoming a cop, and none of these things probably matters all that much, because I'm pretty damn sure I am going to die from fucking AIDS anyway.

Normally, when life is spinning out of control, I go visit my grandpa, the patriarch of our family. I'd go to his beautiful home overlooking the ocean, the one where I had watched all those movies, the one that led down to the breakers, and we would talk. While he was always very firm, and quite clear on the path forward, he was never judgmental. I could sit and talk with him with the ocean as a backdrop, and he would help give my thoughts real clarity. Then I'd spend the night and think about what had been said, listening to the waves break against the rocks, and by the time morning came around, no matter what was going on, I usually felt better and had a pretty clear plan of what I needed to do to make things right.

But my grandpa is dying. He has terrible emphysema and when I'm there I can hear his life leaving him a little more with every troubled breath. I hate to see him like this. I cannot handle it. Anybody that's ever had a loved one with a disease that slowly tears them apart knows the feeling of loss, frustration, and powerlessness. This is a man who has done things. He survived the Great Depression. He fought the Nazis. Then he built a generational legacy in his family and business. Time doesn't care about all that, and lung disease certainly doesn't. He has been there for me my entire life, and there is nothing I can do for him— nothing anyone can do. He is the strongest among us and his body is failing him. I am losing him and I am losing my foundation with him. I feel so incredibly lost and alone.

And that's where I am now. In the middle of the ocean. Tired. Cold. Alone.

I tread water for a while just looking into the fog. I feel it barely roll against my wet face, and even though I'm soaked and my fingers are waterlogged, my lips are dry from the salt. I realize I don't know how long I've been swimming.

Maybe this is the end.

Then I hear something cut through the silence. It sounds like a rumble at first, and my frozen brain cannot place the sound. Then I see the red and green lights cutting through the fog. It is a boat. A Coast Guard boat, to be more specific. Apparently, when I was on the beach all alone, I wasn't alone. An older woman had been up high on the parking deck overlooking the beach taking some photos or watching birds or something, when she saw a muscular guy start stripping naked. At first she was there for the show, but then got really concerned when I stared out into the ocean and jumped in. She waited for a while to see if I was just taking a dip, but when I didn't return, she called the Coast Guard. She told them she was worried—that there was something odd about the way I was acting that felt off. She also told them the general direction I swam using landmarks.

She saved my life.

The Coast Guard boat pulls up next to me and the Chief looks down on me and asks, "Whatcha doing out here, buddy?"

This fucking guy looks bored to be here. I am aggravated about how casual he is and that he doesn't seem to be worried about me, so I just reply, "I'm swimming."

"Oh!" he replies, in a showman tone with a big smile on his face. "Why are you swimming?" I summarize the past year for him. It's almost like I'm in a Catholic confessional. I dump it all out there. He pauses for a moment. "Should we just leave you out here in the drink, then?" He gestures at the vastness of the ocean with his arms as if he's a magician revealing the woman he has just cut in half.

I want to say yes to spite him, and show him I don't need him. I'm that stupid. My pride is hurt and I don't like that he is fucking with me. *I've been through hell! Fuck this guy!* But for once I don't do the old Tim Kennedy thing.

"The water is cold," I respond. "I'd like to come in with you guys."

He leans over, pretending to look at my dick through the water. The sun is now rising.

"I can see that," he smirks. "Climb on in."

Climb in? Now I'm even more pissed. My hands will not work. I literally cannot grip with them. My body is weak from hours of swimming in the freezing ocean. I'm dehydrated and I'm knocking on the door of hypothermia. This asshole wants me to climb in? I try to get on by weakly gripping the side of the boat and throwing my leg over the side as a lever.

"Come on, man, get in! We don't have all day!" he bellows.

I finally get my leg up and am just kind of hanging off the side, completely exposed. "That's the smallest dick I have ever seen!" he says to his crew. I hate him for it, but he's right. I think my genitals have entered my body and climbed all the way up to my throat at this point. I shouldn't care. To be honest, if it had been anyone but this guy, I would have laughed it off, but he had me fired up. "The water's fucking freezing!" I shout, super pissed off.

"Sure, buddy. Sure. Whatever you say," he responds.

He stares at me for a long while and then finally says, "I'm going to treat your life with more respect than you've treated it. We won't be out here next time. I don't want to have this conversation again."

He reaches down and grasps my hand, and then gives me the lift up that my physical body and ethereal soul absolutely need in this moment. His hand is so warm. It almost feels like it is burning me. He wraps me in the roughest blanket I have ever felt and I sit quietly on the boat deck for what seems like forever. I vacillate between almost falling asleep from exhaustion and the hum of the engine, and jerking awake from the clanging of my teeth from the cold and the bounce of my head against the side of the boat every time we hit a wave.

He brings me to shore. I get my clothes and I dress. It takes me forever. My arms just will not work. He makes sure I get to my car and that it starts. And then he leaves.

I turn the heat all the way up and I sit there for hours, warming myself up and thinking. The warmth feels good at first but then hurts like hell as life comes back to my fingers and toes. Eventually, my whole body begins tingling and I almost feel like I did when I was fighting fires. It's a good hurt, though. It is a reminder that I'm still in the game.

An hour ago, I was pretty sure I was going to die. I thought I was okay with that when I started to swim. But by the end, I wasn't. And all of the regret I felt from my bad decisions paled in comparison to the regret I had when I began to realize it was likely all going to end. Now, I have a second chance.

I tell myself that I am lucky. But then I think some more. I'm not alive because I am lucky. I'm alive for three reasons. First, a woman paid attention to her surroundings and, when things did not feel right, called the Coast Guard without hesitation. Second, the Coast Guard immediately began a search that they carried on for over an hour. Third, and perhaps most important, *I never stopped swimming.*

Everyone took action and the outcome changed. I need to do the same.

I am alive. I have a future. I need to do something with it.

A week later I receive a call from the Army recruiter.

On September 12, 2001, the day after the terrorist attacks on our country, I had visited the Army, Navy, and Marine recruiters to try to enlist. There was such a backlog of candidates at that time that I was put on a waiting list. I hadn't thought much of it over the last eighteen months, but my life is different now. Fighting has accentuated my worst personality traits. I am not doing right by my daughters or their mothers because I cannot earn enough money despite my best efforts. Professionally, there is nothing that moves me—nothing to which I aspire now that I cannot be a police officer.

I need to be better. I can't keep living this life.

When I arrive at the station, the Army recruiter offers me access to a new program aimed at athletes who have already graduated from college—it is called the "18 X-Ray program." It is a fast-track way of joining the Special Forces. Typically, the recruiter explains, you spend six years or more in the Army before you are eligible to apply for Special Forces. This program would allow me to cut the line. It sounds perfect.

I ask for a pen, then I sign the contract.

I'm headed to the Army.

CHAPTER SIX

THE BOOK OF TRUTH

"Toes on the line!" the Drill Sergeant yells from his office in that special "evil bass" only members of their guild can muster.

We all sprint to the arbitrary yellow line that runs down the large bay full of bunk beds where my whole basic training platoon sleeps in Fort Benning, Georgia. If you've seen the movie *Full Metal Jacket*, then you can picture the scene. In seconds, we are lined up in two rows, each with our toes on our respective yellow line, facing each other. Whatever this was, it was about to suck. "Toes on the line" was never followed up with, "Hey, guys, great job. Here's a snack. Now go ahead and take a nap!" It was always something shitty: a shakedown looking for unauthorized items that was just an excuse to wreck our gear, a physical smoke session where they make us work out until we cannot move, a knowledge-testing session, or a late-night road march. It was *never* anything good.

Millions of American soldiers know this moment—the feeling of anxiety, coupled with a constant sweat you seemed to have had going for days, finished off with a skosh of resentment at the person who's treating you this way. But while the scene is similar to the one that has played out for generations, this company is a little bit different.

The only people in my basic training company are Special Forces candidates. They are part of the 18 X-Ray program and Ranger Battalion candidates who will attend the Ranger Indoctrination Program (RIP) after, and if, they complete their infantry training. The guys who volunteer for this shit are always a special breed, even if they don't make it through, but this is peak war. Everyone in this room really wants to be here and really wants to shoot bad guys in the face. And it isn't just machismo and blustering. The pain of 9/11 is still very real and super fresh, not to mention the pictures of Americans being hung from bridges by Al Qaeda and the Taliban—their burning corpses still smoking from when they were burned alive.

9/11 is an open wound. This war is making that wound fester. And every time we see a new image of a killed or wounded American soldier, that wound is drenched in lemon juice and salt.

The Drill Sergeant is still in his office. I hear a whole bunch of other young voices. They are laughing, but not friendly laughs. Their laughs are sharper, more mocking, and somehow aggressive. While I cannot make out the words they are using, muffled as they are behind the door, they sound more like the testosterone-laced, bravado-riddled tough-guy talk that you hear in a high school football locker room. The door opens. The Drill Sergeant comes out with five privates in tow. *Yup, definitely an underdeveloped frontal lobe vibe going on from this crew.*

As they walk out, the Drill Sergeant stumbles a bit. Ah yes, I've seen this show before at the fire department. This guy's fucking drunk. He wants to show off for his pack of stooges.

The guys with him are recent basic training graduates that are gearing up to go to RIP (now called RASP). If they pass, they will become members of the 75th Ranger Regiment, a legendary fighting force. Our Drill Sergeant is also a former member of that organization, though the more I am around him, the more I suspect he isn't here teaching us because he remained in the regiment's good graces. I have mixed feelings about him. He's not a particularly kind man, and while he isn't a textbook alcoholic, his regular alcohol abuse has made him crueler than I believe he would be sober. Still, he's been around, has seen some shit,

THE BOOK OF TRUTH

and has a lot of value in terms of things he teaches us, so even with his obvious faults, I generally have a good impression of him . . . well . . . on most days.

As he walks our line, he stops every once in a while to deliver something he deems profound. "Special Operations isn't like a regular unit. Only the strong survive here. You have to separate the wheat from the chaff," he proclaims. He follows that up with every cheesy strength analogy you can think of: iron sharpens iron, you're only as strong as your weakest link, the cream rises to the top, etc. He closes strong with his voice steadily rising to a crescendo, "As I look around this room, I think of it as a blacksmith's forge. We have to beat away the impurities. Who's the impurity here? Who's the weakling? Who's the chaff that needs to be removed?"

While he does most of the talking, the other five guys are his hype guys. It's like walking into a motivated Baptist church and there's the pastor, and yeah, he's the man, but then there's the core group near him shouting "Hallelujah!" and "Amen!" at the top of their lungs getting everyone else going and fired up. In church, that makes for a fun sermon. Here, it is dangerous chemistry. They want to show off for him and he wants to show off for them. This is a train wreck waiting to happen, and my platoon is standing on the tracks.

So at the apex of this chest-thumping moment, he has to find something bigger and better to do. And for him, bigger and better is to start talking shit about all of the smaller and weaker guys in our company. "Do you think you could actually carry a wounded man? Do you think you could kill the enemy in hand-to-hand combat? I don't," he tells one recruit with blond hair. But he didn't stop there. "And all you motherfuckers who are going SF? You think you're smart? You're not. You're pussies. Nation building doesn't work. You hang out with people who will never embrace the American way of thinking and you teach them how to fight their own people. In the end, you make more terrorists than you kill. If you were real men, you'd be Rangers," he closes.

I'm pissed. It isn't even that I necessarily disagree with his drunk ass on some of this stuff. I don't think all of these guys can make it. I don't think they are all tough enough either. But it isn't up to him to decide.

It's up to him to *teach* and *train* them and then it's up to each man to succeed or not. Even at the age of twenty-four, I know you can't judge a man from his appearance or size. I've seen it through fighting, firefighting, and policing: Some badasses simply don't look the part. But that's only about 7 percent of the reason I'm mad.

The other 93 percent comes from the fact that he called out Special Forces and said they were weaker than Rangers. This offends me because I now think of myself as part of the Special Forces family. Of course, this is pure ego since I have nothing to base it on. I have never served with or seen Rangers in action and I have never served with or seen Special Forces in action either. But my frontal lobe is also not completely developed, and as a wannabe SF guy, I am willing to stand up against any wannabe Ranger that dares disparage my regiment! (I'll find out later that I love Rangers; they're amazing, fearless, and indispensable in combat, but right now that's not my concern.)

He continues walking the line looking for weakness. He stops and calls this little Mexican kid named Cortez a pussy and says that he will never get selected. Cortez is unfazed and remains unperturbed by the comment.

When Cortez doesn't take the bait, he returns to the little blond kid standing next to me. That's when he turns up the heat.

"You need to quit right now or you're going to get people killed, do you hear me?" he says to my compatriot.

"No, Drill Sergeant!" blondie replies.

"Who do you think would win in a fight, Private? Rangers or SF?" he asks.

"Special Forces, Drill Sergeant!" he boisterously answers.

"Okay, then prove it to me. Fight one of these guys," he says, gesturing to the pack of idiots.

Flummoxed, he again replies, "No, Drill Sergeant." This time in a softer and less confident voice.

The hyenas immediately surround him. They lean in and shout in his face. I can see the spittle hitting him and making his eyes blink with every syllable.

"You're a fucking pussy, you hear me?" one of them shouts.

"You're gonna get your whole fucking platoon killed!" another chimes in.

The third pretends that he's going to hit him and stops short, making him flinch. They all laugh.

"If you don't fight one of them, I'm going to have all five beat the shit out of you," the Drill Sergeant whispers in his ear, loud enough so the whole room hears it.

Those words are like chum to these assholes. They crowd in even closer.

I'm now officially done with this shit.

"Get the fuck out of his face and leave him alone," I order. The room goes silent.

"What the fuck did you just say, Kennedy?" the Drill Sergeant snarls.

"I told them to leave him the fuck alone, Drill Sergeant," I calmly reply as I feel my adrenaline rising in that sweet way only fighters and veterans understand.

He assesses me and cleverly changes tactics, "He's either going to get strong now or get people killed later. How does that sit with you?"

"Well, he'll figure those things out between now and then, Drill Sergeant," I reply firmly.

He smirks. I don't know if he respects me or hates me, but I'm certain the five morons hate me.

"Looks like we're beating your ass, then," the biggest one says as he moves toward me, his friends in tow.

All rational thought leaves me. I'm doing the math and preparing to engage.

These guys aren't pussies. They've probably gotten into a skirmish or two, but they do not have ten pro fights, thirty-one amateur fights, and years of training with absolute monsters like Chuck.

Give me any reason. Please.

The loudest guy is right in front of me, but he is not the biggest guy. I prioritize. Due to proximity, I am going to hit the loud guy first with a one-two combination (the jab, followed by the right cross) and then go to the biggest guy from there, and then take targets of opportunity as they react.

"You're the tough guy?" the loudest hyena asks. "Why don't you just get rid of the weakest link now and be a stronger chain?" These guys all just kept saying different versions of the same shit and I'm bored with it. I actually hope we are gonna do this, but I know I can't start it.

"You're not fighting him," I deliver in my best leader voice. He gets right up in my face and pokes me in the chest.

Bingo! Physical contact made. It's on like Donkey Kong.

He's too close for my jab, so I just fire my right cross. He goes down, completely unconscious. I'm shocked by this result more than anything. The shot wasn't even that great. I immediately realize I'm in the perfect position to throw over him and land a left hook on the big guy. It's a gift I cannot refuse, and I let it fly. *Thwack!* He goes down and lands right next to his pussy friend. These guys are weak as fuck. Best of all, now there's only three left.

I bull charge the biggest of the remaining dudes. He must have wrestled junior varsity somewhere because he did a level change and tried a double leg body lock, which was trash. I snapped him down into a chin strap, where my chest is on the back of his head and my hand is cupping his chin and wrenching it. Once there, I grip my hands and move into a high-elbow Marcelo Garcia (largely considered one of the best Jiu Jitsu players to ever live) choke—a choke where my grip constricts one jugular, and my forearm constricts the other, as my elbow lies across his back). For the three-to-five seconds that it takes for him to pass out, I use his ass to block the other two guys from closing the distance. When I feel him pass out, I snap him down onto the ground and his head sounds like a watermelon someone dropped on the concrete.

We are eight-to-ten seconds into this thing and there are only two left. They put their hands up and back away like the little bitches they are, while filling the air with a string of "Hey, bro, it's over," and "Got it. All good bro." I'd have a lot more respect for them if they were part of the pile of bodies on the floor.

"We're gonna pick up our friends, okay, bro?" one of them asks.

I don't answer him. Instead, I do a crisp about-face, walk back to my yellow line, and regain my military bearing.

The Drill Sergeant is red-faced, but calculating, and chooses his words carefully. "Being the loudest dog doesn't matter. You still have to be the toughest dog. Pick up your boys."

With that, he walks back into the office. Through the cracks in the shutter, I see him open his bottle and begin to drink. The hyenas leave and he sits in the office for over an hour while he lets us stand on our lines until he finds the bottom of the bottle. I hear the bottle drop into the metal trash can with a clink, then his light goes out and he leaves, never dismissing us. After a few minutes, we relax. He's gone for the night.

I have mixed feelings about the whole incident. I am mad and disappointed none of my friends helped me. They will later claim that it happened too fast or that they knew I was a fighter, but fuck that. Someone should have stepped up. I also know our leader is a bully who is dealing with his own post-traumatic stress, having seen it in the firefighting world, and the alcohol didn't help him in that regard. But in the back of my head, I know that even though he's an asshole, some of what he said and did wasn't wrong. We are going to war and some of the guys in this bay are a liability.

My time at Fort Benning after basic training was a breeze.

Infantry school was super easy, especially for a guy like me who grew up planning missions with friends and shooting with my dad.

Airborne School, where one is taught to jump out of airplanes, should have been exciting, but in classic Army fashion they crammed five days of actual instruction into three long and dumb weeks. The one highlight of Airborne was meeting this hot Marine lieutenant that I got to bang for the month. This was the first time I interacted with another military service, and I hoped all future cross-branch interactions would be this much fun.

But now, as I sit on my shitty Greyhound bus, I smile a little bit. I'm leaving Fort Benning, home of the infantry, and I'm heading to Fort

Bragg, North Carolina, home of the Special Forces. My real journey is about to start and it's time to finally find my place in the military world. I want to bring the fight to the enemy. I've had this feeling for three years and this is the first time I feel like I'm at the precipice of doing something about it.

Everyone my age or older has a 9/11 story. For me, the "Falling Man" is the thing that changed me. I remember watching the news and these things falling from the buildings. At first, no one knew what was happening. Not the news crews. Not the civilians. But the first responders did. As the camera panned the area, I could see it on their faces. The anguish. The inability to make a difference for those people. The utter helplessness. Then the news reporters picked up on what was happening, and in their horror, the world finally understood.

Americans were trapped on top of that building and there was nothing anyone could do to help them. As the world watched, one after one, each person made the decision to either burn alive or jump to their death. To this day, I still wonder how many jumped out of desperation and how many did so out of raw unbridled defiance. I think a lot about what I would have done—wonder how I would have chosen to go out. Even calmly sitting on the bus thinking about it, it's an impossible decision. I don't want Americans to have to make that decision ever again.

As we rumble north up I-95, I look around at my compatriots. What was once a forty-man platoon is down to twenty. Those that left either failed a school or changed their mind when faced with the difficulty of our task. Just about everyone the Drill Sergeant said would come up short did, including the blond kid I defended.

I don't know how I feel about that.

The journey forward isn't an easy one, but I'm excited that my Special Forces journey is finally starting. First, I have the Special Operations Preparation Course (SOPC), then I have actual Special Forces Selection. If selected, I have Small Unit Tactics, then Military Occupational Specialty (MOS) school where I will specialize in one Special Forces element, then language school, followed by "Robin Sage." That's where I will test all my school-acquired skills in a practical exercise. Finally, but certainly not least, I have to attend SERE school, where I will be a POW trying to escape. Listing it out, a practical person would conclude I'm closer to the beginning of my journey than to the finish line, but to me it's a done deal. I'm going to don the Green Beret, the distinctive mark of the Special Forces.

After six hours on a bus that smells like urine and body odor, we are dropped off at the Greyhound station in Fayetteville, North Carolina. As I get off, somehow the smell isn't any better. Looking around, I can tell that this is a strange and dangerous place. The only ones here are bums, prostitutes, and a heroin addict. I now see why everyone calls this place "Fayette-nam." We wait for a while, but no one shows up to get us like they said they would. Stranded, one of the guys in my squad calls his cousin Lloyd, who happens to live here, asking for help.

Industrious and loyal Lloyd comes through. He shows up with his mom's borrowed minivan and we all pile inside. Twenty idiots pile in like we're getting into a clown car. Packed like sardines, we head to Fort Bragg. The only information we have is a building number. We have no point of contact. We have no phone number. Just the building number.

We expect the gate guard to give us a hard time because there are twenty-one people packed into a van, but he clearly has seen it all before. Given the understanding he shows, we ask where this building is. He isn't exactly sure, but he knows a general direction, and we head that way. After many trials and tribulations (military buildings are rarely in numerical order and building 4300 can be next to building 83 and there is never any reason for it), we arrive at 1:00 a.m. Lloyd, who is now in trouble with his mom for being gone so long, leaves.

The building is locked, and there's no one in it. The only sign of life is a white paper taped on the door that says PT starts at 0600. We have no idea if that paper has been there a day or a year, but we all agree risking missing PT while feigning ignorance is a bad plan. As such, we're going to be ready for it. We have nothing with us except our backpacks and the original bag we traveled to Fort Benning with, which at most has a change of civilian clothes. The air is cold, and the grass is wet, so we sleep on the wooden deck attached to the building. At 0500 our watches start going off, letting us know to get up. We all slowly put on our PTs and wait. *Does anyone even care that we're here?*

They did care. Sort of. The Special Operations Preparation Course is about to start and we are about to meet our instructor. SFC Will Summers (one of the original "12 Strong" guys that was captured for all time riding on horseback in Afghanistan in the early days of the war) shows up with a rack that would make Dolly Parton blush: Special Forces Tab, Ranger Tab, Airborne Badge, President's 100, Dive Badge, HALO Badge, and a whole bunch of stuff I'd never seen before, including a Combat Infantryman's Badge.

We didn't know what to do with this guy. He couldn't be real. (Guys like him were the stuff of legends, not our instructors!) And here I am sitting with nothing on my chest, fresh out of infantry training. I've only seen one other Special Forces Tab thus far, but that guy was part of recruiting and he was friendly. SFC Summers does not look friendly. And he's with another guy that might as well be his twin. They have no fat on their face. None. There's a cheekbone, a jawbone, some visible sinew, and something else: hate. Hate is exactly what is all over their faces. And they waste no time in telling us why it's there. They hate the 18 X-Ray program.

These guys all spent six to eight years leading soldiers in infantry units before they came to Special Forces. Most came from Ranger Regiment. They were badasses before they went to Special Forces Selection. Some had deployed to Panama or Somalia, and most had deployed to Bosnia or Kosovo *before* they even started the process we were about to start. They had life experience, leadership training, and most importantly, knowledge of how the military actually worked. After Selection, they spent time in Afghanistan or Iraq or both. They are cutting-edge, tier one Operators in their thirties at the height of the War on Terror . . . and they are stuck babysitting us. We are twenty-three or twenty-four and our life experience has been college parties and part-time jobs, and in my case, fighting. I wasn't mad they hated us. In fact, the more I thought about it, I kind of hated us too.

Nevertheless, SFC Summers was a good Christian, who offered us rides to church every Sunday. Because of that, he avoided the kind of crude language and insults our Drill Sergeant had bestowed upon us in favor of more creative ways to degrade us. "Even when David was on the run from Saul, he wouldn't have used you guys" was one of my personal favorites.

But while his language is less crude and cruel, what he and his fellow instructors put us through is way worse than what our Drill Instructor put us through. Pre-selection for us is to take place May through August 2004. While most pre-selection periods last about four weeks, ours will be four months. Tragically, a few Green Berets died during Selection in the summer months, and the command decided to put us into a holding pattern until it cooled down.

Four months is a long time to be at SOPC.

These guys relentlessly smoke the dogshit out of us. In fact, they smoke us so bad that we become the number one recruiting location for all of the Special Operations adjacent branches. Every two weeks, a new busload of twenty-to-fifty dudes shows up. Every two weeks, Civil Affairs, EOD, and PsyOps would show up to recruit the dropouts. So many guys were quitting the process that in a matter of only a couple weeks, they changed tactics and set up a permanent recruiting station inside our building. Every day we lose more and more guys to these recruiters. In my first three months there, they recruited 400 candidates from our building. It became a revolving door of faces.

We PT twice a day. We do land navigation twice a week. We run and we ruck and we run and we ruck and we run—you get the picture. Everywhere we go, we carry a rucksack with at least fifty-five pounds and two liters of water.

While all of that is hard, the bane of our existence is the "gig pit." The gig pit is a little corner of a swamp that they dug down two to three feet and then built a small walkway bridge over it. The little bridge is for the cadre to stand on. The pit . . . well the pit is for us, and the pit is gross. The Army has a lot of oversight. SOPC does not. These guys pissed in the pit. They spit in it. They threw dead raccoons in it. They dumped food waste in it. The pit is always fucking disgusting, and it was an excruciating part of our everyday life.

"Fall in!" the cadre shout.

We quickly line up in formation, hoping to not garner their wrath. They walk the lines, not with the swarming mentality of Drill Sergeants, but with a calm demeanor that carries a certain inevitability. "Your bootlace is sticking out," one cadre member says aloud. I don't know who he is talking to because I cannot look around. "Your canteen is empty," says another cadre member. "This ruck is not even close to fifty-five pounds!" yells a third who I can see out of the corner of my eye. Whether the bootlace is really out, whether the canteen is really dry, or whether the rucksack is really light doesn't matter. They always find gigs.

"Get in the gig pit," Will says, not quite raising his voice beyond a conversational tone.

We obey. The smart ones among us dive in with enthusiasm. The slower ones are tentative. They will not last.

Jumping in the gig pit has a different feeling than jumping in a pond or lake. The water doesn't just flow through your uniform instantly. It's not really water at all. It's more of a semiliquid ooze. It slowly seeps into you. You're dry for the first few seconds, even though you're completely immersed, but then it begins to flow over your skin. The smell of rot and decomposing matter engulfs you. You feel like you're bathing in disease.

"Roll around! Get nice and muddy!" they shout.

"You can do better than that, Private!" someone yells to a guy who is trying to game the system and stay partially out of the muck. They watch from their perch until everyone is completely covered.

"You have ninety seconds to get in the barracks, change your uniform, and get back here! Ready! Go!" Will shouts.

I leap out of the pit. *Fuck.* I've played this kind of game before and there is no winning, but you still have to play. A horde of men are running in front of me and behind me. We're coated in filth as we cover the grass between the gig pit and the barracks. As we hit the door and try to squeeze in as quickly as possible, muddy handprint after muddy handprint hits the door. Guys are wiping out as they take their first step into the barracks. I'm the seventh or eighth guy in, and the movement of the handful of guys in front of me has left mud on the floor and walls. I get to my bunk and strip off my shirt and undershirt, then sit on the ground and try to rip my disgusting boots off. The mud makes it way harder than it should be. I rip my socks off and then stand dropping my pants in the middle of the room. Everyone else is doing the same.

I grab a clean uniform, skipping the socks so I can be faster. It feels gross to throw a clean uniform over a body that was just soaking in filth, but I have no choice. As quickly as I can, I throw the new uniform on, tuck my pants into my boots, and tie the fastest knots I can tie and sprint out the door. I'm one of the first guys out. As I hit the grass, I hear Will counting down, ". . . six, five, four, three, two, one! You're late!"

I fall in just after his countdown. I'm late. A few other guys somehow made it, which seems impossible. Almost everyone else is still inside for at least another two or three minutes. When everyone finally arrives, the cadre fall right into the routine we all know is coming.

"When I say ninety seconds, I mean ninety seconds. Not ninety-one seconds. Not ninety-five seconds. Not three minutes. Is there something about instructions that you do not understand?" Will asks.

"No, Sergeant!" the whole formation shouts in unison.

"Let's see what condition you all showed up in . . . and I can tell you . . . from up here it is not looking good . . ." Will says, feigning disappointment as if he expected something other than failure.

The gigs come hard and fast. From one corner of the formation I hear "Boots unbloused!" From another, "This guy isn't wearing any socks! Are socks part of the uniform?" "Roger, Sergeant!" comes the response. "This canteen is still empty," comes the comment from the same cadre member to the same guy as last time. "Do you not have the ability to pay attention to me when I am talking to you?" he asks. "Roger, Sergeant!" comes the reply.

The cadre member slowly walks to the front of the formation and then addresses him with disgust and hatred dripping from his every word:

"Then why didn't you do it? Same mistake. Same person. You think you can operate like that and be Special Forces? Right now, my old unit is fighting Al Qaeda. Their lives depend on exacting attention to detail.

They're calling fire missions meters away from their positions. They're clearing buildings where one wrong move gets a member of the team killed. And what am I doing? Trying to get some specialist to put water in his damn canteen. How hard is it? How damn hard is it?"

He walks back in front of the poor bastard catty-corner to me. He honest to God looks like he is going to kill this kid, even as he stays calm. "Put some damn water in that canteen," he almost whispers, making it somehow more terrifying.

Silence falls over the formation. Will leaves it like that for a moment.

"Into the gig pit," he finally says. Not shouts. Says. Calmly. With no human emotion.

We jump back in.

This continues until no one has anything clean left. At some point they dismiss us, and we spend the entire night doing laundry and cleaning the barracks, only to have it happen again the next day.

Every afternoon they bang a gong. Every afternoon Will Summers gets up and reads a Medal of Honor citation or a Silver Star citation. He tells stories of valor. He tells his own stories or asks other cadre members to tell theirs. Then he closes with something like, "My old team right now is knee-deep in grenade pins killing the enemy, and you're bitching about your boots, or this mud, or how you never get to sleep. Quit! It's never going to get easier. This is only *pre-selection*. You think Selection will be easier? It won't be. You think missions will be easier? Hell no. They're doing what you're doing with a hundred pounds on their backs, plus carrying their own food and water. And people are trying to kill them! You're just getting dirty. Quit! You don't want to be here. All of those gentlemen behind you would love to have you join them. You can go and be part of those perfectly fine units and live a good and civilized life. You won't get that here. Quit!"

Every single day, people quit. I honestly didn't understand it. *Didn't they realize this is the game?* But they did realize. They just couldn't take it anymore.

The guys that stay are my people. We start making changes. We alphabetize the barracks to make formations easier. We hide changes of clothes so we won't always be dirty. When we are supposed to have guards up, we run with two guys instead of the 33 percent that was required so that everyone can get more sleep. If the cadre came, the 33 percent were fully dressed on top of their bunks and the two would wake them quickly so we'd never get caught. We get really fucking good at cheating.

For four months forty-to-eighty guys show up every week. Well over 1,000 guys come through here. At the end of all of it, just ninety-one are approved to move forward to Special Forces Selection. Only six are from my original basic training platoon: Steve Coleman, Brendan Hay, Sean Herren, Ian Marone, Luke Jones, and me.

Selection is honestly fun. It really is a mental and physical break for us after pre-selection. And it is even better because we all know each other.

There is no question in my mind that the SOPC cadre saw the 18 X-Rays as a liability (and they were right, as we died at two times the rate of regular Special Forces guys), and so they decided that they would put us through so much hell the guys that made it through would at least be tough enough to make up for their lack of experience.

Their final push was to make us run the Army ten-miler on our last weekend before Selection instead of resting up. We won the whole thing, of course, but still! In the process of trying to make us quit, they actually pre-selected us and didn't realize it.

For most people Selection is an emotional event. Not for us. We are an anomaly. The cadre do not know what to do with us, because we are messing around and having fun. But we can't help it! This is one third of the work we would normally have done, and all of our SOPs (Standard Operating Procedures) are already in place. Like in SOPC, we break the rules and only keep two guys awake. There is a giant whiteboard that we are expected to check at particular times. We have one guy do it rather than the whole unit and everyone else sleeps on their rucks in full uniform so that the second we have a task we could move out and be ready, while simultaneously getting extra rest.

We cheat here at everything too. Literally everything.

During the big Star Land Navigation test, one is not supposed to run on any roads. I ran on every single one I could find. It was so much faster.

The cadre hid in the woods trying to catch people that tried to run on the roads but rather than fear it, I prepared for it. I hid my roster number and moved quickly. When one did see me, they would shout, "Hey, you, stop!" and I would take off sprinting. People are fundamentally lazy, so most of them didn't even chase me. The one that did wasn't as fast as I am, and didn't really want to fight through bramble and thorns. I saved hours by cheating on those roads, as did all my friends.

They also don't tell you how much time you have to finish the Star Land Navigation test. This is true with every other Selection event. The entire military runs on the premise of Task, Condition, and Standard. You are given a task and a condition and you are expected to meet the standard. Special Forces operate on the premise of Task, Condition, No Standard. In other words, the "standard" is your best effort, every time.

Then they decide if it is good enough.

The whole idea is to see how hard you will push yourself without a known goal. In the lead-up to this event, during practice, we stole the standards sheet, so we knew exactly how much time we had available to finish. For those, I ran the entire course, got my points early, then camped out in the woods near the finish point, set my alarm, and took a nap. When I arrived at the finish line, with about ten minutes to spare, they asked why I was bone dry. I simply answered, "I'm not a real sweater, Sergeant." For this one—the real event—Team 18 X-Ray wants to send a message. All ninety-one of us run the entire event. We all finish the Star Course so quickly that the cadre double- and triple-check our sheets and confirm their logs.

We fucking crushed it.

Of the ninety-one of us that arrive at Selection, eighty-eight of us pass. The other three are selected later in the next course. We spent four months preparing for Selection. I don't know why. It was easy. I do know one thing: I've never been around a better group of people.

After Selection, most people return to their old units to wait for the Small Unit Tactics (SUT) course to open up. SUT is considered the second phase of Special Forces Qualification (Q Course), with Selection being the first. If your SUT date is happening soon, then you stay at Fort Bragg and wait it out. Otherwise you go back to your pad, wherever that is, and chill.

Not 18 X-Rays. We don't have a unit and we don't have a home. So guess where they send us? Right back to SOP-FUCKING-C. That's right, we pass Selection near flawlessly and get thrown right back in the gig pit! Will calls it SOPC II. Dick. You'd think there would be some little wink and nod, given that we are now selected, but nope. Same people. Same shittiness. No additional love. On the plus side, the month of additional unnecessary suffering made the Q Course fun!

Before we know it, SOP C Part Deux is over and SUT is beginning. Everyone I know describes SUT as mini–Ranger School with a guerrilla warfare twist. Unfortunately, this doesn't mean much to the eighty-eight of us at the time because none of us have been to Ranger School. Basically, though, we are broken into a heavy infantry squad, which is roughly the size of Operational Detachment Alpha (ODA), which is the main operating unit for Special Forces. ODAs are sometimes referred to as A-Teams.

We, as a heavy infantry squad, are issued M240 machine guns, Squad Automatic Weapons (SAWs), and M203 grenade launchers. I like guns a lot and I am excited. Our instructors are awesome. One is from 3rd Group and one is from 5th Group. They look like elk. Their muscles have muscles, but they are sinewy and lean and I can see all of their veins, as opposed to thick and meaty. They look like they can run or ruck or do anything forever. You can tell that all these guys have done is run through the desert for years chasing bad guys. They both kind of have a thousand-yard stare because they just came back from war. One of the many things I don't know yet is that even guys who are the life of the party in most scenarios need time to find that personality again after returning from combat. You have to be a different person for that long period of time to do what must be done, but I don't know that yet. I just want to smoke this course. Like my SOPC instructors, they think 18 X-Rays are fucking garbage. Also like my SOPC instructors, if they have been assigned a task, they are going to do it to the best of their ability.

I absolutely love SUT. It's the first time that I am doing what I consider to be Special Forces stuff. We are given direct action, special reconnaissance, and recovery of personnel missions to perform. In other words, we either pretend to ambush bad guys, pretend to spy on bad guys, or pretend to save hostages from bad guys. The coolest part, though, is that we aren't given the necessary tools to complete the missions.

If we want to stop a tank, we can't do it with rockets or artillery, because we don't have them. Instead, we must do things like run (fake) piano wire at hatch level to take the tank commander's head off, or place an explosive charge (also fake, obviously) in their tracks to stop them in place. We have to find or forage for those tools, just like we would have to on an actual mission. In a normal class, they apparently don't give you much to work with, but for our class there seemed to be an abundance of random objects floating around or contacts that could provide us with whatever we needed.

I didn't notice the weird man at first. He is walking around and occasionally asking questions of us and seems to be affecting how our class runs. I assumed he was some kind of weird cadre member, but he is too nice. He introduces himself to us as Dick Couch. Apparently, he is a former Navy SEAL and CIA member under George H. W. Bush, and he is here writing a book about the 18 X-Rays. Dick is a big deal and is here with permission from President George W. Bush, so the cadre want to make sure that he has a lot to write about. As such, our training got a little more budget than in years past, which to me is super cool. But we also get driven a lot harder to make sure that Special Forces Selection is seen as appropriately rigorous, and that sucks. Still, it was more cool than it was sucky, which goes to show you that life is always better with a little more Dick. (Years later, I will find out that I am a featured member of this book, called *Chosen Soldier*, under the pseudonym Tom Kendall.)

SUT, just like Selection, is easy and fun. In the blink of an eye, the training is almost over. In SUT, we all have to rotate into different jobs, but in the next phase we will go deep into one job. Right now, we are 18 X-Rays, meaning we are Special Forces members with no actual skill. We need to get rid of that X and replace it with something. 18A means team leader and that's only for officers (yuck). 18B is the weapons specialist. It's exactly what it sounds like. You become a master of every weapon system imaginable. 18C is the engineer sergeant. Basically, they blow stuff up. 18D is the medical sergeant. They are masters of keeping people alive in the worst conditions possible. Given a choice between an actual doctor and an 18D on the battlefield, I would take an 18D. 18E is the communications sergeant. They do all the radio stuff. So I have to choose between B, C, D, and E. I use two criteria to make my selection: Which one is fastest so I can get to war and which one is the most fun? The answer, obviously, is B. I like guns. I like shooting. No-brainer. So I rank order my choices, B, E, C, and D. Medical stuff is cool, but it takes a long time to get good at it, so I kick that one to last.

My cadre also agree I would fit best as an 18B. I get my first choice and I'm off to Phase III: MOS Specialty.

———

"You are in the MOS with the highest attrition in all of Special Forces," our instructor informs us.

I had no idea, but I also don't care. Special Forces training has already shown me why this statement is probably true: Most people haven't grown up with guns, or if they have, their training sucked. My dad made sure that wasn't the case. Shooting is like breathing for our family—from my dad to my little sister, we will fuck you up.

This class is different from all my other classes. This is the first time I'm in a class mixed with regular Army people. Up until now it has been all 18 X-Rays, all young and inexperienced guys. An awful lot of the new guys in the class are five or more years older than me, and almost all of them have been to war. I notice the difference. They aren't as consistently physically fit as the 18 X-Rays (though some have that elk look too) and they definitely aren't as cocky. They also treat the cadre differently. My crew looks at cadre as kind of a cat-and-mouse game to see how much we can get away with. Yeah, we want to learn, but getting away with stuff is really fun and we take pride in it. These new guys are less interested in that and seem to take everything seriously. They are definitely less fun. And they dip nonstop. The class is half them and half us.

18B is four months of SOPC-level hazing with a specific purpose. We are expected to expertly handle any weapon, from any country, made after World War II. We are tested on this constantly. These tests are always in the worst possible conditions. If you're doing a fire mission, you'll be malnourished, sleep-deprived, and exhausted. If you are on the range, you are smoked first so that your heart rate is up and your arms are shaking. If you're doing firing lanes, you're in body armor, not the new Gucci stuff, but old-school Ranger Body Armor (RBA) that weighs about thirty pounds. They yell at you the whole time. Their goal is not to see if you can shoot or maintain weapons. That's easy. Their goal is to see if you can do it *under pressure*. This hazing has a very specific purpose. They want that adrenaline dump. They want that anxiety. And they want to see if we are good enough when both hit.

And being good enough isn't easy. You aren't just timed on assembling or disassembling a weapon. They'll throw parts for five weapon systems into a box, then tell you that you have ten minutes to put all of them together or you fail. Then they swarm you while you're trying to do it, bumping into your arms, shaking your table, and generally making life impossible.

The question they want answered is: What will this guy do under fire? Will he fight through the stress or freeze?

We covered every weapon from pistols to submachine guns to machine guns to AT4s, RPGs, and Gustavs. The pace is relentless and I love it. I feel myself getting better every day.

On our last day, they tell us if we passed or failed with no ceremony whatsoever.

"If you passed, your certificate is on your desk," the head instructor says. There's one there for me. I'm an 18B. The instructor walks up to me as I'm staring at the certificate and whispers, "You have the highest GPA for the course. You're the Honor Graduate. Doesn't matter now. It might matter later."

He starts to walk away, but pauses, looks back, and adds, "Now get your shit and get out."

———————

At some point after SOPC, interlaced with all these other courses, I buy a house in Fayette-nam (not bad for a twenty-five-year-old). It is a total shitshow of a house, but I need to have a place to call my own. The house costs me $53,000. Six to eight of us live in it at any given time depending on what school everyone is in: Brendan Hay, Shawn Herren, Ian Marone, Luke Jones, Luke Heir, Steve Coleman, Mike Ozinga, and me. The house is jammed. Guys grab couches, floors, air mattresses, or whatever, but it is better than the barracks. I charge the guys $200 a month, so they can keep $450 of their $650 housing allowance. Cheap for them, covers my mortgage and then some, and we have a home base.

We are the token white guys in the neighborhood, but we all love living here. The area is so impoverished (again, my house was $53k) that the neighborhood kids would always kind of show up when we were grilling. Since we had so much extra money from the BAH (Basic Allowance for Housing), we always bought a shitload of extra steaks, burgers, and brats and fed them. This just became part of our lives. We had been so hungry for so long, and so focused on being SF, that all we did was eat, work out, and sleep. At first the gangbangers eyed us wearily, but after about a month, we got word our local gangbangers told the other gangbangers from the other neighborhoods that if they messed with their white guys (us) they would fuck them up. In a weird way, this was the first test of our SF skills, but it struck home. We quite obviously weren't naturally part of this neighborhood, but we had built trust by coming through, and not trying to take over. We became part of this community.

We find out that some of the SOPC buildings are going to be demolished along with everything in them. None of us owned anything so we stole four mattresses, a washer and dryer, and a lamp I really liked. I felt it was the least I could do for that organization after the great time they afforded all of us for the past five months of our lives.

I know how this sounds, but the SF mentality is that "it's only wrong if you get caught." We need to think this way because we never operate under black-and-white rules. I've literally never had a mission that was clear-cut. There's always an element of "figure it out" or "You'll know more when you get on the ground." It is important to stress that I'm not joining a conventional force—there's no talking to any military attaché to figure out what is right or wrong. I'm going where we have to go and doing what we have to do. A lot of guys cannot handle this type of structure. If you need rules and a clear picture of right and wrong, then be a Ranger. They're total badasses but they like to have a clear picture of who and why they are fucking someone up before they leave to fuck them up. We prefer to show up and figure out who needs fucking up on the fly, using our own judgment. If you think rules are more like suggestions, come play with us.

If you think this is just a bad excuse to steal government property and feel okay about it, you're probably right, but fuck SOPC, and government waste.

———————

We are at full-out war right now and the Army desperately needs more SF guys in the field, so they introduced an experimental five-week language course for college graduates instead of the normal four months of total immersion. The five-week course was only being offered in Spanish or French. Desperate to get into the fight and speed this process up, I chose Spanish.

"This will be different than all previous Robin Sage events," the instructor tells us as we start the keystone event of our entire Special Forces training, "In the past, the role players have either spoken English, or we have provided translators. For this Robin Sage, it will be a total immersion into your chosen language."

Well. The ultimate, must-pass, final test of all my accumulated SF knowledge thus far will be entirely in a language that I spent all of five weeks half-heartedly learning. *Perfect*.

Abbreviated language school seemed smart at the time; it seems less smart now. There's probably a lesson in here about shortcuts resulting in long journeys or whatever, but there's no time to learn that lesson.

This language change, of course, was all planned by the Army. They wanted to test this concept on us and see the results. My whole team, except the officer, went to language school together. So when we show up for Robin Sage, our whole ODA is already built. We're continuing with the exact same crew, which is cool. For the exercise, our indigenous forces would be played by ROTC cadets who speak Spanish. They are only allowed to speak to us in Spanish. They are fired up to do it and are stoked to be part of Special Forces training. It's a shame they are going to grow up to be officers, because I like them.

Robin Sage is rad. It's exactly what training should be. The entire local population is involved and has been for years. The Army spares no expense in having a strong OPFOR (Opposing Force, aka the pretend bad guys) with the right weapons, vehicles, and relationships to make this feel real. The exercise starts with planning for an infiltration into enemy territory, then moves to linking up and training the indigenous people, and ends with missions. The planning really matters. We have to pack pallets of goods that will be airdropped to us at various pickup points throughout this operation. We need ammunition, food, medical supplies, batteries, gasoline, candles, antibiotics, and a whole lot more. If we don't plan this properly, we simply will not have it. The cadre will not step in and say, "Oh the poor guys screwed up and didn't pack food so we'll drop it off for them." We just won't eat. Everything we plan or fail to plan is on us, and in 2004, this is a must-pass event. So we try to plan our little asses off. I'm figuring out when we will need ammo and how much. The 18E is figuring out where we will need to go to get good communication back to base, and how many batteries we will need to do so. The officer is . . . I don't know . . . golfing or some shit. I don't know what officers do. We never see them. Then the 18C takes all of that information, plus whatever other shit he thinks we need, and plans out each pallet.

We are jumping into a drop zone in Saint Mare that is about thirty miles from our objective, so the enemy cannot spot us as we come in. We expect to be linking up with the indigenous people just off the drop zone, who will drive us to about ten miles from their base. From there we will have to walk to a rendezvous point over very challenging terrain while carrying about 120-to-140 pounds each. At the rendezvous point, if the natives trust us, they will bring us to their camp where we will meet the G base commander (essentially the chief of the indigenous people). If all goes well, we will start to execute missions shortly thereafter.

While all of this is happening, the cadre are grading us and we have must-pass gates. If the pallets are wrong, or the resupply is poorly planned, then the 18C is in bad shape. If we cannot get communications with higher, then obviously that's bad for the 18E's grade, but also he needs those communications to call for the pallets to be dropped in the first place. There's no backstop. If he forgot the batteries or didn't get the right secure fill for the radios, it doesn't matter what the 18C's pallets look like—they are never going to get the message to drop them off, so they won't be dropped off. The 18D handles all of our water purification, makes sure the food we kill in the woods is clean and safe, takes care of the horse, and holds a daily sick call to make sure everyone is healthy, and treats them if they are not. If he does a bad job, we will get sick. This shit is as real as it gets. Once we engage in battles, he will be in charge of trauma care and, in concert with the 18E, evacuation.

For my part, as an 18B, I get graded on *everything*. I must build fortifications like machine gun positions, clear out defilades so we have good intersecting fields of fire with our guns, keep all of our weapons in good working order, build an Escape and Evasion (E&E) plan, and make sure it is rehearsed. And make sure that at all times everyone knows where positions Black and Gold are (two places to fall back to if we need to flee the enemy). I also have to make sure that the weapons of the Gs (indigenous people) are functioning. The people playing the Gs purposefully will take poor care of their weapons, because the cadre can spot-check at any time. So if I'm not on it—if I take their word for it that they are cleaning their weapons and the cadre finds them full of gunk—I fail.

So with these criteria as a backdrop, I happily load into a C-130 airplane and prepare to not be a "Five-Jump Chump."

You see, to graduate Airborne School, you need to jump five times. Until you complete your sixth jump, you are somewhat ridiculed by the Airborne community. They actually call your sixth jump a "Cherry Blast." I'm getting mine at Robin Sage, as is most of my team.

Everyone is fired up and ready to go, which is awesome. Well . . . everyone except the Captain. His wife just gave birth so he got special permission to miss training, which is fine, because officers rarely make things better.

Military jumps are weird. They sound fun, but they never are. You're carrying 120–140 pounds between your legs so you have to waddle everywhere, they always take forever to load up, and by the time you're jumping, you need to piss so bad you don't care how you get to the ground. And there's also the danger of having so many people in the air at once. Specifically: A static line can hit you in the arm and rip your biceps on the way out if the guy in front of you is lazy; a guy can steal your air by moving below you; you can bounce off the side of the plane if you exit poorly; and, of course, the chute might not open.

The jumpmaster stands up and gives us the command to "stand up." We all do. Then he gives us the command to "hook up." We connect our static lines to the wire running the length of the plane and make sure it is secure (if it comes undone, our chute will not get pulled from our backs and it will not deploy). He then opens the door and looks out, visually inspecting the drop zone and the landmarks leading up to it. He has a small window of time to put us out of the plane so we land in the right spot. "One minute!" he shouts. We echo him. "Thirty seconds!" he shouts. We echo again. Our eyes are now transfixed on the light at the door. It is currently red.

It changes to green.

"Go!" he shouts.

One after another we exit the plane. My turn comes and without hesitation I step out into the breeze.

One thousand. Two thousand. Three thous . . .

I feel the pull of the parachute and breathe a sigh of relief. If you get to four thousand, that means your parachute didn't open and you need to pull your reserve. I look up and check to make sure my chute is fully open and there are no issues. *Good to go.* Now I look around to make sure there aren't any assholes getting too close to me. *Also good.* I aim myself in the general direction of where we are trying to land, and watch the horizon. It's always beautiful up here. The world feels small, and there is no sound but the wind whistling past your ears.

There isn't a lot of time to enjoy that, however, as the ground is coming close and I still have 140 pounds of rucksack between my legs. I will have to drop that about 50 feet before I hit the ground so it separates from me and I don't land on it. I estimate my altitude. 200 feet. 100 feet. 50 feet. I release the ruck and hear it hit the ground as I prepare for my parachute landing fall (PLF). PLFs aren't the sexy walk-offs you see with civilian chutes. You basically keep your feet and knees pressed together and then eat shit. There's a whole skill to it, but it always hurts and you always land like you weigh 1,000 pounds. This time is not different, but I don't feel any injuries. I disconnect my chute, roll it up, collect my rucksack, unpack my weapon, and start moving to the link-up point.

Robin Sage has begun.

When we finally arrive at the G base, we are all drenched from sweat. I already have a nice series of salt lines on top of my BDUs (battle dress uniform), which is pretty solid for it being day one. (The ten-mile movement through rough terrain took approximately eight or nine hours. The rendezvous took another hour or so of discussion and another hour or so of movement, so all in, since the jump, we've been going for about eleven or twelve hours.)

The G base is nestled in a valley behind a mountain so that it's very hard to see unless you're right up on it. It's not overly complex, but it's absolutely a working camp. There are tents, vehicles, an aid station with their local medic, and a mini tactical operation center (TOC) with radios. When I first see the G leader, I know he is not happy. I do not know why. Then I notice the guy he is talking to is our Captain. Apparently, our 18A got back from his wife's birth, and they opted to drop him off right here. Were we bitter that we just worked for twelve hours and had to carry his gear in so he could spend that time with his wife? Perhaps. Did we have some compassion for him given the situation? We are dudes under twenty-five, so not really.

The G leader, who is a fifty-five-year-old retired SF guy playing the role of a tribal elder, agrees with us and gave us all a hard time because of it. "Why are all of you guys disgusting and your officer is clean?" he asks in Spanish. "Is this leadership? How can I trust a man who doesn't prioritize his men?"

Our officer tries to make it right with platitudes, but the G leader is not impressed, and his mind is made up. He kicks us out of camp. This blows and we all know it is payback for the Captain's break. We can't waste time thinking about that right now; every moment we are not in camp is a moment we are not training them. We have about one week total to train the G Army and the clock started the second we jumped out of the airplane. This bullshit is going to kill at least a day. But you can only control what you can control, and that is our reaction.

We explain that we totally understand his position and leave the camp but ask if we can speak to him again later. He agrees to talk to us in the morning. *Well, that's one day wasted.* So, we make our own camp just outside of theirs, update command via radio, tend to our weapons, and get some sleep.

In the morning, the G leader tells us he is willing to consider working with us if we do a few things for him. Those things include hunting some game for the base, fetching water, and making some deliveries to some of the other G camps in the area. None of this is ideal, but they're in charge. If that's the price of entry, then that's the price of entry. Over a couple days, we manage to kill a pig, make a number of water runs, and deliver messages and gear to some of the other G camps. Finally, at around midday on the third day, the G leader allows us to enter his camp. Regular military guys would have an issue with this scenario, as they are not in charge.

We have goals. We have a mission. We want to get things moving. But it's not our camp and they aren't our soldiers. It's his camp. So, we need to build rapport. I immediately chum it up with everyone I see. This is the same thing I would do if this were a real mission. I ask about their families. I show them things I know—shooting, fighting, fishing, hunting, whatever. I practice the fuck out of my bad Spanish. And I find the same thing that I would eventually find in all my other travels around the world: people are people. They generally have the same goals, the same desires, the same fears, and they generally don't speak Spanish well. It became obvious very quickly that most of these ROTC kids had significantly oversold their Spanish-speaking ability in order to do this mission; their Spanish was every bit as shitty as ours. That became a little internal joke between us and them, and English started finding its way into conversations when the cadre weren't around. Regardless of all these challenges, I make it very clear that our unified plan is to assist. Whatever they need to reclaim their fictional country of Pineland, my team and I are willing to help them do it.

Our goal is to get them involved to fight our enemies. We are trying to establish a legitimate government in Pineland that is democracy-forward and friendly to the United States . . . you know, as we have successfully accomplished so many times in our history . . .

We have only four to five days left to train them before the missions are supposed to start. We're not here to train them to be Special Forces. We're just trying to teach them basic infantry stuff out of the *7–8 Manual* (the Bible of the infantry): how to react to contact, how to conduct an ambush, how to conduct a raid, how to call for fire, and how to do recon. None of this is all that crazy, but it honestly is the fun part. The ROTC kids are told by the cadre to be dumb and problematic, but all this infantry training is new to them, so they are super excited to learn it. Every time they do anything right, I go out of my way to praise them. I cheer. I whoop. I tell them, "Fuck yeah! That is how it is done!" My compatriots do the same.

After four days of this, they don't want to be role players giving us a hard time anymore. They are our little motivated army of bad-Spanish-speaking cadets. They're sophomores and juniors in college that probably get made fun of for doing ROTC while the rest of their friends are getting high and drunk. They get very little training until the summer, and they don't have cool stories to tell. Now they do. They are getting personally trained by SF guys, who they legitimately consider friends. They don't care what the cadre want. They want to fuck up the enemies of Pineland as much as we do.

When the week of training nears its end, the cadre show up in the middle of the night to blow us out of our G base and disrupt all our planning. I'm one hundred percent sure it is their favorite night of the exercise. They have hundreds of artillery simulators and training grenades, and their plan is to surprise us when we are least prepared and just start ruining our world so we have to flee and leave equipment and intelligence behind. They forgot, however, that we 18 X-Rays are dirty, rotten cheaters. We are not supposed to have cell phones, but we smuggled several in. Plus, we have friends who were hurt and assigned to support duty inside the cadre's TOC. For some reason the cadre trust them. This is super dumb. They have been acquiring information and sending it to us via text message the entire time. So we know that the G base blowout is coming tonight at 2:00 a.m.

The cadre aren't with you 24/7. They check on you a few times a day and then go and check on other people or rack out or do whatever it is that cadre do. They also adhere to a general pattern. Usually, the last time they see any of us is around 10:00 p.m. So, when they take off at 10:00, we immediately load up everything we have and get ready to move. We also leave behind some fake intelligence that disguises our plan. When the artillery sims kick off at 2:00 a.m., we are off the objective in minutes, leaving nothing behind but some fake intelligence and one 240 tripod so it wouldn't look too suspicious, but also so we didn't have to carry that heavy fucking thing. (Note to future cadre: If you recycle someone from the same class and they are aspiring Green Berets, search them—and I mean a prison, four-knuckles-deep search, because I promise they are not on your team.)

We weren't as smart as we thought we were, though. The cadre are also Green Berets and they have been doing this a lot longer, and while game recognizes game, they were none too pleased to be fucked with, so they scuffed us up anytime they could and made our lives harder. As hard as it got, though, it didn't feel malicious the way it did in SOPC. They were having fun with us, and we were having fun with them. I loved every minute of it.

After the blowout, both sides went full "fuck fuck" games, meaning it became a competition to see who could screw with the other side the most. My favorite moment of the entire course is when we are assigned the final sabotage mission. The cadre give us an operation window to perform this sabotage. We are not supposed to operate outside of that time window. The site we are to sabotage is an opposing forces (OPFOR) base that is off the side of the path. The cadre pulled up to this thing to observe in their own vehicles, which they parked a few hundred meters away. Their vehicles were strictly off limits. We knew from our guy on the inside when the OPFOR was arriving to man this base and as such, we ignored the time window and the ROE (rules of engagement). The night before, we sneaked into the base that we would be hitting tomorrow and siphoned the gas out of the generators, leaving enough for maybe ten-to-fifteen minutes, tops. We knew they'd just filled them yesterday and would not be thinking about fuel. When the time window actually hits, we aren't dressed as normal. We go full Mac-Gyver ninja mode. We cover our faces and hands with axle grease and cover our uniforms in charcoal. We are as black as night and there isn't a lot of illumination from the moon.

There we are, completely blacked out, waiting. The OPFOR turn the generators on to light up the night, so we are easy to spot. We see the cadre standing around bullshitting waiting for the mission to go off. We wait. Time is on our side. The generators start to cough, and then one by one, they go dark. We move. But not to hit the OPFOR. We move the vehicles. We steal everything that isn't bolted to the ground, and even then, we check the bolts to see if they are loose.

We were on the objective for a total of six minutes. No one saw or heard any of us.

The next morning, the cadre show up, part pissed, part amused. I am wearing a Black Diamond headlamp that belongs to one of them when they arrive.

"We would like all of our shit back, including but not limited to: my Black Diamond headlamp [he says, looking at his headlamp on my head], our Suunto watches, a Casio G-Shock watch, our SureFire flashlights, our beef jerky, food, dip, and the teddy bear that belongs to one of our kids," he finishes, with a look of bemused judgment.

"This will have to be negotiated," my teammate says to him.

"Indeed, it will," I add, smirking.

We asked for food, purified water, and a pig. They agreed. We slow-roasted it that night and had a feast with our team, our fifty-five-year-old, very impressed G leader, and our Army of ROTC students.

When we finish Robin Sage, unlike every other SF course, where we were shown total indifference, our cadre take us all out to Golden Corral. I know that doesn't sound fancy, but when you graduate from military schools you're usually starving, and food is about quantity over quality (no disrespect to the Corral, mind you). They laugh and joke about our group and talk about how much they enjoyed seeing what we would try to get away with next. I feel like these guys are my people, not just my teachers. We broke every rule, and they think it is hilarious.

There's only one gate left—then I become one of them.

Our rule breaking, disregard for societal norms, and personal discipline reach their pinnacle at SERE School. SERE School, like Monty Python's Camelot, is a silly place. SERE stands for Survival, Evasion, Resistance, Escape. Basically, it's all about learning what to do if you become a prisoner of war, and how to avoid getting caught if you manage to escape.

During SERE, they teach you this stuff, then at some point they let you go and tell you that you have a few hours' head start and then they start hunting you. If they catch you, they bring you to a concentration camp and torture you and try to break you for information. The longer you last without capture, the less time you spend at the concentration camp.

To be super clear, this isn't a fun course. When they catch you they do torture you. You get physically beaten up. You're punched. You're kicked. You're placed in boxes where you can't sit or stand, and they blast music at you. They strip you down and make fun of your dick. And they do it all in these really crappy accents that somehow makes it much worse. No one likes SERE School. Anyone who tells you they like SERE School either didn't go to SERE School, is a blowhard pretending to be tougher than he or she is, or is into some really weird shit.

The first part is all training and there is nothing particularly special about it. The meat of the course starts when they let you go and start hunting you on the evasion lanes. I'm excited. They let us go and tell us we better get moving. Most people spend the week hunting squirrels or eating bugs, and that's cool . . . but we had a better plan. We came out here before the course started and buried Meals Ready to Eat (MREs) at various places along the course. I hid enough MREs so that our twelve-person team could have two meals per day. That's a glorious 5,000 calories per man, and it nullifies the purpose of the entire evasion lane, but fuck it. Cheating got us this far, and we are not quitting on it now. My goal isn't just to graduate SERE School, but to graduate as the fattest SERE squad in the history of the entire school.

When our twelve-man group clears the tree line and is no longer visible to the cadre, I plot a course to my first hidden bundle of joy under this giant log. We move out at a good clip, and in less than an hour we are there, and I dig out our MREs. (I still remember exactly where it was: 251 meters from an intersection at the edge of the drop zone under a fallen tree. Fifteen years later, I think I could still navigate to that exact spot.)

Eleven of us have been together for almost a year now. One dude, an Air Force guy, has not. "Where the hell did these come from?" he asks. "I buried them here," I respond. He falls apart before my very eyes. He is sputtering and he turns red. "This sounds like an integrity violation. I'm not doing it," he says, sticking to his guns. "Are you serious, man?" I ask him. Apparently, he is. No amount of cajoling will convince him. Okay, then. I divide the twelfth MRE amongst us and we all get a little extra. We eat quickly and then bury the trash.

As the days get longer and he gets thinner, I expect him to break. To his credit, he sticks to his guns for seven days. Just because he refuses to cheat doesn't mean we abandon him. We are team players and help him as much as we can. We find him some deer corn, a couple of crab apples, and some roadkill that we think was a squirrel at some point before being mashed by a couple thousand pounds of vehicle. But on the whole, the poor guy just stays hungry. Even though I think he is dumb for doing this, I respect his honesty. If he wants to suffer, and isn't dragging the team down, more power to him.

We avoid capture for the entire seven days, which is a huge win. But the course is designed to make sure you spend at least a week as a POW, so at the seven-day mark, when we arrive at our prearranged exfiltration point, we are captured by the enemy, allegedly because our cadre betrayed us. Black bags are thrown over our heads, we are pushed around, and then we are stuffed into a vehicle of some kind and taken to the concentration camp. Once we arrive, they immediately start beating the crap out of us. And you need to understand, while they aren't trying to murder us, this isn't light slapping. They beat you up pretty damn good. As soon as that pain infliction kicks off, guess who starts singing like a motherfucking canary and rats us the fuck out? Mr. Honest Air Force.

He immediately goes from the honorable guy that we respect to a total bag of dicks in five seconds. But his cowardice just gave us a gift that we didn't know we needed. This exercise just became real.

If we fail SERE School, we are out. We do not get to be Special Forces. *Everything we experienced over the last year is for nothing.* If just *one* of us breaks, even for a second, and admits that we cheated, then we will all be integrity violators, and we will all be kicked out. My entire career is on the line, and these guys have an entire week to torture us and make us admit what really happened.

"Is this true?" one of our captors asks me.

"Kennedy, Specialist, United States Army," I respond from behind the bag over my head. They punch me in the gut and smack my head around, making my ears sting, then move to the next member of our squad.

"Smith, Specialist, United States Army," the next man responds.

One by one, each man responds the same exact way. By giving them the absolute bare minimum. They respond the way we have been trained to respond. I know these guys. For one year, everyone has told us that we are not good enough. That we're just motherfucking know-nothing 18 X-Rays. And here we are. I smile from behind the bag and lick the blood running down my mouth from their strikes.

None of these motherfuckers are going to break. We're golden.

In that moment SERE School went from "just another must-pass course" on my way to the coveted Green Beret to the best school I have ever been to in the military. The cadre now have a real mission. They want to, no they *need* to, break us and admit that we cheated. We have a real mission. If we admit it, not only do we get out of the course, but we get kicked completely out of the SF pipeline and have to join a regular unit. And let's face it, our whole crew would get kicked out of a regular unit in like two weeks.

These motherfuckers beat the shit out of us. They put us in pain positions and leave us in them for hours while they blare loud noises and music at us. They lock us in confined spaces. They spit on us. They stick us in ice baths or spray us with hoses and leave us outside (it's the middle of winter). They are relentless and do everything possible to crush our souls. In fact, they spend so much time on us that it is probably the easiest SERE School in history for everyone else in the course.

After seven days of nonstop torture, not a single guy changed his story. I'm so fucking proud.

Some might conclude, after hearing my story, that since we cheated, we don't deserve to be Green Berets. To those people I would argue simply that we are Green Berets. We aren't Marines. We aren't SEALs. We aren't Rangers. Like them, we will attempt to follow the rules and be perfectly disciplined. We are professionals, after all. But when the rules prevent us from finding a solution, or they flat out don't make any sense and fall under the "this is the way it has always been done" category, well . . . it's our job to find the best solution. We have to get the job done, often while understaffed, outgunned, and in incredibly complex situations far from home, with limited backup. The lessons we learned from constantly trying to get away with shit, and finding ways to achieve mission success where others had not, will keep many of us alive on the battlefields in Afghanistan, Iraq, Africa, and South America.

Funny, the very habits that made me a terrible firefighter are the same habits that make me a perfect fit for this life.

After graduating SERE, we are all brought to the John F. Kennedy Special Warfare Center at Fort Bragg. There's a statue of a Green Beret there. We form up in front of it and are ordered to remove our maroon berets that represent we are Airborne personnel. We then move to our assigned tables and at the corner of each seat assignment is our new Green Beret, with our new unit flash already affixed. Even though I always felt this moment was inevitable, actually being here, looking at my beret, has a profound gravitas I did not expect. The commander gets up and gives an officer speech, but my eyes keep lingering on it—on my beret. When he is done, he sits down, and the Command Sergeant Major stands up and orders us to don our Green Berets. I will never be able to truly describe the profound weight of that moment for me. It isn't just a hat. It's a brotherhood. It's a responsibility. It's a moment that will define me, and the expectations of me, for the rest of my life.

They file us through the museum. Inside we are each given our individual Yarborough knife. Each knife has a serial number and your name. You then sign a book that dates all the way back to the '60s, with your serial number and your name. This book is commonly referred to as the "Book of Truth" because of how many people claim to be Green Berets that have been proven liars by this book.

I learn that I am going to 3rd Battalion, 7th Group, meaning I remain on Fort Bragg.

Before I report there, I am given some time to go home. It's been over a year since I have seen anyone. It feels like a different lifetime.

I'm not the same anymore, but everyone there only knows the old Tim. I spend time with my babies. They have grown so much over the past year. It's incredibly painful to see them and know that I am not a part of their lives the way I want to be, but I also know unequivocally this is the right path.

I stop by the Pit to get in a workout or two with Chuck and the guys. It's nice to be back, but it feels smaller and distant, like I've lived an entire other lifetime since I've been here last. John Hackleman is there, and he comes over.

"Tim, I want you to know that I understand the weight of what you just accomplished, and I know the weight of what you are about to do, and I am very proud of you."

He clasps me on the shoulder, and then he leaves.

I've known John for years. He's said a lot of things to me. "Good match." "Keep your hands up." "Selling parrot meat is illegal." "Nice combo." But never once did he say anything like that. And I knew he meant it. I had never truly felt like I belonged at the Pit until that moment.

———

Months later, with all the training well in my rearview mirror, the cadre from SERE approached me and my former squad and invited us to dinner. They wanted to know what really happened. We tell them the truth and they are blown the fuck away.

They cannot believe that even though we were immediately separated and had no way of communicating with one another, we all kept our stories straight and did not crack. We spent hours that night explaining our methodology. They took notes and explained that they were going to reverse-engineer our methods so they'd be more effective interrogators in future training and in the real world. They ended the conversation and the evening by saying they were proud of us.

This wasn't the Boy Scouts. It was kill or be killed.

I knew I had finally found my tribe.

CHAPTER SEVEN

HUNTING ZARQAWI

It's March 13, 2006, and I am on my way to Iraq for my first combat deployment. Life is fucking awesome right now for two completely badass reasons.

Reason #1: I am the youngest guy to ever get put on Combatant Commanders In-extremis Force (or CIF). It is a specialized force modeled after Delta Force, the highest level of tactical unit in the entire United States military.

After spending half a year in infantry training, and then over a year in Special Forces training learning how to be a contributing member to a normal Operational Detachment Alpha (ODA), I end up bypassing any time on said ODA. Instead, I get added to this elite unit that is focused on hostage rescue and "direct action," military speak for "kicking in doors and shooting bad guys in the face." Basically, the Army decided they didn't have enough Delta Force guys, so they asked each Special Forces Group to stand up a CIF. Ninety-nine point nine percent of the guys on the CIF are either previously from Delta Force or are very seasoned Special Forces veterans. Then there's me, who is a dirty twenty-six-year-old 18 X-Ray, who has never been on a regular ODA, never gone to war, and now is here somehow. Most of my teammates, especially Shane Thompson and Travis Freeman, do not think I belong here. They are right. But fuck it; I took the opportunity when it presented itself.

That magical opportunity was granted by my new boss, Master Sergeant John "Shrek" McPhee, also known as the "Sheriff of Baghdad." Apparently, John's boss, Sergeant Major (SGM) Oquendo, told John that he needed to get some fresh blood on the CIF after several of our guys were injured in a vehicle accident in November. John came from Delta and had the attitude that he would rather be down several guys than have any guys that he doesn't fully trust. He didn't want any of the seasoned guys available to him for the CIF, so he told Oquendo no. Oquendo told him yes. So now he had to pick someone.

Apparently, the guys joked around with him about pulling in some of the cherry guys if he didn't want who was available.

"Hey, isn't one of them a fighter?" John asked

Mario Montesè, the senior 18 Charlie, replied, "Yes."

"I'll go watch him fight, and if he doesn't suck, I will take him," John replied.

And that's how I got here. I'd like to think that my stellar reputation from Special Forces training preceded me and that is why I was chosen. But literally no one cares about that once you graduate. My assumption, knowing what I know about John, is he figured I would make them better at hand-to-hand combat. So, at the very least, I would have some use, and maybe he could teach me the rest. Or kick me out.

John is not a lovable guy. He is not sweet. My guess is he probably doesn't read a lot of books about emotional intelligence or empathetic leadership. More than likely, he is not going to make you feel better when you feel blue. He will not tuck you in at night. But if you're going to war, you want John Fucking McPhee.

Other than John, who employs the "whip people to either get better or quit" methodology, there are two other dudes helping me out a ton. One is Dave Fredericks, who was John's whipping boy before I came here. Dave made the dual mistakes of saying he didn't really want to go to Ranger School and asking John why he did things on a few occasions. He and I share that last habit. The other guy is Ben Rios, my senior 18 Bravo. He basically had to jump in and teach me how to be in the Army. I didn't know how to get a range, to forecast ammo, to request ammo, and all that kind of stuff. I only knew the schoolhouse stuff. Any regular infantry could do that, but not an 18 X-Ray. We're new! Dave and Ben were great at making me feel like a part of the CIF, and I was sure the other guys would come around eventually.

Despite a little hazing, I am really fired up to be part of this unit, heading to this war, with this ogre of a man as my boss.

But this impending deployment pales in comparison to Reason #2 why life is so fucking good right now: I just got married to this girl Ginger.

Ginger is twenty-three years old and has already earned a master's degree and a high-level government security clearance. She is a government contractor, managing radio crypto for one of the most elite Special Operations units in the military. She graduated high school at fifteen and college at nineteen; she is a lot smarter than I am. She is fierce and uncompromising, and loyal to a fault. She presents herself to the world in the exact opposite manner that I do: She's quiet, understated, careful with her words, pretty, and petite.

The first time I saw her was at the Ugly Stick Bar in Fayetteville. Legend has it that the bar got its name because the girls who work there fell out of a tree and hit the ugly stick on the way down. (A cruel naming convention but mostly accurate.) She is with her girlfriends, and she is most assuredly not ugly. She has olive skin, almond eyes, the jet-black hair that comes with the mixture of her Native and Mexican heritage, and an hourglass figure that looks drawn out of a comic book. In fact, I believe that when they tried to throw her out of the tree with the rest of these girls, she began flying, because she is an absolute angel (write that one down, guys). She and her girlfriends are having fun, when some guy with a very tight T-shirt on, slicked hair, and a gold chain walks up to her and starts talking. I cannot hear everything he says, but he definitely makes some kind of comment about her physical appearance, accentuated by a hand motion describing her general shape and curvature. She pours her drink over his head and turns her back to him.

The next time I see her is at a bar called the Graduate. It's a swankier place that has a catwalk for a bar entrance with the tables all recessed into the floor so that as people walk in you're looking up at them. As Ginger walks into this bar looking hot as fuck in six-inch stiletto heels, some random guy reaches up and puts his hand around her calf to get her attention. While balancing on only one stiletto, she removes the other one and stabs him in the arm with her heel. Her agility, balance, and propensity for violence is inspiring—and immediately arousing. I must talk to her.

As I walk up to her and her girlfriends, having watched her previous two performances, I make a mental note to not touch her in any way. Instead, I say, "Hi, I'm Tim!" I shoot for friendly and confident. She looks me in the eyes for a second and then slowly turns around. I walk around so she can see me again. She slowly turns around again. We go through three or four iterations of this, and then with a sigh and an exit phrase that went something like, "Until we meet again, mean dream woman!" I go away a failure . . . but not a quitter.

It's time to use all of my ODA training. I have to crack the code that is Ginger by determining her center of gravity. I enlist my friends and we work our way into her inner circle by creating a target set of the friends that seem most valuable to her and befriending them. Once we acquire her core friends as our own, I start gathering intel. Ginger apparently has a passion for live music. *Now we're getting somewhere!* It's time to construct a plan to get access to my principal.

Ginger is still unwilling to give me any personal attention, but due to "Operation Gingerbread Man," I am now a known quantity instead of some random dude she has to destroy, so that's a step in the right direction. I invite her and all of her friends to a big social event with a live band. I ask her friends to arrive at 8:00; I tell Ginger that it starts at 7:00. She arrives at 7:27, and I hit send on the pre-populated text message I have set up to all of her friends telling them that dinner is canceled. She walks in, looking incredible, and I tell her that the whole thing is an elaborate ruse to finally get her on a date. She is slightly impressed, but also explains to me this is a little creepy. Boldness wins the day, and I take her to dinner.

We spent every single day together for the six months until this morning when I left Fort Bragg for Iraq via Germany. We eloped at a strip mall five days ago. I recognize, and the team reminds me, that this kind of marriage is generally a failed state. But I know it isn't.

The Air Force guys let us know that we are about an hour from Al Asad Air Base. I look out the window of the C-17 and can tell we are slowly dropping altitude. The boys are breaking down the hammocks that they have been sleeping on this whole trip. Putting up the hammocks apparently breaks some kind of Air Force rule, but when they tried to make us take them down, the fifty-five team guys opted for raw intimidation techniques and that won the day.

We put on body armor in case they try to shoot at us as we come in to land and start gathering our things together so we can get moving once we touch down. After thirty minutes or so of waiting, I experience my first combat landing. Civilians are used to a nice, straight, gentle landing. That's not the way pilots do it in war zones (straight paths are easy to target with machine gun fire or rockets), so our pilots execute very sharp circles and a steep descent that sends my stomach into my mouth. It is surprising at first, especially because you can see the hydraulics working the wings on the inside of the plane.

One of the hydraulic lines is leaking. I wonder how important that is and whether these Air Force guys even knew or worry about stuff like that.

Almost as soon as the descent starts, it is over, and I feel the wheels of the giant aircraft bounce off the runway and then come back down again, smoother the second time. In less than two minutes, the plane has completed taxiing and has come to a standstill. I'm ready to get off. This place smells like fifty-five meat eaters have been breathing through their mouths for sixteen hours.

The ramp drops, and I immediately miss the smell of our grossness because I am assaulted with a host of fresh awful odors. I'm experiencing an odd combination of the sights and smells of a military base and a Middle Eastern country. *Is that jet fuel? Is that a burn pit? Is that asphalt? Is there maybe some hummus and body odor mixed in?* This air is not American air. All of these things combine for a potpourri of grossness. I'm not saying it's the worst smell ever or anything, but I never want to see Yankee Candle knock out "Al Asad Air Base 2006." No one needs that candle in their lives.

Our ADVON (Advanced Echelon) meets us at the gate. Mario Montesè is leading the effort and he's been here for about a week.

When I first arrived to the CIF, Mario refused to let me in the Team Room, because I was a cherry. He asked me why the hell I was here, and I told him I wanted to be trained. "I've got some physical training ready for you right now," he said.

"I want you to go to the gym and move everything in it to the left side."

I did it in two hours. When I finished, he said, "Why the hell did you move everything in the gym? It looks dumb. Move it back."

I did that in ninety-eight minutes.

I got a lot more efficient. I made it a point not to complain no matter what they did to me in those first few months. Because of that, over time the ribbing diminished from the original legitimate disgust for an 18 X-Ray cherry joining the CIF to friendly ribbing and insults.

Works for me.

Mario is super squared away, and even though I am halfway around the globe, I appreciate why we do things a certain way. We load this pallet the same way every time. We unload it the same way every time. Unloading it now gives me a sense of familiarity and consistency. I absolutely see why Ben Rios was so anal about doing everything exactly the way he laid it out for me. This was so easy and natural that we might as well be back at Fort Bragg.

Once we finish with the pallets, Mario escorts us to our new home— a giant hangar right next to the runway. We're this close because we expect a lot of short-notice time sensitive targets (TSTs) and traveling from the other side of the base could delay getting to the target in time.

The battlefield in Iraq in 2006 is insane. Our core mission is to defeat Al Qaeda, but in particular it is to find and defeat this total piece of shit named Abu Musab al-Zarqawi. If bin Laden is the biggest piece of shit in the War on Terror, then Zarqawi has to be the second biggest piece of shit. He also demonstrates a cruelty that puts bin Laden to shame, which is saying a lot.

Zarqawi is the face of Al Qaeda in Iraq. To date, he is believed to be the mastermind of the Canal Hotel bombing that killed the special envoy from the United Nations to Iraq. He was in Iran at the same time as 9/11, and there is evidence he was there to help plan the attacks. He personally assassinated three Americans. He shot and killed Laurence Foley, a senior administrator of U.S. Agency for International Development, in Amman, Jordan, in 2002.

Later, in a now famous and horrifying video, he captured and decapitated Nick Berg, and in a separate incident did the same to Olin Eugene Armstrong. He claimed responsibility for killing thousands of Shia Iraqis, proclaiming war against them, causing a rebuke from bin Laden, as he did not believe Muslims should be attacking Muslims. When bin Laden is like, "Yo, dawg, that's too far," you are not a nice man. If all that bad shit isn't enough, Zarqawi is regarded as the godfather of ISIS.

We are here to kill Zarqawi. Although he is currently the number two bad guy on the planet, he is, operationally speaking, number one. This is our CIF's first deployment, and we are regarded as the baddest organization in the world that has never been tested in combat. We need to prove our worth. We are keenly aware of the opportunity this provides to kill two birds with one stone, and by that I mean a terrorist and our hurt unit pride.

As we enter the hangar, I see it is filled with single-wide white trailers, with dripping A/C units sticking out of each one. *Am I in Louisiana or am I in Iraq?* These things are shitty. The wiring is shitty. There is no plumbing or bathrooms. Each is jammed with five or six beds, so each accommodates about half of our ODA. The inside is like a basic training bay but on a smaller scale, with a small walking space in between the beds running to the door. There are no shelves or cabinets or mirrors or anything. It's a shitty tin shell with flickering lights and an air-conditioning unit. To be fair, I've slept in far worse places.

We grab our kit and start unloading everything. Everyone has a job. Our 18 Foxtrot, Shane Thompson, heads out to get the intelligence brief and the lay of the land. Foxtrots used to be one of the regular Special Forces MOS, but they get selected into the role when they are more senior and must complete another course to become qualified. Sounds close to the Team Leader's job to me and I want to avoid that.

Our 18 Charlies are out doing inventories, checking sensitive items, procuring wood for cabinetry and storage, and other shit like that. Our 18 Echos fill and check all our crypto for the radios and make sure our batteries are good to go. Our 18 Deltas are getting our medical bags ready, linking up with the hospitals to learn procedures, and going down to Blue (the dirty Navy SEALs) to claim a med shack and get it set up for when people get off the birds after a mission and need urgent care. At this location, Team Blue is in charge, so we have to defer to the SEALs. While we have our own medics, we do not have our own trauma team. All the tier one folks do. That team consists of a trauma surgeon, an ER doctor, three to four medics, plus three to four 18 Deltas, so basically the most rad trauma team imaginable. SEAL Team 6 had one. JSOC (Joint Special Operations Command) had one. We shared theirs and had a little hut of our own for minor stuff.

As the junior 18 Bravo, I get to work on the busybody stuff. I mount weapons on vehicles. I build drop mags that have thirty full magazines and two battery packs each. I add swing arms to the gun trucks for M240 and M249 machine guns. I do the Mark 19 automatic grenade launcher and .50 caliber machine gun headspace and timing. Finally, I change and check all the batteries on our optics and lasers.

While we are doing all this, our Team Leader, Mike Gomez, is down with the task force targeters trying to figure out what operational tempo looks like and where we can get plugged in. He left for this task super excited. When he comes back, he is super sad.

The sad Captain Mike Gomez episode is the moment that my judgment of all things Navy SEAL begins. I have spent the entire day preparing weapons, vehicles, and equipment for one of the most elite units on earth, and Team Blue decides that it is too dangerous for any ground assault force (GAF) missions. Meanwhile, the Marines (including my future Jackson-Winkeljohn teammate Brian Stann) are driving out the gate every goddamn hour like it's no big deal. To say this is immediately the most frustrating thing in all of our lives is a gross understatement, but the SEALs are running the show so we can't do jack shit.

All the vehicles I rigged are now our Quick Reaction Force (QRF) in case something goes terribly wrong and our guys (or anyone in the task force) need help. All movement will now happen via helicopter.

That, in and of itself, isn't an issue. I will happily fly on to an objective. The problem is that in addition to not wanting us to drive out, they also don't really want us to fly out. We want to work. We want to do hits, which will lead to intel, which will lead to more missions. This is the Delta way that John espouses. This is our way.

This is not the SEAL way. They're waiting for CENTCOM (Central Command) intelligence. They don't want to use their allotted aircraft for fear of missing something if the big one comes down. I don't know what the issue is. Maybe they want bigger missions. Maybe they have responsibilities I don't know about. But to me, they just don't seem like they want to get in the fight like we do. They may not be hungry, but we are!

We're not about that "hang around and wait" kind of life. We are doers with a chip on our shoulder. We need to prove ourselves. We're going to find a gunfight whether the SEALs want us to or not.

So we start to beg, borrow, and steal intel and develop our own target sets. Shane Thompson, our 18F, along with the five other company 18Fs, lead the charge on that. The six of them go to the big meetings, then debrief together at the company level, then at our level. We have a whole separate operational plan that supports the main mission but isn't really on Blue's radar. "Oh, you don't want these targets, SEALs? No worries. We'll go get them. In fact, we're ecstatic to!" was our 18F modus operandi. They stayed with it so passionately that Blue finally said, "Fine. If you can get the air assets."

Okay. That's progress. Mario and I immediately go to schmooze with the Marine aviators to see if we can get some time on their aircraft. We work in two-man teams buttering everyone up. We relentlessly pursue three goals. Goal number one: Get out the door. Goal number two: Find bad guys. Goal number three: Shoot them. But despite our best efforts, we're stuck on goal one.

Two weeks go by. All of a sudden Mike Gomez tells us we somehow have some additional 1/60th assets. We have aircraft! Whether Blue changed their minds because they felt sorry for us, whether they were given more assets, or our 18Fs sucked some dicks for the team, I don't know, but I'll take it.

We receive our first mission: "Operation Bogota." It's a capture/kill mission for a High Value Target (HVT). We're hitting two buildings that are right next to each other. I don't feel anything different. I just go to work. I load thirty magazines with thirty rounds each and then drop one from each so there's only twenty-nine in each one. With one round out, the spring is less compressed and there's less of a chance of the round jamming as it loads into the rifle, and it's much easier to do a tactical reload this way. You don't normally have to do this with nice civilian-purchased magazines, but military magazines are notoriously trash. I put all my favorite magazines directly on my kit. I place all my extra magazines in the speed ball bag that we will drop inside the front door as we hit the building. If the gunfight ends up being long for whatever reason, we can fall back to the doorway and reload. I prep all of my flashbang grenades by unbending the safety on one of the two clips so the safety comes off super easy. To do it, you basically pop the pin out, then place it back in, then only bend one back. Do not try this at home!

I prep all the other equipment. I put brand-new batteries in everything even though we really haven't used any of it. We're running FN M4 rifles with Aimpoint PEQ IIs. Everyone carries a fixed-blade knife. I throw on my altered DCUs (Desert Combat Uniforms) that have regular sleeves sewn into an Under Armour–style body. No one has developed this yet, so everything our team has was custom-sewn by a seamstress back in NC. We all carry two flashbangs and two grenades. For comms, we have SINCGARS and a PRC 119 with helmet mics and a push-to-talk on your shoulder. My callsign is Delta 06, which kind of looked like DOG under night vision, which I thought was really cool.

We load onto Black Hawks at 2130 and wait. Nervous excitement rolls through me. It's been over two years since I put on the uniform. I have been through a lot and overcome a lot. I've gone through some of the toughest training a man can go through. I've defeated the malaise of the SEALs. Now, I finally get to do my job—to represent the CIF.

We take off a few minutes after 10:00 p.m. Our time on target will be 1:00 a.m., so the plan is to drop us a few kilometers away so the enemy doesn't know what the target is and we can walk in quietly. In the air, the doors of the Black Hawk are wide open, pushing wind into my face and dust right along with it. And, with the loud as fuck engines blaring, I do more thinking than I should be doing at this juncture. SGM Oquendo spent a lot of time hammering in the new ROE. Before pulling the trigger, he wants us to make sure our targets are military-age men, that they are holding a gun, and that they are posing a lethal threat before we kill them. This feels awfully close to "don't shoot unless you're fired upon," which is not the message you expect when the mission is literally titled "Capture/Kill."

That thinking fades quickly, though. The high-pitched whine of the Black Hawk coupled with the cool breeze puts you in a pretty chill place and that's where I am heading. That coupled with the fact that when you have a huge spike of adrenaline, and you're used to doing high-adrenaline things like I am, you often get the opposite effect. Instead of getting hyped, you get more chill. It's almost a counterreaction brought on by training. I almost feel sleepy. Am I going to take a nap or go fuck up some motherfuckers? My body isn't quite sure.

My legs are dangling out the side of the Black Hawk as we rapidly touch down. The second the skids hit earth, I step out. As I have been trained to do, I walk five steps away from the bird and take a knee. By the time my knee touches the ground, I can already hear the whine of the Black Hawk engines pick up speed. I feel the rotorwash against my neck and resist its attempt to push me forward. Moments later, the Black Hawk is a distant memory. We wait until we can no longer hear it and then remain in a disciplined posture in place for a moment, exercising stop, look, listen, smell (SLLS). We're smelling for campfires, body odor, camels, shit, cigarettes, or anything that would give away potentially hostile activity. We have our night vision on and have infrared turned on to see if we spot anyone or anything. It seems clear.

I'm super disoriented. I'm not sure on what our direction of movement is supposed to be, even though my GPS is preloaded with our coordinates. For the life of me, I also cannot remember our order of movement. *Am I supposed to be first?* Apparently not, because Mario begins moving. *Whew!*

The guys all stand up one by one and peel off the objective in a Ranger file (a straight line with about ten meters between each of us). Once we are cleanly off the landing zone, we spread out into a wedge formation (think more of a V with the point of the V in the front) so that if we take any kind of gunfire or someone hits an IED we wouldn't be bunched together and all die at once. Even though I have used night vision a lot during training, I have not walked under night vision in a wedge formation in combat with live rounds in my gun waiting for someone to shoot me, and all those thoughts garbled together made me drift too close to Shane Thompson. He, of course, responds with the gentle but reassuring, "Get the fuck back." The whole situation is really fucking embarrassing, and it's the kind of thing you'd expect from a new private, but I am too hyped up to worry about it.

We continue to move toward the objective. It's quiet out. There's not much to be seen—the occasional building, some trees here and there, a stray dog—but really not much at all. I feel just like I did when I broke into that hardware store when I was a kid. At any moment, I expect someone to spot us. My head moves left to right, scanning the horizon and every nook and cranny I see in the darkness. But there is no one.

We are working off of a GRG, which is a satellite image of the target with a built-in target overlay. There are three buildings on the objective, and they are numbered clockwise from one to three. Target one, the main building, is on top of a hill on the outskirts of a little village. There is a small fence, which I assume is for goats. There's a stone pathway from the fence to the front door, which is where my team will be going. McPhee is the ground force Sergeant Major. Major Jimmy Hester is the commander.

Most units at this point in the war just hit the building. They kick in the front door and take the home by force. We are not most units, because we have John McPhee. John learned from CAG (Delta Force) that in most situations, just jumping into a dynamic environment is high-risk and leads to more friendly casualties. Are there still times when kicking in a door makes sense? Absolutely. Hostage situation? Kick it in and hit them hard. Bomb maker? Maybe not a great idea.

So instead, John has us all move about 100 meters back, forms us into an L-shaped ambush on the building, and begins a "Call Out." It's exactly what it sounds like. We get on a megaphone, and we start telling people to get out of the house. Within the five minutes, two guys and five women and their children leave. One of the women tells us her husband is still in there. We ask him to get out for fifteen minutes. It starts nice, but at the end our terp (interpreter) is essentially screaming, "Get out of the house, motherfucker, or we're coming in to get you out!" He doesn't budge. We're going in.

The four of us walk to the front door as Dave Fredericks, Ben Rios, Mario Montesè, and Manny Vialobos move to the back door through the sheep's pen. The rest of the guys are either hitting the other buildings or covering the windows of ours in case the guy tries to squirt out. We're set. As the number one man, Al, pulls the door open and I, as the two man, throw in a flashbang, John, as the three man, covers the doorway with his rifle in case someone tries to take a shot at me or Al as we do our jobs. BAM! The flashbang goes off and we flow into the room, one behind the other.

We see a guy sprint past the door. Our terp yells for the guy to get on the ground over and over again. The guy is not going to the ground. He is defiant. My red dot is on his chest, as are Al's and John's. He takes a breath and makes an athletic movement away from us. I hear Al switch his weapon from safe to semi. It's such a small sound. The tiny click of metal on metal, but all veterans know what that sound means—go time. You can always hear it, through flashbangs, through grenades, through artillery—that little click engages the mechanism in your brain that tells you this event is now real. My eyes see where this man is going, and my brain slowly passes that message to my body. He grabs an AK-47 and starts to spin it toward us. Somewhere between the time he grabs for the gun and the time he turns toward us with it, I moved my weapon to semi, as does John. By the time the man's gun gets two thirds around the half circle from where he grabbed it to where it is pointing at Al, Al squeezes off one to two rounds. Milliseconds later I double-tap the guy. John shoots at almost the same time I do, also double-tapping. The guy falls to the ground, lifeless. There are five, maybe six holes, stacked on top of each other, through his heart. To be honest, if you don't look carefully, it looks like one bullet wound. I just killed for the first time (though I think Al's rounds get the actual credit), but at that moment, I'm actually impressed with how good we are.

I thought this would be a bigger moment. I thought it would have gravitas. It doesn't. He was a bad man. He tried to kill us. Now he is dead. It is that simple for me. What isn't simple is hearing his wife's screams when the shots ring out. There is no sound like the sound of a woman seeing her husband die. It rattles me and lingers.

We collect intel off the entire building. We get blood samples, fingerprints, face pictures, and we take the body with us. There is a ton of valuable intelligence here, and this is a huge, unexpected win, tactically. But his wife keeps screaming at us. She is saying we murdered him. It doesn't matter to her that we gave the guy the opportunity to leave the house. It doesn't matter that he tried to kill us. We killed her husband. I look at the other men, glaring at us. I look at the kids, crying.

Did we just make more terrorists? Will these kids grow up to try to kill more Americans? I probably would if I were them.

The wife complains enough that there's an immediate investigation of Al's decision to pull the trigger. This is a huge shock to me.

Isn't this war? This fucking guy was going to kill us!

Nevertheless, SGM Oquendo took statements from everyone. They did a forensic analysis of the shoot and concluded that what we said happened is exactly what happened. Al is cleared.

When we get back to base, the guys at Blue tell us we did a great job. They apparently watched the whole thing via satellite. There is now a lot more trust. They don't think we're idiots anymore.

We're off to the races.

Our success that night becomes the first domino to fall in what would become a hugely successful deployment. We build four more targets off the intel from that house, which in turn leads to more targets, and so forth. From then on, we will basically do one or more missions every night, with breaks only because of a lack of air, deconflictions of battlespace to ensure there is no friendly fire, or sandstorms.

After our baptism by fire, I think I am the man and that we are all now on equal footing as brothers-in-arms. After all, except for a few of the senior guys, I now have as much combat experience as most of the team. I felt I kicked ass on the last mission. I did it all right. I had proven myself. I am feeling like a total fucking badass.

Then it happens. On our very next mission, we are a bird short because an engine was damaged by small arms fire. They have to redo the load plan, and I get bumped. They literally find a way to squeeze everyone else on one Chinook (which is a terrible idea by the way), except me. I am pissed. McPhee grabs me right before he leaves, and I'm expecting him to change his mind—to say, "Tim, we need you! We cannot possibly do it without you!" Instead, he says, "Hey, man the QRF while we're gone."

I go to the vehicles, turn on the radio, and start working. I check all of the guns. I load all of the ammo. I check fuel. I check batteries. I prep bags. But mostly, I stew on being left behind the whole time they are gone. I listen to the radio traffic and know I would have been an asset. The more time goes on, the angrier I get. By the time they return to base, having completed a successful mission, I'm enraged and have decided to let my Team Sergeant know exactly how I feel. I'm no longer rationally assessing the mission and asking if we completed the objective or celebrating the fact that no one is injured. I'm just butthurt that I didn't get picked for kickball on the playground.

"Can I have a minute, John?" I ask almost immediately as he walks into the hangar. He looks at me for a minute. "What did you get done while we were gone?" he asks. I tell him about prepping everything. "What else?" he asks. "Nothing," I say.

"Huh. Sounds like someone was chilling out while the team was working. What do you want?"

He definitely knocked me on my ass a little with that last comment, but I'm not backing down. "John, I'm the best shot, I'm the most physically fit, and I dominated that last mission. I should have been the first to go, not the first to get pulled. I want to be treated fairly. I know I'm an asset to this team," I finish, my speech now complete.

John just looks at me for a long time, his head rolling from side to side, cracking his old-man neck, but his eyes never leaving mine. "Go grab your boxing gloves and meet me in the gym, and we will hash this out," the crazy bastard says.

Is this guy nuts? Fine, fuck it. As I leave his room, I cannot stop smiling. I mean, John is a tough guy, and he will fuck up just about any normal person or wannabe tough guy in a fistfight, but he can't carry my jockstrap. Not only am I going to smoke the dogshit out of him, but I will confirm to him just how right I am.

When I arrive, my whole team is there wearing gloves. I'm not sure what's up. John tells me that I am not just fighting him. I am fighting the whole team. I see what he is doing, but I don't care. Fuck his old-man life lesson. One after one they come after me. Two-minute rounds. No rest. The second one guy gets out, a fresh guy gets in. Mario, the senior 18C, is up first. I beat the shit out of him and the next few guys. But by the time I get to my fifth teammate, I have taken some shots. I am bleeding a little bit, and my head is ringing. These guys aren't pros, but they are tough as nails, and they are treating this like it is life or death. I keep winning. By the time I get to Shane, I don't have anything left. I can't keep my hands up anymore and he is fresh. I start getting pummeled. John's up next. He doesn't let up and hits me with some big shots. I think it is over. He's the last guy.

John then calls the first guy back in, the guy I crushed at the beginning. I have nothing for him. He gets his payback. They all do. They rotate until every team member has won a round against me.

"Okay," John says. Everyone starts taking their gloves off and they all begin to walk out. Blood is oozing from my pores. My face and hands are swelling. Spittle drips from my mouth. My lungs are on fire, and it is impossible for me to relax and draw breath. Except for Shane, and maybe Travis, the team didn't seem to enjoy doing this, but they also seemed aligned that it had to be done. When everyone but John and me are gone, John walks over to where I am still sitting on the floor, bleeding. He doesn't quite make eye contact with me, but kind of looks over his shoulder in my general direction and says, "I don't want to have this conversation again."

As he walks out, I realize that he just said the same thing to me that the Coast Guard Chief said. I wonder if they're related.

This moment should have left a powerful imprint on me. I should have picked up what he was trying to tell me: that no one, regardless of talent or skill, is more important than the team. I should have realized that I am not an all-star—that quite the contrary, I am a cherry asshole with a lot to learn, and if I don't, then I will be a liability to the CIF.

But I am Tim Kennedy, and my takeaway is, "It took all of those assholes two tries each to finally beat me up."

———

I can feel the rotorwash as I approach the bird and load up. There's something about the engine whine that I find reassuring, almost like a lullaby before drifting off to sleep. A weird feeling for sure because we are heading to a compound with some high-value individuals as we try to ascertain Zarqawi's position.

I feel like Jason Bourne.

I'm sitting in the door of the bird. As the engine whine gets louder and we lift off the ground, I watch my dangling feet get further and further away from the earth as the Black Hawk jolts forward into the night.

On a mission, in the sky, at night, flying toward a target is surreal and almost impossible to describe if you haven't been there. You have pent-up energy and nervousness about what is about to come, yet there is a feeling of serenity about being in the air, about feeling the wind against your face. There's a total calm when you're up there, and sometimes you find yourself asking if this whole situation is real. *Is this war or is this all a dream?*

For this mission, my emotions are in overdrive, and I just keep thinking that I need to make sure I do the right thing. My only real fear is letting my team down. I've been on a few missions thus far and I've done everything right, but I feel I haven't really been tested yet. I want and need to come through when that moment arrives.

As we approach the target, we switch on our night vision, and the transition from surreal to wild magical universe is complete. The static electricity from the rotorwash combined with the dust creates a brown-out effect. The air around us is covered with dust and sand and constant arcs of electricity fire through them randomly and rhythmically all at the same time. These mini lightning storms are unnoticeable under normal light, but they paint powerful kaleidoscope-esque images under night vision. Eerily, there is a green halo rising above us, created by the spinning rotor. I look away from the lightning storms and into the halo. Even looking directly at it, it seems a little evil. It's amazing how different the world looks under a different light spectrum. Snapping back to the mission at hand, I see that we're almost to the ground and I lock my eyes on the horizon, getting ready to exit from the left side the minute the skids touch down. I hear a series of *pffft* sounds and I notice the arcs of light are getting far more intense. *It must be because we're kicking up more dirt close to the ground.*

We touch down and I hop off. This is the first time I've ever touched down on target. Until now, we've always walked it in, but that isn't possible given the layout of the building and the adjoining security. The

Black Hawk takes off as quickly as it landed, but I still hear the *pffft* sounds and I see arc after arc of light coming toward me. Suddenly, it clicks. *These are bullets. These are fucking bullets.*

Al Qaeda is shooting at us and the bright lights are their muzzle flashes off in the distance.

I am not afraid. I am exhilarated. I take off at a dead sprint toward the entrance that I had memorized from our rehearsals. I cannot see anyone with me as I start running, which is not uncommon when you're under night vision (aka seeing the world through two green toilet paper rolls), and after a few seconds I start getting an uneasy feeling that I am screwing this up somehow. I arch my head a little over my shoulder and see the most beautiful image I have ever seen—a line of Green Berets running full bore toward the target. I look over my other shoulder and see the same thing. I smile a big wide grin as I turn back straight. I catch myself and kind of acknowledge in the back of my head that it's really fucking weird to be smiling right now, but I can't help myself. Without hesitation, every single one of us, including cherry Tim, starts running toward the gunfire. On that battlefield, with bullets flying around me, sprinting as fast as I can run, surrounded by guys that beat me up like a week ago, I know that this is now my home. I belong here.

I'm a real fucking Green Beret.

———

The missions over the next couple months get more and more fun, even when they don't go exactly how we expect them to go. The more times we go outside the wire, the more stories we come back with, the more we bust each other's balls, and the more we become a real unit.

There's one night where someone accidentally drops a flashbang body and Mario thinks it's a frag from the enemy and shouts, "Grenade!" and runs away. From then on out, we try to work in the fact that he didn't jump on it into any conversation. Mario "Medal of Honor" Montesè becomes his new moniker. He does not love that.

I'm not immune to getting made fun of either. During one mission, I blow out my boot and the heel is close to popping off. John has Shoe

Goo and I ask him if I can borrow it. He tells me, "Yes, it's on the bed. Return it when you're done." I fix my boot and return the Shoe Goo to his desk. John, who significantly favored those on the team that had come from Ranger Regiment or at least gone to Ranger School, pretended he could not find his Shoe Goo and let me know in no uncertain terms that a Ranger would have returned the Shoe Goo to the appropriate place. As punishment, the dude actually made me do a tactical mission against an actual enemy with a Shoe Goo dummy corded around my neck like the shittiest necklace you've ever seen. Good times.

Another night, Shane Thompson is zip-tying this enormous Al Qaeda dude, and the guy spins on him and elbows him right in the face, dropping him to a knee. I blast him with a right cross, knocking him to never-never land, and say, "No, no, no! We don't do that!" I thought that moment was going to finally quell the beef Shane and I had (or more accurately that Shane had with me), but I was wrong. I remained the dirty cherry in his eyes.

Yet another time, we knocked out a mission and the 1/60th told us they couldn't come pick us up. We were way too far out to walk back to base, so we found the closest thing to us—a small Marine outpost run by Lima Company, 3rd Battalion, 3rd Marine Division. They gave us food even though they were low. They offered us their beds, woobies (our affectionate name for the military-issued poncho liner), everything. They were so incredibly generous. We refused to sleep on their racks because we thought it was fucked up, so we slept on the ground and on a treadmill that they had instead.

We stayed up with them and bullshitted late into the night. No one could come get us during the day, so we chilled with them until it got dark and then the 1/60th picked us up. Iraq worked like that sometimes. We were just random people thrown together for a brief moment, sharing the hell that is war.

Still, on the whole I generally have an odd feeling. It isn't that I have any complaints. Life is generally good, but it still feels like we're not doing the most important work. There just has to be more to this.

Then, after six weeks in Al Asad working for Blue, our world gets shaken up and we get assigned to Task Force Central in Baghdad. Our company is split in half into two troops, with two teams and a recce team per troop. Troop 1 went to Camp Biop. Troop 2, us, is assigned to Building 3 in the Green Zone, halfway between Camp Liberty and one of Saddam's palaces. TF Central is instantly so much cooler because instead of SEALs running the show it's being run by CAG and Ranger Regiment, and like us, they just want to fuck bad guys up and get shit done.

Each troop is given three HMMWVs and three Pandurs, which are six-wheeled armored vehicles with gun turrets. Troop 1 works with the ICFT (Iraqi CAG). Because of that, they get constant intel, which they always share with us. We do the same. This becomes a phenomenal recipe for lots of missions.

We have a much nicer building this time, but we're still on cots, so the juxtaposition of beautiful marble and shitty Army cot is sufficiently weird. I put cardboard with aluminum on the outside up in the windows to reflect the Iraqi heat and keep people from seeing in. Then we got mortared, and I replaced every square inch of that cardboard with heavy plywood.

The missions come hot and heavy. You name the crazy 2006 mission, we did it: Sadr City, Ramadi, up and down Route Irish like it was our job, Samarra, Tikrit, Taji, Khalis, Abu Ghraib, Fallujah. To be honest, it becomes a blur. We do one-to-two missions a night. They all run together, but unlike before, it all makes sense. There is a clear purpose, with clear command and control, with clear directives, with a clear task organization that supports each other. Why is it so different? Because it is an Army operation, and not just Army, but the most elite planners on earth: JSOC.

Now, no matter what is happening, I get to go. Unlike before, I do not care what I do. I'm happy to sit on top of a .50 cal on a HMMWV or Pandur. I'm happy to be on the assault force. It just doesn't matter because there is so much work to be done. I'm always doing different stuff, and I'm always learning. I have become a devoted student of John. It's not that we're boys. His approach to human relationships will never be my approach, but I do respect him as an Operator. There are people that love John and people who despise John, but I've never heard any-one say they didn't want him with them for war. He's just built for it. Observing that respect from literally everyone I encounter, I decide he is my target, much like Tom Way was when I was an EMT. I want to know what he knows.

I begin by memorizing John McPhee's post-assault after-action re-view (AAR) process. I write down all the questions he asks and map out how he runs his AARs. The more I study, the more I understand how it all fits together. When I arrived here, I was a monkey showing up and hitting a target. Now, two months in, I'm not at John's level, but I've at least grown opposable thumbs.

I'm starting to see the value of all these different forces and all these different processes. After we hit a building, we number all the rooms and then we bucket the intel found on site by those numbers (maps, weapons, computers, whatever). This is John's way of doing things, and at first it seemed like an unnecessary waste of time. But when you start to attach rooms to individuals it makes more sense. Who knows who is very important? It isn't enough to know someone in the house has intel. It is important to know the specifics. We take that intel and build a mur-der board in our unit headquarters that ties all of these things together, so we have a good picture of all of it. In a very short time, a bunch of guys that are not experts on the region know the major Al Qaeda play-ers and how they fit together better than a lot of CIA analysts. The wall made it easy to understand. It made it easy to map the next mission. And the wall came from the numbered buckets. *Nothing we do is without purpose.*

We're doing great now and we're jibing as a team. We even get in-vited to do the first bilateral mission with CAG in C/3/7's history (we were outside the perimeter but it's still cool). John and the guys trust me more and more and I trust them. Gone are the over-the-top question-and-answer sessions. It's now more like, "Hey, did you put ammo in the truck?" "Yup, sure did!" "Great, mission brief in sixty minutes."

The dynamic is totally different. There is no extra time. There's only the mission. And it's awesome. I know most people tell you about how awful war is, and it's true, it is awful, but I am loving it. I do not feel guilty about killing these people. They're awful. And we're so good at what we do that I don't even really feel fear anymore. It almost feels like we are in *Call of Duty*. We hit a house, we shoot or capture the bad guys, we reload, and then we do it all again.

My biggest challenge is getting sleep. It's gotten so hard to get to sleep after the adrenaline rushes we experienced every night that I started doing two-a-day workouts. I work out when I wake up to start the day, and then after the missions I work out so I can get some sleep.

Tonight is the night.

June 7, 2006.

Operation Arcadia.

There are twenty-three primary Arcadia targets, each with multiple ancillary targets attached. We know Zarqawi is here, and we are going to get him. Tonight is our Super Bowl. The entire U.S. military has been hunting this motherfucker for years, but he has always eluded us. He cannot now. We have a cordon around the entire area, and we know he's inside our perimeter.

Three nights in a row we came within one building of getting him. We continued to tighten the noose and now there's only thirty targets left as the noose gets tighter and tighter after each remaining target is neutralized. This mission is a who's-who of badasses. Delta, Rangers, SAS (Special Air Service), ICTF (Iraqi Special Operations Forces), and both CIF troops. (There are no SEALs. They are too busy in Al Asad not driving out of the gate.)

This is 2006 peak President Bush "we're not messing around vengeance time." The guy who hung Americans alive and posed with their dead bodies, who beheaded two Americans, who slaughtered thousands of Shia Iraqis, is within our grasp. And to make the situation even better, we have Lieutenant Colonel Tom DiTomasso as our squadron commander. (If you don't know him, he received a Silver Star for bravery in Somalia during what most people call Black Hawk Down.) He gives no fucks. He tells us to hit everything. No breaks. No respites. Hit until Zarqawi is dead. This is exactly where I want to be.

We have been assigned six named targets, covering thirty buildings in one night. We know in advance that it is going to be dynamic, and the targets may change. We know that these guys can't squirt too far, so at some point we'll be fighting desperate Al Qaeda insurgents who have nowhere to go.

Command prioritizes the targets. Most probable targets go to CAG. The second most probable goes to us, then the Rangers, and so on until it loops around again.

We roll out with all of the ammo that we can possibly pack on the trucks. We are not going out for just any mission. In the words of William Wallace from the movie *Braveheart*, "We are going to peck a fight!" And we do. All of us. All night. The more fights we get in, the more Al Qaeda resources are leveraged to try to save these assholes, and the more bad guys come out of the woodwork. It's awesome.

Target 1 is a letdown. It's a giant house in downtown Baghdad that looks like it is going to be packed to the gills with baddies. We're approaching it to do a surreptitious entry because we believe there is a 30 percent chance he is here. So, we're all blacked out, silent, moving under night vision, throwing ladders over walls, and even ninja crawling up to this bad boy. Then we hit it all at once and find . . . nothing. No furniture. No people. Completely fucking empty.

No worries, though, because we still had five other named targets to hit. CAG had more luck in their first hit and the radio was hopping. Everyone was on the net. Company Commander Major Jimmy Hester and SGM Oquendo are even out that night. Things are happening so fast and reported so quickly, it sounds like they are speaking in tongues on the net. Our targets keep changing throughout the night. ICTF gets intel from an interrogation that this other house is a high priority. So CAG flexes to that house and we flex to the target CAG was going to hit.

To this day, that night is still one of the wildest nights of my life. It is like the world's most dangerous Fourth of July. Everyone is shooting. We even hear a Bradley Fighting Vehicle kicking off with the main 25mm cannon. The targets are all close enough to hear and even see the rounds hitting buildings. All of Baghdad is being lit up.

For the rest of the night, we are in a nonstop gunfight. I have no idea how many times I reloaded my rifle. I have no idea how many times I refreshed all of my mags from the go bags I prepacked before the mission. I have no idea how many men we killed that night. I just didn't have time to think about it.

Somewhere in the middle of the night, TOUCHDOWN comes over the net. We all smile and fist bump.

Zarqawi is dead!

On February 24, 2006, Zarqawi was made the number two man on the most wanted list. On June 7, 2006, he was killed. CAG got positive confirmation he was in a building and rather than risk their lives to go in, they did what John McPhee would do. They lazed the target and two F16s dropped a laser-guided GBU-12 and a GBU-38, two 500-pound bombs. After the bombing, they went in and found him. He wasn't quite dead, but he would be within fifteen minutes from all the damage he received.

But there is still work to be done. Usually when you kill one leader, three more pop up, but this is our chance to kill all of them. We are going to work until they make us stop.

Within minutes of TOUCHDOWN, the Iraqi police arrive on scene and start shooting at us. They are Zarqawi's QRF, and before our task force blew him the fuck up, he must have called in for the cavalry. At the same time they arrive at Zarqawi's building, another police force arrives at ours. So these regular shitty Iraqi cops are so afraid of Zarqawi and what he will do to them or their families that they think the better option is to go to war with Delta Force and the CIF. Absolutely wild. They are quickly dispatched with extreme violence.

President Bush flies in the night after the mission to greet us. Only the officers and the senior NCOs get to shake his hand, but we all get to see him and hear him speak. You can tell how much he genuinely cares about us, and the mission. *Holy shit, there's the President.* I'm blown away that I'm anywhere near this level of power. Two years ago, I was scraping together money for pizza and prizefighting on an Indian reservation and now I'm in a room with the President of the United States after being part of arguably the most important mission of the Iraq War.

The next day we take task force pictures. Everyone is saying it is the end of the reign of terror, but I don't think so, and I get shit for saying so. I still see sixty-four people on the murder board without lines through their faces. (I don't know this yet, but many of those sixty-four people would later found ISIS.)

I want to stay and get all of them now, but that's not my call.

———

Landing back in the States is weird. People always say it's weird, but I didn't really believe it until just now. I want to see my wife. I want to have a nice meal. I want to have sex. I want to sleep in a nice bed instead of a cot. I want to go a day without sweating. I want all these things and more. But I also miss the important work. I miss the life or death of it. I keep scanning the horizon for a threat. I keep assessing people who are just trying to be friendly to see what their real intention might be. I'm more stressed here than I was over there.

Suck it up. Ginger is waiting for you.

I finish unloading all my gear and lock up my weapons. I can finally blow this Popsicle stand and see my wife. I'm very much liking this idea the more I think about it.

"Hey, Tim, I need you in my office," John says.

I walk in. I don't know what this is about, but I'm assuming he's going to tell me good job in Iraq or to take it easy for a few days because transitioning is hard or that kind of normal leader stuff.

"What's up, John?" I ask.

"I'll cut right to it. You're not where I need you to be," he says, pausing a moment to look at my face as he delivers this punch right to my gut. Well, if the first punch was a jab, he hits me hard with a cross and a hook with his next comment.

"I'm sending you to Ranger School. If you don't graduate as the Honor Graduate, you're out of CIF."

CHAPTER EIGHT

PRIDE COMETH

Fort Benning, night

It's crisp outside on this lovely November 6, 2006, night. It's significantly warmer where I am, inside, on the ground being smothered by a 220-pound Ranger while his buddies cheer him on from the stands. *This fucking guy has great pressure.*

Damien Stelly, a member of 3rd Battalion, 75th Ranger Regiment, is pinning me to the ground, attempting to knock me out or submit me. This is my fifth fight in two days. The other four I finished. This one is a war, going back and forth at a frenetic pace. Neither of us gets tired. Both of us are good in all positions. I love this guy.

Stelly leaves his arm on the mat for a second and I grab his wrist and catch a Kimura from underneath, wrenching him over my body and getting on top. I try to make him tap with the Kimura, but the tough bastard manages to get the arm out. There's about thirty seconds left in this fight and I know it's close. I've done a lot more damage, but he's a phenomenal wrestler and is the only guy I can ever remember who's able to hold me down for any length of time. I go to knee on belly and start throwing punches. The crowd of soldiers cheers on the violence.

Stelly manages to get me off. We scramble. I spend the last fifteen seconds with him pinned against the turnbuckle and throw punch after punch at his head and body. The bell rings and the whole crowd cheers.

I love the All Army Combatives Championship. It is the hardest tournament on the planet, bar none. The troops in attendance know the sport and appreciate every aspect of it, so you can live through an entire event and never have to hear a single fan screaming, "Sweep the leg!" "Get him a body bag!" or "Stand them up!" What I love most, though, is that everyone competing is representing the warrior spirit in the best way possible.

Stelly and I embrace after the fight. We both raise our arms. The Rangers, who are stationed here, start chanting, "Stelly, Stelly, Stelly!" I think I did enough to win, but it was a good fight and I am in his backyard, after all. The ref grabs both of our arms . . . and we wait. The judges are taking way too long. I look over at Stelly and we bump gloves. I hope the anticipation on his face isn't showing on my face, because I definitely feel how he looks. I want this win. I won this event last year, shortly after SERE School. He won too, at Heavyweight. No one's ever won it twice. Tonight, one of us will.

The tension is palpable. This is a big deal. There are generals here and both commands want to be able to claim victory. After all, it's two storied units going head-to-head. SF versus Rangers for all the bragging rights.

Finally, the announcer comes on. "And the winner of the 2006 Army Combatives Championship at 205 pounds, by split decision is . . . TIM KENNEDY!!!"

Split decision? I need to get back into the gym!

Still, I got it done. I am now the only person ever to win this thing twice, which is pretty cool.

I don't have a crew here, and the clock is ticking. I leave the ring, and I hear them announce the beginning of the heavyweight match as I push the door of the locker room open. It looks like a high school locker room. A mirror has a crack in it. One of the faucets is dripping. Even though there is a perfectly good trash can, apparently everyone missed it with wads of paper towels. I look in the mirror. Not too bad. No cuts. I peel the tape off my hands. They are swollen.

I strip naked and turn on a hot shower. *Ow!* I realize my knees and feet are skinned raw from the rough canvas floor of the ring. I give myself a few minutes of grace and reflect on what just happened. That was one of the most competitive and violent fights I have been in up to this point of my career, which is now sixty fights deep. I'm happy it was Damien who pushed me like that. Another combat veteran, a Ranger, and by all accounts a good dude.

I automatically revisit and critique the match in my mind. *He shouldn't have been able to keep me controlled that long. I need to be more dynamic on the mat.*

I push those thoughts out of my head. Back to the task at hand.

I finish my shower, ice my hands, and pick the remaining tape off my hands and hair. I rinse out all my gross fight stuff in the sink and squeeze it out. It's going to be in the back of my car for a couple of months, so I'd like to minimize the amount of bacteria that grows during that time. I then put on my pressed BDUs and rush over to Ranger School to check in. The class starts in the morning, but I am required to check in the night before. As I drive the back roads of Fort Benning to the Ranger Training Brigade and look at my swollen hands, I ask myself what's wrong with me. What fool cuts weight, enters a fight tournament, and fights five fights the night before he starts Ranger Training?

I pull up to the compound. As I walk in, I stare at the ominous sign that every Ranger student knows well, "Ranger: Not for the weak or fainthearted." Tomorrow morning, I will be here wearing blank BDUs. No rank. No badges and tabs. Nothing. Every student is equal at Ranger School. You're defined and judged only by your performance. It's kind of cool, actually. But cadre are people, and people can be influenced, so I show up with all my bling on: Special Forces Combat patch, Combat Infantryman's Badge, Airborne, and SSG rank. As I walk in, a few of the cadre know who I am. One of them, apparently, was just at the gym. "Wait, didn't you just fight? You're starting Ranger School? Fuck, man," he says, a little awe-stricken. Mission accomplished. It might seem cheesy to do this, but I need every edge I can get. If I don't finish as the Honor Graduate, it's no more CIF for me.

Six hours later, at 0330, I'm back. This time, my BDUs are blank except for my name and U.S. Army. I have my duffel bag and rucksack filled with the prescribed packing list of items. The second I step foot into the compound, I am shark attacked by the Ranger Instructors (RIs). "You beat Stelly, huh? You think you're something special because you beat an Army Ranger? Do you think that was a good idea before coming to Ranger School?" they bark at me. RIs are much louder than my SF instructors. They're not afraid to yell.

"That motherfucker was tough, Sergeant. I barely beat him," I reply, meaning it and also trying to placate them at the same time. It does not slow them down.

"Do you think a Ranger Tab needs a little umbrella over it?"—referring to my Special Forces "long tab"—"No, it does not. We can stand the rain on this side of the fence," one says. Another chimes in with, "Why don't more Green Berets have Ranger Tabs? You girls scared of leadership and a little suffering?"

I'm unscareable from this kind of shit at this point in my life, but I do find myself agreeing with the last guy. *Yeah, SF guys really should go to Ranger School.* I hate that I just accidentally agreed with John McPhee. I'm still pissed at him for sending me here with an ultimatum. I wanted to come here anyway. Seemed like a no-brainer to come to what is widely considered the best leadership school in the entire world. After all, if I'm going to be the best, I can't duck a school just because it's hard. It's just that John took some of the shine off of it for me: he made it his decision instead of mine.

They leave me alone for a few minutes and go back to messing with everyone else. At precisely 0400, they bring us into a formation, and roll call starts. They get about three names deep when I hear them call out a surprisingly accurate representation of the name Afshin Abusadih Aryana. *Now that's a name I've not heard in a long time.* As I hum the *Star Wars* music in my head, I peer over. Afshin calls out that he is present. *I recognize that voice too.* I step out of formation and walk right over to him.

When I arrive at his spot in formation, I see a little brown Persian that is three apples high off the ground like a Smurf. He wears his trademark smug insulting smile on his face that starts at the undercarriage of his nose and crawls all the way up to his eyes. And if you peer too long into his ocular cavities, you see a little glint in those eyes that tells you that he knows something you don't. The last time I heard that name was five years ago in college while I was working as a bouncer in downtown SLO. My buddy told me Afshin Aryana had just left the bar with a girl I was dating. As if that didn't create enough friction, he was also a wrestler, making it to the All-State tournament in California.

"I know you," I say.

"I know you," he answers, smirking.

The moment of contention melts away when I ask, "What the fuck are you doing here?"

"I just left Bragg to come to Ranger School. You?" he replies.

"I also just left Bragg to come to Ranger School. What unit are you in?" I ask.

"3rd Battalion, 7th Special Forces Group."

"I too am in 3rd Battalion, 7th Special Forces Group."

"Huh."

"Huh."

Through the smirk I recognized from so many years ago, I notice something else, something new: He has the same look in his eye that all combat veterans have; that agedness that doesn't exist in people who haven't seen war. I know we are going to be friends.

As the sharks descend upon me again, asking me what the fuck am I doing out of formation (and to be fair, after eighteen months of SF, I barely know what a formation is anymore), we smile, and Af says, "We're gonna have to continue this conversation later."

I walk back to the line, thinking about what a small world it is. Two guys from the same town, join the same program, go to the same unit, have almost the same deployment, and now are stuck at the same school.

I wonder if he has a little Persian John McPhee making him come here too. I stand until the RIs call my name. Then the shenanigans begin.

Ranger School is broken into four phases:

1. The Ranger Assessment Phase or RAP Week
2. Darby Phase
3. Mountain Phase
4. Swamp Phase

The first two phases take place at Fort Benning, Georgia. Mountain Phase takes place in Dahlonega, Georgia. Swamp Phase takes place at Camp Rudder at Eglin Air Force Base, Florida. The entire school takes sixty-two days if you go straight through. You are graded several different ways. During RAP Week, there are must-pass gates like the PT test, the five-mile run, the fifty-meter gear swim, and other similar events. For the other fifty-five days of the course, however, it's three things: peer ratings, patrol grades, and demerits.

Peer ratings are exactly what they sound like. At the end of each phase you force rank your peers 1–9 (or however many you have in your squad). Those scores are tabulated and averaged. If you get below 60 percent on your peer score, you fail.

Patrols are a little more subjective, but the Rangers make that "subjectivity" objective with a checklist. There are specific things you have to do by mission and by position to be successful on a patrol. If it's an ambush and you are the weapons squad leader, you know your role. If it's a movement to an ORP (objective rally point) and you are the alpha team leader, you know your role. And so do the RIs. If you miss too many elements of your job, you are a NO GO. At any given point, there are only a few people in leadership positions. When you're given one of those positions it is "your patrol." To graduate a phase, you need to have at least one GO and at least a 50 percent GO rate in your patrols. To graduate the course, you need to have a GO in every phase and at least a 50 percent GO rate.

Demerits are less about passing or failing and more about differentiation. The Honor Graduate will have some major and minor pluses stacked up. I will need some of these to hit my goal. It is possible to fail on demerits, but you would have to really want it.

First up is the PT test. I start doing push-ups. You need to do a minimum of 51. This is a joke for me. I do 50 unbroken push-ups and the RI counts each one. When I get to push-up number 51, the RI counts, "50." I do another. "50." No matter how many I do, he keeps saying, "50." He gets right up in my face and smiles as he says it. I smile back and keep going. I do a lot of push-ups. Finally, he says, "Get up, Ranger." The sit-ups are uneventful. Then we have to do six pull-ups. Also easy. Lastly, we have to do the two-mile run. Again, comically easy for me.

As I wait for the rest of the class to finish their runs, I realize that as easy as this was for me and anyone in shape, I watch guys fail on every single event. Everyone here knew the standard before they came. Ranger School makes it very clear. And yet these people showed up and failed. And they are shocked, especially some of the people with a little rank or status or a combat deployment. The ones who failed from the push-ups and sit-ups and pull-ups requirements are sputtering excuses and talking about how the RIs gave them a hard time. Clearly, that isn't what happened.

When the two-mile run hit the cutoff time, the RIs just yell out, "Anyone still on the track, come see me. Your school is over." I love the coldness of it.

Ranger School is hard but fair. There is one standard: the Ranger Standard. You either meet the standard or you go home. This is a meritocracy. There's no rank. There are no favors. There are no exceptions to the standard. It's a simplicity I immediately respect. I'm a combat-deployed Special Forces Staff Sergeant, and if I fail the push-ups at the beginning of this course, I go home, just like a cherry Second Lieutenant would.

After the PT test, there's an obstacle course. Then there's combatives. And all of these RIs know I just beat their boy. It starts with grappling and stuff and I'm winning easily, and then at some point pugil sticks enter the mix. Most fighters would naturally be better at pugil sticks than the average person because they are just an extension of boxing skills, but I have a lot more training than most because of my Japanese

Jiu Jitsu years with Barry and Terry. It becomes a revolving door for me in the pugil pit as the RIs send in a new person every few seconds. I'm smoking everyone. These guys are all trying to find the hole in my game and I'm just running combos. My favorite is the jab, cross, hook, followed closely by the tap to the low body, paired with a nice uppercut.

The whole time I'm engaged in these battles, in the background, there's a voice doing Joe Rogan–type commentary, mostly mocking me as I am murdering a dozen classmates. The voice is relentless, so I look over to see which RI is making the comments. Instead, sitting there with his little legs dangling over the edge of the pit like a premature baby is Af, running his mouth with his snarky clever comments. "And they said apes didn't know how to use tools!" he says as I crush one guy. Then when the next guy comes out and we circle each other, "Look how much the chimp resembles the human here, almost as if he has a strategy. Fascinating!" Then when I beat the guy a moment later, "As you can see, in the wild, it is not always the smarter ape that wins, but the one that is too dumb to feel pain." I didn't know him well enough for him to be making these jokes, but for some reason I couldn't be mad at the asshole. It was funny.

RAP Week sucks, but it's mostly just physical hazing and a lot of physical gates. It ends with a road march from Camp Rogers to Camp Darby, where we will begin the patrolling portion of Ranger School. It begins easy enough but frankly, I'm aggravated at John. *Why am I here?* I'm an 18B and I'm being graded on how to assemble and disassemble an M240 machine gun? I can do this in my sleep. This is dumb. Everything I'm experiencing here, I have already mastered. I don't understand how anyone is having problems, and I am feeling arrogant about being SF. I receive five major positives between RAP Week and Darby Phase. I get one for the pugil sticks, one for weapon assembly, one for crushing everyone in the combatives pit, one for reciting the Ranger Creed perfectly while at the pull-up bar, and one for crushing the Darby Queen obstacle course, which I found way easier than SF's "Nasty Nick" obstacle course. *What a waste of time. This is what you thought would develop me, John?*

Things change when I get to Mountain Phase. It's colder here. Much, *much* colder. It's also called Mountain Phase for a reason: everything is a hill. The standing joke at Mountain Phase when someone asks how much further a movement is going to be is to say, "It's just past that next hill." The brutal terrain takes its toll on everyone. Small guys struggle because proportionally they are carrying a huge amount of weight. By the time you load ammo, food, and a tripod, most Ranger School rucks weigh 80-to-100 pounds. If you're a 140-pound dude, that fucking sucks. The big guys have problems too. They struggle because there's not a lot of air up there, and they have a lot of muscle to lug around, so it doesn't take too long for their bodies to start telling them they need to stop. Lucky for me, hairy-handed trolls are pretty good in the mountains.

In time, even I feel a little worn down. Every day I start to smell something different—almost like ammonia. It's coming from my skin. It's coming from my squad. I realize it's the smell of my body eating my own muscle. I try to think of a way out of this. *How do I set the conditions so that this can be easier for us?* I've been able to do this over and over again throughout all of my training . . . but here I cannot find the answer. The Rangers are different. There is no easy way to cheat, and there will be no recourse if you are caught cheating. There's no buddy to call and ask for a favor. There are no hidden MREs. All you have to see you through is you, your Ranger Buddy, your squad, and your will to continue. The important questions you need to answer are not about external factors that you can affect, but about internal ones. How well do I know infantry tactics? How well can I lead? How well can I lead when it's fucking freezing, everyone is hungry, and everyone is tired? And last but not least, how tough am I?

Cliques also start to fade away quickly in the mountains. During Darby, the 82nd guys tended to hang with 82nd guys, the Ranger Regiment guys tended to hang with the Ranger Regiment guys, and the officers tended to hang with the officers. Those relationships melt away in place of a different clique system: Are you good, or are you a piece of shit? In the beginning people try to figure out how to game the system so no one gets peered out. By the end, a lot of guys wish they could peer more people out.

Suffering is the great equalizer. The cadre, the missions, the lack of food and sleep, and the elements bring everyone to a place where they no longer hide their real feelings. You might be my best friend in the world in real life, but so help me God if you fall asleep on that SAW (Squad Automatic Weapon) one more time, I am going to murder you.

Realization sets in that this school is serious. If a butterbar Lieutenant in the infantry doesn't pass this course, he can only go so far in his career. If a Ranger Regiment Specialist doesn't pass this course, he's out of the 75th Ranger Regiment. If I don't pass, I'm out of the CIF.

We have now spent over a month suffering and you better believe no one wants to go home empty-handed. We all have real skin in this game.

But there is lots to do.

One January 2007 evening, a huge blizzard comes through, and they freeze training (pun intended). Weather conditions are one of the few things the cadre take seriously when it comes to our suffering. Why? Occasionally, students die at Ranger School, usually from hypothermia or heat stroke. So when a combination of weather factors moves the RI's threat assessment from yellow (caution) to red (NO GO) they are quick to move. They may pretend to hate us, but these NCOs are professionals, and we are their responsibility. Besides, it would really look bad if one of us died on their watch.

They bring us into a tent with a small space heater, and we all huddle together for warmth. The problem we now have is the guys in the middle have it good. They are nice and toasty and warm. The guys on the outside might as well be outside but without the windchill. "We have to keep rotating" I propose to my miserable brothers. They all agree. So every couple minutes the center guy goes to the outside and everyone pushes in one. We get a couple hours in there, and thank God for it, because as soon as the conditions go from red to yellow, they kick us out and we are right back onto patrols.

The mission that night is an ambush along a road. There's supposed to be a HMMWV with a red mark on it driving down the road at 2100 hours. As cold as it is, it's not so bad when we're moving, but when we finally get to the ambush line and into the prone position, lying on our bellies, the rock-hard frozen ground sucks the heat right out of us.

By 2015 hours, the whole ambush line is in place. The next forty-five minutes are excruciating. A small part of me wants to just die right here so I don't have to feel this anymore, but I know weaker men than I have made it through this course, so I try to suck it up and think about fun things I am going to do when I get out of here. 2100 comes and goes . . . and goes . . . 2130 arrives. We are hurting bad. If I wasn't fucking frozen I'd probably surmise that this HMMWV is probably used on lots of objectives and the pause for the cold probably slowed them down for everyone, but instead I think about how much I need the fucking bad guys to show up already so I could fucking (fake) kill them and be done with this mission!

"I quit!"

The words shock me. The dude immediately to my right stands up. We have been at this school for about forty days. He has weathered a lot but he cannot take it anymore. The Ranger Instructors immediately run over to him. Gone are their harsh tones. Gone are their stern looks. "No problem, buddy. Here you go," one offers, handing him a hot cup of coffee. Moments later, another shows up with a warm cup of soup. "Make sure you eat this. You'll feel better, man."

I'm trying to process what is happening, as the RIs wrap this guy in a blanket, say nice things to him, and walk him down the road. I can smell the coffee. I can taste the soup. But something is weird about the whole incident and I can't put my finger on it.

I look down the line of the ambush and every asshole here is yearning for a taste of either. I hear a clattering sound and look around to see what it is. I look and I look, but I can't seem to find it. Finally, I realize it is my tiny little frozen pecker that has reduced itself to the size of a Tic Tac, coupled with the clatter of my teeth.

I refocus on the RIs, who are loudly explaining to him how great a decision leaving is. In the same high voice, they ask if he wants another cup of coffee or some more soup. He does. I can see the steam rising off of it. *This motherfucker is smart! Why am I on this fucking ground? Will my nuts ever drop again?* I know we are all thinking it, but none of us move.

We finally hear an engine, and we snap back into mission mode. The HMMWV with the red mark on it comes into view. We wait silently for it to hit the X—the optimal point of the kill zone. When it does, our M240 machine gun kicks off, as do our fake claymores, then the whole line starts firing. Sixty seconds into it, the squad leader calls for the assault. The machine gun stops firing and we spring across the objective and search the bodies of the bad guys in the HMMWV for intelligence assets.

We walk off the objective and the Ranger Instructors call for a "time-out" so that they can review our mission and how we did. The guy who just quit is standing off to the side of the road with his coffee, looking at the ground. The OPFOR (the bad guys in the HMMWV) are now back to life and they are loading the vehicle back up to go be the bad guys for someone else. One of the RIs runs over to the coffee guy and ushers him over to the HMMWV. "Hey, man, these guys are gonna take you back, okay?" "Roger, Sergeant," comes the response. Then he gets into the vehicle and they leave.

Then it hit me. The weird thing that threw me for a loop earlier: They weren't calling him "Ranger." From the moment you start this course, you have that title. You lose your rank and your awards. But they lend you that title. Ranger Kennedy. Ranger Aryana. Ranger Smith. Ranger Whoever. They lend it to you with the expectation that you'll actually *earn* it. That guy spent forty days earning it, and then the cold ground was too much for him, and he gave it back. They started calling him "man" and "buddy" but not "Ranger," because he wasn't going to be one.

We finish our after-action review (AAR) of the mission and get up. We have a few hours of movement to go before we get to the new patrol base and can camp for the night. I'm still cold, but I don't feel so bad now. In fact, I felt better the second the ambush kicked off and haven't really thought about the cold since. That guy would have been fine if he could only have held on a little longer . . .

There are food Rangers and there are sleep Rangers. Some people can live without sleep. Others can live without food. Sleep is arbitrary for me, but I need food. Even with the misery they dish out, I am very good at most things. My squad and platoon mates start coming to me asking me to put in extra effort to help them get the GOs they so desperately need. I want to do this, but I cannot push every night for everyone on low calories. So we come up with a deal. I go way above and beyond. I carry the machine gun or the tripod. I make sure the guns are running. I write the operations orders. I pull extra guard shifts when people are hurting. In return, they kick me extra food. Some guys give me whole meals because in a previous life they were wrestlers who were so used to cutting that they didn't even feel that bad from food loss. Other people give me pound cakes, peanut butter, and Skittles. It was a great arrangement.

Every single person in my squad got GOs.

At the end of Mountain Phase, we get to eat in the actual chow hall instead of eating MREs. The story I heard coming into this place is that the blueberry pancakes here are legendary. When I finally get to eat them, I realize all the stories are false—the blueberry pancakes are beyond legendary. *Honestly, this might be the best meal I have ever had.*

Florida Phase is miserable. It's never cold unless you're up to your neck in swamp water, which we are for fourteen hours a day. Plus the water is disgusting . . . you know . . . because it's swamp water. It's hard to explain Florida. By the time you get there, the quitters are gone. No one just up and walks away in Florida. Moreover, most of the shitbags have been peered out as well. So you're really down to people that have what it takes, generally speaking. If you fail here it's because you were injured or you got nothing but NO GOs. So the fear of failure is in many ways diminished. On the other hand, you're so close to getting something you want that you don't want to fuck it up at the last minute. The pass rate for Ranger School is about 33 percent and the class is already well below that. The winter storms broke a lot of hearts.

So, on the one hand, Florida sucks because it's cold and wet, and sandy and miserable, and the missions require you to stay in those conditions indefinitely. But on the other hand, everyone by now knows that the sure way to graduate is by helping and contributing to the team. We all understand servant leadership is the process by which to do that. The missions run smoother. Everyone knows their job. You'd happily go to combat with any of the guys still in your squad because you know what they are made of. You know you can count on them.

Everyone who fails during this phase is a legitimate loss. They've contributed. They earned their spot. We don't want to lose anyone. By the time we finish, all with GOs, we are a very cohesive team. I feel about these guys the same way I feel about the SOPC guys . . . but without all the rule breaking. I'm genuinely going to miss them, but I'm also ready to get the fuck out of here and eat my weight in food.

After completing Florida, we fly back to Fort Benning. Most guys are down thirty to fifty pounds from the weight they started at. I'm only down about fifteen thanks to my meal plan. We out-process for a day and a half. During this time they let us actually eat as much as we want, letting us fatten up a little so we don't scare the shit out of our parents and wives and kids because we look like concentration camp survivors.

Graduation day comes. I've got to hand it to the Ranger Training Brigade: they do graduation right. They have guys jumping out of helicopters into lakes, people zip-lining, fast-roping, doing combatives. It's a cool, festive show. My parents are here and my dad proudly pins on my Ranger Tab, which I will eventually sew on with white thread, signifying that I am a winter Ranger. My Team Leader Mike Gomez shows up too! He is legitimately proud of me. I'm completely shocked. I think this is the first time he has acknowledged my existence or shown any interest in my success. I honestly didn't know whether he cared if I lived or died prior to this moment. I don't know how to deal with his happiness. It actually causes me physical pain. But he's not who I'm here for. I want to see John Motherfucking McPhee so I can rub my NCO Honor Grad status in his motherfucking face.

"Where's John?" I ask Mike.

Mike looks at me sideways. "He didn't tell you?"

"Tell me what?" I reply.

"John left right after you did. He's got a new assignment. But I want to introduce you to your new Team Sergeant, Ed Weams." I look at the man to which Mike is gesturing. He's like 6'5" and an actual mountain of a man who comes from the old Puerto Rico C-37 days. He seems very cool. There's a smile on his face and his mouth is moving, but I am barely hearing the words coming out of it, even though he is apparently telling me to take some time off and not come into the office for a few days.

That motherfucker. That motherfucker wasn't even going to be able to kick me out of the CIF because he wasn't even going to be there.

I realize Mike would have been happy whether or not I was Honor Grad, as would Ed, as would the team. And John either sent me here for his own amusement or because he thought I needed it. But you know what? Either way, this Ranger Tab looks pretty fucking good.

Four days after Ranger School, a sound is interrupting my dream. I slowly open my eyes. Ginger has already gone to work. My cell phone is ringing. It's not a number I recognize. For some reason I answer and am greeted with a thick Russian accent.

"Hi, my name is Leo Khorolinsky. I represent fighters that fight for a league called the International Fight League. I'm one of the owners of the Chicago Red Bears. We have a fight this weekend in Atlanta, and we lost our middleweight fighter. We need someone to fill in for us. You'd be fighting Dante Rivera, a BJJ black belt under [legendary MMA/Jiu Jitsu fighter and coach] Renzo Gracie."

"When do you need me in Atlanta?" I ask him.

I head into the office to see my new boss. Nice as always, he says, "I thought I told you that you didn't need to be in today?"

"Yeah, I know. But actually, I was going to ask you if I could have a four-day weekend with my wife in Atlanta next weekend instead. I've been away a lot and it would be good to have a weekend with just us," I offer up, thinking this is a better, and not completely untrue, pitch compared to "I want to head out to Hotlanta to moonlight as a professional fighter not having trained at all since I won the All Army Combatives Championship."

"Sounds good, Tim," he says.

Man, this guy is cool. I better not do anything to damage his trust in me.

I call Leo back and say, "Yeah, I can come." He's really excited and says a bunch of things in that thick Russian accent that I can't quite understand. He doesn't know what leave is or that I had to ask my Special Forces Master Sergeant boss if I could go to Atlanta. And he doesn't have to know. Just like my Master Sergeant Team Sergeant boss doesn't need to know that I just agreed to a professional MMA fight representing a questionable Russian business owner on national television.

The whole thing starts off a little sketchy. Leo asks me to book my own flight for convenience, which usually means I will never see the money. I also book my hotel "for convenience." I'm living on Staff Sergeant pay, so this expenditure isn't insignificant. I'm not at a point in my career where I'm making real money. Since I've been in the military, other than the two All Army Combatives Championships I won, I have only fought once, against Hector Urbina for $2,000. I was cornered in that one by Brandon Garner, the human personification of a bulldog, a walking muscle with a raspy voice all wrapped up into 170 pounds, and Greg Thompson, a Royce Gracie black belt who runs Team ROC. I don't get them for this one. They already have a coach for me. Apparently, the structure for this is that we are all on one team and each individual fighter win gets us a team point. Our coach is a notorious bare knuckle fighting Russian guy named Igor Zinoviev.

I fly to Atlanta. When I get to baggage claim I don't know what to expect. This is my first televised fight, so I'm thinking maybe there will be a little class to this, like there was with Chuck's UFC fights. Maybe some press. Maybe a limo. A guy with a tux and white gloves holding a placard. Instead, there's an unshaved Russian who looks like he was out all night on a bender holding a three-ring binder with a white piece of lined paper and the words "Tim K" spelled out on it in bad penmanship.

I walk up to the dude with the placard and introduce myself. He has the worst coffee breath I've ever smelled. He doesn't help me with my bags even though I have my carry-on, my regular bag, and my huge fighter kit bag. So, as we walk out of the airport, I'm completely wrapped in luggage that smells like sweat and ringworm and this guy is speed walking in front of me talking to someone on a cell phone in Russian.

I am regretting my decision.

Once we get to the fighter hotel, another Russian with a shaved head, glasses, and wearing soccer warm-ups, a $15,000 Rolex Submariner, and some really fly shoes comes and introduces himself. "Hey! I'm Leo. I'm the guy you spoke to on the phone!" He has a lot of energy. Assessing my situation, I am uncertain if they are going to drug me and take my organs or if I am simply going to fight and never get paid. But the more we talk, the more I like him. He is endearing and sincere and grateful that I came on short notice.

In the middle of our conversation, I offhandedly tell him that I just finished Ranger School. "Oh that's great!" he says in his excited manner, not really understanding what he is congratulating me for. We finish our conversation, and it is time for me to get to work. I have to cut weight.

Cutting weight always sucks. It's never fun or good for you. But it's especially shitty after Ranger School. Your body is not normal after Ranger School. The average person takes six months to recover completely, and some people never do. Your back is shot. Your feet are shot. You typically lose 20 percent of your BMI. Most units don't require guys to participate in physical events for a month or more after graduating. In fact, the best part about graduation is getting fat for a little while and eating anything and everything you want. I have been doing that for the past week, and I got my body back up to 220 pounds. I have to get to 205 over the next day and a half.

My body tells me to go fuck myself. It was liking the getting fat part a lot and it thinks I'm trying to drag it back down to Ranger School mode. Everything is harder than usual and I have to use all the old wrestling tricks. I wrap myself in trash bags. There's no sauna. I am not tub and alcohol sophisticated yet. So, I sit on a bike, shadow box, and do mountain climbers wrapped in trash bags, occasionally wetting my mouth to trick myself into thinking I'm drinking.

Friday night I'm a little dizzy and my skin is dry, but I'm still under my own power when I get on the scale. It's an old-school high school gym–style sliding scale and it takes a minute to get to the weight: 201 pounds. *Fuck, this scale is four pounds off!* I lost four more pounds than I needed. Oh well, time to eat. I drink water and Pedialyte immediately and have some watermelon and other sugary fruits. I instantly start to feel better. The first food and liquid after a cut is always the best-tasting food in the world, but it is doubly so after going back-to-back with Ranger School. All I want to do now is link up with Ginger and go eat! But Leo the Russian stays on me like a moth to a light.

"How're you feeling?" he asks.

"I'm fine, man," I answer him. He looks at me for a minute and his face seems very concerned. He is really put off by my lack of stress. "This is a big fight, you know," he tells me. "I know," I reply, not feeling it was a big fight at all. "You need to get hyped for this, Tim," he says as he whacks my arm. "I am, don't you worry, Leo," I say with a smile, before adding, "I'm gonna go take my wife to get some sushi now." "Great!" he almost shouts. "I'll go grab my jacket."

During dinner he has lots of questions about who I am and what I do and what is going to happen in the fight. He has a vested interest in my success as an owner of the Red Bears, and he keeps bringing up the fact that I am not hyped. I can see it is giving him anxiety. "Don't worry about me, Leo. I just am not the kind of guy who needs to get angry to fight." I can tell that doesn't help.

———

I warm up in the back in an old gray sweatshirt. I haven't really met my coach yet, and I don't have a warm-up partner, so I just kind of shadow box and work some takedowns and sprawls. This is nicer than I'm used to. No one's smoking. No one has a glass eye. No one's wearing Drakkar Noir.

I can hear the matches going on outside. I know I am up next whenever this fight ends.

The International Fight League (IFL) is a pretty cool idea. It's set up like a wrestling dual meet. Both teams have a set of fighters who get points for winning, and more points for finishing fights. If your team wins, everyone on the team gets a bonus on top of their regular pay.

"You're up, Kennedy!" says some skinny dude with a headgear mic.

I walk out to the ring in a gray sweatshirt. I have nothing military on. I told them I am from the Pit. As I walk up to the ring, I expect to hear, "Tim Kennedy, a Kempo fighter from the Pit in Saint Louis Obispo!" Instead, I hear, "Tim Kennedy, a U.S. Army Ranger from Fort Bragg, North Carolina!" *Crap. Hopefully, no one I know heard that.* I look over at my coach. He says something to me in Russian; it sounds like, "You go first." I'm not sure. Hopefully this match doesn't require much coaching.

I'm fighting Dante Rivera, a Renzo Gracie competitive black belt who has been touring internationally, winning high-profile BJJ events. He's muscular. He's got chunky ears. He's the embodiment of the New York high-end BJJ practitioner. Renzo's a legend. He's old-school and his guys are always tough. If there is a betting line in Vegas, I am a −1,000 underdog. No one, including my new friend Leo and my coach, have any idea who I am. I'm weird in that I hear everything anyone is saying when I'm fighting. So before the match even starts, I hear the ringside announcers say something like, "Kennedy is going to want to keep this off the ground and use his kickboxing, as Dante Rivera is a talented black belt." *I know Jiu Jitsu too, announcer guy.*

The bells sound. I'm on national television for the first time.

I take him down right off the bat and go from side control to mount in a couple of seconds. I hit him with a short elbow and the ref tells me they are illegal and I can only use hammerfists. *That's news. Time to change the strategy.* I just keep dominant top position and dole out punishment. At this time in the fight world, there are guys that can wrestle and do a few subs, and there are guys that can do Jiu Jitsu and do a few takedowns. Not many guys can wrestle and do Jiu Jitsu.

Surprise, Dante!

I feel like a pit bull that hasn't been fed and then suddenly is given a 200-pound piece of rib eye. It isn't personal. But I need this fight more than I thought I did. He gets up for a second and I kick him in the face, then knee him, and then take him back down and regain the mount position. I immediately start throwing strikes. As I'm punching him, I notice Evander Holyfield in the crowd. *Woah. Wild.* Dante makes it out of the first round.

I go to my corner. I spot Ginger in the crowd. She looks hot. *I need to sit her further back next time.* I look over at Dante to see what his coach is telling him. I cannot quite make it out, but I think he is telling him he needs to move more standing up, probably to avoid the takedown. I have no idea what my coach is saying. *Evander Holyfield. At my fight. That's really rad.*

The bell rings and I walk to the center. Dante is bouncing around like a little rabbit. He's coming out with game plan 2.0. I take him down again in the second round with an outside trip, regain mount, and proceed to just beat the shit out of him. He taps to strikes. The ref pulls me off him. I'm smiling. This is a real crowd. Bas Rutten is commentating. Legends are in the audience. *This feels very, very cool.*

I was not supposed to win, and it definitely wasn't supposed to be a beatdown. Everyone is surprised. The team is thrilled. But all I want to do is get more food. My Ranger mind is telling me to fucking eat. The good news is that Leo wants to take me out to dinner. He takes Ginger and me to the best steakhouse in Atlanta. I order the porterhouse, which is like $150, two servings of mashed potatoes, and a side of bacon. It's amazing. I kind of want another one, but I don't want to be that guy.

Leo pays me the $4,000 I was promised and asks if I am interested in fighting in the future. I say yes.

When I get back on Sunday from my amazing weekend in Atlanta, there is a note in my Army email account asking me to show up bright and early to SGM Oquendo's office. Once there, the email explains, we will be walking over to the group CSM's office. I am to make sure I bring my leave form.

I don't know it yet, but this is the beginning of what would become an arduous battle within Special Forces Command. One faction loves the idea of an elite prizefighter on one of their most elite Special

Operations Teams, and the other faction wants to kill me and use my body as fertilizer in their tomato garden.

————————

I love shooting. So when I get the chance to go to the Special Operations Target Interdiction Course (SOTIC), aka "SF Sniper School," I jump at it. I have to admit, I didn't expect it to go this way.

In SOTIC, you pass or fail as a team, not as an individual. I have the highest individual score in the class. My partner has the lowest. He's a great guy, but he is absolutely not a natural sniper, doesn't have the right temperament to train himself to be one, and is dealing with some post-traumatic stress. In 2008, these things are not talked about the way they will be later, so he likely is in a very bad place worrying about people thinking he is weak, with the additional stress of the schoolhouse stacked on top of that.

The field shoot is our last must-pass event. If we finish this, we're golden. We need to stalk up to a target without being seen, take a shot, and hit the target using no more than three rounds. I am the shooter. He is the spotter. We walk, crawl, and drag ourselves into position, inch by inch, quietly over a matter of hours. I have an easy shot ahead of me. I can virtually hit this blindfolded. I call the shot, meaning I tell him we're taking it here, and ask for a read, meaning he estimates the range and reports the wind speed and direction. He takes a moment and gives me the read. I look at him. It's a terrible fucking read. I know it is completely wrong. The range is long and he has called the wind in exactly the wrong direction. If I fail to hit the target, we fail. I cannot take the shot with that read. I whisper, "Hey, brother, can you check that again? I think the wind is in the wrong direction."

His eyes fidget. He looks at the target and then looks at me and says, "You're right. I'm freaking the fuck out." Then he stands up and walks away, announcing to the cadre that he is quitting sniper school, while simultaneously giving up our position.

What in the actual fuck just happened?

The cadre are about as shocked as I am, but are also greatly amused,

whereas I am not. "Looks like you fail. Your partner quit, Kennedy."
"Hell no, Sergeant," I reply. "I'm not quitting. I still have a shot to take."
They mess with me for a while, taunting me for running my partner out
of the course. I am the last guy left to shoot. When I'm done, everyone
gets to go home for the day. Everyone else has passed and are all sitting
in the bleachers watching and waiting.

Finally, given that we are at an impasse, one of the cadre walks off to
the bleachers. "Does anyone want to spot for Kennedy? There are two
caveats: I'm only giving you one round to hit the target, and I get to pick
it. Given those conditions, who wants Kennedy's pass/fail to be on your
shoulders?"

I scan the bleachers. I know my chances are not good. Who would
want to do that? But I don't wait long. A burly Asian on the far-left side
stands up immediately. Picture the Batman costume, but Asian, and
that's basically Mike Glover. This dude isn't worried at all. He walks over
like he's about to choose a salad dressing at a salad bar, not making the
decision that will affect whether I pass or fail.

"What if I put your graduation on the line, Glover?" the Sergeant asks.

"I'm making the same decision, Sergeant," Glover responds.

I like this guy!

"Well, I guess it's lucky we aren't doing that to you, Glover."

The cadre take one M118LR round out and place it on a little dish,
proffering it to us like they're serving dessert at a fine dining establishment. "If you get a first-round hit on our target, Kennedy, you graduate.
If you don't, you fail Sniper School."

They choose the 788-meter target. It is the furthest one from our
position.

Mike looks at it very quickly and gives me the adjustment. His confidence and speed scare me a little. I'm not used to it after spending
the whole course with my partner. "Are you sure?" I ask. Calmly, Mike
repeats the exact wind call he just said. I make his adjustments. I squeeze
the trigger.

I see the impact, and then a second later hear the *ping*!

Dead. On. Balls. Mother. Fucking. Accurate.

Mike claps me on the back and says, "Good job."

I pick up my gear and smile at the cadre and strongly resist the urge to break into an MC Hammer–style breakdancing session while singing "Too Legit to Quit."

———————

I get another IFL fight right after Sniper School in June 2007. My opponent, now at 185 instead of 205, is Ryan McGivern, who trains under Pat Miletich, an absolute legend of a coach. Miletich is responsible for UFC Champions such as Jens Pulver and Matt Hughes. Incidentally, those are the other two guys that will be in McGivern's corner. He is currently 7–2 and fights for the Quad City Silverbacks, the winningest team in the IFL. He is undefeated in the IFL with wins over Dennis Hallman, Matt Horwich, and Dan Molina. This is absolutely the biggest fight of my career. If I was most guys, I would probably be nervous right now, but I grew up with Chuck Liddell, and I spent my last year in combat, Ranger School, and Sniper School, so it's hard to worry too much about this stuff.

The bell rings and I do pretty much the same thing I did in the last fight. McGivern is a better wrestler and striker than Rivera, so the standup is a little more dangerous and he's a little harder to get down, but once I do get him to the ground, I beat him up. He makes it through the first round, but in the second round he takes an extremely bad reaching shot on me with his head down. I lock up a guillotine choke and win.

Because the fight is televised, I get texts from a ton of people congratulating me on the win, including one guy I recently met through Greg Thompson, a former infantry officer named Nick Palmisciano who recently started a military apparel brand called "Ranger Up." Nick is a 5'8" Italian guy with almost black dark-brown hair. His shoulders are about as wide as he is tall, and he still has that wrestler walk, even though he's been away from it for a few years. As a rule, I don't like officers. I'm not sure about him either, but I had just done this photo shoot with him for a charity fundraiser for the Wounded Warrior Project and it was fun. Basically, it was me and a bunch of hot models on motorcycles holding guns.

Not unlike when Af was commenting at the Pit at Ranger School, this cocksucker was heckling me the whole time I'm posing. As I mounted a Harley and a buxom woman named Grace got on the bike behind me, Nick casually asked me if I'd ever had anything that big between my legs. Grace giggled. Ginger did not. But it was funny, so I didn't kill him.

Even with Ginger's reluctance to appreciate the humor of the situation, her being there was great . . . until one of the models told Ginger she loved her shoes and asked her if she could borrow them for the next shoot. Ginger said yes, but I instantly knew there was a problem. At the end of the day, the girl handed them back to Ginger, thanked her, and walked out the door. Ginger, while maintaining eye contact with me, walked over to the trash, dropped them in, and walked out. Nick said, "I'm sorry" and I just said, "Yeah."

I answer Nick's text, and a hundred others like it, with "Thanks."

If your team wins, you get a team bonus. I never got one of those in the IFL because we never won. The Red Bears disbanded after that season. It probably wasn't a great investment for my new Russian friend.

But the Red Bears' loss is my gain. Leo, the mad Russian, is now my manager. Our deal is that while he is helping me, he won't take any money. He says fighters don't make enough to pay managers yet. He's not wrong.

The more I am around Leo, the more I appreciate him. Leo never talks about his success, but he's wildly successful. Leo never makes promises he cannot keep and never tries to upsell his connections. When he tells me that he wants to introduce me to someone, I do not expect that someone to be Mark Cuban. Cuban is about to launch his own fight promotion at the end of the year called HDNet Fights, and Leo pitched me to him as a possible fighter. I let Mark know I am absolutely interested. But first, I have a title to defend.

———

This 2007 All Army Combatives Championship will be my last attempt at this event. I've felt myself getting markedly better over the last year, and after beating a guy like McGivern, it doesn't feel right to be throw-

Here I am proving
that habits start early.
Kennedy Family Archives

Me with my dad,
Mike Kennedy, in
full uniform.
Kennedy Family Archives

Celebrating my birthday with my friend Jared.
Kennedy Family Archives

Learning Japanese Jiu Jitsu
with Terry and Barry.
Kennedy Family Archives

Here I am at the Pit, training with Chuck Liddell.
Kennedy Family Archives

Graduating from the police academy.
Kennedy Family Archives

Me and my baby girls, Sabrina and Julia.
Kennedy Family Archives

Swearing to defend the Constitution.
Kennedy Family Archives

After basic training with my family.
Kennedy Family Archives

Me and the boys training at SFAS.
Dick Couch

Receiving the Green Beret, an honor of a lifetime.
Kennedy Family Archives

My first mission in Iraq.
Kennedy Family Archives

Flying to combat on a Blackhawk helicopter in Iraq.
Kennedy Family Archives

Graduating from Ranger School, with my parents, Ginger, and Sabrina.
Kennedy Family Archives

Me winning my third
and final All Army
Combatives Tournament.
Kennedy Family Archives

Here I am before heading to the Valley of Death in Afghanistan.
Kennedy Family Archives

In a sniper position, overwatching the Jingle trucks in Afghanistan.
Kennedy Family Archives

The nicest poop ever, in the middle of a gunfight in Afghanistan.
Kennedy Family Archives

Leaping on top of the cage after I knocked out Nadal at "Fight for the Troops."
MMAWeekly

Me with Mike Winkeljon, Greg Jackson, Nick Palmisciano, and Brandon Gibson at "Fight for the Troops."
Kennedy Family Archives

Michael Bisping wishing me all the best before our fight.
Sherdog

Training local troops in Africa.
Kennedy Family Archives

About to dive a Nazi submarine on my television show, *Hunting Hitler.*
Anthony Eslami

Emerging from frozen waters on *Hard to Kill.*
BJ Golic

Having a laugh with Randy Couture on the set of *Range 15*.
Range 15 Archives

Me and Nick at Hamid Kharzai International Airport
during the evacuation of Kabul in August 2021.
Nick Palmisciano

Evacuating Afghans during the fall of Kabul.
We were able to get 12,000 people out of harm's way.

Kennedy Family Archives

The Kennedy clan.
Kennedy Family Archives

ing down with other soldiers. This year's a little different, though, because I have a sponsor: Ranger Up. Nick approached me right after I got home from the McGivern fight about doing a shirt for the event. *I said yes. Why not? I've never had a sponsor.*

I figure he'll do what all MMA brands do and set up a table and sell shirts. Instead, he comes with hundreds of shirts that say, "Ranger Up Combatives," half of which have me on them, and gives them out to every fighter that entered the tournament, no matter how they fare. This is the right way to do it. I immediately feel good about representing the brand.

I blast my way through the tournament. With more time at home, and more time preparing for fights, I had built a small group of very tough guys. As a collective, we dominate the tournament, placing in almost every weight class. In fact, the guy that I beat in the finals, 1LT Carpaccio Owens, is one of my students.

I am now the only three-time All Army Combatives Champion. I'm very proud, but it's the last All Army Combatives Championship for me. Nick, who I didn't know could write, places a bunch of articles about the tournament on various MMA websites. MMA fans now start connecting me more and more with the military. The combination of the IFL wins and press around the Combatives gets me increased attention and additional opportunities begin to arise.

Mark Cuban reaches out to Leo. They want me to fight a guy I have already fought and beaten badly: Jason "Mayhem" Miller. Miller has become a celebrity since we last fought. He's popular with the skater crowd, and people love him for his WWF-style antics. I take the fight.

I arrive in Dallas. The treatment I wanted in Atlanta (but didn't get) for my first IFL fight is exactly what I receive from HDNet. Mark Cuban is fucking amazing. He treats us like real valued professionals. Everything is first tier. A limo picks us up at the airport. We are taken to a fantastic hotel and our rooms are suites. We also have paid access to a nice gym. Whatever food we want is available. Frankly, the way I was treated that week is the best I have ever been treated before or since in the fight world.

Fight night, I feel great. But the fight itself is unexpected. Mayhem is good. He's much better than when we last fought. I can tell that he has been working hard. He's slippery. I get in eight submission positions throughout the fight, but I cannot finish. I land a lot of shots, but not enough that do real damage. But in my head, while I get the same cut on the bridge of my nose that I get every fight, he never has me in any danger. I won this fight.

But I didn't. My head wasn't thinking about it like a point fight. I was thinking about it like a soldier. What we do in Combatives, while it may look the same, is not the right strategy for a prizefight, especially a close one. I am super pissed. The way I see it, I get a huge shot in front of Mark Cuban—a chance to establish myself as a contender—and I blow it.

Fortunately, Cuban doesn't see it like that at all. The next day I am in a private box at the Dallas Cowboys football game with him and Randy Couture. It's the first time I've been able to hang out with Randy since the Pit days. He used to come down with his boys or we'd go up to Team Quest, a gym. We were the strikers. They were the wrestlers. And we made each other better. "I've been following you since that Dante Rivera fight. You're doing it right. Don't let this one set you back. You just need to get in a real fight camp next time," he offers up. Having been in the military, he understands how hard it is to do both jobs. "You've actually been following me a little longer," I tell him. Randy doesn't realize I'm the kid from the Pit until I remind him. His eyes go wide when he does the math. "You were just a kid back then!" he says. We had a good time. He's a genuine guy and it's cool to be around someone who gets it and who knows both of the worlds I live in.

This past year, starting in November of 2006, had been fucking perfect until two weeks ago. Ranger School. Undefeated in the IFL. Sniper School. Third U.S. All Army Combatives Championship victory—the only person to ever do it! Then I lost to Jason Miller.

My friends told me to let it go. After all, I am deploying to Afghanistan in two weeks. I need to focus on that. But I couldn't. I needed a win. I needed to scratch that itch. So I asked Leo to get me another fight. And here I am, two weeks after losing to Miller, and two weeks from a deployment to Afghanistan, once again in the IFL, this time at the Mohegan Sun Casino in Connecticut. I am fighting Elias Rivera. Brandon Garner is my corner, two days before New Year's. My wife Ginger and Nick are up in the stands.

The crowd for this fight is different from my last three pro fights. The previous fights were all in real event centers. This is in a casino, albeit a nice one. This crowd isn't here because they are fight fans. They are here for the spectacle. They want blood. *Good. Me too.* I'm ready. It's time to get back in the W column. The bell sounds and I move forward.

Right out of the gate he stings me with a right cross. I don't buckle or anything, but it was a good shot. A sliver of concern runs through me. *Fuck no.* I shoot a reactionary double leg, pick him up high into the air, and slam the fuck out of him. Thirty seconds later I am mounted. I'm not calm the way I usually fight. I want to throw shots. And I do. I connect with eight power bombs in a row. The ref pushes me off him. He's unconscious. It only took me two minutes to end this fight. I jump up and celebrate. The crowd cheers. Then the crowd gets quiet. He's still out. *Fuck. Some of those shots at the end were really big shots.*

At the same time that I'm worrying about him in the ring, his wife, who is sitting right next to Ginger and Nick, screams and runs into the bathroom. *Fuck. Did I just kill this guy?* Ginger follows to comfort her, not telling her who she is. The whole thing is incredibly scary. Finally, Elias starts moving and the crowd cheers. I expect him to get up, but they decide to take him out on a stretcher. He stayed unconscious for a long time.

It was scary. I didn't want that. It might surprise most people, but I fight to win, not to hurt people.

I enjoy the night with my wife and my friends. We have a few drinks and a decent meal, and I go to bed, allowing myself to revel briefly on the happiness that the silly little world of cage fighting brings me.

Because I know when I wake up in the morning, it's time to switch gears.

I'm going back to war.

CHAPTER NINE

THE VALLEY OF DEATH

January 2008

Rot. That's what invades my nostrils and floods my throat as I exit the aircraft. Stagnant rot like the smell that hits you when you're trudging through an algae-filled pond as a kid, trying to catch frogs. For a second, the scent brings me back to those childhood summer days mucking around in the creek. There is a burning smell in there somewhere too, but the rot dominates the argument my nose is having with my brain. Even though I know this isn't Iraq, I am still surprised not to feel the smoldering heat I have grown accustomed to on these trips. The only heat I feel as I come down the metal ramp of the aircraft is the warm air coming off its engines.

The sky is foreign as well. I cannot see the sun the way I always could in Babylon. It is bright out, but the clouds completely shroud the big orange ball in the sky. I squint from the brightness, though, the same way I would on a cloudy day at the beach and reach for my sunglasses. The light is different too. The blue hue I'm so used to from the States is replaced by a gray one. Afghanistan is going to be a new adventure, that's for sure.

I am here in Kandahar with my partner Billy on pretty much the coolest, most international mission imaginable for me at this point in my career. We are tasked by the United States Army Special Operations Command (USASOC) and the Joint Special Operations Command (JSOC) to supplement "tier one coalition units." In other words, if the toughest dudes on the planet from either the British, Czech, French, or Italian Special Operations communities are about to get into a gunfight, Billy and I are going along for the ride. This is a volunteer mission, and we are both stoked to have been chosen—working with the best of the best on nonstop missions as an elite two-man sniper team. This is exactly the kind of mission I was born for.

Unfortunately, life had different plans. More specifically, Jody had different plans.

In military parlance, "Jody" is the generic name we use for the guy or girl who swoops in and steals your significant other while you're deployed. These individuals are a detested (but common) part of military life. Usually, Jody is just a side piece. Sort of a "while the boys are away, the girls may play" kind of thing. But not for Billy's wife. She decided to take the normal Jody situation and up the ante. She entered the old-school Nintendo Konami Code into Jody. Up, up, down, down, left, right, left, right, B, A, Select, Start, and boom! Within hours of arriving in Afghanistan, Billy's bank account is emptied, he is served with digital divorce papers, his credit cards are maxed, and his possessions are stolen. She took everything from him.

Look, people get divorced. People cheat. Those things aren't ever okay, but they're a normal part of life. But this bitch (and she deserves the word) is pure evil. She did him so dirty, so unexpectedly, and so brutally, that one of the toughest guys I know is, for the first time ever, not in the right headspace to execute the mission. And, in an absolutely shocking twist of events, the Army looks out for him instead of telling him to suck it up and drive on.

So here I am, a sniper watching my teammate get on a plane to head home. I am now an Army of One and I am not exactly sure what JSOC has in store for me. Turns out, they kind of don't know either.

For a few days, I basically sit around doing nothing or working out at the on-base gym. At first, I thought I was going to be sent a replacement but was alerted that wouldn't be the case. That led to a brief period where I thought I'd be sent back home, with my dream mission completely falling apart. Finally, though, they decide to assign me to a coalition command reporting to Sergeant Major Flaherty in Kandahar. This is great news! Not only am I not getting sent home, but now I am a one-man band, not unlike Antonio Banderas in *Desperado*, except not quite as dark and handsome, but with much bigger guns. (Also, I'm more of a piano guy.) But just as that good news hits me, I get some more bad news: Before I can do a single mission, I must take a one-week, forty-hour course on the RG-31 Mine Resistant Ambush Protected vehicle, or MRAP.

I hate classroom work. I especially hate Army classroom work because the Army is incredibly skilled at cramming five hours of instruction into a forty-hour class. It is always taught at an eighth-grade level and, hence, takes longer than it should by a factor of five. I hate classwork with the fiery intensity of a thousand suns, especially when that classwork is keeping me from doing something I want to do, and make no mistake, I *really* want to start hunting bad guys.

The RG class became mandatory that very week because right before Billy and I landed in country, four members of 1st Battalion, 7th Special Forces Group, rolled one into a canal, resulting in an absolute tragedy. Sergeant James Treber, Sergeant Shawn Simmons, and Sergeant First Class Jeffrey Rada Morales lost their lives to drowning. Sergeant Joe Serna was the sole survivor but only because Sergeant Treber dove underwater, released Serna's seat belt, and dragged him to an air pocket. Treber then tried multiple times to find more air or a way out but could not. Serna blacked out, was rescued, and still doesn't know how Treber finally expired.

Forty-year-old Tim knows how precious life is and is in absolute awe of the bravery of Sergeant Treber. He saved his brother-in-arms and gave up his own life in the process of trying to find a way out for the two of them. But twenty-eight-year-old Tim didn't want to go to a stupid RG class and was bored out of his mind.

That week was dumb. I ignored most of the things they went over except for the Common Remotely Operated Weapon Station

(CROWS). The CROWS was basically a universal platform you could use to mount a .50 cal machine gun, a Mark 19 grenade launcher, an M240 machine gun, or pretty much any other crew-served weapon (these weapons are the ones that actually fire thousands of rounds per minute and can saw trees in half) and fire it from inside the vehicle so you would never be exposed to enemy fire. The CROWS also had a cool targeting system that let you use a laser to find the range of the target. The gun would adjust automatically, and as a result you could accurately hit targets, even on the move, far faster and without a lot of adjustments. So, I played with that the whole time. I wasn't supposed to, but I was the big scary Special Forces guy that was in Afghanistan alone without a unit, which added an ominous air about me no one wanted to mess with. Ultimately, the guys teaching the course were just happy I cared about anything to do with the RG, so they left me alone to play with my targeting system.

That misery of a course finally ended, and I was free as a bird, and this bird you cannot change. I wanted to find the bad guys as quickly as possible and shoot them. I had been here for weeks and had been repeatedly denied this opportunity, and my frustration was at its peak. I reported to SGM Flaherty and begged him to help me start finding some missions. He was all too happy to help.

Flaherty basically became my pimp, and I was his special boy. When a CONOP (concept of operations) was submitted by a coalition partner, he'd walk over and offer up my services and discuss my capabilities, as either a liaison or a sniper.

It was a great relationship. In a very short time, I got involved with missions from everyone in our area of operations (AOR). Nothing meaty really happened, but I was keeping myself busy and enjoying the operational tempo. I'd get a CONOP, link up with my point of contact, figure out how I'd be employed, do the mission, then come back and work out. It was also instructive to see how other militaries worked. While we all had different policies and procedures, at the highest level, we were all the same guys.

Except the Czechs.

The Czechs were the same guys, but genetically engineered to be twice the size of normal men. Honestly, those guys were rad. Watching them do missions was like watching "tactical *Baywatch*." Everyone was a specimen and you wondered how they could find so many enormous, chiseled, good-looking dudes with a penchant for crushing the souls of their enemies.

The Czechs were why I got super excited when I found out I was going to be the liaison for a multinational mission involving U.S. Special Forces ODA 7182 and a Czech Special Forces company, in addition to Afghan troops. I couldn't have asked for a more badass group. Our mission was to resupply Forward Operating Base (FOB) Anaconda. Now I appreciate a resupply mission doesn't sound too cool or dangerous but sit back so I can paint this picture for you.

FOB Anaconda is located in the heart of Oruzgan Province, the most Taliban-centric province in Afghanistan. To add some flecks of gold paint to that picture, it was being supported by Iranian freedom fighters. The base wasn't even safe in the way we typically think about Army bases. The Taliban had tried to overrun the FOB three times in the past year and had actually breached the wire, resulting in Green Berets being engaged in hand-to-hand combat in their own base. Landing an aircraft for resupply was challenging because the FOB sits in a valley surrounded by towns friendly to the Taliban. Any aircraft that came into range would immediately draw enemy fire. Even doing parachute drops of equipment was a bad idea, because if the wind picked up even a little in *any* direction, our troops would have to fight their way to the drop and then fight their way back. If it was way off, then we basically were resupplying the enemy. That left trucks as the only viable resupply option.

When I say "viable," I'm stretching that word as far as it can be stretched. Anaconda is a glorious 251 kilometers (156 miles) from Advanced Operations Base Kandahar. There are only two ways to get there on roads big enough to handle armored vehicles and the large trucks that would make up our convoy. When I say "big enough" I'm not talking about superhighways either. Both roads can barely fit two cars across and are hewn out of the mountainside in winding paths in deep valleys on either side of a mountain range. The mountain range is littered with towns loyal to the Taliban on the high ground alongside the roads. The roads do not have safety rails the way we do in the U.S. If you drive too close to the edge, you can fall to your death down the side of a mountain. There are limitless places for bad guys to hide and set up ambushes. If I was drawing up a mission that was going to result in catastrophic loss it would absolutely have been this one. The whole thing was terrible. The Taliban had every single tactical advantage imaginable, but we had no choice—we had to get our guys resupplied.

Since this mission was incredibly dangerous (and one not to be taken frequently), we were bringing enough supplies to last an entire year. Food, ammunition, medical needs, etc. Anything and everything was coming in with us. That meant we needed trucks, and lots of them.

Eighty trucks to be precise. And since this was Afghanistan, it was eighty Jingle trucks. If you don't know what a Jingle truck is, try to imagine any movie where the main characters are lost in some third world country, and they get on a bus and the people on board are a carnival of colors and smells. There's one lady holding a chicken, and a goat with a bell walks by, and then imagine that a semi hit that bus at 80 mph and everything inside just kind of stuck to the outside of the truck permanently. That's a Jingle truck. They have no armor. They have questionable maintenance practices. And they are driven by people who were not particularly loyal to our cause.

Each truck had three drivers, because we were anticipating we would be losing some along the way, either from cowardice, treachery, or enemy bullets. The drivers were not allowed to have phones or any other communication devices because we were worried some of them might tip off the Taliban to our makeup and timelines.

So there we were, an A-Team and me with RGs and up-armored HMMWVs, the Czechs in their unarmored gun trucks, the Afghans in up-armored HMMWVs, and eighty Jingle trucks full of a year's worth of supplies, getting ready to go at zero dark thirty, with a bunch of drivers we didn't trust, into an area where we were moving to certain contact at a massive disadvantage. Oddly, I didn't even consider we wouldn't dominate the situation, whatever it turned out to be. I was the guy that came out on top in MMA fights I wasn't supposed to win. I passed the 18X program I wasn't supposed to pass, I made it on the CIF team no one had ever made it on without being on an A-Team first, I chased down Zarqawi alongside a bunch of other trigger pullers *Call of Duty*-style on my first deployment, and I had just finished Ranger School as the Honor Graduate when challenged to do so. I was a fucking juggernaut. I was absolutely unstoppable. This was going to be just another few days of awesome for Tim Kennedy.

Everyone always says there is a calm before the storm, but in Army movements it's more like a storm before a different storm. As I look out at this line of vehicles going back as far as the eye can see, I am grateful I am not the one organizing this clusterfuck with the next storm coming. That honor falls on the shoulders of Captain Kevin Key, a short, auburn-haired, intense former Ranger officer who is now on his first Special Forces deployment. Every soldier knows that feeling of sitting in a military vehicle with the low vibration of the engine lulling you to sleep, while JP8 diesel fuel hangs in the air, sticking to everything it touches. I enjoy this last cozy moment without responsibility, as poor Kevin runs up and down the convoy making sure everyone has everything and all is as it should be. I check one last time to make sure my SR-25 sniper rifle, short-barreled rifle, and shotgun are ready to go, that all my ammo is accessible, and that I still have my rucksack full of grenades. With the knowledge all of those things are as they should be, I nod off to sleep.

I wake up as the vehicle starts to move. A HMMWV isn't the smoothest ride and, even if I wanted to sleep, it was time to be alert. I am riding shotgun in the second vehicle in the convoy with three guys named Mike. We'll be labeling the Mikes as Irish Mike, Mike G, and Mike Keller. Irish Mike is driving the vehicle. Mike Keller is on the .50 cal machine gun in the turret. Mike G is in the back. The lead vehicle in front of us houses an Afghan team in a U.S. HMMWV. The Afghans always lead in the first vehicle as a sign of trust. The lead vehicle is most likely to get hit in an ambush or run over an IED that has a pressure plate trigger; this is their way of showing us they are not the enemy. Pretty baller. Plus, we wouldn't trust them if they didn't do it.

As I look out the window into the countryside, I start to feel worse and worse about the mission. Sure enough, immediately upon beginning the movement, we start intercepting cell phone calls from the drivers, who aren't supposed to have phones. They are informing the Taliban we are on the move. So, we have to stop and search the trucks. We find and take a ton of phones. This is a very bad sign.

As we approach the first village, we are shocked to find it abandoned. It is a complete ghost town. The Afghans know we are about to get our ass kicked, and they are either getting their butts out of Dodge so they won't be in the line of fire, or more likely, they are Taliban themselves.

A call comes over the radio. We have to stop because some of the trucks have overheated. That doesn't make sense at all. We checked every truck thoroughly before beginning this trip, and we have only been driving for an hour or so. *How are multiple trucks already overheating?*

When we stop to investigate, we find radiators with screwdriver holes in them. We aren't in a position to make repairs, so for each truck that "broke down," we have to rush to cross-load its supplies to another truck using nothing but manual labor, even though these pallets and parts are extremely heavy. Then our wrecker, a giant truck with a crane attachment, picks up the broken vehicle and literally throws it down the side of the mountain. There is no room to drive around them, so this is the only choice we have.

Finally, we are ready to move again. Except we can't, because some of the trucks now have no drivers. While we were cross-loading, they went off for a smoke or a piss and just never fucking came back. Now, I'm sure some of them are just cowards and when they saw the ghost town, they lost their nerve, but most of the guys are actively working to slow us down to give the fighters a chance to set up for the ambush we now know is coming.

It pisses me off, but I also respect it. These aren't the usual Taliban riffraff. These guys are being led by Iranian fighters. And the Iranians, unlike the incompetent hodgepodge of farmers, goat herders, and angry teenagers that make up the Taliban, are well-trained elite troops. They employ good tactics. They set up near- and far-side security elements to ensure they know when we hit critical checkpoints. They build fallback points after first contact to ensure we can't zero in on them quickly and blow them to hell with artillery or close air support. They mark kill zones so that when we hit the big X on their maps, they can unleash maximum firepower on us. We are fighting a foreign army, not a militia. This situation repeats itself often in the Middle East and it is the big reason military people don't understand why the U.S. cuts Iran so many breaks—these guys have been killing us for years. They just take their uniforms off right before they do it, then put them back on when it's done.

As we continue to pass ghost village after ghost village, the RG picks up the Taliban's far-side security element on thermals on the back side of a village. The amazing thing about thermals is that much like in the *Predator* movies, you can feel very hidden but be shining bright as day in those glorious sights. Now none of this is announced over the radio yet, so when the 40mm grenade launcher starts going, I don't know if this is real or not. Are they probing? Are they fucking around? Then I hear the machine gun start barking. It is real. When the RG team picked up the outline of AKs in their thermals, they lit the bad guys up and cut down the whole team in an instant. *This is exactly how we should start—with dominant and overwhelming force.* Then I hear the shouts for "Medic!"

It is unclear whether it was a .50 cal round that had ricocheted or a piece of shrapnel from the grenade launcher, but a piece of metal had come back toward the Czech vehicles and hit one of their men in the leg, severing his femoral artery at the groin. Blood is pouring out of him. I've never seen so much blood leave a man so quickly. The medics rush around him working their magic as fast as they can. They do everything possible to stop the bleeding, but he is in bad shape. Fortunately, because we aren't under fire, a MEDEVAC comes quickly and airlifts him out. To this day, I don't know whether he lived or died.

Our demeanor changes after losing that man. *We're in the shit now.* I feel like I am living in some old Vietnam movie. I don't realize how prophetic my feelings are. If I did, I'd probably turn the whole goddamn convoy around. That is the last village we will see before we hit the Cho-kazoid Pass, an unknown little valley in the middle of a hole-in-the-wall country made up entirely of dirt, rot, and pain that would break me in a way nothing ever had or has since.

As we turn the corner in the narrow pass, something feels off. It is quiet. I can't hear birds or animals or anything but the hum of the diesel engines. I don't like where we are. The area is no more than sixty meters across from valley wall to valley wall. There is a runoff stream along the right side, which has sprouted thick overbrush, shrubs, and healthier trees than we had seen elsewhere, so much so that we cannot see through any of it, even with thermals.

That's when the explosion rocks me. It is so big that at first I thought our vehicle had been hit. My vision goes completely white and there is a ringing in my ears—a gentle whine—as my brain reignites and starts working again . . . sort of. It is the same feeling I had in the old days when Chuck Liddell used to hit me. Sure, I am conscious, but I am not quite right. My brain doesn't feel like it is processing at full speed. My vision slowly returns and white flecks of light frolic through my eyes as my situation comes back to me in a jolt. I realize we're okay but immediately know we are totally fucked. The vehicle in front of me hit my roof. I don't know if it hit a pressure plate or what, but a two-and-a-half-ton ar-mored vehicle just did a backflip twenty meters in the air, is completely shredded and missing everything from the front wheel forward, and is now sitting on top of my vehicle.

Bullets from machine gun nests high above us start to hit the ground around us. I can hear rounds pinging off our vehicle. The RPG nests come seconds later, but luckily the assholes shooting them at me suck and they fly over our vehicle. I can now see that the firing positions have been built up. These aren't hastily made. These fuckers planned on killing us right here.

I need to move. The whole fight is right here in the front. The guys in the back are so far away that all they can do is listen to the gunfire. The pass is so narrow that you can barely fit two vehicles in the gap while they are able to hit us from every conceivable position and angle. There is no way to reinforce us. Wisely, like the grizzled combat veteran he is, the ODA Sergeant Major starts pushing all the units to the high ground to take the fight to them and get the guys out of the line of fire. That is great and all, but it doesn't do jack shit for me. The lead three vehicles, one completely blown up, are stranded with nowhere to go while death rains down around us.

I fucking know I am about to die. I am not going to see my wife again. I am not going to see my kids again. I don't want it to end like this.

Irish Mike agrees. He slams us in reverse and turns the vehicle so it can back up the hill. I don't know if we will make it. The axle is bent from the explosion and we have an extra few tons on top of us, but we slowly crawl backwards as the metal of the axle strains and whines. Bullets keep pinging off us. An RPG misses us by a few inches in front of me. If Irish hadn't started the move, that would have been a direct hit.

We are now in a total brownout from the dust. We cannot see anything but the muzzle flashes and whatever is two feet in front of us. Keller is in the turret shooting at everything. If it is in the hills and it moves or blinks it gets six to eight rounds of .50 cal coming its way. I have no idea if he is hitting anything, but he is letting his presence be known to these cocksuckers. I am sitting next to my shotgun, my SR-25, and my SBR, but it feels like they are so close that they will emerge from the dust right next to us, so I am holding my shotgun. Mike G has the M249 Squad Automatic Weapon hanging out the window firing like a madman. He dumps at least two nutsacks (400-round canisters) through that thing. I don't know how he didn't melt the barrel.

Maybe he changed it while I was dumping rounds out my window, but I sure as shit didn't see it happen.

The HMMWV hanging off us finally falls off and we rocket back just as another RPG whizzes past us. *Another* near hit.

We finally get to the base of the hill, after zinging backwards for the last sixty meters. For the first time we have the slightest bit of cover. I don't know when it happened, but I traded my shotgun for my SR-25 sniper rifle and am now using it as a spotting tool. I look through the scope and find a machine gun nest, plink a round so Keller sees it impact, and then he lights it up with the .50 cal.

Mike G is covering the other side, shooting anything and everything that moves. I see the Czech guys closest to us take off into the woods to claim the high ground and flank the enemy to take the guns out from up above. It's a great plan, but it leaves us isolated once again.

Dust is still fucking everywhere, but a lane of light clears from us to where the front vehicle had fallen off of ours sixty meters away when we backed up. It is eerie, kind of like when you're sitting on your couch on a lazy day looking out the window and you catch a beam of light and watch the dust particles whirl around inside it. The beams are on either side of us, full of dust, but the lane to the vehicle is clear. It is almost as if God cleared a path for us, but that path didn't make my life any easier.

"Those dudes are still alive! They're still fucking alive!" Irish shouts out.

He's right. I see it too. One guy is moving.

"I'm going to sprint to them, man!" Irish yells to me.

"That's a bad fucking idea, man, and if you do it, we're all gonna die," I tell him. There is no lack of seriousness in my voice. I do not think we have any chance of surviving that run right in the heart of this ambush.

Irish looks right at me and says, "I'm going." He takes off in a dead sprint. I hear the guns pick up. They see him. I'm still holding my sniper rifle. For some reason, I don't grab my AR as I take a deep breath and sprint after Irish. I do not want to be doing this. I do not want to expose myself. But I don't want to fail my comrades even more.

We get to the vehicle unscathed, and I look inside. Fuck. They are in bad shape. The first guy has lost both of his legs at the quads. They simply aren't there. I pull him out in a sandbag carry and his bile and blood and guts spill out onto my uniform, rolling down my stomach and soaking my legs. Even with the adrenaline and the fear and the explosions and the bullets, I acknowledge this is the most disgusting thing that has ever happened to me. Irish grabs the other dude, who is in rough shape but is still breathing. As we start moving the sixty meters back to our vehicle, I see a squad of six to eight guys moving out of the woods to finish us. They are the assault element getting ready to fight to the X and kill those of us standing on it.

I have a choice. I can drop this guy and leave him for dead so I can fight two-handed, or I can fire my cannon of a sniper rifle one-handed Rambo-style in their general direction while trying to move my wounded guy to a high carry with one arm on the other side. Whether it is courage or because I knew Irish would have just picked him up and carried two guys, I opt to fire one-handed. I know I am not hitting anything. I know I am not even close. They see us. A squad against two guys who are carrying wounded Afghans and have no real ability to return fire. We are dead.

Then, thank God, Keller sees them. The sweet melody of the .50 cal fills my ears and they evaporate. When I say that, I need you to understand what I mean. They didn't die. It wasn't like there were corpses sitting there. They fucking *evaporated*. There is just a pink mist floating in the air where they had just been. It is like that Jake Gyllenhaal scene in *Jarhead* where he says he wanted "the pink mist" you see after pulling the trigger on a sniper rifle. I had never wanted it before. But right now, I have never been happier to see anything in my entire life. Keller just saved me for what proved to be the first of many times over the next few days.

As happy as I am to be alive, I find myself acutely aware of the overpressure sickness I received from the initial explosion. That's because every round Keller fires from the .50 cal feels like a baseball bat hitting me in the head. The pain emanates everywhere, from the crown of my nose through my eyeballs, into my ears, and down my neck. And there is nothing to do about it. I have to push it to the back of my existence and control it as I keep driving myself forward to get back to the vehicle.

Before we're all the way back to relative safety, the ODA medic is sprinting to us to help the wounded Afghans. He is 6'6," 250 pounds, and we will call him the "Ginginator." He takes immediate action to keep them alive and calls in a MEDEVAC request to get them out of there. The request is denied because there are no Americans or Czechs also wounded. That policy still pisses me off. These guys were fighting side by side with us for their country, putting their lives and the lives of their families at risk, and we couldn't get them an asset that we knew was readily available and on standby. It felt evil, to be honest, and I wondered if the Afghans knew.

For his part, while we were all fighting the Taliban, Ginginator relentlessly worked on the wounded and kept them alive for six hours before they finally succumbed to their wounds.

Moments after my Hail Mary sprint to get back to the vehicle, I realize Keller had taken a huge but necessary risk to save our asses. Those rounds were leaving that gun at 3,000 feet per second and were traveling only three-to-five meters over our heads. At that range, with that weapon, a small miscalculation would have been the end of us. A lack of focus on hitting the enemy in order to give us more of a safety net would have meant the end of us at the hands of the enemy. Looking down his barrel, that window was so goddamn small that I have no idea how he did it.

I generally live by the rule you don't rise to the moment but rather fall to the level of your training. I'm going out on a limb here and saying Keller had never trained in threading the needle with an 1,812-grain round over two of your best friends' heads and accurately hitting six-to-eight moving bad guys that wanted to kill them all within a few milliseconds. Keller made that parable his bitch. He rose to the occasion, then rose over it, and then framed it and hung it on his wall. Irish and I would both have died on that battlefield without Keller, and without us, many more would have died.

Enough about Keller's bald eagle catching a fish while fireworks go off and an American flag waves vigorously in the background heroism. Back to me.

I can't see straight, my head is killing me, and I want to puke. I'm covered in another man's shit and guts, and I'm at the beginning of a three-day gunfight. So far, I've only been able to play defense.

It is time to fuck some shit up.

That's the last thought I remember for a little while. I lose time, most likely from my concussion. When I "come to" I am hanging off the side of a Czech gun truck driving up the edge of a mountain trying to get to these fighting positions before the Taliban have the chance to bound back to their next preplanned spot, where they have more weapons cached.

I find my way to the Czech Commander's vehicle to improve command and control. We aren't all speaking the same language, and even when we do, it isn't easy to understand each other on the radio because of accents and inflection, but in person it is much easier. So, I'm hanging off the side of this vehicle with my sniper rifle, my SBR, and a rucksack full of grenades. We're driving around looking for a fighting position when we come upon a bunch of tents and mud huts. Lo and behold, there are a dozen Taliban just sitting there looking at us, absolutely frozen in place. It is like early morning hunting where you're looking at the feeder just waiting for a deer to come up to it. You hear the feeder go off and you feel the wind hitting you in the face and you think, *Man, this is perfect.* Then you hear the crunching of bramble over your shoulder, and you see the deer behind you and you think, *Hey, what are you doing THERE? Why aren't you in the perfect feeder position?* If we reversed that scenario, where they are the hunter, and we are the deer, I'm pretty sure that's what they see.

The problem for them is that these deer have lots of guns and are fucking pissed.

When it comes to vehicles, Americans believe in armor and Czechs believe in speed. You can argue which one is better, but in this case, speed is glorious. Let me paint for you the picture of their final moments. A Land Cruiser comes flying over the hill that is supposed to be your exit lane. A mongoloid American who is as wide as he is tall is hanging out the window pointing an SBR at you. Next to him are four Viking gods, but instead of carrying Mjölnnir the hammer, they have a turret-mounted machine gun, a swing-arm machine gun, and more service rifles than you can count, also pointed at you.

Sometimes in a firefight, there is an awkward moment where you surprise each other, and shock, recovery, and reaction time sort of decide who goes first. We don't give them that moment. We just fucking go. If you are the three guys closest to us, then that's where your journey ends, because the four of us that are not driving shred those guys to nothing in less than two seconds at twenty meters. If you are one of the remaining nine guys, you run into a building expecting a fair firefight with some standoff. Instead, before you even get the chance to find a shooting position, the mongoloid runs up to your building throwing grenades in, and then the truck lights your building up until there is no building left.

We don't clear a goddamn thing. There is no surgical close quarters combat. They don't deserve it. We make them rubble.

And then silence.

After an insane half hour of fighting for our lives that kicked off with a mind-crushing explosion, had me almost die twice, and culminated with a fast-as-fuck Czech counterattack with me as their sidekick, we have a moment to pause and assess what the hell is going on. I have been in a lot of firefights before, but I had never been in one like that.

I couldn't believe it when I opened my rucksack: I was already halfway through my grenades—I only had about twenty-five left. Not in my wildest dreams did I think I would have to ration grenades with as many as I had brought, but now I am already worried I will run out. The story is the same everywhere in our convoy. We don't have any more linked ammunition other than what is loaded on the gun in the truck. The rest had been fired into that mountainside.

Three Czech dudes are injured. Two additional Afghans are dead. Two more are badly injured and about to die. One American is full of shrapnel. This is an absolute "oh fuck" moment and we are only thirty minutes into a three-and-a-half-day firefight. And just so we're clear, this battle wasn't a spend-ex (ammo-wasting) or a grenade-throwing party. We weren't wasting ammunition. Everything we did was doctrinally correct. But the enemy kept coming.

It is time to move again. We cannot stay here to refit (garner new supplies and prepare for what's next) because we are still in a kill zone and we know they will regroup. We cannot go backwards because there is no way to easily turn the Jingle trucks around and if even if we could, we'd be failing in our mission, so we have to push on through the valley. I can't tell you how many truck drivers we lost. Some were killed in the firefight. Others melted into the woods with the Taliban. Others simply fled on foot back the way we had come. Some of the remaining drivers do not want to continue forward. Arguments break out. Men are screaming at us and each other in dialects I do not speak. Finally, it takes Team Sergeants pulling out service pistols and telling guys to get in the fucking trucks or they are going to die here anyway to get this clown car cavalcade moving again. But that didn't mean they stayed. We had drivers literally leap from moving vehicles as we started again and disappear before we could react. More trucks had to be offloaded and more Jingle trucks got thrown off the mountain by our wrecker.

As the sun goes down, the situation gets more dire. We cannot keep moving because the Jingle trucks do not have night vision and we are skirting a dangerous ravine along a mountain. So, we are sitting ducks. We don't know this land. They do. Shittier than that, though, we are dangerously low on ammo. My rifle has nothing left. It is now a very expensive baseball bat. We barely have any linked ammo left on the machine guns. The SAWs are dry except for a canister or two floating around. I hug my service pistol because that's all I have left to defend myself. I use the scope on my sniper rifle to try to find a bad guy with an AK so I can go kill him and grab it. I am that desperate.

I am scared. It isn't the kind of scared I felt when I was sprinting to the downed truck to help Irish save the wounded Afghans. That's the "watching a horror movie and jerk from a sudden shock" variety of fear.

This version is much worse. I am watching my options disappear. My choices are being taken from me, and I do not get a vote as to what is going to happen next. If they attack full force right now, we are going to die. I know it. We just do not have the juice to stave them off. So, I constantly anticipate that attack. It is a helpless kind of fear, like a dream where you just can't move fast enough or you're frozen in place and can't move at all. It is like those moments surfing where you bite off more than you can chew as you chase the perfect wave, and you get flipped and caught in the undertow. The fun moment unexpectedly turns to panic as the wave keeps crushing you further and further down. You can't breathe. You can't see. The board hits you as you tumble. You have no control, and you desperately want to see the sun again and take one more good, solid breath. But you don't know if it's coming.

But there is one little bastard amongst us that seemed to show no fear. He doesn't give a single fuck. The least imposing guy in our entire convoy is a tiny, little pasty white Air Force guy who held the job title of JTAC, who we'll call Gizmo. JTAC stands for Joint Terminal Attack Controller and they are a new toy in the Air Force arsenal, having only been stood up a few years earlier. JTACs are basically forward air controllers on crack. They can rain death on the enemy from any aircraft, helicopter, naval gunship, field artillery piece, catapult, ballista, you name it. If it can fire a projectile through the air and hit a target on the ground, these guys can call for it and make sure it hits the right place at the right time. I'd been around a few of them over the last couple of years and they were worth their weight in gold, and then some.

But I had never seen anything like Gizmo. I watch him holding three different radios and he is going from one to the other speaking tongues. His mouth is moving and I keep expecting English to come out, but instead it is just math, numbers, equations, and angles. It is like they plugged him into the Matrix and while the rest of us are busy dealing with reality, he is just seeing floating binary code. He makes those planes sing. All night long, the AC-130, which is basically a floating monster gun equipped with a 25mm cannon, a 40mm cannon, and a 105mm freaking howitzer cannon, makes gun runs for us. They come on station and keep a continuous steel rain going on the valley until they go red on ammo, then they fly back to reload and come right back on station and do it all again.

Every time I hear those engines above us, it is like being wrapped in a warm blanket. I know we have angels of death looking out for us. And every time they fly away, my stomach is an empty pit. Will they be back in time?

In the absolute middle of the night, we have a very close call. The AC-130 let us know they were red on ammo and are heading back, but as they are leaving they pick up 200 enemy moving in our direction on their thermals. Gizmo the JTAC hopped on the radio and convinces them to head out and then come back like they are a new aircraft and run the guns empty in a show of force. It does the fucking trick and holds the bad guys frozen in place. No one wants to fuck with Spooky. The AC-130 is such a badass airframe that while it has been updated many times over the years, it's basically the same plane that was running missions in Vietnam. I always knew it was good. We'd used them before. But now I fucking love them. I love how they look. I love their crazy pilots. I love the JTACs that call them. They are the absolute shit.

Finally, after I don't know how many gun runs, the sun starts to peek over the horizon, and that's when I fully understood what we had been up against the night before, and the carnage that our JTAC had caused.

If you've seen *Braveheart* or *Game of Thrones*, you can picture that moment after the battles where there is a sea of humanity lying on the ground: some dead, some wounded, some pretending to be dead to avoid being slain. And there's always that throwaway shot of the plungers walking the lines of bodies and stabbing anyone that didn't look quite dead enough to make sure they wouldn't live to fight another day. As the only sniper, today this is my job. It is a terrible job I do not want. We had barely lived through the night, and we couldn't afford to have these guys reengage us as we drove past, so the RG used its thermals to identify bodies that still had heat signatures and they dialed me in. I'd get on target with my scope and if that body had a weapon, I put a round through it. Young or old, it didn't matter. If they had a gun, they died.

I am very proud of being a sniper. I'm proud of the training I put myself through to be able to do what I do. I'm proud of our profession. We save a lot of lives, and I'm convinced I saved American and Czech lives that day, but there's something most people don't understand about our job. Our kills are up close and personal, even though we're often very far away. We see their last breath through that scope. We see their faces. It's one thing to kill a man who is actively shooting at you, or even to shoot a leader responsible for atrocities. I never lost any sleep about those shots. But these shots are awful. There is no satisfaction. There is no rush of knowing you quieted the gun that was hunting for American lives. This is just killing. With every trigger pull, I lose a little bit more of my soul. But the target calls kept coming from the RG and I have a responsibility to keep my team safe.

I shot for two hours.

It haunts me still. I wish I could forget everything that happened through that scope.

I hope every one of those people I killed meant to kill me too, but I will never know that. When you're in Afghanistan you don't know who is good and who is bad. *Who is an insurgent? Who is a villager? How do I identify a combatant?*

One of my favorite scenes in any movie is from the film *13 Hours* about the fight in Benghazi. The CIA contractors head over to the ambassador's house, which had been overrun by insurgents. As they come out of the house, there are people pouring out of the bushes with guns, but there are just as many friendly faces waving at them. And they all look the same. There is no rhyme or reason to it. There are no uniforms. There isn't a guy speaking German wearing a swastika on his arm. Everyone looks like regular people, scared out of their minds.

So, this whole thing is hard as hell. The sun is coming up and the battlefield is clouded, and I mean that emotionally and physically. It's gray and you see movement, but is that a grandpa trying to recover his son who was fighting or an Iranian fighter? You don't know, but you have to make the call over and over again to the best of your ability. I try hard to get it right, but I know it isn't likely that I do every time.

When people say war is hell, they mean *this* moment. Half of my friends are covered in their own blood. Some of us are dead. I still have some-one else's shit and bile running down my chest and pants. My head is pounding from overpressure sickness, an adrenaline dump, and dehy-dration. The exhaust that was coming off the HMMWV all night as I camped underneath it trying to maintain security probably added to my throbbing head as well. Just for good measure, my stomach decides it is fucked, and I am trying like hell not to add my own shit to the mixture of human fluids already covering me. And we're surrounded. And we want to live.

I want to live.

I squeeze the trigger the last time overlooking the Valley of Death. There are no more heat signatures, and it is light enough for the Jingle trucks to start moving.

I will give the Taliban props—there is almost no collateral damage to the drivers. This is either because the drivers have an impeccable abil-ity to hide where we Americans and Czechs do not, or because they are Taliban themselves. I'll let you decide. The trucks, however, are in bad shape. We are down to thirty or so fully functional trucks from our original eighty and they are cross-loaded to the gills with supplies. But the remaining drivers do not want to move. They refuse. Some even seem smug. *Fuck that.*

We go vehicle to vehicle by gunpoint and tell them to get in the trucks and drive. We do not care if they are scared. We do not care if they are plotting to kill us. If they do not move, we were all going to die in place. A few of them get roughed up. For once, it isn't me doing the fighting.

The wrecker, the vehicle that had kept us moving as the drivers had fled or sabotaged us throughout this journey, throws some thirty-odd vehicles off the mountain that morning. It does so much work that it dies. Our convoy is now less than half its original size.

The next day is mostly a blur. I definitely lost a lot of time due to my concussion, but there are keystone moments that stay with me. Our resupply almost brings me to tears. I grab as much 5.56 as I can carry and I refill my rucksack full of grenades. Then we overload the vehicles with .50 cal, 40mm grenades, and 7.62.

My personal condition deteriorated, limiting my effectiveness. My massive headache got worse, my vision got blurry, my diarrhea came full force, and vertigo decided to join the party. My hands are shaking so badly that I cannot figure out how to get the rounds for my SR straight enough to get them into the magazines.

We lose more men. Two MEDEVACs come today, at least. A round hits my vehicle about six inches from my head, almost killing me.

The battle rages on. I burn so much ammo that by midday the limitless rounds we had packed our vehicles with are almost depleted. When I'm not fighting, I spend the day on the radio coordinating with the command, our trusty JTAC Gizmo, and the Czechs. I send Land Cruisers into the woods repeatedly to scout the high ground before the main element moves through. We receive a second ammo resupply.

What sticks out most, though, is that one of us would see a target and call out distance, description, and direction, and then everyone would lock in and shoot. We did this all day. It becomes so repetitive it feels like folding a pile of shirts or pairing a pile of socks. It isn't cognitive thought anymore. I am robotically going through the motions of eliminating the enemy. So, all of that stays with me, but that day remains blurry to me compared to the first day and the days that follow. I'll leave it to you guys to decide if that is because of blood filling my brain, a lack of sleep, or some psychological issue associated with everything around me being the absolute fucking worst.

Things start to get clearer for me toward the end of that second day of combat, and as night is closing in on us, we desperately do not want a repeat of the previous night. First, the Team Sergeant builds a clear geometric perimeter now that we have enough room to set one up. The gun trucks are at the strong points and the movement vehicles are in an even line. He isn't fucking around with the truck drivers either. After the bullshit from earlier in the day, coupled with watching a couple of these guys low-key try to do a pace count from a large hilltop to our vehicle position and then call that in on a cell phone they weren't supposed to have, when it came time to button down for the night, the drivers were told not to leave their vehicles for any reason or they would be shot, and he meant it. If they need to piss, they are allowed to roll down the window and stick their dick out, but if they crack those doors for any reason, as far as we are concerned, they are Taliban.

But even a bigger issue than the rent-a-Taliban we have with us is that we know we cannot weather another night like last night. We radio command and call "Broken Arrow." Broken Arrow means that ground units are under threat of imminent attack and need air support on station. We need the birds running all night long. Words are not minced. "This isn't just a TIC [troops in contact]. If you don't send us everything you have, and keep it running all night, we're all going to be dead in the morning."

And they do, thank God. As the sun disappears, I slide on my night vision and watch that Spooky AC-130 shoot. It is melodic, peaceful, and magical. It almost feels like I am not actually here—like I am a kid sitting with my parents on a blanket looking up at fireworks on the Fourth of July. It is a soothing lullaby, and my eyes feel heavy as these glorious guardian angels hammer the Taliban and the Iranians that want to kill us all night long. I don't want to sleep, but it's like when your laptop is on 3 percent and it tells you that you have fifteen more minutes of computing, but then it says "go fuck yourself" and just shuts off. After fifty-seven hours of nonstop combat, my brain tells me to go fuck myself, and I finally pass out.

When I wake up three or four hours later, I realize I had unconsciously burrowed eight-to-ten inches into the ground I was lying on, which was made up of dirt and light gravel. I don't know if I had some crazy dream, or if I subconsciously cast my mind back to basic training where we dug fighting positions all the time, or what. I don't remember doing it, but I woke up in a perfect dirt hole. "Unconscious me" is probably a better soldier than "conscious me."

I also woke up to a fresh rucksack full of grenades, which filled me with absolute joy. One of the SF guys must have hooked me up.

I know how dark that sounds, but when everything is bad, you have to cling to the little things. Thankfully, there is also a big thing. The birds had killed 400 insurgents that night. Up until this point, the Taliban command and control had been exquisite. They had remained a step ahead of us the entire time, and we had paid for it in blood. Last night, they had been on their way to the next village to regroup and reinforce so they could finish the job of taking us out completely. Well, the AC-130s took their bowl of Cheerios and absolutely filled it with piss.

As the sunrise hit us and beams of light start strutting across the valley, I take a deep breath. The RG rolls up and it is time for me to be the plunger again. Luckily, though, the AC-130 crew had been very thorough, I don't have to fire a single round. There is nothing alive in that valley. Relief washes over me and I think I almost smile. I have already given up enough of my soul on this mission. I tell myself that today is going to be a much better day.

I will be proven wrong.

I will not realize it for three hours, though. The sharp edges of the mountains are now in the distance, and the terrain opens way up. We are moving through a long stretch of rolling hills, and there is a nice breeze running through the vehicle. A small part of all of us thought that maybe the worst is over and we might be able to get to FOB Anaconda without too much trouble. They lost 400 fighters to AC-130s last night and hundreds more the night before. Today has to be easier. How much more could they have? Plus, an ODA from Anaconda is pushing our way and will be linking up with us soon, increasing our lethality by about 30 percent. Yes, I tell myself, today will be easier.

As we hit the third hour, I can see a village about ten miles in the distance. Without the mountains in the way, visibility is crystal clear and the naked eye can spot a hell of a lot at a great distance. But we have a lot more than the naked eye; we have some cutting-edge optics available, and immediately begin to scan the town as we drive. We spot a building with several military-aged men looking in our general direction and talking on radios. My heart sinks, but I hold out a little hope. Maybe they are just a general watch. After all, Afghanistan is tribal. Their presence doesn't necessarily mean the worst.

Mortars explode about 600 meters away from us. *Well, so much for the idea of them being fucking friendly.* That's the bad news. The good news is our indirect fire is light-years better than theirs. We start dropping some mortars of our own, while Gizmo calls in for the big guns: 155mm howitzers and CAS (close air support), which is a combination of Apaches and AC-130s. We use our eye-in-the-sky optics to identify them, laze the target giving us an exact grid coordinate, and watch entire compounds get vaporized from miles away. You know how earlier I told you how hard it was to pull the trigger looking through the optics? This is not that. There is glee every time our boys and girls behind the guns or in the aircraft light these fuckers up. Every building they destroy marks a bunch more dickheads that I do not have to deal with, and I'm a big fan of not having people try to kill me and my friends.

But the main building they are fighting from is a large modern school that we had built for them. It is clearly their headquarters. I want it blown up, but the Team Leader refuses. I'm sure he has excellent officer reasons for not wanting to do so. I'm sure it is a pivotal part of "winning hearts and minds" on some fucking PowerPoint slide in some TOC somewhere. I'm sure that PowerPoint was converted into a division PowerPoint and that PowerPoint ended up in the Pentagon and then on the President's desk. I'm sure a whole bunch of people who have no idea what it is actually like on the fucking ground are patting themselves on the back telling each other that they have hit the goal of building 347 schools in Afghanistan and that the mission is being accomplished, and that we are winning. But I don't have any of those guys to yell at. I have this poor Captain who probably feels the same way I do and has his hands tied behind his back, but I don't care, because he is here and they aren't. I am insubordinate as fuck and tell him he is a pussy for not doing it. I add a bunch more colorful insults about his height, weight, hair color, and anything else I can think of and close it all out by basically telling him he is prioritizing officer bullshit over his men. I can tell you that 99 percent of him doesn't deserve it, but I also wish he would just blow off whatever orders he has and make the call to demolish that thing, because it is the sturdiest, most bullet-resistant, hardest-to-breach building in the entire town, so it's still 1 percent his fault.

To his credit, he doesn't seem to hold a grudge. He tells me to fuck off and we move on. My dad reminds me this reaction is the mark of a good leader. But I think a good leader would have listened to me and blown up the damn school.

At this point we are already supposed to be linked up with the ODA from Anaconda, but they have essentially been living through our situation in reverse, so we start fighting in their direction so we can combine into Special Forces Voltron. Now we're hearing all their radio traffic and we know they're in contact, plus as we get closer, the gunshots are echoing through the valley. I'm riding shotgun in a Czech truck, and then rounds start flying our way. The Taliban have a PKM machine gun nest running out of a cave firing at them. The PKM machine gun is okay, but compared to what we have available, it sucks, so they have good standoff and unless the enemy gets lucky, they are in a pretty good spot. At this point, my ammo is low and I need weapons and their trucks are loaded with them! While the Czech truck I'm on is still moving, I throw the door open and start sprinting toward them. Later they will tell me it was one of the funniest and most surreal moments of the deployment. "We saw these Czech Land Rovers pulling up and then on the horizon a wire-haired gorilla covered in blood and wearing an American uniform came sprinting at us. Do we shoot or do we let the beast get closer?"

They obviously don't shoot me. I am sprinting so hard I literally run into their vehicle. Before my ricochet off the three tons of metal truck is complete, I am pulling two AT4 rocket launchers and a Carl Gustaf recoilless rifle off of it. One of the shocked dudes inside the truck is a guy I knew from the Q Course. It is nice to see a friendly face! "Tim, what the fuck are you doing here, man?" he asks me with a surprised look painted across his face. "No time to talk," I respond. "I need this Gustaf."

I now have three missile launchers. Between these weapons, the AT4 is by far the more accurate one. The Gustaf has never been considered "precise." In fact, it's a pretty common joke that once you fire the Gustaf you really have no fucking clue where it is going to land. So being the Special Forces elite weapons sergeant slash tier one sniper that I am, I grab the first AT4 and aim it at the cave. The adult professional soldier in me wants to take out the threat and complete the mission, but the child slash meathead in me desperately wants to blow this cave up. War is the worst, but if you're gonna do it, you might as well leave with some amazing stories.

So, no shit, there I was: After leaping from a moving gun truck, sprinting through PKM machine gun fire like Carl Lewis, bouncing off a vehicle, and majestically pulling an AT4 off the side of it in a nanosecond, I am about to save the day for the Czechs and two ODAs, like the hero that I am as the music grows to a crescendo. I fire. The AT4 rocket bounces off the entrance of the cave. Okay, this is going to be less majestic than originally planned, but as long as the mission is completed, I'm still the man. I grab the second AT4. I spend more time aiming but am also acutely aware I now have the Czechs and two ODAs watching me. I fire. Once again, I bounce the rocket off the edge of the cave. By now my buddy from the Q Course has exited the vehicle. He picks up the Gustaf, that inaccurate, never-hits-the-same-place-twice-might-as-well-shoot-blindfolded weapon, and casually fires it at the cave. Dude, it might as well have been Luke Skywalker shutting off his targeting computer and blowing up the Death Star. Perfect goddamn shot. So, my hero story is now a "laugh at Tim" story. I think those AT4s were faulty.

When the laughing subsides, it becomes obvious that we need to take this village. They have overwatch over the entire road for miles. If we try to get those Jingle trucks through here, they are going to get eaten up and we are going to take a lot of casualties. We stage the Jingle trucks out of gun range in a "ready to go when the village is clear" position. The Czechs are going to provide security on the trucks and take care of anyone that squirts out of the village as the two ODAs plus me move in. They are super pissed about this because they want to kick ass too. The problem is we haven't worked with them long enough and door-to-door fighting is a lot more complex. With different tactics, techniques, and procedures (TTP) plus a language barrier, having us both running around in there is going to increase the chance of friendly fire casualties. We don't need that on top of everything else. They understand it and agree with it, but they don't like it. I love that about them. They are warriors through and through.

———————

It's hard for me to explain the feeling of linking up with the ODA from Anaconda and getting ready to go. The last three days shredded us. We do not feel like badasses. We do not feel elite. Any semblance of believing we are invincible like I did in Iraq is gone and will never return. We feel like our body armor won't stop bullets. Our confidence has crumbled. But we aren't thirteen Green Berets doing the best they can with a bad situation anymore. We are twenty-five pissed-off Green Berets and it is time to get ours. It is *our* turn to deliver some pain—to show these fucking Iranians what we can do. They'd beaten our asses for sixty hours. It is time to kick the shit out of these assholes.

The truck-side briefing is aggressive. The word "fuck" is used often, and with great passion, and the mission is clear: By no means are we going to deviate from our rules of engagement, but we are going to push that ROE to the absolute limit. At this point, we know the assault line that ambushed us on our way here has retreated into this town. Our planes watched them. We also know that no one has left, so the bastards are in there. We have ammo. We finally have numbers. These guys have been killing us for days. To use a sports analogy, we're on the eight yard line. No first downs possible. We have four downs to bang it in or we lose the game. Green Berets don't like to lose.

Here comes the violence.

Moving toward that village, I am scared and I am angry—the worst emotions to have when you know a brutal fight is coming. When I fought MMA, I always did my best when I was emotionless, when I was just in the moment, without judgment, simply executing my game plan. War is the same. You want to be cold and calculating. You want to do the right things because they're the right things. That dispassionate approach, even while someone is trying to kill you, is one of the reasons we are so damn good at what we do. But I am not that right now. I am pissed and I don't care, and that creates risk. You see, door-to-door is an extremely different fight than the valley fight we had experienced thus far. It's closer. It's faster. There are more distractions. You can see and smell everything. You're not shooting at guys in the distance; you're shooting at them in their living rooms. It's extremely personal. To add to the stress and complexity of the situation, this village is not empty. We can see cows and chickens. Civilians are here, and that makes it harder. The patriarchs of the family take the most risk to protect the family, so grandpa is the one sticking his head out the window to scout. They know they are the most expendable because they cannot work anymore. But if grandpa is setting me up to die, then grandpa can go to hell right along with his terrorist son and Iranian best friend.

This is dark. This is scorched-earth shit. I don't just want to kill these guys. I want to salt their fields so nothing will ever grow again and throw goats down their wells so the water is never drinkable. I want them gone. If shots are coming at me from a house, then everything in the house is going to be dead. The fighter, the donkey, the chicken, the cat, everything. Our timeline is shortened too. The natural human pause between assessing the threat and pulling the trigger to take another human's life is now at the absolute minimum amount. If you haven't been in it, you can't understand. Believe me: I know how dark it sounds. But think about watching a video where a cop is arresting someone and everything is fine, and then the criminal goes for his gun. There's that split second where the cop realizes this just went from a regular day to a fight for his life. He gets faster, meaner, more brutal. This is the same. I want to hurt everything that wants to hurt me and my brothers around me.

In a building-to-building fight, you can't leave any stone unturned. You have to know, have to be abso-fucking-lutely sure there is no one behind you, because that is how you die. When people think about the great urban battles—the Battle of the Bulge, Ramadi, Fallujah—this is an area that is never considered. You don't see it in film. It isn't spoken about. But it's what makes this hard. If we hit a building but don't keep the buildings we already cleared secure, or we miss someone that was hiding in an attic or under the house, they can either shoot us in the back or create a new strongpoint behind us, and then we have to clear everything all over again. We do not want to do that. To clear a town properly takes a lot of time. We don't have any of that either. Our Jingle trucks are on the road. We don't want another night outside the wire. That means we have to go hard and fast.

In a perfect world, we could have fought this fight like Floyd Mayweather—smart and calculating with great defense until we found our moments to strike. Instead, we are forced to Mike Tyson this bitch. Remember Tyson in his prime? He was a raging bull, moving forward with lightning-fast hips and power. When his momentum was going forward, he was unstoppable. People cowered and hid, backing up the whole time, until he finally connected, and it was over. His opponents beat themselves because they didn't want to get in the way of the juggernaut.

That is us. We aren't throwing flashbangs into buildings. We are throwing grenades. We throw smoke in between buildings to hide our movement, but as we are moving to the next building, the RG is lighting it up with 40mm grenades or machine gun fire. We are punching holes in buildings before we arrive at them, then blowing them up from the inside with grenades, then cramming guys into the door right after the explosion to take out any fighters that are still moving.

Even as we flow from building to building fast as hell, we're still missing out on any major resistance, which puts me on massive edge. I know we are going to have a fight. I just don't know when. Another thing that makes this hard is the structure of the buildings gives them more time than if this were in the States, or Europe, or really anywhere that isn't the Middle East. The walls here are built in a really rudimentary fashion. They don't have a lot of structural support like our homes do in the way of wood or metal. Instead, they take that brown dirt and combine it with rock and water and create an ugly stucco-style concrete. Because there is no support structure other than this earth mixture, they need to pile this on to support the weight of the roof and to keep it from breaking down over time, so the walls are about two feet thick. Two feet of concrete is tough. It even takes the .50 cal a long time to get through that. Our small arms just bounce off it. So even with our shock and awe, they know that when we start hitting a building it is their time to bail, which keeps their core element a slight step ahead of us.

I finish clearing a building to no avail, and the RG-33 MRAP moves up to support our move to the next building. As soon as it moves, the RG starts taking fire. We assume it was from the next building and run up on it, getting ready to breach.

Ginginator, the medic who had spent six hours trying to save the Afghan wounded during our first battle, is on the gun and he is screaming he can see tons of guys squirting out of the building we are stacked on, heading into the next compound. Nevertheless, we still have to clear the building. We cannot assume they all fled. In fact, I expect a fight. As I move through it, I feel like every room has death waiting for me. I expect the guy in the prone, lying in wait to kill the first guy through the door. I expect the guy who has cut a hole in the ceiling so he can shoot me in the face from up above. I am stressed out of my mind. The adrenaline is gone and I am now sweating acid. You can tell when you get there, because you reek of ammonia.

Nothing. The building is empty. Fear and anxiety eat away at all of us as we move forward. The relative emptiness of these buildings, coupled with the size of the force we know was here, foreshadows a reckoning we both desperately want and dread.

We start tactically moving to the compound Ginginator saw them enter. Mike Goble and I are at the front. There are two approaches: a large wooden door that can fit the RG, and a smaller gardener's door hidden away to the right. My first instinct is to hit the large door so we can get the RG through, but Mike G motions toward the smaller door. Six in one, half dozen in the other, so we turn to approach the small door.

We are three paces from the entrance to the large door we had just turned away from when the door starts splintering from the thousands of rounds getting pumped through it from a PK machine gun on the other end. Once again, I missed death by an inch. If Mike G had chosen the big door (or simply had no preference), we'd be dead. If we had been a little slower, we'd be dead. But we aren't and now we have to do something with it. The PK is unloading on the RG, and while the rounds are bouncing off of it, we don't know what else they have in there. The RG is a sitting duck. Game time players that they are, though, the boys in the RG do not retreat. They start ramming the door with the vehicle while they are getting shot at. With every hit the giant wooden door splinters some more and groans at the edges. The whole ground shakes. And by being the crazy sonofabitches they are, those boys give us a gift.

You see, when a twenty-two-ton vehicle starts ramming your wall, it gets all of your attention. Hell, it has my attention. Little splinters from the door float in the air and are being pushed around from the force of the rounds coming through it, as well as the force of the vehicle hitting it. It almost looks like it is snowing. I worry I need to be careful not to get any of it in my eyes, as if that is the biggest problem I have. But the threat to my vision from floating snow splinters aside, when the bad guys are all looking at the big mean vehicle with the grenade launcher on it, they don't notice the two Green Berets that quietly sneak to the gardener's door. My hand grabs the knob. Mike G is pointing his rifle at the door. I open it.

Nothing. I stick my head around the corner quickly and retreat. Empty. I check again, a little longer. I scan right and left. The alley is barren of any people, but I can see the barrel of the PKM sticking out of a small window in the courtyard twenty-five meters away. The RG is still smashing into the wooden gate, but the door will not give, and the rounds are pouring out of the PKM into the vehicle. It's only a matter of time before we start getting killed. I need to take out that gun.

I reach for one of my frag grenades, pull the pin, and take aim at the tiny window twenty-to-twenty-five meters away. If this wasn't combat, my friends would be laughing at me at this moment. You see, I suck at throwing. I mean, *really* suck. Yes, I'm a professional athlete. Yes, I can do all measures of physical activity at a level that most people can't fathom. But you know what I never did growing up? Ball sports. It was so bad that when I joined the Special Forces and had to throw something to one of my teammates, I believe a roll of 100 mph tape (green duct tape), they were so horrified that they began instituting football-throwing practice as part of my training regimen. I might be the only SF guy ever that as a new guy, in addition to the normal tasks of shooting, planning, and physical fitness, had to work on my spiral.

But here I am, grenade in hand, with my team counting on me, and I launch it. And it is perfect. It isn't a lob that lazily floats into the window. It doesn't bounce in. It is a fucking Aaron Rodgers laser that flies from my hand and connects directly to that window. It is the best throw I ever made. In a weird, fucked-up way, it is one of the happiest moments of my life.

A grenade going off in the movies is very different from what happens in real life. It's not this giant fireball. It's not dramatic. It's a hollow thud. It's that late-night sound of opening the refrigerator to see what's in there, and the watermelon rolls out and hits the ground. That's all a grenade is after you throw it. A little hollow pop. And after you hear that pop, you either want to hear nothing, or you want to hear men screaming. You do not want to hear women or children scream. You absolutely do not want to hear that. Yet that's what I hear.

My soul churns inside. The helplessness tears me apart. I want to take that fucking grenade back so badly. I can hear kids screaming. They don't understand why this is happening to them. I can hear mothers screaming—mothers that are punctured by fragments of metal and can barely hold air in their lungs. Their screams are the sounds only a parent can understand—of desperately wanting to help your children but not knowing what to do to help them, or in some cases, knowing it is too late to help them. Every scream tears me apart. After everything I have been through, I thought my soul was dead. I was as hollow as the thud of that grenade. I thought there was nothing left. It all comes flooding back. I am a raw nerve of emotion, and each sound coming from that room burns me worse than anything that has ever happened to me. Shame, horror, and guilt at what I have just done envelops me. I have seen this before in others as an EMT. The drunk drivers that had killed someone. They sat there on those street corners crying, trying to sort out in their heads the disparity between who they thought they were—

a decent person—with what they had just done. But I cannot stop and cry. I have to move.

Mike G and I flow into the courtyard. With the PKM out of commission, the RG gets more aggressive, and I see the wall start tumbling down. Everything is moving fast and Mike G and I do not want to lose momentum. I flow right. Mike flows left. This mission never would have happened in Iraq and goes against doctrine in any unit. In Iraq we had a whole company of CIF working together to clear buildings. A normal infantry unit would have at least four on a door, followed by another fire team right behind them at a minimum, with another squad or platoon in support. We have a whole compound to clear and it is me and Mike G—that's it.

When I hit the first doorway, I instantly see food everywhere. It's a kitchen. I can smell the tea kettle with the clove tea that everyone here drinks. It has just been made. I can smell it right now as I write this. It's amazing how smell stays with you. You can forget details and images, specific words and conversations, but the smell of a moment is forever.

Curry, clove. The screams are louder now and I move toward them. I follow a hallway to a 90 degree turn, and as I hit the edge of that corner I get the first traces of the smoke and dust from the grenade. At this point, I'm in this room somewhere between thirty-to-sixty seconds from the moment it exploded, and the scene is awful. It is worse than I expected. When you throw a grenade into a building that has walls two feet thick, all that overpressure has nowhere to go. This isn't America where the pressure will break the drywall or blow the door off. Their bodies took the brunt of it. There are two women, six kids, and an old man inside. I am once again that kid standing on the street looking at a crashed church van, so desperately wanting to help, but not knowing where to start. Except this time, in addition to being the guy who so desperately wants to fix it all, I am also the guy who crashed the van. I scream for Ginginator to come in and help. Why the fuck isn't he in here? Because there is no reason for him to be here, but I need this fixed. I cannot have this on my ledger. They have to be okay.

He screams at me to come back and man the gun because he is running the grenade launcher and cannot abandon his post. I take one last look at the room. It is so dark. The floors are dirt and dust floats in the air. I am standing in a real-life nightmare, a horror film. The smell of death, emptied bowels, and vomit hangs in the air. The hot machine gun is right there. Someone was shooting it, goddamnit! Who? The old man? One of the women? Someone else? Everyone that can scream is screaming. Some aren't. They aren't all going to make it. I did this.

I am the bad guy.

I cannot do anything about any of that now. I don't know what to do. It has been so long since I didn't know what to do. I've been so confident for so long, and now I just want help. All I can do is sprint out to the truck to man the gun so that Ginginator can get in this room.

In a daze, I get to the vehicle. Ginginator hurdles out of it at full speed, med bag in tow. I drop into the gunner's seat. It's all so familiar. Why is this so familiar? Forty hours of mandatory CROWS training. I know this system cold. I flip to thermals to check out the next building and make sure Mike G and Ginginator are safe. As I do, I see the dudes that were just in this building squirting out the back of it and running to the next one. I do not pause. Not for one second.

I laze the running dickheads and my grenade launcher automatically makes the angle adjustments. I make sure to aim where they will be in four seconds based on their running trajectory just like I had learned in class and let loose with the Mark 19 grenade launcher. I don't know how many grenades I have loaded in this thing, but I decide that every one of them is going to land on these three dudes. I hold the trigger until I hear the gun run dry. I switch to normal sights to confirm the kill. All three are lying strewn apart on the ground, their bodies separated into pieces.

I wanted it to feel better when I killed these guys—these pieces of human garbage who used women and children as a shield. I desperately want my pain to be washed away, but it isn't. This isn't like the movies, where vengeance is the cure. Reality is awful. The pain of what I have done is overwhelming, so I descend into an emotional void. There is no Hollywood moment of vengeance and them getting what they deserve and me getting my hero moment. The kids are still wounded or dead. These deaths cure nothing. Help nothing.

Now we have a decision to make. We're about half a mile from FOB Anaconda. We still need to get the Jingle trucks to the base, but now we have badly injured women and children that need to be treated. We have to make a tactical decision about whether we start treating these women and children now or go secure the route into the firebase. We still need to get the rest of the supplies to these guys to sustain them for the next six months safely.

We have to complete the mission, but none of us are willing to wait on treating these casualties, so we opt to separate and accomplish both. Ginginator immediately does triage on site and then takes the most severely wounded ones into the back of the RG. He makes a beeline to the main road into FOB Anaconda. Since the wounded situation restricts our ability to clear the town all the way through, we opt instead to provide supporting cover to keep the Taliban from fighting their way down. We take an up-armored HMMWV with a .50 cal to a hill behind a house on the main road, where we have overwatch over any avenues the approaching enemy could take, and put down supporting fire.

I jump back on my sniper rifle. I am in hunting mode. The .50 cal is manned behind me on the main route, and I am slinking from window to window with my rifle looking for someone to shoot. While we haven't cleared the whole town, we have cleared every building that has the ability to fire on the main road, so we are in a strong position. We have also taken the momentum firmly back, as the second ODA has bounded back into a support-by-fire position with the Czechs, and they are killing anyone that even looks at the trucks the wrong way.

One ODA is a substantial amount of firepower, even though it is only twelve guys. The skill, the weapon systems, and the ability to call for fire or get CAS prioritized all make it an exceptionally lethal force. Now we have two ODAs that are super pissed off, plus a bunch of raging Czech Hercules gods. Our plan has not been perfect, but it has been violent as fuck. We're taught over and over again that a good hasty plan executed violently is far better than a flawless detailed plan executed with hesitation. We hit them hard with absolute violence of action and we destroyed their will to fight. We took them from "kill mode" to "flee and regroup mode." We aggressively took the high ground and key terrain features and cleared everything from that point to the main supply route (MSR). And if you were a man and you were outside, you are probably dead. It was absolute dominance.

But we aren't done yet. Those drivers that have fucked us over and over again on this journey are taking their sweet time getting ready. And this last leg of the trip is the longest part. As the convoy starts creeping by with apparently no motivation to get to safety, I keep wondering if I am going to die now, so close to the end. Will there be a big counterattack? Will there be 400 more men hiding around the corner? Sitting here is torture. I imagine this is what the guys at Dunkirk must have felt. Their lives depended on them being able to move, but they couldn't. They were just stuck there. I just want to get in. I want to rush for the firebase and have a hot meal, and get clean, and know I am fucking safe, if only for a few hours. I just don't want to keep waiting for death to come.

But we cannot abandon the convoy, and if we leave, there is the chance they will get shredded. We cannot risk it. These guys desperately need the food, replacement parts, and ammunition that these Jingle trucks carry. We are not going to cut corners. I hold my post.

It takes five hours to get all of the trucks into Anaconda. It feels like five days.

We started this mission with eighty trucks. Four days later, we arrive with twenty.

I am one of the last guys into FOB Anaconda. As I walk in, emotions roll through me like a hurricane. I am alive. Part of me cannot believe it.

I have also killed. This wasn't Iraq. It wasn't *Call of Duty*. I pulled the trigger many times when I didn't want to. And I had killed kids. Kids the exact age as my daughters. I know what that will mean to me as a parent. I know everyone we touched will hate us forever. Not only had we not won any hearts and minds, but we further entrenched their loathing for us.

I look over at the truck drivers. I hate them, but I also pity them. I doubt very many are on Team USA, but whether they meant to or not, they had completed their mission for us, which makes them an enemy to the Taliban. They cannot stay here. If they do, they will be tortured and killed, so their only option is to head back with the ODA through the same hell we just lived through.

As I am still wrestling with everything that has just happened to me, and the plight of these drivers, the Team Sergeant from the ODA at Anaconda walks up to me and does a health and welfare inspection.

"Show me that you're not bleeding or leaking fluid." "Show me your skin so I can see for sure." "Do you know who you are and what you're doing here?" He then did a roll call of battle roster numbers to see who actually made it here alive and uninjured.

As he moves on to others and his voice trails off into the distance, I lie down on the floor. I don't even remember what floor. It is plywood with dirt on top of it. I cuddle my backpack of grenades and magazines like it is my wife and I sleep for twelve hours. I'm still covered in shit and blood but I don't care. I am alive.

It is the best sleep of my life.

CHAPTER TEN

RETURN TO THE VALLEY OF DEATH

I don't want to move as I begin to feel the light peeking through my eyelids. Everything feels cozy and warm, like I had passed out in a hammock on the beach after one too many beers. My eyes slowly blink open, and I am trying to figure out where I am, and what I am doing. Something stinks. I ignore it. This is too comfortable. I slowly start picking up the sounds of voices and movement. *Why are these people bothering me?*

Ah, that's right. I'm in Afghanistan and that smell is another person's innards and shit baked onto my uniform. That realization doesn't make me move, though. I take another thirty minutes to just lie there and think. My head is pounding, but nowhere near as bad as it had been. It is more of a dull ache now instead of an all-encompassing throbbing. The sleep has done wonders for my concussion.

The camp is bustling. The ODA assigned here is cranking on their priorities of work. Focusing on this sector is a matter of life or death for them until they get relieved. The guys I came in with are doing essentially what I'm doing—recovering. The Jingle truck drivers are off in the corner by themselves, smoking cigarettes and probably talking about how screwed they are.

I dig into my rucksack and pull out my ACUs, which is the worst uniform the Army ever created. It is only effective in two places: hiding out on your grandma's '70s fabric couch undetected, or Afghanistan. Here it makes you nearly invisible because it looks like someone took regular clothes, threw up on them, wiped it off, and then covered them in dust, which is a good approximation of the Afghan terrain.

I trudge into the shower facility and peel off my DCUs. I check the pockets to make sure I didn't leave anything in them and then throw them away. No amount of cleaning is going to get them back to normal, and even if they look washed, I don't want them touching my skin ever again. I make the water as hot as I can handle it, then watch the dirt, blood, shit, and grime that had seeped through my uniform and onto my skin run down my body, onto the cement floor, and down the drain. The shower is like a massage. It helps me get rid of a lot of ache that is still attached to the back of my head. I just rinse for fifteen to twenty minutes under the hot water before I even lather up. I think I just want to be alive for a little while longer and feel some comfort before I embrace what I have to do next.

Fully clean and feeling refreshed (with only a hint of the pain I had felt in my head twelve hours ago), I walk outside. Everything now seems a little clearer with the fog of sleep washed away. My eyes fall back to the ODA running this place. I know some of these guys from my 18X Selection class. It's weird to see them out here, because it seems like yesterday we were all together breaking the rules and trying to graduate. I still picture them like that, but they have all had their own adventures since then, some a lot more harrowing than mine. They are different now—just as I am different.

But it is great to see them. I feel a strong kinship with my 18X brothers. For years, we weren't looked at as equals to the traditional SF guys, so we all have massive chips on our shoulders. The older guys stereotype us as cherries that are physically fit and tough but don't have the tactical knowledge and experience necessary to make good decisions. Unfortunately, there is probably something to that stereotype because we are dying at a significantly disproportionate rate to our traditional counterparts.

Traditional SF guys have to be leaders in regular units before coming to Selection. They are already trained not only to think of themselves, but of others. When you think about other people, you tend to take less risk. You don't want to get anyone killed, and you also realize if you get killed or injured, you put the rest of the team in a bad spot. Most of us in 18 X-Ray land aren't quite there yet. We are young, aggressive, and itching to prove ourselves. To be honest, and this isn't an insult because I love the 75th Ranger Regiment, we probably have more of a Ranger mentality at this point than an SF one. There's a lot of great stuff that comes with that mentality, but a lot of bad stuff too, when instead of a platoon or a company rolling up in support if something bad happens, you only have a dozen guys.

Whether anyone likes it or not, in 2003 we simply do not have enough SF guys to do the mission, so the 18 X-Ray program is needed. And the situation will keep getting worse. From 2012 to 2020 the average age of a Special Forces soldier will drop by seven years. That means the average team will lose eighty-four years of tactical experience in less than a decade.

After grabbing chow, I do my part of contributing to the lack of experience by building my own priorities of work in a vacuum. A seasoned guy would begin by walking into the TOC and getting the details of the current battle plan and posture, the current base security plan, the base emergency plan, and the mortars and fires plan that had been beautifully set up. My priorities are different: I want to climb up in the tower and pink mist some of the guys I know are out there trying to kill us, and then I want to get in a workout.

Before being able to do what I want, the base Team Sergeant gives us a tour. That's when I realize my good friends had played a huge role in setting this place up. The mortar positions had been set up by my friend Af, who had been in this base before the current ODA with ODA 782. I could see his exactness and attention to detail in every range card, laying out the fields of fire for each weapon system. Seeing his signature on this beautiful setup made me proud. He whole-assed this job just like he did everything.

The last part of the tour is the med-shed that I know my buddy Peter built as part of the last rotation. I can almost smell the booze from his constant battle with alcohol as I think of him, but that feeling is cut short the second I walk past the entrance into the larger bay, and I hear the Afghans. There's screaming babies and weeping mothers and it's all because of me. Instantly, the emotions that had been playing in the background come racing out, and I am overwhelmed with crushing sadness once again.

I know in movies they make it seem like we turn our brains off—like we're some kind of killing machines that do not feel. But the opposite is true. The more time you spend in bad situations, the more exposed you become. Think of a normal person with a good, healthy view of life—love, family, friends, empathy—all those positive things. They are your shield. Every bad situation is an arrow in that shield—is a sword blow against that shield. Eventually, if you take enough hits, that shield is splintered or broken, and you're just getting shredded. You're getting cut wide open. Every scream from these kids drives a spike right into me, sending electricity through every nerve ending in my body and jolting my conscience. The pain and guilt is absolutely unbearable.

In my mind, the other guys are all judging me. The reality is that they probably don't notice the change in my demeanor. After a few minutes in the bay, we walk out.

I desperately want to change mindsets and my eyes fixate on the "Eye of Sauron" at the top of the tower in the center of the camp. It is an amazing orb that can accurately magnify and laze distance and direction on anything within two miles of the base in any direction. It's essentially a sniper's dream come true, and I want to use it. Mike G and I grab a .308 and a .408 Cheyenne Tactical or CheyTac and climb up into the tower. Mike is going to be my spotter and I'm behind the gun.

The Eye of Sauron is controlled from the TOC, which is about forty feet below us. Mike is on the radio so we can talk to them. The plan is that they will identify a potential target, then I will get in position for it, while Mike calls out adjustments. Mike won't be able to be behind the glass much, though, because he is more effective as a relay with the

Eye that is acting as a spotter, instead of spotting himself. Comparing the two is kind of the difference between an iPhone camera and an old-school flip phone camera.

We are up there for about thirty minutes scanning the perimeter when I spot a guy with a radio and binos looking at us. He has an AK leaning up against the wall. Mike calls in over the radio and lets them know what we are seeing. I want to know if we have any friendlies in that village. The TOC comes back that they are definitely not friendly, that they have eyes on the target, and that we are absolutely clear to fire. The TOC lazes the target and it comes back 1,460 meters. I dial it in on my rifle, get a perfect sight picture, and gently squeeze off a round. This is the longest shot I've ever taken on a human being.

I miss.

The round splashes about a foot and a half away from his head and hits the wall right above where his AK is leaning. We're far enough away that he hasn't heard the shot yet, only the splash. I chamber another round, about to make an adjustment to take another shot, when the dude leans in to see what just happened to the wall and places his head exactly in front of where the last shot just landed. So I just hold position and squeeze off the second round. Pink mist. A perfect headshot.

Whoever is downstairs on the mic keys it and starts laughing his balls off and says, "That worked out!" Mike asks, "What happened?" "I hit him on the first round," I lie. He pauses for a second and asks, "Why'd you shoot twice, then?" "To be sure," I respond. He seems satisfied with this answer, and we look for the next target.

We stay pretty active up there and hole up in that tower for between four to six hours. Toward the end of our first day there, close to dusk, but still way too early to be operating "under cover of night," two idiots start emplacing IEDs about 900 meters away. I am absolutely flummoxed because that's shockingly close. I mean, it isn't an easy shot necessarily for a dude with normal equipment, but for anyone with any kind of sniper rifle, this is pretty straightforward. I ask Mike if there are any other snipers on this base because it is clear that having Mike and me up here is a wrinkle these clowns hadn't factored into their equation.

At the time I didn't get it, but the real reason they felt safe at 900 meters is that just like with the massive shortage of SF guys that even allowed me to exist in the first place, there is an even greater shortage of snipers. But man, did this place need one. And it especially needs one now.

I drop them both.

Intel says we have a thirty-six-hour window to get some Black Hawks in before the Taliban will be regrouped and back in the area. We are already seeing an increased amount of activity outside the wire. If you're asking yourself why we didn't just land Black Hawks instead of doing our crazy eighty Jingle truck march in the first place, you have to understand that this place is dangerous as hell. Now that I'm at FOB Anaconda, it is even more apparent to me why Black Hawks cannot effectively resupply this location. Landing here is almost impossible without engaging the enemy outside the wire first. There's no airstrip for a C-130 to land. You can't drop supplies via parachute from a C-130 because if you screw up the math or the wind changes, the supplies are going to land somewhere else and then the guys have to fight to them, which adds a whole new level of danger. If they don't get to them in time, then the enemy is getting food, water, and ammo. And every time the guys leave the wire, there is a risk. The base had been nearly overrun three times already. And when I say nearly, I'm not talking about they were outside the fortifications and were stopped. I mean, they climbed the barriers, got inside, and were in hand-to-hand combat with Green Berets. The ODA claimed a couple of guys killed Taliban with rocks in the midst of a life-or-death struggle. Rocks. We're not talking war stories here. We're talking about three times every American inside came close to being killed. When you're talking about bashing a guy's head in with a rock, you're talking about the primal need to survive and nothing else.

And now we have a window. Our nonstop runs with AC-130s, Apaches, artillery, and mortars on the way through the valley bought us a little time. We are going to evacuate the wounded, including the Afghans, and do a short resupply of ammunition and parts. Thus, Mike and I need to keep the bad guys away from the wire as best as we can.

We shoot about twenty times over three days. Even though my head-aches are dull now, I am still losing time, so I don't remember the details of the ones that weren't memorable, but the TOC logs it every time we pull the trigger and they say we engaged about twenty targets. The only reason I know I spent three days in the base is because I worked out three times, and I always remember workouts. Day one I deadlifted engine blocks and then closed with a little CrossFit-style workout. Day two I took a transmission and did modified Olympic-style lifts with it until I was depleted. Day three I sprinted up a hill at the back of the firebase holding two jerry cans full of water for resistance.

I know it sounds weird that I don't remember everyone I killed, but I remember those workouts. It's weird for me now. The closest regular-life thing I can compare this time to is when your wife is about to give birth and you go to the doctor. You get the ultrasound and they are worried about the baby, and now it's go time. You have to make deci-sion after decision about the health of the baby, about the health of your wife, about everyone's safety. Everything moves so fast, and then all of a sudden the baby is coming, and you get hit with this whole new set of emotions. It's healthy, isn't it? It kind of looks like an alien. It's not all cute and chunky like I expected. Is there something wrong with my kid? Then you hold the baby for the first time and it looks at you and the nurse reassures you and your wife that you just created this amazing person, and you're flooded with emotion. A lot just happened. Do you remember it all? Do you remember everything you said? Everything you were asked? Everything you did?

That experience is one of the happiest moments in your life and you still can't recall the details because it was new and overwhelming. Every-thing out here is bad. Still new. Still overwhelming. But bad. Then stack a concussion on top of that.

I think I remember about half of what happened. Mike probably had the other half, but we lost him in Afghanistan a decade later, fighting the same unwinnable war, so I'll never be able to fill in the rest.

After Mike and I finish shooting, we eat again, and I knock out my workout. Afterward, one of the dudes from the TOC lets me know I need to stop by to receive a message. Sergeant Major Flaherty called in on red side comms (two secret systems communicating directly via encrypted connections) and let me know that I am Mike Charlie, or Mission Complete. My piece of this operation is done. The message said I have two options: Option A, which is what he made clear he strongly wants me to do, is to fly back on the Black Hawk because I am a coalition asset, and it is time to do more coalition work. Option B, which he made clear is not his preference, is to head back with the ODA that I fought in with and help them fight their way back. The sergeant that just gave me the message stares at me waiting for me to let him know what I want to do. Instead, I absorb this information, thank him, and leave the TOC.

I walk around for a little while, checking on the ODA that's gearing up to go back out, walking past the Jingle truck drivers jabbering about this and that. I know these guys are going to have to leave soon, even though they all would have preferred a few more days relaxing. Every day we stay here cuts into that one year of food, water, and ammo that we just delivered. Twenty drivers plus a twelve-man ODA plus me, plus the Czechs, plus the Afghan fighters all adds up pretty quickly. Every couple of days of us being here kills about a week and a half of their rations, and no one wants to be making the trip we just made any earlier than needed.

I keep walking and kind of give myself a little tour of the camp, thinking about my time in the tower, picking at the edges of the HESCO bastions with my fingers, wondering how many bullets they have absorbed from the enemy, when my legs carry me to the one place I didn't want to be. I stand frozen, staring at the med-shed. I know I have to go in there and check on the kids again, but I don't want to.

I feel tons of shame. This one horrible moment took away my entire vision of myself. No one is going to be able to convince me that I'm not the bad guy. I'm afraid to face them. I'm afraid to face their moms. I'm terrified to face the Ginginator, the 18D medic who was first on the scene when the grenade went off. He knows more than anyone what I have done to these kids.

I walk in.

The Ginginator walks up to me. I wonder if he will spit in my face.

Instead, he hugs me, and asks me if I am okay. This amazing man is the quintessential medic. He has no anger. No frustration. No judgment. He has spent the last forty-eight hours taking care of these kids, and still has the empathy left to worry about me. That's not what I want. I want him to punch me or slap me in the face or scream at the top of his lungs that I'm a piece of shit. I want penance of some kind. I want to do something that will make it okay. But there isn't anything I can do. Instead, he tells me to hold on a minute so he can go change the gauze in a little girl's stomach where my shrapnel had entered. After about an hour, he asks me if I could hold down the fort while he runs to get some food. Of course, I can.

Almost immediately after he leaves, the tiniest little girl starts moaning and crying. It is the helpless sound that only a little kid can make. She doesn't understand why she is in pain. She doesn't understand what is happening to her. Her mother is handcuffed to a bed on the other side of the med-shed, and she can't provide her comfort. So, I walk over and stroke her head. She quiets just a little, but is still sobbing. Her mother, across the room, is leaning forward, extremely worried. Men are different here. It is considered unmanly for a man to deal with children, especially girls. If a man is touching a child, more often than not, it is not for a good reason. I do my best to assure her I do not mean her daughter any harm as I gently lift this tiny baby into my arms.

I don't know if I've ever moved slower. I pick her up so gently because she is in so much pain and has so many little holes in her that any sudden movement sends her into fits of sobbing. I have not moved this slow since Sniper School. I just don't want to inflict any more pain on this tiny little baby. I want to make her feel better and wash away all her suffering. After what feels like an hour, I finally have her cradled in my arms. I lower myself into one of those tiny metal chairs the Army seems to buy in bulk that no actual adult can fit in and rock her and talk to her. I sing lullabies. I tell her stories. She finally falls asleep and for one moment that beautiful little baby girl looks just like any happy baby I'd ever held. My legs are now numb, but there is no chance that I'm going to risk moving her or placing her down. I want her to stay in this comfortable baby sleep for as long as she can. So I don't move—for six hours. I cramp and I hurt, but it is my mission not to move. Eventually, everything numbs, except my shame.

When she wakes, I know it's time to go. I give her a tiny kiss on the forehead and look at her for one moment more. Then I turn, clap the Ginginator on the shoulder, and walk out.

I know I will never see her again. If I sit with this emotion long enough it will probably rip me apart, but I have to shut down that part of my brain and go back into Green Beret mode. It is time to prep. I'm leaving in the morning, and I will not be doing so on a helicopter like my boss wants me to.

I have to see this mission through. I thought about it all night while holding that little girl. There is a recurring pattern that is forming in my life, and I don't like it. I don't necessarily run from my problems, but I'm definitely not addressing them either. I've always found a path around the thing that scared me, hurt me, or upset me. It is the same unhealthy coping mechanism that I have used ever since Jared died. Fireman problems? Cool, no big deal. I'll become a cop. Screwed up my chances of being a cop because I paintballed a kid? Cool, I'll go Army.

And now my boss has teed up a perfect scenario for me to do that again. I can leave right now, safely, and go on another mission with the Brits or the French and get some cool combat patches from their militaries and pad my résumé. No one would judge me. My boss is literally telling me he would like me to head back. I do not want to go back into that valley. I am scared as hell. But I can't shake that night in Iraq when John McPhee made me fight the entire team after I mouthed off. I said all the right things back then. I said I understood that the team can accomplish anything, but the individual is weak. But I also thought that I had beaten up eight of them, and that even though they all beat me up, no single one of them could have taken me. I let myself cope with the humiliation by protecting my ego. I ignored the reality that no one man, least of all me, is that big of a deal.

I'd heard the sayings before, and I thought I understood them. *You don't leave a man behind. You fight for the man next to you.* But I didn't understand them until this moment.

I'm afraid of letting these guys down. But I am also having an awakening. I am finally taking the red pill that I have refused to swallow for years. I wasn't good enough. I wasn't fast enough. I wasn't a good enough shot. And neither was anyone else around me, even my old boss John. We weren't unstoppable as individuals, but together we had a chance.

I'm not going to be the savior of this mission. Odds are, they won't need me. But one more Green Beret gives them a better chance. So, they are getting it.

No, I don't want to go back to the valley. My headaches are coming back from the added stress, I had just stopped shitting myself, and I am scared. But for the first time ever, I'm doing the thing that I know I *have* to do, even if I don't want to do it. I am going into the valley and people are going to die. I hope it isn't me, but I have made my peace with that too.

I spend this last day getting prepped for the journey to come. I wash my clothes. I clean my guns. I take my first phenomenal totally regular dump in ten days. I work out with my water-filled jerry cans. I get a good night's sleep. I am trying to get my body right for the fight I know is coming.

The sweet smell of JP8 diesel fuel fills the air once again as the Jingle trucks fire up their engines for the journey back. The drivers have a much different attitude now. Whatever their intentions were on the way here, the Taliban now know they are complicit. If they fall behind, they're dead. They also know that we don't give a shit about these trucks, so if they were to try to slow us down by purposely damaging them, we'll just keep on driving. I believe the pre-drive speech actually included the words, "So go ahead, stab a radiator. Good luck with the Taliban." Our mission is to get back, and we are done messing around with these guys.

Personally, I ignore them entirely. They can check their own trucks. Instead, I spend the morning helping Daniel Carlton and Mike K load radios and prepare guns and ammunition. I make sure the headspace and timing on the .50 cal is set properly and prep all of the ammo for the RGs. The CROWS system on the RGs is pretty amazing, but there is one dangerous moment where you are completely exposed: on reload. To make that faster, we unpackage the ammunition from the cans they come in and reroute them in a snake pattern with the feeder round on top. This way, instead of having to be hanging outside of the turret for a long period of time with a big sign that says "Hey, Taliban, shoot me!" you can just pop up, open the gun, slap the feeder round in the chamber, close the gun, and drop back down.

Our crew heading back is very different from the one that came up. The Czechs are staying at Anaconda, so our team is now an ODA of twelve guys, twenty Afghans, twenty Jingle Truck drivers, and me. We have two RGs, one with a .50 cal and one with a Mark 19, and three HMMWVs, each with either an M240 machine gun, a .50 cal machine gun, or an Afghan PKM in the turret. All three have an M249 Squad Automatic Weapon (SAW) mounted on swing arms on both sides. We know we're outnumbered and we know what the enemy is capable of, so we're ready for the fight. This is "ride or die" mode.

The gates open up. I take one last look back at Anaconda. Getting here was one of the happiest moments of my life. I hope I never see this place again. Unlike on the way out, I am not being lulled by the engines. I'm already scanning the horizon past the other vehicles before we even leave the gates.

The Czechs and the ODA that is staying here lead the way on this convoy and they are heading out the same direction that we came in. We're following close behind with the Jingle trucks in tow. The plan is to get the Taliban to bite on the advancing Czechs and engage them on the right, then we'll turn left at the last second and take the upper route to the north. We do this for two reasons. First, we are hoping that they stay engaged with our friends to the south so we can go north unscathed. Second, we want to make sure we don't get flanked and split apart. We're hoping this confuses them. It feels like a great plan. As we head to the intersection, I am definitely feeling like I am slow playing an ace-high full house in poker. I just want that guy with the ace-low to push all in.

To add to my feeling of excitement is the fact that our Joint Operations Center (JOC) left us in a troops in contact (TIC) this entire time, even while we were at Anaconda. This gives us greater access to the ISR (intelligence, surveillance, and reconnaissance) feeds from aircraft and satellites. Now to be clear, this isn't the "President Obama watching the bin Laden raid in real time" level of support. It is more like the occasional snapshot is taken and then relayed to us via radio level of support. The good news is we have a solid idea of how many bad guys are out there and where they are hanging out. The bad news is we now know that no matter which way we go, we are getting into a fight. The other bad news is that we can tell these aren't just Afghan farmers. We are once again dealing with Iranian freedom fighters.

Conventional wisdom tells us not to separate our units, but we are shying away from that and learning a lesson or two from our Czech friends. Split into two groups we have mobility and speed. If they engage to the south, then we should be able to slide right past them to the north. If they engage us to the north, then the Czechs should be able to flank them and we'll tear them apart. We have an AC-130 and two A-10 Thunderbolts on station, so as far as I'm concerned, we're in good shape.

The first inkling of a potential problem is only about fifteen meters outside the gate. As I'm scanning the horizon, I pick up an old man with binos walk out onto his balcony and look at us. He doesn't have a radio or a gun, so I send a warning shot a few feet from his head. Then the most eerie thing happens. He glances over at where the splash happened and shrugs. This isn't even close to the first time this old man has been shot at. He very casually and indifferently looks out at us, stretches a little, and then walks slowly inside. He knows we could have hit him (and that we might still), and he wants to make sure we know he doesn't give a shit.

I have a bad feeling about this now. I am starting to think this fight might kick off at great distances. I adjust my zero from 200 meters to 500 meters.

Within minutes of leaving the gate, we hear the Iranians launch an ambush to the south. I hear the south getting hit with enemy machine gun fire. I instantly recognize that it isn't ours. The caliber is the same, but the cadence is different. The guns sound meaner, harsher. *This is what we wanted.* They've sprung the trap.

That's good news. The ISR told us our route was clear, at least until the first village. The only fighters they've picked up on are to the south. The north only has field workers in the orchard. We still expect an ambush, but we figure it will be a mile or so up the road and will be far weaker now that the main enemy is fighting to the south with the Czechs.

As we take the northern path, something is odd. The buildings are still full. I see men, women, and children, all looking at us. This sends our anxiety spiking through the roof. Our heads are on a swivel as we come upon the orchard we saw in the ISR. I'm three vehicles back from the front of the convoy when I notice a little kid on the roof. He's maybe eight or nine. No threat. I go back to scanning the houses and tree line. Then I hear *clank, clank, clank!* A grenade bounces off the back of our truck and explodes right behind us. I didn't see him do it, but I'm 99 percent sure it was that nine-year-old.

Fuck. My brain is already recalculating a threat assessment and my own personal rules of engagement. It isn't like a lot of true healing has happened within my soul over the past three days. I didn't get a soul transfusion, just a little food and sleep. I don't want to shoot an eighty-year-old man on his balcony, and I sure as shit don't want to shoot a nine-year-old kid on a rooftop, but that's the message these guys are sending to us already. They want everyone to be a combatant.

Fighting an insurgency is brutal. The grenade I threw on the way to Anaconda that killed and injured women and children is the best-case scenario for them. That's months of propaganda to be used against our country and our mission. At no point will they state that I threw the grenade because an Iranian fighter was shooting at us while using women and children as shields. They'll just say that the American invaders tortured, maimed, and killed women and children. We have a lot of evidence that they often would simply kill women and children on their own and then blame it on us for the same effect.

And in SF, you have to take this nuanced look and always weigh the effect of not only collateral damage, but the *appearance* of collateral damage, for its long-standing effects, as your goal is to free the oppressed, to turn the tide, and have the people rise up and fight for themselves. It isn't just to kill the bad guys. That's the easy part. I'm convinced that if a regular infantry unit drove through this town and had been hit by an ambush, they would have killed everyone and anything that moved, and they wouldn't have been wrong. But every bit of collateral damage is going to come back on Anaconda. Every dead man is someone's father, brother, or son. Every dead woman is someone's mother, sister, or daughter. Every time you kill someone, you create five new passionate enemies.

As the clanking grenade explodes off the back of our vehicle, I wish I was having all of those deep and nuanced thoughts—thoughts that separate SF from everyone else—but the truth of the matter is I'm now distracted because all hell has broken loose around me.

A dozen RPGs kick off in our direction in less than ten seconds. Another five or six grenades rain down from the rooftops. Machine guns start to unload on us from fortified nests. Rifles start poking out of every window. We're now in a point-blank gunfight. I can literally reach up and grab some of these rifle barrels.

When I first told my mom about the next part, she just smiled with a smirk of satisfaction. As a devout Christian, she had a prayer chain for me throughout my entire deployment. Sixty women called each other and prayed for me every day, asking God for a bubble of protection around me. I'm not saying she's right. I'm not saying she's wrong. But twelve RPGs—and RPGs aren't quiet with a shooshing sound like they are in the movies—bounce off our vehicles, go over our vehicles, and slide under our vehicles. Twelve. There is also machine gun fire, but it hits no critical targets. Rifle fire is ineffective too. The best way I can describe what is happening is the scene in *Pulp Fiction* when the guy jumps out and fires at John Travolta and Samuel L. Jackson and he misses with every shot. It's impossible that he misses. It is point-blank range. But he still misses. The Taliban shouldn't have missed. Some of us should be dead. But we aren't. So whether it is guardian angels knocking back RPGs with shields and swords or just the absolute fucking luckiest thing that has ever happened to every single guy on this convoy, they miss. Thank God.

And because they miss, they are about to realize who the fuck they are dealing with. They thought we'd try to run when we hit the ambush, but that's not what we do.

You can't explain violence of action. You have to see it. After the initiation of an ambush, it's almost impossible to turn the tide, but we do. I jump off the back of the truck and sprint to the building. Out of the corner of my eye, I see a couple other guys doing the same. They do not expect us to dismount the vehicles. Mike G is on the main gun pumping hundreds of rounds into the side of the building, while I run from window to window dumping grenades inside. I shoot several guys at point-blank range inside of four feet. It is absolute pandemonium. And that's when the A-10s come in. Daniel Carlton and our JTAC Gizmo are swearing at the A-10 pilots on the radio. They are screaming at them to "just fucking do it." What exactly they are screaming "to fucking do," I am about to experience, which is to do two gun runs directly off of our position.

I was scuba diving once in Catalina when I was eighteen or nineteen years old. There were these beautiful orange fish there called the garibaldi. I was following them around and watching the sea otters chase them through this amazing underwater kelp forest. It was so beautiful. Suddenly the sea water felt weird. It felt heavier. Darker. The sea otters and orange fish seemed to have disappeared and the happy kelp forest felt like a dark enchanted one. A pall had just fallen over it. I turned my head and there was a shark. It looked enormous. In reality, it was probably a seven-footer. But that shark serves one singular purpose in nature and the ocean knows it. Its presence changed the entire chemistry of the water.

And suddenly there it is. Death incarnate. The A-10 Thunderbolt, aka the Warthog. And it is coming right at me. Gizmo screwed up and he called this thing on our position, didn't he? After surviving all this bullshit, I'm going to get ripped apart by friendly fire. I see and hear the Vulcan cannon start to spin. And then it lights up the enemy in the most ungodly way I have ever seen. Gizmo didn't screw up. That little bastard called a danger close mission right off the edge of our trucks and those absolute magicians that most people call A-10 "pilots" had the balls and skill to execute it. It feels like the rounds are impacting ten feet away from me. They cannot have been more than thirty feet away. The ground is shaking like a California earthquake.

For you civilians out there that don't understand what this means, that A-10 run was the rough equivalent of Robin Hood shooting the apple off the guy's head. It's not a high-probability move (especially under pressure), but these pilots nailed it and saved our lives.

Anyone who has ever seen an A-10 in action is forever changed. They emit an unbelievable amount of power. Anyone who was ever in a danger close mission with one knows what it is like to almost taste death. Anyone who was ever targeted by an A-10 has nothing to say, because they are very, extremely, unequivocally dead.

From that moment on, the tide completely turns in our favor. As the Taliban try to flee, the Czechs and the other ODA show up with an incredible flanking maneuver. Then the AC-130 arrives on station and is cleaning up any guys who try to squirt into the woods or down the road.

I am living the scene in *Braveheart* when William Wallace goes to pick a fight. That initial English assault with their cavalry is the Taliban ambush. Once they are impaled on the spears, they don't know what to do. They never considered that their charge wouldn't work. So we step over their dead horses, stick pikes through their helmets, and then charge. In my life, before or since, I have never seen a battle turned more quickly or brutally. We go from being totally outnumbered and surprised, to a dominant crushing victory in less than fifteen minutes.

Daniel Carlton apparently receives the first of his three Purple Hearts during this battle when he is hit in the hand and arm with shrapnel from an RPG or an enemy grenade, severing an artery in his hand. Naturally, badass that he is, he chooses to ignore it and keep going.

We continue fighting down the road and up the dominant hill in the area, which takes about two hours. Horrible as it all is, I feel so much pride in our boys, and I mean both the Green Berets and the Czechs. They put on a clinic of violence of action, speed, and communication that should be an example for years to come.

At the top of the hill, we have the dominant position for miles and take the opportunity to regroup, assess casualties, and redistribute ammo. We can still hear the Czech boys and the Anaconda ODA kicking ass in the distance.

After our battle assessment, we identify three casualties. We lost an Afghan fighter. I didn't know the guy too well, but he was a favorite of the ODA that had been training him, and they mourned him heavily. Daniel is the second. He now has a tourniquet on his hand. He wants to stay, but the Ginginator vetoes it. He is getting a MEDEVAC out.

I am the third. Apparently, at some point that I didn't notice, I took a bunch of shrapnel in my neck, shoulder, trap, and arm. The biggest piece of shrapnel bounced off my 5.11 ballistic calculator watch, destroying it, but probably saved my hand from a fate like Daniel's. The most dangerous piece of shrapnel missed my carotid artery by three millimeters, or about the thickness of two pennies stacked on top of each other. Later, I would be told that the right side of my body looked like it got hit with birdshot. Honestly, it isn't a big deal to me, but Mike G is worried. Despite me telling him to shut the fuck up, he goes and tells on me to the Ginginator.

The Ginginator, true to his calling, walks up to me with his usual calm demeanor. "Hey, man, Mike said you have some holes in you and you're bleeding. I'd like you to go back on a MEDEVAC." I say no. And I get away with it for the same reason I get away with lots of things—I'm alone out here. I have no Team Sergeant. I have no supervisor. My official boss is in Bagram and probably still thinks I'm flying back to him on a Black Hawk. If my Team Sergeant had been here, I would have been sent back with no say in it. But he isn't.

Carlton doesn't want to leave either, but we all tell him he is going to lose his hand if he doesn't. Grudgingly, with his Team Sergeant's foot in his ass, he gets on the MEDEVAC with a few of our Afghan friends and some bad guys we bagged.

They ask me again if I want to go, and I get pissed off. I am actually insulted. They are not going to cut me from this team. "All of you working together cannot pull me out of here and you know it, so you might as well start moving," I snap, not at all joking.

The MEDEVAC takes off, and suddenly it is quiet again. Even the distant sound of gunfire from the Czechs has subsided. We are alone.

Then someone yells, "Mount up!" We all jump on our vehicles and are once again on our way.

We spend the next two hours in an oddly quiet time, where we see almost no one, and there is no aggression toward us. That change in itself starts to play tricks with our minds. *Are we done? Is the rest of the trip going to be easy? Or is this the eye of the storm, and when we come out the other side, we'll be right back in the shit? Is this fight done? Is Big John McCarthy going to run out and wave it off or signal another round?*

We see a village on the horizon. As we approach, we start having potshots taken at us. This is nothing like the ambush we lived through, but a bullet is a bullet and we have to respect it. We return fire in places, but as most of the village does not seem engaged in this fight, we are extremely careful. My impression is that there are a few guys trying to cause trouble and the rest of the village just wants to live their lives, but for those few, it is the insurgent mentality. Their buddies in the last town just told them we had a knockdown, drag-out fight, and that we would be on edge. If they could get us to engage and kill some innocent people that would be good for them.

And we are on edge. I look up at one point and Mike G has come off the machine gun and is holding his pistol. I don't know what he is doing. Maybe he fears another close-quarters fight? Maybe he wants to hold his pistol? Who knows? But instead of asking like a regular person, I ask him what the fuck he is doing and tell him to get back on his fucking gun. He asks me who the fuck I think I am talking to. I say the pussy holding a pistol when he should be on his gun. He says he is going to come down here. I tell him he knows what will happen if he does. And yes, the next thing you know, two "Quiet Professional" Green Berets are having a fistfight in the middle of a gunfight, because we're morons. The other guys roughly break us up, and we all go back to work. To be honest, I still don't understand that one. I love Mike G. None of this is his fault. We are great friends. But adrenaline is up and we've just been through a hell of a lot and it got a little primal.

As we get to the heart of the town, a crowd of people start lining up along the edge of the road, all watching us while saying nothing. It is in-

credibly unnerving. I dismount and grab my shotgun and keep my SBR
slung. I'm watching for aggressive movement. I'm scanning the crowd
for weapons. I'm looking at faces to see if I can spot the aggressors. We
are all reading into their actions from the unreasonable perspective of
what we have just gone through. What is actually happening is that
we are slowly moving out of Taliban country. Unlike the towns we had
come through on the way to Anaconda (or the ones we encountered
from Anaconda thus far), this town doesn't allow the Taliban to operate freely. They aren't fighting them or anything, but they do not want
trouble. For whatever reason, the Taliban seem to respect that "treaty."
They shot at us on the way in, but once we hit the main street, it ended.
Likewise, as we leave the main drag on the way out, the gunfire picks
up again.

We keep traveling and the gunfire keeps coming. It's ineffective.
There definitely isn't the commitment or the expertise that had occurred
earlier, which leads us to believe that these are just Taliban and not the
Iranians. The Team Leader calls for a halt in order to develop a plan of
action for the next town and deal with some bullshit going on with a
couple of the Jingle trucks, so I take the opportunity to send a little message to our fine Taliban friends.

The place we stopped at is gorgeous. We are at the top of a hill and
crops are being grown all the way down it on a series of well-irrigated
plateaus, almost like a giant staircase. This isn't modern farming. This
represents years and years of knowledge passed down from one generation to the next. This is growing lush and full crops out of land that
isn't good for much of anything. It is awesome. And at the very top is a
field that you can see for miles. It is wide open. In a different world, this
would be the perfect place for kids to play and families to have a picnic.

I reach into our vehicle and pull out the throne that we have not
been able to use yet. Before this mission, we had taken a metal chair
and cut a big hole in it so that when we were out here in the middle of
nowhere, we could take a nice poop without being uncomfortable. You
know how when you go camping and you have to poop, you go and
find a quiet secluded place—maybe you find a mossy tree to lean against

or a stump to hang off of—and you take your time and enjoy nature? Well, that isn't what we got to do on these missions. We went under a HMMWV with an MRE bag and uncomfortably tried to fill it without spilling. Or maybe our vehicle pulled up to the side of a hill for cover and we hung our asses off the side of it, while all our friends watched us. There's no Zen in that. For weeks I experienced nothing but shitty poops (pun intended) and I am sick of it. And I am sick of the Taliban. I am sick of them shooting at me. I am sick of the way they torment their own people. I am sick of the terrible way they poop in little gross holes in the ground.

So, I grab our chair, and I grab my Bible, and I walk out to the middle of the field. I can feel the eyes watching me. I set my chair up, and with my back straight, with perfect posture, I proudly look out over the gorgeous fields this town has cultivated and poop. I read my Bible. I relax. I enjoy the moment. And I hope they are all pissed and insulted, because that is the icing on top of the cakes I am dropping on this field.

Rounds come every once in a while as I sit there proudly shitting like an American. It is my way of telling them, "Go fuck yourself!"

My moment of tranquility ends as Mike G calls me back to the convoy. The Team Leader is about to give us the warning order on the hood of the HMMWV. I collect my throne, take one last look at my field, and jog back.

The plan is simple. Once we make it down the road and into the valley, we are going to spread out as much as the terrain will allow so we cannot get bunched into a chokepoint for an easy ambush. We will enter the village from three different directions, and the RGs will provide overwatch, so if we start getting lit up, we still will hold the dominant position over the enemy. After a couple of quick questions, we go back to our vehicles and start to move to our various positions.

As we hit the bottom of the hill and start spreading out, some guys dismount. I opt to stay on the back of the HMMWV going down the main road of the village. As we get closer and closer to the village, something is bothering me. Something just doesn't feel right. And then it hits me: for the first time since we left Kandahar, we are approaching a village and no one is shooting at us. *Where are they? Where is the ambush?* I know it has to be coming.

It is uncomfortably peaceful. I can hear the singing of birds. I can smell the fresh-tilled soil and the manure that had carefully been worked into it. I don't smell campfires, gun oil, or unwashed men like I did everywhere else in this country. These guys are disciplined. My senses are heightened.

As we crest a small hill that brings us to the edge of the village, my mouth drops. I see the guys around me stiffen. There is a large, thick, scary tree that looks like it is right out of a Hans Christian Andersen book. The tree isn't dead, but it is somehow almost black. It looks like it has been tormented for years and has grown wicked as a result. But the tree isn't the story—it is just the backdrop. Hanging from the tree on a rough hemp rope is a rotting corpse.

This is some horror movie shit. This is jarring. I'm waiting for a guy with human faces sewn on his face, or a hockey mask, or maybe the headless horseman to pop out and try to harvest our souls. It's especially disturbing because the skin falling off the bones and leaving a pile of gelatin for the carrion to pick through is such a sharp contrast to everything else I am seeing.

We now know it is going to be on. We are all on edge. The sight and smell of that body and even the way the rope creaks as the wind rocks it ever so slightly is seared into my memory, and it is definitely what we are all thinking about as we move down that road.

My vehicle is the pencil that is going to trip the rat trap. We are going to move to the center of town and draw out the fighters so the RGs from the overwatch positions can eradicate them.

We start driving in. I hate the slowness of it. I'm tired of the anxiety and want this thing to kick off. I'm looking for movement . . . and I see tons of it manifested in the weirdest Afghans I have ever seen. I blink a few times and look around to see if the other guys are seeing what I'm seeing. These people are wearing brightly colored scarves instead of black, white, or tan. The kids are wearing cute and colorful sweaters and boots. The women are not covered. What is this place?

The best way I can describe these people is that they look like the descendants of Genghis Khan had made babies with a bunch of Russians, because they have freckled skin, almond-shaped green eyes, almond hair, and they seem stunning compared to everyone else I have met in this country. Then it hits me. They are weird because I am looking at people. Everywhere else I have been, the villages were empty, or filled with fighters trying to kill me. These people are happily living their lives.

As they spot us, old men, women, and children begin to walk toward us. This is nuts. I get out. I'm not going to fall for some trick and get us killed. I grab my SAW. They keep walking. *Oh, shit.* Their approach off-balances me. I don't know what they are trying to do. Is this a diversion? Are they waiting for the Taliban to show up? Are they buying them time? Do they have IEDs on their bodies? No matter. Whatever it is they are about to do, I'm ready for it.

Except I am not.

A little boy gets to me first. He just walks up and grabs my hand. It's an immediate human connection—a touchpoint. I can feel his soft little kid fingers on my hard calloused hands, and my brain cannot compute what is happening. I have felt nothing but pain for two weeks and I flat out cannot comprehend what this kid is trying to do.

Then the old man reaches me. I feel like I am looking into eternity when I look into his eyes. I can't tell if he is 110 years old or if he is immortal or what, but this is an old man. He looks so fragile, but beyond his physical form, I can see in his eyes that he will fight like hell for this kid, for his family, and for this village. He stops for a brief moment and looks at me. This is pure conjecture on my part, but I think he looked at us and saw broken men. I think a man who has spent a century in a place like this knows all too well the look of shell-shocked young men. He's seen these faces for seventy years, whether it was us, the Russians, the British, or his own people.

My parents always told me there is a clear line that distinguishes right from wrong. Good people stand up for what they believe is right. They stand up to bullies. They embrace those who are suffering and protect them.

The old man wraps his arms around me and embraces me. I won't tell you that I melt. I'm still who I am, and I am still leery of strangers, but I trust this man for some reason. As he holds me in his embrace, so many layers of hate and rage that have built up over the last two weeks start dissipating. The anger and the burdens that have been crushing me fade away.

I start crying. And that shocks me. I had no idea how much I had bottled up inside, but once the floodgates open, they do not stop.

As the tears roll down my cheeks, girls bring bowls of water and start washing our faces and our hands. We are disgusting. We are covered in dirt, grime, gun oil, blood, and even pieces of Taliban thanks to the A-10s. But they continue, ever so gently, to scrape the layers of grime from us. Then men bring us bowls of food filled with nuts, berries, and fresh pomegranate. They are so friendly. The men embrace us. The girls kiss our cheeks. None of it is sexual or forced. It feels more like you're walking into an Italian family reunion or a Mexican quinceañera. They just want to deliver joy.

I am completely overwhelmed. Why are they being so kind? I don't have anything to give them. I have nothing left. I don't deserve this attention. I want to tell them what just happened to me. I want to tell them all of the horrible things I have done. But as I look at the old man, I know he wouldn't judge me if he knew. If anything, I think he and his village would give me even more love.

I am not the only one confused and emotional. All of the guys are trying to make sense of this development, including the interpreter and the guys in the Jingle trucks (them most of all). They frown at the uncovered women and the playing children. These are not good Muslims as far as they are concerned. But fuck them.

The interpreter sits down as the other vehicles roll in. He doesn't understand what exactly is going on, but he assures us that we are safe. As he gets situated in front of the elder, our first couple of questions are mini-interrogations. Are the Taliban here? Is there any reason we should be afraid? Are we putting you in danger by being here?

The old man starts laughing with the kind of guffaw we haven't seen since Sean Connery in *Highlander*. "There's no Taliban here," he assures us.

As delicately as we can, we mention that, "Hey, there's kind of a rotting body hanging from the entrance of your town." The old man quickly corrects himself. "I guess there is one Taliban here, then."

I start doing the math. I don't see any military-aged men in this group around me, but when I expand my vision, I can see that they are either in the fields working or are situated in craftily hidden military fighting positions, and robust ones at that. This place would have sucked to try to take by force. They have their own defense, their own customs, liberal values by Afghan standards, empathy, kindness, and generosity. They have created their own paradise in a sea of hate. This was Shangri-La.

I think about this town often. When you realize that you have something good and amazing and special, you don't want to just keep it to yourself. You want to shout it from the rooftops. You want to share it with everyone. I don't want freedom for Americans. I want freedom for everyone. We don't own freedom. When I go hunting and harvest an elk, I want everyone to taste my elk tacos because they are the most delicious things on the planet. Everyone should be able to savor that level of exquisite taste. These villagers are the same way. They know how good they have it. They know what they have created. They want to share it with us, and anyone interested in the bounty they have to offer.

Conversely, though, if you fuck with them, if you try to take what they love and value, they will fight like demons to preserve it. They will fight to the death. And you will be walking past the remains of your dead comrades strewn up on a tree on your way to try to take what is theirs.

We stay for the afternoon. It's wonderful. We eat. We talk. We learn that the village has been Taliban-free for generations. They have the perfect location. It's big enough to self-sustain, but it's small enough that fighting for it just isn't worth it for the Taliban. The only resource the village really has that the Taliban desire is military-age men and breeding-age women, but it is very clear that every man, woman, and child in this village is willing to fight to the death to protect what they value. For the Taliban, the juice just isn't worth the squeeze.

As the afternoon turns to evening, it is time to continue our journey. I think the old man could sense that we were once again putting ourselves in warrior mode as we prepare to leave Shangri-La, and he walks over and lets us know that we will be safe from here to Kandahar. He assures us there are no Taliban fighters past his village.

We believe him and it provides an incredible calm over our group. Now don't get me wrong, there is nothing anyone can say at this point that can make us drop our guard. We have gone through too much to be lackadaisical now. But we all begin thinking we may just have made it.

My memory from this moment on is much better. My lizard brain— the primitive brain that focuses on keeping you alive—relaxes a little and lets my higher functions join the party. As we drive, I let my brain slip into highway mode just a little. I'm still looking out the window. I'm still scanning my sector. But the pit in my stomach is gone.

After a while we come upon a British outpost we need to coordinate with. We park outside while the team leader and team sergeant do their thing and my vehicle is right next to a pomegranate tree. There is no one around—no homes or farms or stores. The tree looks out of place—almost lonely. I've got an hour to kill while we wait for these guys, so I grab a shovel and a bucket, and I dig my little tree up. I pluck a pomegranate off it and let the juices flow down my chin. It reminds me of home.

The rest of the drive back is uneventful. My brain has prepared me to feel like I imagine the guys felt after the Mogadishu Mile at the end of the Black Hawk Down battle, but the exultation is missing. Everything I have just gone through has faded to the background. It feels like I am in a completely different world now, only a couple hundred miles from the places that brought me so much pain.

When we get back to base, I drop my stuff and my tree off at my hooch, and then Mike G, Mike K, and the Ginginator bring me to the SOF med-shed. Bases this size have large medical facilities, but they operate under different rules. I don't want to get dumped into the big Army system. I would lose control.

They put me on the table and I stay there for six hours. There is lots of iodine, lots of tweezers, and lots of metal pulled out of my body.

After they remove it all, they still want to send me to the hospital. Apparently being concussed, blown up, and having shrapnel in my neck, shoulder, and back, while having a hand swollen to twice the normal size (thanks again to the 5.11 watch for saving that hand), is cause for concern. I'm not going. I'm not done in Afghanistan yet, and that's exactly what will happen if I get admitted to that hospital. I call SGM Flaherty and let him know I'm okay. He sarcastically thanks me for letting him know I wasn't coming home on the Black Hawk from Anaconda. The other guys already told on me and let him know I am injured. Thankfully, he isn't forcing me to go to the hospital, but he wants me to take the rest of the deployment off from active missions and instead take a Liaison Officer (LNO) position in the JOC. I tell him I think the best course of action is to let me heal for a week or so and then reassess. He thinks that's reasonable. I have no intention of being the LNO in the JOC. My plan is that I'm going to Wolverine my way to health and get back out there.

The guys drop me off at my hooch so I can rest and heal. I wait for them to leave and then I leave the base and head into town and buy a case of Jack Daniel's, violating several rules, including General Order Number One.

There's kind of a "turn a blind eye" mentality in Kandahar between the officers and senior NCOs and SOF when it comes to this shit. We go out and get them the good coffee, the good bedsheets and utensils, and all the nice things they crave and don't have access to, and they pretend we follow the same rules as everyone else. If we get caught, there is no protection. They will pretend they have no idea it was happening, and we will get hung out to dry.

I get back to my hooch with my booze and I start to drink. Drinking downrange is stupid, childish, and unprofessional and I shouldn't be doing it. I have been overseas twenty times with the military in Iraq, Afghanistan, Africa, and South America and I've never touched it on any other mission. Nothing good comes from it. And I'm not making excuses for it. I just want the pain to stop for a little while.

Dulling the pain only postpones healing. I wish I could take that week back, but unfortunately, that isn't how life works.

Ten days later I convince SGM Flaherty that I can work again. I do missions with the French, the Brits, and the Italians for the rest of my tour.

But that mission to Anaconda defined me, and in many ways still does. It was the honor of my life to serve with these men. Every member of the ODA that fought through that valley received at least a Bronze Star. Every member of the Czechs was awarded at least a Silver Star, with one guy receiving the Czech Medal of Honor. An extraordinary number of men were awarded the Purple Heart.

When I landed in Afghanistan, I wanted these things on my uniform. I wanted the bling that told people I was a badass. Now, I felt like I didn't deserve any of it, and didn't want it if it was offered. I didn't even report my wartime injuries to my actual chain of command.

Everything I had done thus far—Ranger School, Sniper School, deployments, fighting—were no longer accomplishments meant to stand alone. They were tools to make me better. And the only thing I proved on this deployment was that I wasn't good enough. And I never wanted to "not be good enough" again.

I decide as I board the plane to fly back home to Fayetteville, just as the UFC Fight for the Troops event is starting at Fort Bragg, that I am going to spend the rest of my career stacking the deck in my favor so the men around me will never have a liability in their midst. I will never live up to being the man I once thought I was. And I will certainly never be perfect.

But I can be better.

CHAPTER ELEVEN

TIME TO FIGHT

As I fly home from Afghanistan, the UFC Fight for the Troops 2: Fort Bragg is happening in my own backyard. The event is taking place on December 10, 2008. I land early morning December 11.

I was offered a fight, which would have been my first UFC card. The UFC's matchmaker reached out to Greg Thompson, the owner of Team ROC, where we all trained MMA and Jiu Jitsu. Greg immediately reached out to my senior sergeant, Alex Ortiz, to see if we could work something out. Ortiz, excited for me, asked if I wanted him to do some drug deals so I could get back early for the event. I told them I would happily fight if I was back in time but that the mission overseas comes first.

Even though this would have been a huge opportunity for Greg Thompson's program to be featured in the UFC, he respected my decision, and I will always appreciate that about him.

At first it looked like I was going to return in time to fight, which would have been super. However, I was in Afghanistan and I had asked SGM Flaherty to keep finding missions for me until I had to go home. He came through and I kept doing them.

I missed the window for the fight.

It looked like I was going to at least be home in time to be a guest of UFC President Dana White at the event and maybe even speak or introduce the last fight. That would have been cool, because Ranger Up is throwing the only afterparty for the event at Huske Hardware, a great downtown bar and restaurant owned by a former Operator. I've now joined Ranger Up as an owner, along with Nick, a couple 75th Ranger Regiment guys named Tom Amenta and John Tackett, and a former 1st Special Forces Group Chemical Officer named Kelly Crigger. The guys from ODA 782—the unit I was supporting in Afghanistan—got back just in time to make the fight and the afterparty, and between their texts and the texts from the Ranger Up team, I have a pretty good idea of the crazy-good time that I missed. Apparently the afterparty was so good that even Brock Lesnar showed up.

I'm happy for everyone, but I don't regret missing any of it. Sure, it would have been cool, but I was able to go on one more mission with the Czechs, and it was worth it. It might surprise some, but as I hated leaving Iraq, I really fucking hated leaving Afghanistan. I definitely didn't want to leave before the Czechs left; I owe them. But the Army doesn't care what I want any more than the Czech Army cares what they want.

The trip back is very different than the trip over. On the way to Afghanistan, we stopped in Germany for a couple days. On the way back to the U.S., there is no stop, only a brief refueling in Ireland. Normally, there is also a week or two period where you stay in country and do not do any missions so you can come back to normal a little bit mentally before heading home. Because it's just me, no one planned for that. I did my last mission twelve hours ago.

When I get off the plane at Fort Bragg, Ginger is waiting for me. She is beautiful, and I get hit with how much I love her, and how much I have missed her. My eyes well up, which is not how I am built. She walks up and gives me a kiss. I drop my shit on the tarmac so I can wrap my arms around her. This is the woman who drove the five hours from Fort Bragg to Fort Benning while I was at Ranger School to share my four-hour break with me and hand deliver my dad's famous post-Thanksgiving turkey sandwiches. This is the woman who gives me constant intentional love. She is my anchor, and my whole world. I squeeze her a little too long, and she studies my face.

"Are you okay?" she asks.

"Yes," I lie. "It was just a tough trip."

I spend most of the day with Ginger, but I have a lot of friends who are here to see me too, so I jet out to link up with some of the guys that are here for the UFC fights and are still here waking up in hotels and shit after a late night partying at Huske Hardware. The plan is just a quick "Hey, what's going on?" because I have been gone too long from my wife, and if I know the Army, I will be somewhere else before I've even had a chance to breathe.

I pull into the parking lot of their hotel and meet the guys in the lobby. Mike G plus a couple guys from ODA 782 are there, plus Ranger Up's COO Tom Amenta, Rob Hallford, who is a friend of Nick Palmisciano's, and Nick. I'm happy to see Rob isn't carrying a guitar. He's a super nice guy but it seems like every time I meet him, he starts strumming an instrument like he's opening up at Coachella, and I'm not up for that right now. Tom, on the other hand, always retains his largest noise-making device—his mouth—and he jumps right in with it. "Bro, you look like shit. I felt the same way after I got back from Afghanistan. Did I ever tell you about the time that . . ." Tom keeps talking, but I no longer hear the words he is saying. Tom is a machine. A workaholic. Tough as nails. He is also a 5'6" Italian guy from Chicago with two deployments with the Rangers, who absolutely loves CrossFit and music bands no one has ever heard of. He is genetically predisposed to talk. It's not his fault. The only way it could be worse is if he was vegan or a Marine.

We all grab cappuccinos (yes—cappuccinos) and shoot the shit for a while. I hear all the stories from the night before. Dale Hartt, our sponsored fighter, won when his opponent broke his leg kicking him. It sounded like someone snapped a baseball bat. The whole place apparently went silent. Rob, who was exceedingly drunk that night, apparently challenged Lesnar (tongue in cheek) to a fight after Lesnar knocked a plate of chicken wings on him. When Rob asked, "Do you want a piece of me?" Lesnar thankfully (for Rob) replied, "No, sir. I do not."

The stories are funny and I can tell they are all happy to see me, but the moment is weird. This is the first time my worlds have come face-to-face. It's always been my fight world and my military world. Sitting here with components of both at the table feels like I've crossed the Rubicon, and I do not think I will be able to go back, for better or for worse. My brain is also still in mission mode, and I start to get uncomfortable just sitting here. After what feels like an appropriate amount of time, I excuse myself. "I need to get going, guys. Gotta get back to Ginger."

"I'll walk you out, man," Nick says.

"Sounds good,"

When we get close to my car, Nick jumps in with what I like to call "officer shit."

"Hey, man, your buddies got pretty ripped last night. They came to the party and told me that they just deployed with you, and that you were some kind of superhuman on this trip. Mike said you stepped out of a car, just as it got blown up killing three Afghans, and then, pissed off, you sprinted into some building and killed everyone inside. Basically, they said you should be dead, but that for some reason you just kept not dying. Sounds really fucking intense. You good? Need to talk?"

I vaguely remember what he is talking about. That event had not popped back into memory until this moment. I am not sure it went down quite as heroically as my ODA buddies remember it. Kind of insane that so much happened that even something like that is foggy.

"Nah, man. I'm good. Thanks for asking," I reply.

The truth is I do need to talk, but not to him. We are not there yet.

I park my car a few blocks from my house, and I call my team phone. Alex Ortiz and Sean McClure are there. I dump it all on them. I shot a lot of people. I hurt women and children. I got shrapnel in my neck. I got blown up several times. We lost a lot of guys. I should have been one of them. What's the point of all this? Are we making more terrorists? Are we winning? Is it worth it?

They listen to it all with no judgment. Then they tell me that they know I went through a lot and they are super proud of me.

"You could have come home right away when you lost your partner. You didn't."

"You went through hell on that mission and could have flown back instead of fighting back. You didn't."

"When you were mission complete, you were wounded and could have come home. You didn't."

"You asked for more missions and you stayed until they made you leave, even though it meant missing the fights last night, which I have to tell you, were awesome."

"You're a dick," I laugh.

"You did good, Tim. You represented us well. Feel good about it," Alex continues.

"I appreciate that. It means a lot. I know this sounds weird, but I don't know if it's good for me to just sit around right now. I'm going stir-crazy and it's kind of eating me up thinking about everything that just happened," I say, waiting to be made fun of or something, but not:

"Well, good news, buddy. When you come in tomorrow, there's a new mission. We're going to leave in a couple of days. Nothing hard, but it'll keep you busy."

"What?" I ask, not quite believing they are deploying me again already. Ginger is not going to be happy, and I'm afraid of an unhappy Ginger even more than the mission!

"I'll tell you about it tomorrow. Call us again if you need it," Alex says. I thank him and hang up.

———

One of the things I will never get over about this job is how quickly the scenery changes. Ninety-six hours ago, I was leaving the Afghan desert, and here I am in the Caribbean nation of Trinidad and Tobago as ADVON for a pre-deployment site survey for the Secret Service, under the auspices of a JCET (Joint Combined Exchange Training). President Obama will be speaking here in two weeks, and we need to ensure security is in place before he arrives.

It's a testament to the flexibility and ability of Green Berets that we can go from a nonpermissive war zone like Afghanistan and immediately transition to the sophisticated nuanced world of foreign internal defense (FID). Our mission is to assess the reliability of the police and military and the extent of organized crime to determine if they pose a credible threat to the President.

As expected, Ginger is not happy that I am here, but I am. I won't go as far as to say I was falling apart back home, but I am not a "sit around with my thoughts" kind of guy. I wish I was. I respect people that can do that and derive a good outcome. I need to *do* shit. I need to sweat. I need to put my mind to a good purpose. And protecting the President of the United States definitely checks that box.

I keep looking around for my rifle, and remind myself it is not here. I feel naked without it. It was my lifeline for the better part of the last year, and now it sits lifeless in our armory back home. I check the pistol under my jacket and mentally run through drawing it. To be fair, doing so is like breathing for me. The chances I will need to do so on this tropical paradise are close to zero, but complacency has killed better men than me.

The first part of our mission is to train the local police and military to secure the area properly and protect the President, while simultaneously assessing them for threats. The second part of our mission is to assess the underworld here and see what level of dirtiness we have going on. To that end, one of the first things we do is hire a bunch of prostitutes.

We drive around the city, and it doesn't take long before we find three girls that fit the bill. They're happy to come with Americans because they know we will pay more, but they're very surprised we don't want to have sex with them. We tell them we just want beautiful ladies as company for a while. What they don't know is that part of our team is tailing their pimp. We keep them with us for a while and then we overpay them by thousands of dollars for their time. Our tail watches them cough up the fortune to the pimp. He now has way more money than he is allowed to carry. If he's more shady than afraid, he'll keep most of it for himself. If he's more afraid than shady, he'll bring it to his big boss.

He's not dumb, so he immediately starts cutting through the city to meet with his boss. We follow him there. A dumber person would keep the money and just pay the boss the expected amount, but when you're talking three girls and a city that has eyes everywhere, the chances of that story not getting back to him are slim.

He goes in, drops off the money, and heads back to his streets. Now we know the main hub for all illicit activity in this city. You see, bad people tend to do most of the bad things. If someone is comfortable running drugs, they're probably comfortable running guns, and they're probably comfortable running girls and boys. You can put those three in any order, but chances are if you can sleep at night doing one of those for profit, you can sleep well with any of them. And then it just becomes a matter of the optimal mix for the optimal profit.

We set up shop nearby and watch these guys for days, developing target packages on all of them, checking their accounts for deposits that might point to a problem for the President, or anything else that might be of interest. As you can imagine, in a place like this, the police cross paths with these guys almost as much as the pimps and the dealers do.

There is a ton of corruption, but no real threat. These guys are small-timers who want to make money the lazy and evil way, not zealots willing to trade the opportunity to hurt America for the consequence of having guys like me kicking in the doors in the middle of the night.

Nevertheless, our assessment isn't the final assessment. We map the entire city for the Secret Service and identify every café that becomes a brothel at night, every legitimate business they can safely take the President to, and every illegitimate business that might either pose a threat or place the President in a potentially embarrassing situation. We also build a brief on the level of security this government can provide and what we believe they will need to do in order to get that security up to our standard. Finally, we learn that Carnival in the Caribbean is fucking amazing.

The whole exercise rehabilitated me in a way that sitting around Fort Bragg and hashing out my feelings never could. By the time we are about to head back to the United States, my head is back.

––––––––––

Leo has a fight for me. It's going to be June 16, 2009, against Nick "The Goat" Thompson in Strikeforce. In the fight game, there is always a fighter and an opponent. If you don't know which one you are, you are the opponent. I know exactly who I am. Nick Thompson is a stud in every sense of the word. He wrestled in college, trains with UFC Champ Sean Sherk, Josh Barnett, and future UFC Champ Brock Lesnar, who has only lost twice in the last twenty-four fights. He lost once to Karo Parisyan at UFC 59, about three years ago, and to my good friend Jake Shields, who pulled me into this godforsaken sport in the first place by tapping me back at Terry and Barry's place for the Elite XC Championship. As if Nick Thompson wasn't busy enough, he also put himself through law school while fighting, which I respect tremendously.

I've never had an opportunity like this.

Plus, it's Strikeforce, which has a partnership with Showtime. So my fight is going to be broadcast live on Showtime! It's a huge moment for me against an elite opponent. It will be his fiftieth fight.

While only about five years have passed since I trained with Chuck Liddell, a lot has changed in MMA. Gone are the days of rinky-dink gyms and tough-guy rooms. Now there is an emergence of real Fight houses: Jackson's MMA, AKA, American Top Team, Team Quest, etc. There's money in fighting now, and the best gyms get 10 percent of the fighter's purse.

I'm still in the Army and there's no fight house in North Carolina. Instead, I have my friends: a bunch of tough-as-nails Army or Army adjacent guys who want the best for me:

Greg Thompson runs the Special Operations fight house. He's a Gracie black belt and the owner of Team ROC.

Brandon Garner is a human bulldog in every sense of the word. He's like 5'5" or 5'6" but 170 pounds of solid muscle, and even at his size he is by far my toughest test for grappling. Brandon also has the highest fight IQ of this group and a low-key coaching style that works for me. Because of that, I like having him in my corner.

Jason Palacious is a two-time world Jiu Jitsu champion and a civilian contractor. He's a 170-pound Polynesian dude from Guam who's really fun to move around with.

My best kickboxing instruction comes from Aitor "Spencer" Canup. Aitor is a very skilled purple belt in Jiu Jitsu as well, but his striking skill is invaluable. He spends a lot of time helping me clean up some of the bad habits I developed from five years away from the Pit.

Finally, there's Jeremiah Futch, who looks like a Greek god and won the world championships in Olympic lifting. He's a pro fighter and kickboxer.

It's a great group of guys and I love them. They go all out for me every single time. But as skilled and tough as they are, I know and they know that it is not an elite camp for a guy my size with my skill. These guys can make me work, but they can't really put me in a position to lose, at least not consistently.

We train in the original Team ROC, Fayetteville. It has shitty blue wrestling mats taped together in a tiny cement building. Greg is too cheap to run the air-conditioning, so not unlike my original time at SLO Kickboxing back in California, it's always gross in here, with mats so wet with sweat that they are like a slip and slide. Greg breaks down his hot box of a gym into three areas: one corner is for takedowns, one is for grappling, and one is for rounds for me before my fights. I know you're wondering what the fourth corner is, so I'll tell you: it's the entrance. We leave a little room there for people warming up and walking in.

If it sounds like I am talking down this team and this place, I am not. Of all the camps I have had in my life, this one is my favorite. They aren't fighters, with fighter problems, and fighter drama, and fighter stupidity. They are men. They are what boys should aspire to be. They have real jobs, and real commitments, and yet they, in their spare time, are genuine high-level professional fighters. They want the best for themselves, and for me, and they are selfless. When I first started training here after leaving the Pit I was a little bummed. I missed Chuck and Gan and Jake and the crew. But after a couple combat tours and a little perspective, maybe these guys have taught me more about what living a good life means than anything I could learn from elite guys on the mat or in the cage. I'm proud they have accepted me as one of their own.

My slight emotional growth doesn't mean I'm not still an asshole. When Greg Thompson tells me he is going to give me a black belt in Jiu Jitsu, I say no. It isn't that I don't want one; it's just that Jiu Jitsu people get weird about belts. For many people, it's like claiming someone. So, if I'm a Royce black belt, it might not be okay for me to train at a Machado gym. If I'm a Machado guy, it might not be okay for me to train at 10th Planet. And I'm not about that life. After all, what the fuck do I care about the color of a belt! I'm going to do whatever I want to do.

Greg is not happy. "Well, you have to start wearing a belt, and it's not appropriate for you to wear a white belt or even a brown belt and just be in here smoking all of our black belts."

"I understand," I tell him.

He nods, believing this heart-to-heart has solved everything. After practice, I head to Walgreens. The next day, I show up at practice wearing a pink belt. I train with this belt the entire time I am at Team ROC.

I arrive in Kent, Washington, the location of StrikeForce Challengers 2. With me, I have Brandon Garner and Nick Palmisciano. I'm meeting Andrew Chappelle, a former combatives instructor who is now in the reserves, there. Andy was Damien Stelly's (the dude I beat in my second All Army Combatives Championship) principal sparring partner. Both trained under Matt Larsen, a former Army Ranger who is widely considered the godfather of modern Army Combatives. Matt made a couple of monsters of these guys. Both are having impressive professional careers of their own, winning big fights in Bellator. Andy is a beast, but he's also a beast that I trust, which is critical. A lot of times, elite fighters make terrible sparring partners before fights because they want to win. You have to lose if you're in that role, and you have to prioritize the fighter's safety over your own. It's very selfless. Elite fighters tend not to be selfless. Andy, a Ranger-qualified infantryman and noncommissioned officer, put the team first.

Strikeforce is the dream world I have always wanted. While the IFL fights were on national television, the behind-the-scenes was every bit as shitty as every fight I have ever been to. Scott Coker's Strikeforce is different. When we get off the plane, there is a man with a professional sign that says "Tim Kennedy, Strikeforce." He and his assistant grab our bags and lead us to a black Suburban. It's not quite a limo, but it will do!

He brings us to a nice hotel. My corners all get nice rooms with double beds, and I get a suite. I am immediately given a schedule and a person to call 24/7 if I need anything. Brandon links up with them to ask about workout areas. They have the workout room for my corner (so that my opponent is never in the room with me) already available, and they give us passes to local gyms that have saunas. This is an organization that cares about fighters.

This is also the first time I have done real press. It's hard going from "Hey, shitbird, what the fuck are you doing?" in the Army to "Right this way, Mr. Kennedy" at Strikeforce. *Do I belong here? Am I a fraud?* There are champagne pyramids at the press events. There are multiple stations set up for different interviews. The fighter stays in place, but the press rotates. Then there's an individual video and photo shoot. The whole thing is surreal. This is the first time I get a glimpse of what Chuck's life was really like all those years ago. Now older, it makes me appreciate a little more that he actually gave me a lot more of his valuable time than I thought back then. *I'm an opponent on a small Strikeforce card. He was the UFC Champ.* But as excited as I am to finally feel a taste of the big time, I'm not the same kid anymore either. War has changed me. At the top of my head, in every interview, at every dinner, in every workout is the thought, *I have to make my Army brothers and sisters proud.*

I arrive at the big press event with that thought in mind, where we sit opposite each other and talk about the fight to come. I say nice things about Nick Thompson and talk about how it's an honor to be fighting on Strikeforce. He does something different. He tells the press that I haven't really earned my stripes enough to get in the cage with him. After all, he had just beaten Paul Daley, an absolute monster, and I hadn't fought in a year and a half, with my last fight against a tough fighter being a loss to Jason Miller.

As shit-talking goes, this isn't even that bad. In fact, objectively, he is completely right. I don't belong in the cage with him based on my record or credentials. But nice adult Tim Kennedy, who knows this is just a sport, disappears with those words. In his place, War Tim Kennedy, the guy that was just in gunfights for his life nonstop for months, arrives and he is not happy. He wants to fuck this guy up. He convinces himself this is personal.

That night, working out with Andrew and Brandon and wrestling a little with Nick, I go hard. Probably too hard. Brandon tells me a few times to chill out. I try to listen, because Brandon is just as evil as I am on the mat, so I know if he is telling me, I need to slow down. But I'm holding on to so much anger. I hit Andrew too hard a couple of times, and he fires back a little. I'm happy about it. I want to step it up. Brandon steps between us and tells us both to settle down. Andrew apologizes and immediately takes it down a notch. He doesn't need to. This is my fault. I know he is a safe partner, so I know I must have cracked him. After my rounds are over, I sit on the side of the mats and watch the other guys train.

Dave Camarillo, a legendary grappling coach from AKA, is training Luke Rockhold, an up-and-coming fighter in my weight class. He's very good, and I can tell he is dangerous, but I'm more impressed with the way Dave is coaching him. He's very different from other Jiu Jitsu coaches because he doesn't come at it from a wrestling or Jiu Jitsu mentality—he is a judoka or Judo player. When he was young, he won all kinds of Judo tournaments and was working his way toward an Olympic berth when he blew his knee out shortly after winning his first major tournament—the Canadian Open. He recovered, but the impact of Judo on the knee was too much for him, so he switched to Jiu Jitsu, where he received a black belt under Ralph Gracie. I had watched him from a distance for a while, and I admired how his style was inclusive, not exclusive. A lot of coaches at the time argued wrestling over Jiu Jitsu or their style of Jiu

Jitsu over another style. Dave absorbed. If one of his guys beat his game with wrestling, he became a wrestler and learned what he didn't know. I wished I had access to him and said as much to Nick and Brandon.

Brandon, an elite purple belt, knows him a little from some seminars. He says hi to break the ice. Dave instantly recognizes him and is happy to see him. Brandon then introduces Nick. Dave has a job to do, so they leave him to it, but when Luke is done working out, Nick starts talking Judo with him. They know a lot of the same guys and did Judo at the same time. Apparently, back in the day, they were in the same weight class at the same time at the same level but never competed against each other. They shared a small world that somehow never intersected, which they both found amusing.

This is the first time I had ever heard that Nick knew any Judo. He told me he was a mediocre wrestler who loved MMA (I would later find out he was a high school state medalist who was recruited at a couple of D1 programs and wrestled briefly at West Point before joining the Army Judo team). I'm gonna have to use him for more things.

Anyway, I don't know exactly how it happens, but after Brandon and Nick shoot the shit with him for a while, Nick just throws out, "Dave, we were supposed to have another corner this weekend, but he had to stay home for personal reasons. I'm here more to manage issues than anything, so I feel like Tim is a corner down. I'm definitely not anywhere near your level. Is there any chance you could help us out and corner Tim?"

"Absolutely! It would be an honor!" he replies.

Holy shit, Nick and Brandon just got me one of the best coaches on the planet. I would never have asked him myself—I would have been too embarrassed. Neither one of them would have asked Dave for themselves, but they did for me. It's not lost on me.

The weight cut was hard. I had to cut 40 pounds to make 185, as I had been at my Special Forces "Operator" weight of 225 for this deployment. The last fifteen really hurt and I did that with the guys in the sauna. Nevertheless, as they announce my name and I realize for the first time that I am the co–main event, I look back one last time at Brandon, Andrew, Nick, and Dave fucking Camarillo and grin. I have never felt better right before a fight. I walk out and a fog machine is blowing fog and people are cheering. I can smell the fog and wonder what chemical is in it. It's got that weird semi-sweet but semi-acrid smell to it that you only think about on Halloween. *Am I inhaling some kind of carcinogen right now?* I always have weird thoughts at this moment. I never think about the fight.

We get to the edge of the cage and I strip down. I see my corners collecting all my sweaty clothes and my shoes. It seems like I'm watching them on television as opposed to them being here with me. The overhead lights are bright and there is a haze around me. Mostly, though, I just feel a little cold now that I'm shirtless in this air-conditioned arena. It's been a wild night of fights. Jorge Gurgel just won a barn burner, and before that Sarah Kaufman beat Shayna Baszler in the first women's fight to go for five-minute rounds. That was kind of historic.

"Mouthpiece?" the ref asks.

I show him my teeth.

"Cup?" he asks.

I tap my cup.

"Okay, say goodbye to your corners."

I hug all of my corners and I climb into the cage.

Shortly thereafter Nick Thompson gets in the cage. He's huge. I'm usually a big 185-pounder, but he seems to tower over me. *We'll be the same height on the ground.* I try not to listen to analysts before a fight, mostly because this is the first time I have had analysts writing about one of my fights, but the majority think I need to keep this standing because "The Goat" has an impressive ground game. *Well, we're about to find out who has the better ground game.*

They announce us. The bells sounds. We touch gloves.

I take him down, easily.

Just as easily, he rolls for a Kimura, a move where you trap the guy's wrist in a figure-four, which threatens to break the shoulder. He's good at it, but I've been here before. After thirty seconds of a positional battle, I get my arm back and am in control. I spend the whole first round trying to stay on top of him and hitting him every once in a while, and he spends it trying to get off the bottom. When the bell sounds to end the first round, I can tell he is frustrated and maybe a little tired. I feel fucking great. I get back to my corner and Brandon and Dave take turns speaking while Nick and Andrew stay quiet—it's best to only hear one or two voices. Dave tells me to watch the wrestling tight waist in order to stay away from the Kimura and to take him down against the cage and to the rear, where I will be able to keep him from an offensive position. Brandon also wants me to land some shots standing if I can, especially an overhand right masked as a shot.

The second-round bell sounds. As I said, he's very tall and I don't want to get caught so I'm tentative coming in, throwing a high kick and a few testing jabs. Then, I see the opening Brandon wanted, and I fake the shot and throw an overhand right, connecting. I push him into the cage following that right, and I take him down to the rear, avoiding the Kimura opportunity for Thompson. *Good corners fucking rock.* Thompson keeps scrambling well, and this round looks a lot like the previous one, until about halfway through I start landing some shots. I know they hurt him. I feel him slowing. Finally, I spin behind him off of a double leg attempt from his knees and land a powerful shot on his ear that puts him to his belly. I keep throwing and I see him start tapping and the ref pulls me off.

Holy shit, I just made Nick Thompson tap to punches!

I pop up and see my corners going nuts. I look down to make sure Thompson is okay. He is. I just beat a real contender on the second largest stage on the planet.

I'm now officially in the mix.

Showtime brought my relationship with the Army to a head. Some of my upper-echelon Command Sergeants Major and officers did not like the fact I was both a fighter and a member of an elite Special Operations unit.

I plead with them to allow me to do both. They tell me I have to choose one or the other.

Enter Mark Gross, an Army veteran and the owner of the government contracting firm Oak Grove Technologies, who pairs up with Nick Palmisciano to do an awesome presentation of my position to the Pentagon. I met Mark through Dave Camarillo and Bob Cook from AKA. He sponsors all of AKA's fighters (that weren't assholes—Mark had an integrity clause) and he wants to help me through this situation. Nick is there because he's Nick. Up until this point, I had never seen the guy in anything but jeans and a T-shirt. Today, he's wearing a custom suit, a West Point ring, and he's holding a Duke MBA pen. I make fun of him to Mark, but I also know he's playing the right game. We have to show that we're adults and not a bunch of Neanderthal fuckwits.

Mark and Nick crush it. They essentially pitch me as a recruiting tool for the Army. Mark is a master of government contracts and knows what buttons to push and Nick is great with structure and talking in general. The answer has to be a yes.

But it isn't. The Pentagon loves it, but my command has the final say and they say no.

I have to decide now between the only job I have ever loved and the chance to be a world champion.

After my failed meeting at the Pentagon, I have ten days to decide. I ask Mark and Nick what I should do. They both tell me some version of, "I cannot make that decision for you. You're great at two things. You have to pick the one you love more."

I spend a couple more days talking to guys on my team. No one wants to tell me what to do. Some of them want me here. Some of them want me to win championships. Ginger would love for me to walk away from the military but believes that it is such an integral part of who I am that the cost of leaving the military will be higher than the cost of staying in. But no one is giving me the key to making a decision I can live with.

That's when I bump into my first senior 18 Bravo, Ben Rios. I explain my conundrum. He thinks for a minute. "You ever try to date a girl that doesn't like you, and you try to like her enough for the both of you, because you just like her so fucking much?" he asks me. "Yeah," I respond, not sure where he is going. "If the Army loved you, they'd give you a way to make this work. They'd make you sign a longer contract. They'd outline recruiting things you had to do or deployments you have to take. Could you do what they are doing to one of your guys? Would you make someone you loved choose? That's not love. That's envy. Are you going to let someone else's envy dictate your life? Meanwhile, how long can you be at peak performance? How long can you do this thing that you have been gifted—truly gifted—to do?" He stops for a minute and lets me absorb the words.

I don't know what to say back. After a pause, he starts again. "Tim, you don't owe anybody here anything. Just get out there and become a champion. Do not love anything that doesn't love you back. We're all expendable. If you die on the next deployment, the Army will not mourn you. Only your friends and family will. As your friend, I'm telling you to prioritize what's best for you and your family. And I gotta say, I think that's fighting."

The next day, I let my command know that I will not be reenlisting. The same dickhead Sergeant Major that started this whole problem is legitimately surprised. He tells me something along the lines of, "This decision will ruin your life."

I thank him for his comments, and I mean it. *I made the right call.*

August 2010

19th Special Forces Group, out of Austin, Texas, has been a dream come true. When I decided I was leaving the Army to focus on MMA, the commander of the 19th Special Forces Group reached out and asked me to come to them. I told him I wanted to keep fighting. He said, "I'm counting on it! You're going to be our number one recruiter!" And he was right. It turns out that the presentation that Mark and Nick had made worked out great, just not for the Army, but for the Texas National Guard.

My fight camp changed from the Team ROC crew to a more MMA-centric crew in Texas. I have some great UFC fighters to train with in Yves Edwards and Kamal "Prince of Persia" Shalorus, but I also have Gracie Humaitá, a Royler Gracie affiliate under Paulo "Coelho" Brandão. I like this place. I'm not married to it yet, but Paulo is amazing, and I love that it isn't the bullshit "fall on your ass and scoot underneath someone" flavor of Jiu Jitsu. Everything taught here is with the intention to win a real fight. Plus, I'm not too far from guys like Andrew Craig, Dustin Poirier, and Mike Chandler, who I typically get together with every week or two.

Two other things made this move great. First, when I made the call to leave, Justin Lakin, one of my 18 X-Ray brethren, made the same call. We literally drove here together in a truck. He was my strength and conditioning coach in North Carolina, and now he is my strength and conditioning coach here. He also started dating Ginger's sister, which I think is great because he is a great dude. Second, I met country and western star Shane Steiner. Shane is rad. His grandfather is in the Cowboy Hall of Fame for riding bulls. His dad is a champion bull rider. His brother and mother are both rodeo champs in their own right. And even though Shane had the skill for it, as well as for football and track, he chased music. His career peaked in the early 2000s, and he decided to walk away from it all to get out of the party lifestyle and focus on business endeavors.

I am a freak when it comes to workouts. That's always been the case. Because of that, now that I'm in a place where a lot of celebrities live—whether they're professional athletes, music stars, or actors—they show up to my workouts to see what they are really like. Because these visiting celebrities tend to be aesthetically fit, they assume they will be able to hang. They are so very wrong and I love showing them over and over again. No one ever comes twice. Except Shane. Even though he's eight years older than me, the motherfucker just keeps coming back. I love it.

The great thing about having Shane and Justin here is ever since the Strikeforce fights started, and the media exposure got bigger, everyone I meet wants something from me. I cannot really trust people anymore, because right when I start to like them, they ask me for something: tickets to a fight, an introduction to someone they want to meet, or money. Justin wants nothing from me (except my sister-in-law).

When he isn't serving in the 19th SF Group, he's a contractor making more than I do fighting, and he's an old friend. He would have dumped me ages ago if he wanted to. With Shane, he's more famous and richer than I am, by a wide margin. He just wants to hang out. I know I sound like a bitch complaining about making money and being a little famous, but it really gets lonely when you can no longer make friends without wondering what they want. I still have my amazing friends Nick and Brandon, but they live in NC, so it's nice to have solid relationships close to my new home.

In the last year, I've choked out Zak Cummings and Trevor Prangley, which has set up my biggest challenge to date: Jacare Souza for the Strikeforce Middleweight Championship on August 10, 2010. Jacare is an ADCC (Abu Dhabi Combat Club) Champion, and he just won a Brazilian Jiu Jitsu Superfight against Robert Drysdale. On paper, he is a better grappler than I am by far, and that's my strongest aspect of fighting. This is a huge fight. I try to pretend it isn't, but I can feel the pressure mounting. I want to be champion so badly.

Even though this fight is in Houston, Texas, and there are plenty of guys I can bring in from my new home, I ask Brandon and Nick to corner me once again. I trust them both. Brandon has as much ring wisdom as anyone outside of a handful of truly elite coaches, while Nick handles everything that is needed before I have to ask for it and is good enough and big enough to warm me up before a fight. Plus, they like and trust each other. There are no egos or drama. They both want me to win. For this fight, I've also added a new guy to my corner: Jason Webster. Jason's older than everyone else in the corner by ten to fifteen years, but he was an elite kickboxer in his day and he's an excellent trainer. He's also a guy who has been through some shit, so he maintains that calm element that I prefer in the corner. I don't need anyone yelling at me. I need information. Additionally, Andy Chapelle is coming out. He's not going to be in the corner, because Strikeforce only allows three, but he's going to be there to work with me for a couple of days. Two other guys were supposed to come as well, but they bailed at the last minute.

Having Brandon, Andrew, and Nick should have been enough. After all, I just need to sweat. You're not getting any better the week before a fight. You just have to move so your body doesn't leave its optimal cycle, but you shouldn't be pushing yourself. But for some reason, the stress of this fight has me out of sorts. To make matters worse, Brandon gets hurt right before he comes out. He's not going to be able to move with me. Now it's down to just Nick and Andy. I'm more aggravated than ever.

Doesn't anyone care that this is my title fight? This is my chance to get to the next level.

The first couple of days of preparation are fine. We mostly do grappling and pad work. Andy is his usual stud self, but I can see he is getting a little annoyed with me. Deep down, I know it's not fair, because he cannot go all out, but I feel I need to push hard. I need to be at championship level. I'd expect the same from him. Nick gives me everything he has, and I am no less forgiving than I am to Andy, even though Nick is not a professional fighter. I know that's fucked up, but again, this is my title shot. Standing, he is solid because he's very hard to move and his Judo style somewhat mimics Jacare's. But once I get him to the ground, I murder him. For any other fight, I'd be flow rolling with both of these guys, but for this one, I feel the need to punish. I know Nick and Andy are miserable, but they both stay quiet and grind through it.

The Thursday before the fight, I have to do some real striking drills. My plan with Jacare is to do a lot of clinch work, push him into the cage, and knee the shit out of him. We're going to alternate grappling and striking rounds. Andy will be my grappling rounds and Nick will be striking rounds. Nick puts on a belly pad so I can work my knees. They both look a little tired of my shit, but they don't complain. Brandon speaks up: "Tim, we're only going 50 percent with this. Do you hear me? Fifty percent."

"I got it."

Andy is up first. We work clinch stuff and I take him down, over and over again. "Slow it down, Kennedy," comes Brandon's raspy voice. *I'm going slow!* At the end of the round, I look at Andrew, and there's a scrape over his eye. Nick's up next. We fight for head position, and I move from the basic over and under clinch to a Thai plum clinch, rocketing knees into his gut and ribs anytime the opportunity presents itself. I feel his strength weakening as I land more and more and for some reason this pisses me off and I get more aggressive with them.

By the time we get done with three rounds of both, Andrew just says, "Good job, Tim," and walks off. Nick slumps down on the side of the mat with his hands on his head. I hear him say to Brandon, "Bro, I am a pussy, because those knees hurt so much that I was wincing before they even hit by the end. And that's only 50 percent. Fuck." Brandon replies in his slightly Southern twang, "Bro, that weren't no 50 percent. That's more like 110 percent. Go get a shower." Nick nods.

I head off to my room.

The rest of the day is crazy. There's a press conference. There's a workout for the fans, where I wear my pink gloves that I bought to match my pink belt. The whole time I just keep picturing what it's going to be like to be the Strikeforce Champion.

Unlike the past, where I had to cut from my healthy Army weight to my fight weight in a week or two, this time I was able to use a nutritionist and do it slowly over six weeks, so I only have to squeeze out the last ten pounds, which for a fighter is very easy. Nick, Brandon, and I knock that out in the sauna, and then we head to the weigh-ins.

For other events, I have just been one of the fighters. For this one, I'm on the poster. There is no hiding. I'm everywhere. On the wall. On the billboards. On the promo constantly running in the arena while fight fans wait for us to get on the scale. And there's an energy that I cannot help but get caught up in.

The air is electric. There are tons of people waiting just to watch us weigh in!

I'm bouncing around backstage even though I am tired and hungry. I run up and say hello to Daniel Cormier. It's my second Strikeforce card with him on it, and he's fun to talk to. Mostly, though, I'm just trying to pass the time. We get the two-minute warning and the Strikeforce staff start calling names to line us up in fight order so we come out the right way. We're allowed one corner to come with us, so Nick waits in line with me. He's carrying a small bag with him that has Pedialyte, water, watermelon, and plain bagels. I did not ask him to get this. He just made sure I had it after getting the breakdown from the nutritionist. KJ Noons and Jorge Gurgel are currently weighing in and Jacare and I are up next. Suddenly, Mötley Crüe's "Kickstart My Heart" comes on and they announce Jacare. Then me. The crowd is all kinds of fired up. Jacare and I bow to each other. No crazy antics. Then we smile and hug and walk off stage. Nick immediately gives me Pedialyte and water, followed by a ton of watermelon. I feel my body getting stronger instantly.

We get back to the hotel room and there's food waiting for me. Pasta with chicken in it. No oil. No butter. Nick ordered it in advance and Leo, my amazing Russian manager, picked it up and brought it to the room. While I start to eat, Nick sets up my IV. Two bags of saline. He's been doing this for me for a while now, even before he cornered me. Every fighter does the same thing, but most people wing it and have no training, so the process of getting an IV from their team is a shitshow. Nick learned the dumb Army way. First from combat lifesaver training, then as an idiot lieutenant living in Germany drunkenly giving himself or his buddies IVs after nights out, and finally, when he realized this was something I needed, he got lessons from a bunch of nurses, so he was sure he was safe.

I'm antsy.

"I want to move tonight, Brandon," I tell him.

"You don't need to," he replies. "You need to relax."

"Let's just do five easy rounds, same time as the fight is going to be. I need to move," I tell him strenuously.

He looks at me and weighs the pros and cons of arguing versus letting me.

"Okay, we'll go easy," he finally says as he nods to Nick.

Nick calls Andy and lets him know that I want to move, but he's out on a date. It's not his fault. I told him he wasn't needed tonight, but I'm still aggravated.

"Fine, I'll do five rounds with you," I say to Nick.

"Okay, Tim," he answers.

Ninety minutes, a pasta meal, and two IVs later, we are at a gym owned by Andy's friend. He let us in late and we have the whole place to ourselves. Nick is not allowed to hit me, but I'm allowed to lightly make contact. The goal is to move around the cage. He's supposed to try to take me down or put me into the cage and I'm supposed to play my game: put him into the cage and then pepper him with knees and get him to the ground when he's softened up.

"I need you to go easy, man. This is just to sweat," Brandon reminds me. I nod. The bell rings.

Nick moves in and immediately locks up with me. This is what I asked him to do. I asked him to try to throw me, as that's a big part of Jacare's game. He fakes a right throw and comes back left, off-balancing me for a second. I don't get thrown, but I see red. *If Nick can do this, then Jacare can.* I turn up the intensity. By the time the bell sounds for the third round, Brandon gets in the cage with pads on. "We're hitting pads this round," he says. "But you're hurt!" I bark through my mouthpiece, sending a muffled group of syllables at him. "So's he," he says.

I look at Nick. He ended the round desperately holding on to a single leg that he was never going to finish. Brandon moves with me for two rounds. Nick gets back in for the fifth and gives me everything he has left, which isn't much after about two minutes. The final bell rings.

"Thanks, guys," I say to Brandon and Nick.

"Sorry, I didn't have more for you, man," Nick replies.

"Fuck that. You're a better friend than I am," Leo chimes in with his thick Russian accent. "It hurt me to watch you get hit."

I don't say anything. We all shower up and go to dinner. Ginger joins us. It's a good meal and we have a lot of fun. It's the first time I feel a little more low-key this entire time, but I still wish we could just fast-forward to tomorrow and be done with it. Nick excuses himself from dinner a few times and sticks to water the whole meal, which is odd for him. The night before a fight is usually when the corners let loose a little and have a few drinks. When he leaves the third time, I ask Brandon, "Was I that bad today?" He replies, "Don't worry about it. You did what you needed to do." "Is Nick okay?" I ask. Brandon pauses for a minute. "He's pissing blood, man. You beat the shit out of him the last two days. But he's fine."

———————

Twenty-five minutes of fighting against Jacare was intense as hell, but I feel great and could go twenty-five minutes more if needed. I ask Brandon, "Did we win?" "It's close, Tim," he replies. I'm doing the fight math in my head. He didn't take me down. I took him down a few times. The only shot that dropped anyone in this fight was mine. *That's enough to win, right?* Still, his game plan was not what I expected. We all thought for sure that the most decorated grappler in MMA was going to try to take me down and grapple, but apparently he respected my game as much as I respected his. Instead, he came in with crisp boxing and counterpunching. He never hurt me, but he scored points where I didn't think he could. I did more damage, but this is a 10 point must system. Damage in one or two rounds isn't enough.

Finally, Mauro Ranallo has the judges' scorecards. He announces that the judges have scored the contest, 49–46, 48–47, and 48–47, all for Jacare Souza. My world drops out.

You know how you've wanted something to happen so badly—to get the job, for the girl to like you, for you to catch the one break you need to make it through the month—and then not get it? My brain is racing to figure out a way to reverse time, to make an argument on my behalf, to fix it. But there is nothing I can do. I lost.

When I get backstage again, I rip my gloves and hand wraps off and I throw them away. Usually, a fighter keeps these, auctions them off, or donates them to charity. I want nothing to do with them. I shower, put on a suit, and go to the press conference. I'm absolutely miserable. I want a rematch, but I know one isn't forthcoming.

When I leave the press conference, Leo brings Ginger to the back. Nick walks over to her and hands her my check, which he must have picked up for me while I was sulking, along with a plastic bag that has my gloves and wraps in it.

That asshole fished my shit out of the trash.

I go to the afterparty even though I don't want to, because I have so many friends and family here, plus a host of troops who came all the way from Fort Hood to see me. They all tell me it was a great fight and that they thought I won and that I'll come back stronger and all the cliché stuff that everyone says when they're trying to be nice. But I didn't want that. I wanted to fix this so I wouldn't be here ever again.

When I find him away from everyone else, I corner Brandon. "What did I do wrong?" I ask him. "You need a real camp, man," he answers quickly. "It's not enough to run your own camp with good fighters around. You need an elite coach who is only thinking about you and how to make you better. AKA, American Top Team, Jackson's, whoever. Pick one."

I ask Nick the same thing. "Bro, there's no camp on earth that would have had me as your training partner for this fight. I'm honored and I will always do it, but you should be with Rashad Evans or Georges St-Pierre or Jon Fitch or some shit. Not a guy like me. You know this. I'm one hundred percent with Brandon on this one. We want you to do the best you can do."

I ask Leo. He agrees.

Ginger is more abrupt. "You're not allowed to lose anymore. I don't like it. So either win all the time or quit this dumb sport." She absolutely means it. She doesn't give two shits about MMA or me being famous.

Looks like I need to find a real camp.

CHAPTER TWELVE

PRIZEFIGHTER

Jackson's MMA is rad. It's not crappy like SLO Kickboxing or Team ROC Fayetteville. Everything here is quality, taken care of, and extremely clean. It's just all . . . old. Everything feels worn in. It makes me feel like what I imagine Mikey's gym was like in *Rocky*. The bags might look old, but champions have sweat on these bags—are still sweating on these bags. The mats may have some of the color worn off their surface, but the best of the best have bled on them. Yeah, there is something awesome about this place. I feel good here.

Greg Jackson and Mike Winkeljohn both have offices in the front of the building, and Julie Kedzie, Greg's assistant, has a desk there too. Julie, a professional fighter who has fought everyone there is in women's MMA, is an MMA pioneer in every sense of the word, and she keeps Greg's life on track. Outside the offices, there is a little waiting area covered with piles of belts, medals, ribbons, swords—basically shit that shows you won something in the fight world. It doesn't seem like this stuff is too important around here. Greg literally has a few UFC Championship belts lying around in his office the way most people have magazines and throw pillows.

Greg is in some other state or country right now cornering someone, so I'm kind of finding my own way.

I traveled around before deciding to come here. It came down to here and AKA. Either one would be great for me. While I really like Bob Cook and Dave Camarillo, and I like the idea of having Jon Fitch, Josh Koscheck, and Mike Swick around—all guys near my weight at the top of their game—I chose this place.

There is just something about Greg Jackson. I trust him. I can tell he is smart in a different way than everyone else. And one cannot argue with the results. Greg currently has welterweight champion Georges St-Pierre and light heavyweight champion Rashad Evans in his stable. But that's not even close to the end of it. The fighters here are a who's-who of top contenders: Jon Jones, Carlos Condit, Cowboy Cerrone, Nate Marquardt, Damacio Page, Holly Holm, Phil Haas, Alistair Overeem, Lando Vannata, Keith Jardine, and the list goes on and on. The craziest part is anyone is welcome in the gym. Any dude off the street can just walk in and start training . . . but there's no mercy here either. The guys that do walk in don't come back after the first workout. Everyone in here is a straight killer.

Before long, though, I notice some tension whenever Jon Jones and Rashad Evans are in the room together. It's definitely a different feel than what they have said publicly about each other. Publicly, it's big brother and little brother. Privately, it is clear Jon does not see himself as anyone's little brother (other than his actual NFL lineman brother, Arthur).

Oh well, they'll work it out on the mats. This doesn't affect me.

I work out with Rashad first and it is fun. He's the prototypical power wrestler, with really tight boxing. I love how he disguises his strikes and takedowns. It's hard to know which one is coming. *I will work on that.* On the ground he's tough, "wrestling tough." However, I can blanket him and wear him down with my Jiu Jitsu. We're very similar with some different strengths and that's exciting. I feel our wrestling is about equal. He's a little slicker standing; I'm a little slicker on the ground. He's going to be a great partner and with GSP at 170 pounds and him at 205 pounds, I'm already thinking I will have the right partners to get that 185-pound strap.

Then I work with Jon. *Oh fuck. This is something different.* Jon is fucking amazing. It's insane. I've been doing this a very long time, but I have not felt this level of potential danger. It isn't that he is necessarily more skilled than Rashad. It's that he has more tools *and* is as skilled. In MMA terms, he's still a baby. He's long but packs a ton of muscle into a very light weight. He's powerful and he's fast. And he's just starting to learn. I give him great rounds and get the better of him on the mat, but I can already feel he is more dangerous than Rashad. If you ask me to pick one of them to fight for a title tomorrow, it is . . . not Jon Jones.

When you come to a new gym as a high-level pro, people are usually nice to you. They want you to feel welcome. They want to acquire you as a partner so they can learn what you know. They want to be part of the reason you like the gym. Rashad and Jon take that to a different level. They aren't just being nice to me. They wine and dine me, then pee on me to mark their territory.

Rashad makes the first move. At the end of my first day of training, he takes me to a Korean barbecue place with his wrestling coach Mike Van Arsdale. They're good company. Rashad is a good, smart guy with a college education and a lot of drive. We talk about all kinds of things. He asks me about the military. We talk politics. Mostly, though, he tells me how it is at Jackson's. He's taking on a mentoring role, and I take no offense. I absolutely believe he sees me as an asset rather than competition, and he wants to make sure I feel comfortable here. This part feels a lot like going to a Special Forces team (maybe not first team, as an 18 X-Ray, but definitely second). He wants me to know how the unit works, what will piss people off, and what to watch out for.

That last topic is where it is very unlike an SF team, because according to Rashad, the thing to watch out for is Jon Jones. Rashad doesn't overtly say he's bad. In fact, I'm not even sure he dislikes him. It's more like, "Jon's talented, but he has a big ego, and only looks out for number one, so be careful." Or he'd say something like, "Jackson's is like a family . . . with a pain in the ass stepbrother," and laughs. Again, nothing vicious. There is respect for Jon's skill, but it is clear that Jon's lack of acceptance of Rashad as the top dog is a problem for Rashad. I've never heard teammates talk like this—certainly not mine. If Brandon was going to talk shit about me, it would be to me. If Spencer was going to complain about my attitude, he'd tell me. If I was being a dick to Andy Craig, he wasn't going to tell Dustin Poirier about it. He was going to tell me.

I know that Greg and Mike want to coach both of these guys, but I can already tell that's not how this will end.

Rashad and I head to get some water-soluble vitamins, and then we head home. Even though parts of the conversation were weird, I really like him. In the fight world, oftentimes the greater the fighter, the crazier the lifestyle, but Rashad has his shit together. He's exactly the kind of dude I want to be around.

The next day, I get some alone time with Jon at lunch. He tells me almost exactly the same thing! "Rashad is a stud, and I respect him, but he's an old dog trying to stay on top. There's a new dog in town and he has to see that." *This is so weird. It's like they were dating, broke up, and are trying to build alliances.* The whole thing is just super odd to me, but again, it's really none of my business, or my problem. These two guys will figure it out. It's only fighting, after all—not life or death.

One thing I immediately notice is with Greg out of town, we are truly left to our own devices. That leads to a lot of wasted time. I am not okay with that. The first class we have, some fighter I have never heard of, who is not an actual coach, who is not great at wrestling or Jiu Jitsu, gets up and starts teaching wrist locks. You're not wrist-locking anyone in MMA. We wear gloves and wraps and it's just not happening. I think there have been a total of two in the UFC's history.

I'm sure as shit not putting both my hands on one guy's arm while he punches me in the face as I try to bend his wrist through his wraps. So, I take over. I focus on transitions, starting with bad wrestling takedown attempts from an opponent into a wrestling chin strap, into various submissions or positional improvements for strikes. No one tells me to stop or complains, so I assume they are good with it.

After class, I go into Greg's office and create a schedule for the next three days. We're going to do wrestling class at these times and Jiu Jitsu class at these times. I'm going to teach them all unless someone else wants to. No one else does. Jon and Rashad are cool with it, and actually both thank me for adding some structure.

So when Greg Jackson and Mike Winkeljohn return from wherever they were, they come back to this new guy running their classes, and they kind of don't know what to do with me. Greg thanks me and apologizes for not being here when I arrived and sets a time to meet tomorrow at 9:30 a.m. for our first one-on-one session. *Great! I get to learn from the master himself!*

I arrive at 8:45. I warm up. I stretch. I do drills. When Greg walks in at 9:35, he's surprised to see me. "Tim, what are you doing?" I'm equally surprised at his question as he is at seeing me. "You told me to be here at 9:30, Greg."

He looks at me for a second and kind of cocks his head to the side. "Mr. Kennedy, I don't know how to say this, but fighters are never on time. If I tell a fighter to be here at 9:30, he wanders in at 9:45. He bullshits until 10:00. By 10:10 he's moving around a little, and by 10:20 we're starting."

I understand what he is talking about. I used to have some of that in me. Not anymore. "Mr. Jackson, if you tell me 9:30, I'm going to be here at 8:45. I'm going to warm up, stretch, and prepare myself mentally, spiritually, and physically for your instruction so that I do not waste one minute of your time or mine."

Greg kind of laughs and says, "Well, okay. Let's get going!"

The Jackson/Winkeljohn dynamic is interesting. They shouldn't work. Greg is a nerd, first and foremost, and I say that as a compliment. He's the guy who's read *The Art of War* and *The Book of Five Rings* over a hundred times. He's the Bill Belichick of fighting. He watches the tape. He looks for the patterns. He looks for the tells. He enjoys taking the strengths of his fighter and attacking the weaknesses (or strengths) of the other fighter. The strategy matters to him. He doesn't teach a fighter generally how to get better. He files the strategy down to a fine point to exploit a specific weakness. He wants you to execute a specific plan with specific timing with specific purpose.

Winkeljohn is a smart jock. He's a hard-as-nails, old-school kickboxer with a glass eye, because one of his eyes got sliced out by a toenail. Because of that, he always wears shooting glasses when he holds pads. He's blunt, uses few words, and has no time for weakness or complaining.

Neither of them knows what to do with me. Fighters do fighter things. They drink. They womanize. They go to strip clubs. They buy expensive jewelry and cars. They waste money. They stay out late. They have orgies with ring girls and almost get AIDS.

I used to be that fighter.

Now, I'm a grown-up who happens to fight. When I have camp, I bring my family to Albuquerque. After training, I hang out with my wife. I go hiking on my day off. I explore museums and restaurants and parks. Because of this, my life stays easy and stress-free. My wife and I live off of my Army pay and her paycheck and we save anything I make from fighting and from my sponsors to invest in the stock market or in businesses. It's not as exciting and wild, but I feel a hell of a lot better than I did then.

It's also safer. Albuquerque is a cesspool with limitless opportunities to get in trouble. The city is so bad that the television show *COPS* was permanently set up here for a while until the mayor kicked them out. It was just too easy to find drama. The fighters who get in the fastest trouble are the eastern bloc guys or the dudes from Muslim countries. They come here to fight and all of a sudden, they can get booze, drugs, and girls at literally the same place. Shit gets dark real fast. One of the saddest stories of squandered talent is Karo Parisyan, the former WEC Champion and absolute Judo and MMA stud. He was prescribed painkillers for an injury and took a liking to them and Albuquerque did the rest. Years later, he got clean and was able to return to the sport, but never again in the UFC or anywhere near his previous level.

But none of that grossness touches me or Ginger, because we are boring. As a team, we do kookie things, though. A weird group of us, all dressed differently, will go and play Frisbee football in the park: Cowboy as a cowboy, Lando as a hippie, Overeem in a tracksuit, Nick Jordan and Phil Haas in jeans and tees, and me in Ranger panties and a tank top. We looked like a '70s rock band aggressively playing a sport that was never meant to be aggressive. That's as wild as I got there.

A month after I arrive, Rashad leaves. I am really disappointed. He's a big reason I came here. He's a really cool guy with a good head on his shoulders, a phenomenal wrestler who hits like a freight train, and he was very good to me. I get along with everyone, but wrestlers have a certain personality that I tend to jibe with. Elite college wrestlers, especially, go through a forging process that makes their minds different. You don't see wrestlers making excuses like you see from Jiu Jitsu guys. Wins and losses rest fully on their shoulders. I respect that attitude. Rashad has all of it and then some.

But he is also the champ, and wants the recognition of being the champ, and wants the gym to cater to him. That isn't Greg's way. I'd have no problem with that. I can train with a guy I'm eventually going to fight. Rashad cannot. Again, for me, it's just a sport. This is life or death for him.

The situation is tough all around and it takes a toll on the camp. Rashad was a real leader and a motivator around here. Assessing it as the new guy, I think Rashad and Jon were both treated equally, but Rashad had paid more dues, believed he had earned more loyalty, and wanted to be treated more equally than Jon.

I already miss him as a partner and hope it doesn't change the place.

I'm hitting pads with Mike Winkeljohn's protégé Brandon Gibson, while Nick Palmisciano and Julie Kedzie half watch and half shoot the shit off in the corner, when I'm interrupted by Jon Jones. He's holding a gym bag full of cash. The zipper is broken so I can see stacks of twenty-dollar bills. "Tim, I need you to watch this for me. No time to explain."

"Do I want to know?" I ask.

"It's not what you think. I'm buying an exotic cat in the parking lot down the street later, but right now I have to take the U.S. Anti-Doping Agency test. He just stopped at my house and he's on his way here. I don't want him to see me with a bag of money. He might get the wrong idea."

I'm actually relieved. "No problem, man."

"Thanks, Tim," he says, before stashing the bag under the cage and running off to drink water before the USADA guy shows up.

It's October 2013 and I've been at Jackson's a couple of years now with mostly good results. I fought Melvin Manhoef, a striking assassin capable of knocking anyone out with one punch or kick, and beat him in the first round. Then I fought future UFC Champion Robbie Lawler, another guy capable of knocking anyone out in one punch, who also happens to be a great wrestler, and had a barn burner with him. Robbie hit me with an uppercut that split my nose wide open and left me with a permanent scar. That was the hardest hit I've ever eaten, which is saying a lot. But I won, setting up another Strikeforce Championship fight, this time against AKA's Luke Rockhold.

I lost the fight.

Second championship opportunity.

Second failure.

But unlike the first one against Jacare, it wasn't a lack of training that cost me the win against Luke. It was a lack of risk taking. I simply didn't engage enough when my "A" game plan—to put him into the cage and take him down—didn't work. It was the lowest percentage of takedowns I have ever had in a fight. Once it became a standing battle, instead of driving past his length and doing damage on the inside, I was content to stay outside, where he had the advantage. I cannot even tell you why. The fight ended and I didn't even feel like I had fought. That one sticks with me. After the fight, I remember Greg telling Winkeljohn, "Cormier has made a big difference in their wrestling over there. We're going to have to adjust." It wasn't meant for my ears, but I heard it. *Thanks a pantload, Cormier.* That one stung.

After that, I got back on the horse with a submission win over Trevor Smith, and then I got the best and worst news ever: The UFC bought Strikeforce. It was the best news because now I could fight anyone! The best guys in the world were either in the UFC or Strikeforce, and now we were all together. It was the worst news because I hated the UFC control mechanism. I know fans think the UFC is the best thing ever, but I don't. Their contracts are restrictive, they pay fighters less than Strikeforce, you cannot have your own sponsors, and they just generally are not nice. In fact, one of the first things they tried to do was reduce the number of tickets I was allowed to have. My Strikeforce contract called for ten free tickets, but UFC contracts only allowed four. What a great start to a relationship!

Scott Coker, the Strikeforce President, is a gem of a man. He loves fighting and fighters. Dana White, the UFC President, is a hell of a businessman. He's a pit bull. I respect both of them for different reasons. They are both winners, but their approach to winning is different. Scott wants to put on the best show he can. He wants people to like fighting for him.

Dana wants to dominate the market, destroy anyone in his path, and deliver the best return to his investors. A Scott Coker motivational speech is a lot like something you'd hear from a high school football coach, or maybe a *Rocky* movie, with some nuggets of wisdom baked in. A Dana White motivational speech is like the Alec Baldwin scene in *Glengarry Glen Ross*, where he tells everyone to "fuck or walk" and tells Jack Lemmon he can't have coffee because "Coffee is for closers."

I learned the difference in motivational techniques firsthand in my very first UFC fight. I had already annoyed all of their matchmakers by the time the ink was dry on their deal, and my manager was trying to renegotiate my deal as my contract was coming up. It did not go particularly well. I was asked in an interview about fighter pay, and I said, "I'd make more money working as a trashman than fighting in the UFC." It was a throwaway comment, but it went viral. Naturally Dana White wasn't super appreciative of his brand-new fighter (who hadn't even stepped into the UFC octagon yet) talking shit about the organization.

Now I'm not saying any of this was planned, because no one would do that in the high-integrity world of prizefighting, but all of a sudden Tim Kennedy, the loudmouth fighter known for being a great grappler, was paired with Roger Gracie, the most elite Jiu Jitsu fighter that has possibly ever lived, in a loser goes home match. Right before that match, Dana kicked all of the coaches out and said something to the effect of, "Maybe instead of talking shit about your pay, you should all go out there and fucking fight! Give the fucking fans what they fucking want! Maybe then you'll get fucking paid the way you want. That'll get you money. Not whining to the press like coward fucking faggot Tim Kennedy. Go put on a fucking show! Don't grapplefuck your opponent like fucking Tim Kennedy. Do you fucking understand what I'm saying, everyone? Tim Kennedy?"

Now, I may have forgotten a word or two, or maybe the exact sequence, but that was the gist of it. It was a really nice moment.

Anyway, after an early scare where Roger Gracie, the greatest grappler who has ever lived (in case you forgot), had my back and was trying to rear naked choke me, I escaped his submission and then grapplefucked him to a dominant victory. (Roger was a gentleman, by the way, and it was an honor to share a cage with him. He deserved to stay in the UFC, but obviously, me and my trashman salary didn't get to make that call.)

That was the night that Anderson Silva, possibly the greatest MMA fighter of all time, lost to Chris Weidman, so Dana's anger toward me got lost in the excitement of that moment, which was nice. Thankfully, it never came back, because only a few months later, he offered me the headlining fight against Lyoto Machida at Fight for the Troops 3 at Fort Campbell, Kentucky, home of the 101st Airborne Division.

Unfortunately, Machida sold me out and went to fight Mark Muñoz instead after Michael Bisping, my least favorite fighter ever, got hurt. So I challenged every single 185-pound fighter to a fight. They all ignored me except for Rafael Natal, a Renzo Gracie black belt with extremely heavy hands. So that brings us up to speed.

I finish my pad session with Brandon. "Tacos?" I ask him. "Sounds good, man!" he quickly replies. "Tacos?" I ask Nick and Julie. Nick is in. Julie is not. She has work to do.

"Nick, can you watch Jon's giant bag of money while I shower?" Nick sighs. Years of being my friend has taken its toll. "Yes, Tim."

─────────

The door bursts open.

"Here we go, baby! It's your time now, Mr. Kennedy! It is show-time now, soldier! Here we go!" comes the powerful voice of Burt Watson, legendary UFC hype man. The sixty-four-year-old former Marine stands in front of me with his salt-and-pepper stubble against his weathered, dark skin, wearing his trademark backwards ball cap, and there is fire in his eyes. "Here we go, baby! This one's for the troops! This is what we do, baby! We roooollllllliiinnnng!" he shouts into my face. If anyone else did it, this moment would be cheesy as fuck, but when Burt Watson looks you in the eyes and tells you it's go time, you fucking go.

I'm so fired up, in fact, that I can barely feel my torn quad. I fucked this thing up a week ago training, and by the time I got to the event, my leg was black-and-blue from my junk to about six inches above my knee. I paid a makeup artist to hide it before the doctor checkup and weigh-in, and the guys and I did the best we could with some basic makeup tonight.

I march outside the trailer and my hot, wet skin meets the brisk November air, forcing it to tingle with goose bumps. I can hear the roar of the crowd through the tin airport hangar as we approach the makeshift stadium that is the home for Fight for the Troops 3. Nervousness swims through my stomach. The fact that I am nervous fucks with me. I haven't felt jitters leading up to a fight since before my first deployment. They have always felt like games since then—a play fight with nothing but pride on the line. I look back at my corners. Greg and Wink are cool as cucumbers. They've done this a thousand times. Brandon Gibson, my striking coach, is amped and nodding. "Here we go, man," he says. Nick is bouncing from one foot to the other as if he is the one fighting. He's usually pretty stoic before these things, but as a veteran, I know he's feeling it too. This fight is different. There's something bigger on the line.

I am the main event, and the last chance for the military to get a win tonight. The other two military members on the card, who also happen to be friends of mine and Ranger Up–sponsored fighters, Liz Carmouche and Colton Smith, had lost their bouts. *I need this win.*

Natal's walkout song comes on and the crowd starts cheering in a respectful way. *I'm proud of you guys. That's the way to represent the military.* If this were a civilian fight, he'd be getting booed or I would be getting booed, and some dipshit would be yelling, "Sweep the leg!" or "Put him in a body bag!" But not here.

I really appreciate Natal. He is a good guy and he knew he was not going to be the fan favorite if he took this fight. The troops in attendance are showing a lot of discipline, but I know they wouldn't boo even if they wanted to. There's too many First Sergeants and Platoon Sergeants patrolling the event making sure no one embarrasses themselves. I wonder how many fucking briefings these poor bastards were forced to go to before this fight, and how early the formations were in order to ensure everyone arrived on time. My guess is something absurd like two hours beforehand, but three wouldn't surprise me. *The Army really does the dumbest shit.* It's funny what goes through your mind when you're two minutes away from someone trying to bludgeon you repeatedly about the head, neck, and shoulders.

And then boom.

Alice In Chains' "Rooster" comes blaring into the hangar. The mechanism is engaged. My song is on. I chose it years ago because the band's guitarist wrote it about his dad, a Vietnam vet, and the hell he went through to get back home. I chose it back then because Nick told me the backstory and I thought it was cool. The more I listened to it, the more it became a part of me. I'd almost died so many times—as a firefighter, in Iraq, in Afghanistan—but nothing has stopped me and I remain defiant. I know Jerry Cantrell wrote the song about his dad, but when I hear it, I feel like he wrote it about me. *I am* the Rooster, and no one on this blue ball floating through space has found a way to kill me yet. As I let the song flow through me, worry dissipates. My adrenaline crawls up as the guitar whines into the night. By the time they say the words, "Ain't found a way to kill me yet," I'm transported to a different place. I am absolutely unstoppable.

But tonight transcends those feelings. Those opening words don't just fire me up. They send a bolt of lightning through the whole crowd, and the resulting thunder is thousands of soldiers and airmen, including guys I had served with, screaming at the top of their lungs for me. I've never felt more invincible in my entire life.

I jog down to the cage and am met with a sea of high-fives. On the way to the octagon I embrace a flight medic I had last seen in Afghanistan when I handed him some of my wounded teammates.

My connection to this crowd is so personal—so powerful. It feels like I never left.

Overwhelmed by emotion, I soak in the support and the gratitude of my fellow soldiers and allow it to charge me up. When I get to the referee station, I rip all my clothes off in about 0.5 seconds, deliver a heaping pile of sweaty cotton to Nick, which has to be gross, tap my cup to show it is present, show the referee Herb Dean my mouthpiece, and climb into the cage.

The lights are red hot and I am pretty stoked about that because the hangar is fucking cold. Bruce Buffer comes in and his bellowing voice shakes the place as he announces us. If Burt Watson is the king of firing a man up, then Bruce Buffer has to be a close second. I actually feel bad for all those guys in boxing stuck with his brother. I'll take the over-the-top flamboyance of Bruce any day. When he finally gets to my name and points at me, the place erupts all over again. It is so loud that I feel like I might lose equilibrium. It's like the end of *Rocky IV* when all the Russians start rooting for Rocky instead of Ivan Drago, except I am getting that treatment from the very beginning.

The bell rings, and just like that, the fight begins.

Natal comes right at me with some very clean striking. He splits my nose early with a good snapping jab, but because my face is basically scar tissue from over 100 fights, that isn't saying a lot. Nevertheless, his hands are what I am worried about as he circles me. Even though he is a Brazilian Jiu Jitsu black belt, I welcome a ground fight. At this point, I haven't been subbed in a match or in practice in about seven years, and I am coming off a win against Roger Gracie, so fuck it. Bring it on. Let's sit down and do some Jiu Jitsu. But standing, Natal has real power in both hands and some slick kicks.

As he catches me with a couple more minor strikes, the crowd, in an attempt to help me, starts chanting, "Ranger Up! Ranger Up!" followed by, "USA! USA!" The chants do the opposite, though. I become so worried about whether they are going to affect my timing and encourage me to attack based on adrenaline and excitement, rather than choosing the right moment, that I hold back a few times when the "right moment" presents itself. And in case you are wondering, the right moment is a microsecond of opportunity that Natal creates when he advances, where he drops his right hand just a little to gear up to throw his left. Greg and Brandon identified that microsecond because they are really fucking good at what they do, and Brandon drilled that moment into me nonstop for weeks. By my count, I have missed two chances to hit him because I am overthinking this fight.

I can hear Brandon yelling, "Tomahawk!" which is the code word for a lunging left hook I had practiced about a thousand times over the last couple months at Jackson's. I dial myself back in and look for the next opportunity, as Natal throws a leg kick. Typically, I eat those and use them to throw a counter, but because of the weakness of my quad, I have to check it. As I do, I slip on the mat and hit the ground. Even though it is just for an instant before I am back up, it pisses me off. I lock back on to him. No more fucking around. I just need that moment. The one I have practiced a thousand times.

The world slows down. I can hear his breath. I can see the flutter in his eye. I pick up the barely perceptible tensing of his shoulders as he moves to throw that punch. And there it is.

I see him twitch forward and I know his hand will drop. Before it even does, I explode forward with a leaping left hand. It is so fast he doesn't see it coming, and I catch him flush, right on the button. I will realize later he was completely unconscious on his feet, but at this moment I follow him to the ground and punch him two more times before Herb Dean tackles me, ending the fight.

A sonic boom blows the roof right off the building. The roof still might be in orbit. It is absolute fucking pandemonium. I scream and celebrate like I never have before. I look over to my corners and point to them and by the time I do, Nick is already getting reprimanded by the Tennessee Fighting Commission for jumping clean off the stool and screaming his ass off when I connected. Even normally emotionless Greg is caught up in the moment, shouting and hugging everyone in sight. I sprint toward the cage and jump on top of it to salute the troops, my brothers and sisters in arms.

I instantly realize that jumping onto a seven-foot cage with a torn quad is dumb. That little number will cost me a month or so of rehab. But at this moment, I don't fucking care. Joe Rogan, realizing the significance of this fight for the audience, is carried away by the emotional avalanche. Years later, he will tell me he recognizes this night and this knockout as one of the most exhilarating and significant in his UFC career. His excitement in the post-fight interview draws even greater emotion out of me, and as soon as it is over I fight my way past the athletic commission and walk into the waiting crowd.

I skip no handshake or picture request. I hug every single one of my brothers and sisters in uniform. I am so happy to be amongst them, and I am so emotional I apologize to almost everyone I meet for no longer being on active duty. UFC staff start yelling at me to leave the crowd, because I am late for my post-fight physical and for the press conference. I don't care. I did what I came to do, and I'm not leaving until they want me to leave. This isn't my night. This is our night.

I stare out into the sea of humanity and lose myself in it, the same way I stared out into that lonely California sea so many years ago, and think about how much life I have lived since then. I have had so many amazing moments. So many things that I never could have imagined then have now transpired. In my wildest dreams, I could not have created this night. I let the waves of exhilaration crash over me, and I keep swimming.

Michael. Fucking. Bisping.

I have waited three years for this opportunity, and it is now mine for the taking. On April 16, 2014, in Quebec City, I will be fighting "The Count" in the main event of UFC Fight Night. I have fought many men over the years. I have a hard time thinking of any I do not like. Most elite fighters are respectful and cool. I'm also not generally a shit-talker when it comes to opponents, so I rarely have encountered anyone that I have a real beef with.

Then there's Michael Bisping.

I do not like him. He does not like me. And it will probably always be that way.

To be fair and totally transparent, I started it all.

In late 2010, Jorge Rivera wanted to get a fight with Michael Bisping. Jorge was one of our first sponsored fighters at Ranger Up, and we love him. He's a man who, not unlike me, has been through adversity, has weathered some bad life decisions, has served his country, and has achieved success. And while he was a great fighter for years who only had losses to top ten fighters, he never got the attention he deserved. So when he came to Nick and me and talked about wanting to fight Michael Bisping, the Ranger Up team basically launched a right-out-of-the-pages-of-Army-manuals psychological operation on Bisping. The guy cannot take being made fun of. He predictably overreacts, which makes for great content and a lot of hype. So, we created a whole series of videos about him: We made fun of how softly he hits. We created fake interviews with him, where the character of Bisping was played by Jorge's boxing coach, Matt Phinney. We redid the "Brave Sir Robin" Monty Python sketch where Bisping was the main character who ran away a coward. And we wrote a whole song about how he was a dick. We actually decided not to use that one because it went too far and then Bisping did an interview where he called Jorge a "retard" and said he wasn't a real American because he was Hispanic, so we said fuck it and launched that one too. In each video, Jorge Rivera was the guy calling him out.

Every video we made went viral. It was the first time this kind of comedic campaign had ever been used in MMA. Jorge got the fight.

Not only did he get the fight, but it rose from an also-ran fight on the undercard to the co–main event because of the hype we created! One of our videos even aired in its entirety on ESPN. The fight got so big that Jorge got a pretty significant bonus for creating all of the fan interest around it. We were very happy for him and felt like we did our jobs supporting our friend and athlete.

Come the day of the fight, Jorge and Bisping were neck and neck. It was very hard to score. That is until Bisping illegally kneed Jorge when he was on the ground. It was so flagrant that if Jorge had opted not to continue, he would have won. Jorge lay on the ground flat on his face, holding his head for a long time. Then he got up to his knees. Joe Rogan and Mike Goldberg, the announcers that night, said the fight was over. But then something happened. Even though he was badly concussed, he got bullied by the ringside doctor to continue in a truly fucked-up display of "the show must go on."

He could barely focus his eyes after the illegal knee and Bisping finished him shortly thereafter. The guy ran around like he won the Olympic Gold Medal and ignored the fact that he needed to cheat to win. Then he walked over to the corner and spat on Matt Phinney. And finally, just to be more despicable, he told everyone that Jorge had made fun of his girlfriend and kids, something Jorge, nor any of us, did do or would ever do. Jorge lost his daughter a few years ago, and family is the most important thing to him. Nick is Italian. You know he isn't going after anyone's family. I'm Irish. Same thing. Our cheesy comedic videos (and they were cheesy) were focused squarely on Bisping and Bisping alone.

We expected shit-talking after Jorge lost. That was Bisping's absolute right. We didn't expect cheating. We didn't expect spitting. We didn't expect lying. We didn't expect him to just be a continuous fucking cunt. But he was.

I'm a martial artist. I know shit happens in a fight. Maybe your hand accidentally gets stuck in the fence, or you pull on shorts on a takedown, or the guy turns and you hit the back of his head unexpectedly. But you still try to show respect, for your opponent and for the art. Bisping full on blasted an obviously downed opponent and then celebrated it unrepentantly and suffered no retribution. So, what started as a little comedic hype for our man Jorge turned into some genuine bad blood. This guy needed to get a little justice, and I decided I would deliver that punishment.

Now this was a weird decision at that time, because I was not in the UFC. There was no direct way for me to fight him. But Nick and I (and Tom and Kelly) just decided that we would chip away at that problem a little at a time until it was inevitable. From that moment on out, if I did an interview, I'd try to find little ways to slide his name into it. If someone cheated in a fight and I was asked about it in an interview, I'd refer to it as "pulling a Bisping." Anytime he was fighting someone, we'd put out a video asking that person to punch him in the face. And we always used Matt Phinney for the videos—the guy he had spat on.

I directly reached out to him for the first time on Twitter in May 2011 about three months after the Rivera fight by tweeting, "It is disrespectful and unprofessional to illegally knee someone in the face while they have their knees on the ground." Naturally he overreacted, asking me, "What the fuck has it got to do with you and why are you piping up now? You missed the bandwagon. It left two months ago." I kept pushing. Jabs here and there. Every interview. Every article. Nick kept pushing. Videos. Graphics. Even a full animated cartoon where animated Bisping refers to hamburgers as "Meat Biscuits." He got to the point where he lost it one time and did this whole interview on Fox Sports where he just talked about how much he "fucking hated Ranger Up and Tim Kennedy." We sold $125,000 in T-shirts that day because he just couldn't help but talk about us. (Thanks, Mike!)

After I beat Natal, I knew it was the right moment, so I tweeted that he was chickening out of fighting me. That did it. Minutes later, he replied with, "Listen, pussy. It's real simple. I've never 'chickened' out of shit in my life. Just ask Dana White and the UFC for the fight."

I did just that, and they gave it to me. It's so wild to think that we spent three years selling a fight. After all that effort, the opportunity to dole out justice and leap forward in the rankings is all on the line.

Bisping referred to our fight as Jorge Rivera II. To him this meant the chance to shut up Tim Kennedy and the Ranger Up boys once and for all. To me this was a lot bigger than that. This was the one chance to make the world right, to avenge what happened to Rivera, and to shut this fucking guy up. Losing wasn't an option. It just wasn't.

To make it more personal, I had just spent the last six weeks training with Matt Phinney. He and Nick had become good friends and he recommended Matt to me to come train at Jackson's, and I recommended him to Greg. So, three workouts a day, every meal, and even hikes through the mountains on the weekends with maybe the only guy that wanted Bisping beaten more than I did further cemented what I need to do.

April 16, 2014, came quickly. Almost every human being I know came out to Quebec City, the location of our fight, even though there was a storm ravaging Canada. My wife couldn't even fly in because the hurricane conditions shut down the airport, so one of my other friends, a former SF guy named Matt Burden, linked up with her in Michigan and drove her the rest of the way. It felt like the entire military community was here in this one hotel where all the fighters and fight fans descended on. I feel the pressure, but it doesn't eat at me. This moment is inevitable. It has to happen. Now I just need to claim it.

The bell rings.

The game plan is to keep my knees bent so I can explode forward with either an overhand right or a right hook and follow it right up with a left hook or uppercut. When he's buttered up with a few of those, I'm going to take him down and do damage from up top. And I do. I land a few nice shots. Nothing crazy, but I'm controlling the distance and I'm connecting with my hands. I see my opening.

I shoot! I get deep on his legs and drive him into the cage, finishing the takedown. His defense is great. He gets the stand-up. I immediately drag him back down. After several iterations of this, the bell rings, and the round is over. I feel good.

In the corner, Greg reminds me to keep my knees bent and to keep moving my head and feet. I go back out there . . . and listen to nothing he says. I do fine. I believe I won the round. But it is not anywhere near as dominant as round one.

When I sit back down on my stool, Greg is mad. Greg is never mad at me. He's the quiet type. "Specialist Kennedy!" Greg calls me, dropping me many ranks and invoking the kid that once had to fight through SOPC for four months, "Why do you want him back in this fight? He doesn't deserve that. I don't care how tired you get, Tim Kennedy. Bend the knees, move the head, and I don't want to see you near that cage! Relentless, Tim Kennedy! Relentless!"

His anger lit a fuse in me. I didn't want Luke Rockhold again. I want to secure the victory. For the next three rounds, I am relentless. I hit Michael Bisping with everything I have. He absorbs it. I take him down. He gets back up. I beat him and beat him and beat him, but he does not submit.

When the final bell sounds, there is no question in anyone's mind who won, but rather by how much. Only two judges gave him a round. The other gave me all five.

This was a different happiness than the Natal fight. That fight was raw emotion. That was an athletic act with a special crowd. This fight was the culmination of three and a half years of strategic planning by multiple people to avenge my friend and give me this opportunity. Standing there, giving the respect to Bisping for being a tough-as-nails fighter (he is, even if it hurts to say), I felt like I had finally accomplished my big MMA moment. The UFC did too.

I was now in title contention.

September 27, 2014
The MGM Grand Garden Arena, Las Vegas, Nevada

Every muscle in my body is engaged. Every iota of my being is locked on Yoel Romero, the muscle-riddled Olympian Silver Medalist in wrestling, who I am now fighting. If I win this fight, I get a title shot. Everything about this fight is why I love this sport. He's so fast. He's so powerful. One millisecond of not paying attention—of missing a cue—of reading a feint incorrectly—and one of us is going to be unconscious. His wrestling is a little better than mine. My Jiu Jitsu is better than his. We both throw power in both hands and legs. I can hear the crowd react every time one of us makes contact. Even when the shots hit me, I hear them as an outsider—as if they are happening to someone else. I don't have time to think about the pain or the blood or the danger. I have to focus on the dance that is this fight.

It's hard for me to explain this, but while I have won and lost fights before, I have never been truly tested by a fighter the way I am being tested right now. This feels dangerous. Every punch that misses me by a millimeter ignites my soul. Every shot that almost drags me to the ground wakes up something primal. Every kick that glances off my arms engages something within me that no other fighter ever has. These strikes could all end me, but they don't. I've never been better than this.

I see the opening . . . and I take it. I throw a monster uppercut and connect! He's wobbly! Left hook. Right uppercut again! Left! Right!

The bell rings. He is saved, but he can barely stand. He wobbles over to his stool. He looks out.

Greg tells me to stay focused. I'm watching Romero. He's fucked and I know it.

The timer sounds to start the third round. He doesn't get up! I won the fight! I am getting a title shot!

But wait . . . his corner is saying something to John McCarthy. Twenty more seconds have gone by. I walk over to ask McCarthy what is going on. He points me back to my corner. *What the fuck? This is over. Why haven't they called it?*

By the time Romero stands up, 1:47 seconds have passed. His corner pretended not to speak any English and spilled water all over the ground to buy him some more time to recover. And somehow, some way, McCarthy, typically the best ref in the game, let it all happen. I'm fucking pissed.

"Reengage Kennedy!" Greg yells.

This isn't fair. This is bullshit! Why the fuck does he get to come back out? I already won this fight!

The bell sounds and I have to get back out there. My brain is not here. It's back there, thinking about the unfairness of this call, thinking about the cheating from this asshole, thinking about how they got away with it. I miss the movement that is imperceptible to most people but oh so obvious to elite fighters. I eat a powerful shot. Thirty seconds later the fight is over. I lost.

How did this fucking happen?!

The crowd is booing. People are literally throwing things at the cage. Romero is running around like Michael Bisping at the Jorge Rivera fight. My corners are in the cage now. They help me up. I look into their eyes. *How do we take this back? I won this fight.* Greg, Nick, and Brandon all have the same look. It's not disappointment. It's sadness. They all feel awful for me right now. They've all seen me lose, but this is different. It's an injustice. And it's one they know I will not be able to endure.

Ginger and I had already decided that if my title fight run gets stopped, then I am done.

I've started my own training company, Sheepdog Response, and it is taking off. I am still employed by the National Guard, and I'd like to get back to running missions. I also have several other business interests. Lastly, fighting pays me the least of everything I do, especially since I left Strikeforce, so there is no good reason to keep doing this. I'm thirty-five. Almost no one stays good past thirty-seven.

But I wanted this so badly. I wanted to be world champion. I wanted to follow in the footsteps of my first mentor, Chuck Liddell.

I will never get to.

We walk out of the cage to the back room. Nick follows right behind me. The second the fans cannot see me anymore, I scream "Fuck!" as loud as I can. I look at Nick, then Brandon Gibson. "Fuck, man. I had it." "I know," Brandon says. "You were fucking amazing out there to-night," Nick adds.

Suddenly, Romero appears with an entourage and says, "I want to talk to him!" and points at me. I don't want to see him. He comes up to me and starts to tell me something, but I don't know what. It seems well intentioned. He is trying to show respect. I don't give a fuck. "If you don't get off the stool, you lose!" I yell at him. His head drops and he won't make eye contact anymore. He knows. One of his corners starts yapping at me. Romero tries to calm him, but corners like to yap. Security starts walking over and Nick stands between me and Romero. Brandon joins him a second later. "Tim, let's go, buddy."

The two of them gather up all my stuff. I don't get to do a press conference, because I, Nick, and my four bags all get loaded onto an ambulance. I apparently need to get checked for brain trauma.

We spend six hours together in that emergency room. I sit in a puddle of blood, sweat, and some very fresh tears and think about my life. Every once in a while, I let out an emotional outburst or a pensive thought. "I think I might be done, man," I tell Nick, wondering what his reaction might be.

"That's good, man, because I'm getting fucking sick of these emergency rooms." I laugh. It really could be a lot worse than this, and I know it. I just wanted it so bad. Objectively, I know I should have stayed sharp. Regardless of what the ref fucked up, I still had the opportunity to win that fight. But I also know if Herb Dean had been the ref, I would have won. An amazing opportunity was stolen from me by a combination of Yoel Romero, John McCarthy, and Tim Kennedy.

I remind myself I can only control one of those variables, and I blew it. That is calming in a weird way.

So what are you going to do now, Tim?

I want to leave this ER, for one. So, we do. I never got checked that night, because Las Vegas ERs suck, and six hours was more than enough waiting. We hail a cab, find a late-night pizza joint, and Ginger and Brandon meet us there. The pizza is delicious. With my wife and friends around me, the loss stings a little less. *Maybe life will be okay without this.*

I would fight one more time. I came back two years later unexpectedly when my old teammate Rashad Evans was looking for a fight. That might have been the only fight I would come back for, other than another shot at Bisping. He ended up not passing the physical, and I ended up fighting and losing to his replacement Kelvin Gastelum, a younger me with shittier Jiu Jitsu and better boxing. Nick and I ended up right back in one of those ERs again, and that fact wasn't lost on either of us. The only difference is that this time I didn't "think" I was done.

"That was the last one, man," I tell Nick, four bags slung across his back.

"You sure this time?" he asks.

"I'm one hundred percent sure. I don't want this anymore."

"Good. Let's do something else."

CHAPTER THIRTEEN

TV AND A MOVIE

I didn't think the "something else" Nick mentioned would be television.

By the time the offer came to join the *Hunting Hitler* cast on the History Channel in 2015 (about a year after my Romero fight), I had already done a few redundant one-off episodes of other TV shows like *Deadliest Warrior* (August 2011), *Ultimate Soldier Challenge* (2013), and *Celebrity Fit Club Season 7: Bootcamp 2*. Those experiences were not exactly as good as they sound.

Deadliest Warrior was a pretty cool show that matched up warriors throughout history. I was part of a new concept: to compare modern soldiers instead of ancient ones. I have to tell you this concept ended up being markedly less cool. They billed me as an Army Ranger sniper who had to take on Korean Special Forces snipers. Behind the scenes, the Koreans couldn't make the more challenging shots, so the producers asked me to shoot their targets, but shoot them less well than my own target. They needed it to seem close so it would make good television. I did it, but felt dirty doing it, and also wanted to teach the Koreans how to shoot better! So if you watched that show, I shot every shot that hit a target.

I left the show with a bad taste in my mouth, and the feeling that television producers are just a bunch of liars.

The *Ultimate Soldier Challenge* was a little better. It was a competition show with a reality TV component. In my episode, they had three pairs of guys compete. My team was me and an active-duty 5th Special Forces Group guy named Matt representing the U.S. Special Forces against two guys from Norwegian FSK named Thor and Tom, who both looked like they were from Asgard, and a team of two contractors focused on protecting high-value targets named Leo and Ryan. Leo was a former Russian Spetsnaz and Ryan was a former Marine. There were several different scoring events. The first one was a target shoot where you had to shoot all the orange targets (the bad guys) and none of the white targets (the good guys). Whoever did it fastest without shooting a white target won. It was easy. We beat the contractors by about ten seconds, which might not seem like much, but it is a lifetime on a shooting exercise. The Norwegians sucked bad on that and finished like a minute later.

The next challenge was a sniper tower. You had to shoot the sniper and shoot the three legs of the tower to win. We won again so we didn't have to do the next challenge. That sucked, because the next challenge was knife fighting and I wanted to stab these guys. The contractors won again, beating the poor Norwegians, so they got eliminated.

Now it was just us and the contractors. We had to drive through a small town in less than two minutes and hit as many targets as possible without shooting a hostage. The contractors hit ten out of twenty targets and killed one hostage. We hit eighteen out of twenty targets and were mad we didn't see the other two. That set up the final challenge. We had to go to an enemy compound with five bad guys and kill them, acquire a laptop and a hard drive, and get back to an extraction point. If you shoot the bad guy, he dies. If he shoots you, you die. The contractors went first with a frontal assault on every building, dumb, but they somehow didn't get killed and completed the mission in 32:19. We did it smart and fast and were done in 12:50.

In short, my Green Beret partner and I murdered everyone and won every single event handily. There were no close calls. Because of that, they asked us to reshoot some things so we would look less competent, and the events would seem more competitive. We grudgingly did. Even with those bullshit edits, we beat everyone so bad it was terrible TV. Once again, I left feeling television is full of liars and cheats.

Celebrity Fit Club Season 7: Bootcamp 2 was the worst. That show was about a bunch of Z-list celebrities trying to get fit. I was a guest coach. It's not even worth talking about. Everyone sucked, especially the actors. They had disgusting aloof attitudes, all talked down to me and the film crew, and all needed to be punched repeatedly in the face. It was frustrating. If the purge happened right at the moment, most of them would have been in bad shape. *The Purge* is a movie where for twenty-four hours you can kill anyone you want.

All three of these shows pretty much convinced me that television was not for me. I hated every experience and swore I was done with it. Then one day sometime in early 2015, a production company called Karga Seven called me. They were looking for consultants for a hush-hush television program and someone had referred me to them. They called and asked a bunch of weird questions.

"What do you know about South America, Tim?"

"I've deployed there six times, and I have buddies in Chile, Argentina, Brazil, Colombia, and Peru. Why?"

"No reason, Tim. Do you know how to use ground-penetrating radar?"

"Yeah, I used it repeatedly in the Middle East to look for caves filled with Al Qaeda. Do you want to tell me why you're asking me this?"

"We will . . . later. Tim, can you fly a drone?"

"Yes, I can."

"Do you speak Spanish?"

"Yes, I do."

"What are some examples of when you have hunted people?"

"I've hunted Zarqawi, the number two terrorist in the world, and was part of the team that got him. I've hunted Al Qaeda throughout Afghanistan. I've hunted sex traffickers on three continents, rhino poachers in

Africa, and drug syndicates in South America. I also hunted my wife for a long time before I finally bagged her."

Apparently, there are not a lot of people on planet earth that can sufficiently answer those questions. They chatted for a while and then asked me if I would be willing to be on camera for a television show instead of being the consultant. *Oh fuck no. I'm not doing this shit again.*

"Guys, I appreciate the offer but unless this is absolutely the coolest show ever, with a real purpose, and no bullshit in the edit room, I am out."

"Tim, we are going to retrace the steps of World War II Nazis, legitimately hunt them down, build target lists on them, and turn those lists over to the authorities to have any living Nazis arrested, and the assets of any dead Nazis seized. We're calling it *Hunting Hitler.* Are you down to do that?"

They got me! Dammit, they got me!

"I am indeed down with that. There is truly nothing I want to do more."

Our first production meeting, in the Karga offices in Burbank, California, was like nothing I had ever experienced before. It didn't feel like a show. There weren't directors and producers running around talking about drama and eyeballs and what they could do to make it more interesting. It felt more like a military operation.

I wonder who is financing this thing, because the room is full of lawyers, law enforcement, and government agencies. More interestingly, there isn't a single actor here. Typically, television shows, even unscripted ones like this one, hire actors. Instead, these guys hired some of the best hunters in the world.

Bob Baer is heading up headquarters for the show. He hunted bin Laden and other HVTs. Dr. John Cencich is an international war crimes investigator. Lenny DePaul is a U.S. Marshal. Steve Rambam is a private investigator hired by the richest Jewish families in the world to hunt Nazis for the past two decades. James Holland is a well-known World War II historian with a focus on the Nazis. Gerrard Williams is an investigative journalist and historian who focuses on the pathways Nazis (and potentially Hitler) may have taken as they fled Germany. These men are real hunters. This isn't the B team. This is the best and brightest in the world at this shit. *Very interesting.*

The show is television, and of course the editors are going to do their best to add excitement and drama, but it really is unscripted. There is so much real shit happening, there is no need to fabricate anything. I immediately love working on the show. There's a real purpose. The showrunners care about that purpose. We start, as anyone should, with open-source materials and informants. We need to figure out where the most likely locations are to track down the cowards who fled the Allied invasion of Germany. We're also well aware that the people we were now hunting have been hunted since 1944. The Mossad and the KGB have hunted these guys for decades.

The Mossad is an Israeli paramilitary group with the mission of getting retribution for the crimes of the Nazis. The KGB (not so unlike the Americans) hunted them for either public relations wins for finding the men who killed so many of their citizens or to capture their best scientists to get ahead during the space race or the Cold War. Avoiding capture is now in their DNA. That makes our mission much harder— and more exciting.

These Nazis wrote the book on how to disappear into populations and stay off the radar. Before the mujahideen, before ISIS, and before the IRA, there were the Nazis. An entire generation of them avoided capture and spread throughout the world like a virus. And that virus has almost no discernible symptoms unless you look closely enough. We want to find every instance of it, and cut it out of its host, leaving the world a healthier place.

I will say this: I don't know what the rest of the cast of the show think, but I am pretty sure Hitler died in Berlin. The title of the show and the ominous voiceover throughout implies that we are going to find him or his progeny. I do not believe that, and I don't think most of the team does either. But it's a catchy title, and the show gives us the means of finding those who did get out.

We start our journey in Misiones, on the hunt for what some people believe is the place Martin Bormann, one of Hitler's top officers, fled to.

Misiones is in the upper northeast edge of Argentina, a little finger darting out between Brazil and Paraguay. It's covered in lush jungle, the kind of place that's easy to disappear to. We begin by building a war room in our hotel and asking ourselves: *If you were a Nazi, where would you hide?* We build a murder board on the wall with the faces of Nazis who have never been found and believed to have fled here to South America. The plan is to continue to update our wall with linkages and evidence as we find it.

Our overseas team was Steve Rambam, Gerrard Williams, and me, plus two cameramen, an audio guy, a producer, and a local fixer. Steve was our ground force commander. He's the guy negotiating with people, planning, strategizing, and giving the orders. I'm the guy executing. I'm talking to the locals, climbing things, sneaking around, scuba diving, and doing whatever Steve thinks up. Gerrard is the brain. He is generally at the hotel analyzing our findings. He's like a human super Google for Nazi shit. "Hey, Gerrard! We just found this Nazi medal! What is it?" "Ah! This is the equivalent of the U.S. Bronze Star and is only given to officers in the African Campaign." That interaction is fictional, but it was like that all the time. He just knew things that would take hours to research online. His job was to analyze our data as quickly as possible and report back to Bob Baer to put the whole picture together.

As we set up in our hotel, before our real work begins, I'm already trying to place myself in the mindset of a fleeing Nazi in 1945. *Did they just want to disappear or were they after something bigger? What's their purpose? What's their desired end state? Do they just want to live or are they biding their time waiting for the Fourth Reich?*

But back to the mission at hand: Martin Bormann was Hitler's right-hand man when he died, often referred to as his deputy. He was the guy that gave the Gestapo total power over the Jews. He was the guy who masterminded the plan to begin to eliminate Christianity in Germany upon the end of the war. He was the guy who created a separate penal code for Slavs and Jews in the conquered territories that was far harsher than the German one. And he was the guy Hitler left in charge of the party in his final will and testament. In short, he is evil incarnate.

The questions about Bormann's final destination exist for good reason. We know he didn't die in Hitler's bunker. Hitler ordered him to fly out several days before the Soviets took Berlin. While historians believe his remains were found in Berlin in 1972, based on DNA evidence from 1998, questions remain. Was the body his or a family member's? Was his dental work done with dental technology that did not exist until the '50s? Was the red clay found on his body in 1972 a type of dirt only found in the Americas? Why were authors who claimed they had evidence of Bormann's existence threatened?

I don't have the answers to these questions. I'm not going to pretend that at the beginning of this thing I am any kind of expert in Nazis, but I know the U.S. allowed Nazis to emigrate and be scientists, and I know the Soviets did, as well. I believe it is entirely possible that through some drug deal, Bormann was allowed to live, spill the secrets of the Reich, and then, upon his actual death, get deposited back to where he supposedly died.

Did that happen? Probably not, but it's possible.

So, let's go look.

Misiones is gorgeous, and right in the heart of the jungle. It's lush and green, teeming with life, and it smells fresh. Losing oneself in here would be the easiest thing in the world. The team is looking for Nazi artifacts, but I am more interested in an equally important story: the German pattern of life. What do I mean by that? James Bond drinks vodka martinis. Jocko Willink gets up every morning at 4:00 a.m. to work out. Winston Churchill smoked cigars after dinner every evening. These things are part of their DNA. If you follow me around for a day, every day looks pretty much the same no matter where I am on planet earth. I get up after a good night's sleep. I eat a small meal—usually eggs. I brew a basic cup of good black coffee. Then I work out for sixty to ninety minutes. After that, I get a more substantial meal—tacos if they are available—and grab a "fancier" coffee. My personal favorite right now is a cappuccino. Then I work hard all day until about dinnertime, eat dinner with my kids, spend time with my wife, do a little more work after she goes to bed, and then crash. Sometimes there are more workouts. Sometimes there is more work. But the general pattern is the same.

This is true of most people. "Pattern of life" is one of the hardest things to change, even for people who know how to hide. To me, pattern of life is almost as definitive as fingerprints or irises. Misiones looked and smelled like every other small village in Argentina: fresh ground, wet soil, and native foods.

We drive our rented trucks to a town just outside of where we flew in, closer to the archaeological dig that we're here to investigate. I stop at a coffee shop, grab a cappuccino, and get a workout in (my pattern of life). My workout is outside using bodyweight movements and some old car parts floating around, and the little kids in the village are watching me. When you work out, your senses are heightened, and I smell . . . bread. Every place on the planet has its own type of bread: naan, bagels, focaccia, tortilla, croissants . . . the list goes on and on. But this does not smell like local bread—it smells European. It stands out. When I finish my workout, cappuccino in hand, I follow my nose to find the source of the smell.

I locate it a few minutes later and walk in. The guy behind the first counter stands up with spectacles and says, *"Guten Morgen."* I look up and I see the war flag of Germany. I do not need to be Sherlock Holmes to figure this one out.

"Hablas español?" I ask him.

"I speak a little," he replies in English.

"But your English is pretty good!" I answer him with pep and gusto. I'm always annoyingly energetic after a workout. "I have some English." He smiles. He explains that his family had come here in the late 1800s. This makes sense because everywhere Nazis fled there were German settlements first. But it's wild that this guy has been here for three generations and barely speaks Spanish. This is a proud German.

I find pride can be the fuel and excuse for horrific actions. There's good pride, like believing in the quality of your work, or the generosity of your church or something like that. Then there's bad pride, where you feel some imagined or real injury done to you or your people, and you create excuses and scapegoats for that injury. History shows us example after example of this: the Nazis, the Soviets, the Balkans, Iraq, Syria, ISIS, Armenia. Where there is genocide, there tends to be an aggrieved party that cannot come to terms with their own failures, or just the general unjustness of life, coupled with charismatic leaders that offer up a scapegoat. Pride tells them that they, their friends, their nation, and their actions cannot possibly be to blame. The propaganda starts. Then the bullying. Then the laws. Then the incarceration. Then the killing. I see glimpses of it here.

These families moved here in the 1800s when information barely flowed to them, but by the 1920s, they knew Germany was struggling in the aftermath of World War I. Their pride in their ancestors placed that burden on their shoulders and they carried it. Then they heard about this charismatic leader Adolf Hitler. They watched Germany's rise to a power never before seen in every sector: science, manufacturing, and of course the military, and they once again felt pride. They were no longer the world's whipping boy. When Germany fell in 1945, they assumed the talk about the camps was propaganda. Germany had grown too powerful and the world united once again, as it had in 1914, to reduce the greatness of the fatherland. These people are still proud of being German. So it is genuinely interesting to meet this guy.

News travels fast in small towns. Within a few hours of picking up our rental trucks we start hearing, "Oh you must be the Americans!" or "I heard from my friend you have camera equipment! Are you doing a show?" But after talking to the baker for a little while, that all changed. Now we were the guys asking odd questions, in a place where there is little trust of outsiders. We were being watched, for sure. Not by pros. They thought they were being slick, but they were extremely obvious to me. Still the tone changed. We'd see the same motorcycle go by dozens of times a day. There'd be a car that stayed with us in the distance even if we were in the middle of nowhere.

Finally, we catch a break. Our local fixer lets us know there is a family that is willing to let us look at their bunker.

Why would a family have a bunker? It was the German style among the well-to-do to build them after World War I. After living through trench warfare, the Germans always thought it could happen again, and they would need to be prepared. Someone carried that belief here, although trench warfare in the jungle was unlikely.

The plan was for me to use the ground-penetrating radar to examine the area and take a look at the bunker, but that idea goes to shit when the production company guys decide to fly a drone ahead of us to film our arrival at the farm. These people have never seen a drone before, and it freaks them the fuck out and they kick us off their property. A few hours later, I am able to convince them to work with us. Once they make that decision, things go better.

These are Germans living in the middle of the jungle with a main house and a second house with a bunker affixed. This is not normal, and I ask about it. They are very proud and tell me that it is a root cellar. He tells me he dries meat in it after hunting. I tell him I am also a hunter and I wish I had one. I notice a distinct line on the side of the bunker. Underneath the line, everything looks weatherworn and old. Above the line, everything looks new and bright. "Was there something built here that got ripped down?" I ask him. He tells me there used to be a sunroom on top that covered the entire bunker, even the sides, and that the only way to get into it before was to climb in through a panel in the sunroom floor.

"So, you wouldn't even see it at all before?" I ask again.

"No, it was completely hidden," he says, smiling.

That smile slowly turns to a look of concern. He weighs me. He weighs the crew. He kicks us off his property again.

Now we're more curious, so we decide to fly the drone over the property again. This time, he grabs a shotgun and shoots at the drone. *Okay, looks like it is actually time to go.* As we head out, two dirt bikes come out of nowhere and start following us. I know you're never supposed to confront your pursuers, and the reason you are not supposed to is because of exactly what happens next. I flip the vehicle around and wait.

They both hop off their bikes and pull out machetes. "You need to leave or we're going to kill you! Do you hear? No more questions about Nazis!" one of them yells in English, but with a German accent. This is where riding solo sucks. I'm the only man of violence here. Everyone else will die in place. There's two guys and they have big fucking swords. I can kill one easily, but I'm worried about getting both before the other guy cuts me or someone else. I like my chances, but I don't love them. Plus, I don't think stacking two bodies is going to help our cause or endear me with the production company.

We get back in the vehicle and head back to the hotel, but this is the turning point for Tim Kennedy. I was doing a job before—making a television program. Now I'm hunting motherfucking Nazis. This is fun now.

The next day, the crew drives around town and waits for the motorcycles or cars to show up. But this time when they do, I am hiding a distance off in a different vehicle watching them. We run the same playbook that Special Forces guys and spies have run for generations: follow the people following you. Just like it worked in the Caribbean when we followed the pimp, it works here. And after a few days of playing this game, we realize the majority of the activity is coming from a little MMA-style gym not too far away.

So naturally, I avoid the place and keep my nose clean. Just kidding. I head straight to the gym to see what's going on.

When I walk in, I feel at home . . . you know . . . except for all the obvious Nazis. It's like an MMA gym from ten years ago in the States. There are some crappy mats taped together, a few weights lying around, and a couple of mediocre heavy bags. Most of the work happening here is Jiu Jitsu and catch wrestling—basically no Gi submission fighting. There's a very German feel here. It's not the Argentinian chill vibe. It's German intensity. I take note of the men in the room. All white. Lots of blond hair and blue eyes. They have plenty of tattoos: lightning bolts on their lats, the Nazi African Palm Leaf Campaign on one guy's thigh, swastikas on hands or poking out from under shorts at the thighs. These kinds of clubs hark back to the old days of the Nazi Party. They'd go to rallies and have boxing matches or bare knuckle fights. Everything was about testing your manhood. Martial arts are about self-improvement and self-testing, not showing off for others in a hate-filled rage. All eyes lock on me. There is a combination of anger and fear.

When Adolf Eichmann's kids were found, all their bank accounts were emptied. All of their property was taken. While they were not arrested for their father's crimes, they were left destitute. When Nazis are found by the authorities and linked to Nazi money, their entire lineage pays the price. None of these men wanted to pay that price.

I quickly introduce myself and realize some of them know me from the UFC. I use that. "Yeah, I have been fighting for a long time." "Yup, I beat Michael Bisping!" "No, I think I'm done fighting professionally at this point, but I still like to work out whenever I can!"

All of those quick conversations lead very naturally to why I am here: I just want to get some grappling in. They seem to accept this, but follow up with "Why are you in Misiones?"

"I'm here for a travel show about German resettlements throughout the world. So far I've spent a lot of time in Canada and the American Midwest, and I'm heading to Africa from here," I tell them. "Are you here to investigate Nazis?" they ask. "No," I lie. "We thought you were here with the Jews. You know, paid for by the Jewish bankers to give Germans a hard time," the one with the lightning bolts tells me, now seeming more at ease with me. "I don't even know who pays me, to tell you the truth! It's all Hollywood assholes!" I tell him, laughing, and this time not really lying. At least about the part where I didn't know who was paying me. The asshole part is thus far undeserved.

They ask me if I will roll with them, and I tell them that's why I'm here. I beat the crap out of every one of them, but in the nicest way possible. I had to be the big dog to build trust and establish domination, but when I take people down, I'm not lifting them to the sky and smashing them with the earth; I'm gently placing them to the ground. I choke them, but I don't rip their heads off and leave them unable to drink water or speak. I'm showing off, and giving them some stories, but I'm not embarrassing them and making them feel like bitches. By the time I leave, we're laughing and smiling. They feel good about my presence.

Just like that, the harassing stops. We get to talk to people. There is now a degree of civility everywhere we go. We finally get to link up with the archaeologists and see the site that some people believe was Bormann's hideout.

———

When I get there, I spend a lot of time mentally trying to figure out what I am actually looking at. This doesn't look like much of anything anymore because the jungle eats things. A dilapidated house in a city will last forever. Yeah, maybe the roof will leak and the windows will be broken and animals will have found their way inside, but it's still a house. The jungle is far more vicious. The whole structure is all but destroyed. Only the walls and fixtures remain, and they are decidedly European. The lights, the toilets, and the tile scream Germany. When we begin to use our radar, we find treasure troves of Nazi paraphernalia. Not a few things here or there, mind you. We find a *fuckload*. Nazi coins. Nazi jewelry. Nazi plates. Apparently, if it got made any time from 1933 until 1945 there was a swastika emblazoned on it, because that's what we found. It felt evil being around all this stuff.

And as we walked around the town that was now comfortable with us, we saw more and more of it. We even found a bar with a picture of grandpa in his SS uniform hung up like it was a source of pride. The resounding echoes of past evil tarnished everything they touched.

I report everything I find and wait for my next mission from Bob. We had gathered everything we could here.

———

I drop into the icy Norway waters, and even with a thick dry suit on, I instantly feel the sting of cold. I wait for my dive partner to enter the water, check my gear one last time, and begin my 217-foot descent to investigate the German U-boat. We are not the first to see the boat, but we would be the first to see it up close and personal. A tech diver had been working in the area and had noticed something big that he believed might be an old submarine and reported it. In Norway, the cold minimizes the algae content in the water, so on a clear day with slow waters, you can see pretty far, even in the deep. His observation became our opportunity. And that opportunity was that we would be the first to lay hands on the vessel and explore it . . . but first we had to get there.

Diving in any condition is dangerous. Diving into icy waters at the underbelly of a fjord at 200 feet using mixed gases is really fucking hard. Add making a documentary while doing that to the mix, and let's just say I had to be on my best game. For this dive, we are taking three tanks each, each with different mixtures. As I descend into the depths, I pause at intervals to acclimate and leave a tank tied to the cable. We placed the cable by sending a submersible. We were not going to have a ton of time on the bottom and thought it best to locate the wreck and have a fixed point rather than free swimming. We had rehearsed this dive ad nauseam. We did a talk-through and a walk-through on land, then we did the whole dive in shallow water to work out communication and the general plan of action between the two of us. We even practiced what would happen if one of us got the bends from coming up too quickly or nitrogen narcosis for being at depth too long. If that happened, whoever got hit would be thrown into a decompression tank that we had borrowed from some local Special Operations types. Now that we have thought through all the ways we could die, we are heading into the depths.

Every thirty-three feet is one atmosphere of pressure, and you feel it. Two hundred feet is a very short distance on land, but it feels like forever as you drop into the vastness of the ocean. The deeper you go the less direct light is available and the little that you can see is refracted light, removing the sharp edge to anything you see, leaving your mind wondering what is real and what is imagined. As we get closer and closer to our destination, the eerier it gets. When you think of iconic shapes of World War II, you think of the Panzer tank, the P-51 Mustang, the *Iowa*-class battleship, the Spitfire, and the German U-boat. And there it was. Nightmarishly preserved in the cold waters, covered with a creepy glow, is a perfect specimen of the last version of the U-boat.

Being around Nazi stuff is weird. I don't know how people collect vast quantities of it. I don't even like holding the coins because it feels like you're touching evil—like it might suck you in—or you might be somehow touched by the depraved hate. This is all of those feelings and then some. It feels like I am coming up on the Death Star from *Star Wars*, caught in the tractor beam and heading into something I want nothing to do with, but I cannot stop it. I have to go there.

Norway was a huge Nazi port during the war. They had giant naval cannons with interlocking sectors of fire, land mines everywhere, and this technological marvel. I shudder from the cold. I'm being hit both with the external cold water and the internal breathing of air, which at this depth is mostly helium and helium is cold. My partner and I are slowly heading to hypothermia, and we know it. Our dive table allows us to be in the water for one hour, but that's pushing it by every dive rule.

Finally, I am upon it. I lay my hands on it and it's like I am opening a time capsule. There are Nazi markings everywhere. I trace them with my fingers and then look around the boat. The hatch. That's where I am heading. I find the hatch at the end of the tower, signaling to my partner that I am going there. When I arrive, the hatch is closed, but unsealed. *Did they scuttle this ship? Did they crash it? Did they purposely leave the hatch open? Did they go down with the ship or simply sink it?* I open the hatch and realize I will not be able to fit inside of it with my tank on. I consider disconnecting it and re-creating my lobster mission from twenty years ago, but I am pretty sure my partner will have a heart attack and die, so think better of it. Instead, I push my face inside, letting my headlamp do the work it is meant to do.

One of my questions is answered. They went down with the ship. At various places throughout the cabin are floating uniforms that seem to be held in place by something, I presume their skeletons, but with the flowing nature of their jackets, I cannot quite make them out. The unsealed hatch has made this a habitat for creatures, and I could see a ton of bottom-feeding crabs moving around inside. I know the fate these men's bodies met.

I signal to my partner, and he peers inside, briefly filming. At this point, we both know that there will be no more discovery of this ship. It is now a war memorial gravesite and international law prevents us from going in or taking anything from the wreck. I say a small prayer for them, even though it's hard for me to find that grace within myself given what these men represented. This was a sad and lonely death.

We spend the rest of the time taking pictures—of the tower, of the torpedo tubes, and of the entire boat from a distance. I swim the length of the ship to estimate its length, height, and tower size. Finally, I signal to my partner that it is time to go up.

We ride ever so slowly up the line, switching tanks as we arrive at them. I start to feel nauseated, which is normal upon ascent as the helium works its way out of your system. It expands, making you feel like you have to shit and puke all at the same time. Incidentally, that's the same feeling you get from all other forms of dive conditions, so as I come up I wonder if I'm just normal dive fucked or, as the Brits would say, "proper fucked." I finally surface and as actual air gets into my system, I start feeling better almost immediately. *Whew!*

I have an unnatural feeling about hovering over the wreck, even 200 feet above it on the surface. I don't want to be in this water. I don't want to be in this place. I want to get away from here, get to the hotel, and wash this experience off my skin.

Season one of *Hunting Hitler* went so well and we unearthed so much information that it became the number one show on the History Channel. Before the season was over in late 2015, they had already ordered a second season. I loved everything about doing the show. I was hunting bad guys, traveling the world, and challenging myself mentally and physically. So, when they came to me to ask what would make season two better, I told them I needed another Green Beret to play with. It's hard to do dumb things by yourself. And when you want to do dumb things and the only people around you are erudite historians and camera crew, you can get really sad.

It just so happened that the show wanted to build out more investigative capability, and they wanted to add people to the team so that we could do more in-depth investigation or split into two teams. They let me bring in my friend Dr. Mike Simpson. Mike served in the 75th Ranger Regiment, then in Special Forces as an 18 Echo, then went to medical school, then served as an emergency physician for JSOC. He likes to warn people that if they piss him off, he can kill them, bring them back to life, and then kill them again.

Mike gave me options to get things done I did not have in season one.

When we hit Chile, one of the first things I do is visit this elderly Chilean couple who claim their parents were involved with the Nazis. The plan is to go do this interview and then link up with Mike for a workout. The crew and I go to this beautiful gated house and the couple offer us coffee and we sit down, and they jump right into it. The guy tells us that escaped Nazis used to come through here all the time and stay at the house. He says it wasn't hidden, but all out in the open. Everyone knew and no one cared. His wife is agreeing right along with him and we're having a nice conversation. These two are not Nazis. To them, it's a thing their parents did. I won't go so far as to say they are embarrassed by it, but they want to set the record straight.

Then the front door opens and it is their daughter and her husband or boyfriend or whatever. She's apparently a politician or some powerful member of society and she asks what we are doing. They casually tell her that they're telling us about their parents' Nazi past. I thought her head was going to spin 360 degrees around and she was going to start spitting fire. This woman lost her shit. She runs off somewhere and all of a sudden doors lock, gates close, and windows shutter. *Well, this is unexpected.*

"We're respected members of the community. You cannot just harass us. We cannot have this getting out. You and your vehicles are locked in here and we are going to call the police. I want your camera memory cards right now!"

My crew is freaked out, but I'm reasonably sure I can kill everyone in the room without breaking a sweat, so I am less worried. "You're not getting our memory cards. Your parents signed a release. We didn't coerce them. They reached out to us willingly," I tell her calmly.

"You give me $10,000! For $10,000 I will let you go," she screeches.

I did not see that one coming.

"Okay, just to be super clear, you're telling me that you are holding us against our will, but we can leave if we pay you $10,000?"

"Yes," she answers firmly.

"Great. Call the police," I answer.

It's right at this point, while she's weighing what to do, that I get a text from Mike. "Are you coming to the gym soon or will you be a while?" he asks. "There's a problem," I respond. "The family/source has gone hostile. Refuse to let us leave. Police may be involved."

"What can I do? Can you get out of the house?" Mike asks quickly.

"It's a compound and they have locked the gates," I answer. "On my way," comes his response.

A few minutes later, he's back online. "Okay, I can see it. I can steal a cab and ram the gate. Confirm if I am a go?"

There is no way in hell I am going to let Mike steal a cab and ram the gate. Chile is not the Wild West, the police here are generally reasonable, and this lady is fucking crazy. In this instance, I'm good with letting the authorities handle it, but I love the fact that there is a crazy sonofabitch outside who is willing to commit two or three felonies on a moment's notice to get me out.

The cops show up, and I can tell they think the whole situation is nuts. I explain that we are being held hostage here and that we have been told that we cannot leave without paying her $10,000. They ask her if this is true, and she tells them, "Absolutely," with a smug look on her face. The cops are shocked that she would admit this, and for them this event just got messy. Then one of them looks at me and asks, "Are you military?" "I am," I respond, "but I am not on duty right now. I'm here as a civilian working on a television show about German settlements for the Travel Channel."

He hears none of that last part because as soon as he realizes I'm military he knows this will be a shitshow that will involve his military, the U.S. military, and the U.S. Embassy, and none of that will be good for him. "You can go," he says to us, adding, "I'm sorry for the trouble." I head back to the hotel and Mike and I grab a workout.

"This is a really interesting system you run here. How do you deal with a mass casualty event?" Mike asks the nurses at the clinic that was once called Colonia Dignidad and is now called Villa Baviera.

Colonia Dignidad was the home of an evil Nazi-inspired cult run by a pedophile named Paul Schäfer. Schäfer moved here in 1961, and somehow came with enough money to buy thousands of acres of land and build a compound on it. He allegedly spent close to $5 million in 1961, which is an astronomical amount of money for any time, but certainly that day and age. What is peculiar is that he was in trouble in Germany for assaulting children, so it's very unclear where his money came from. However, many members of his leadership team were former high-ranking Nazi officers. Rumors abound that the notorious Josef Mengele, the "Angel of Death" of Auschwitz, had been among them. Mengele was the guy who ran experiments on children, twins, and pregnant women. It was said that he could be playing with a child, remembering intimate details about what the child liked and giving him a piece of candy, and thirty minutes later be killing that same child in the gas chamber without remorse. While other SS members often blanched at the task of choosing those who would be killed, Mengele was known to smile and whistle as he did it.

As the nurses explain that as a clinic they don't really have to deal with mass casualty events, Mike launches into a predictable diatribe about the need for them to be prepared. He's charismatic and charming and American, so the nurses give him their full attention . . . which allows me to steal a couple of keycards that they left on the counter. I excuse myself to the restroom.

The restroom happens to be perfectly situated next to the records room. I let myself in with my new keycard and then get to work. I'm looking for the oldest documents I can find. I don't have a ton of time to sort through this stuff as I have to return the keycards before anyone notices they are gone. I give myself a clock of ten minutes tops. I fly through the file cabinets and figure out the order. The older stuff is the back left. I pull out yellowed paper with German names on it and I start taking pictures as fast as I can with my phone. Two minutes gone. Now three. Someone walks by. I crouch down and go quiet. They pass. I wait a moment longer to make sure they are clear and rifle through the papers again. At seven minutes, I pull out a paper to snap a photo and I feel my skin go cold. The signature . . . Josef Mengele.

He was here. He was fucking here! I grab every paper in the vicinity of that one and take photos, then pack everything back and slide into the bathroom.

I flush the toilet and make a big deal out of slamming the door. When I return, Mike is telling war stories. Something about stuffing bullet holes on the battlefield and whatnot. The stories are probably true, but I've been gone long enough that maybe he's in embellishment mode. Either way, I'm stoked. I drop the keycard on the floor near their station. Better than risking them seeing me replace it and they will simply think they dropped it or it got knocked off the counter.

When we get back to the hotel, now with evidence that Mengele, one of the few big Nazi war criminals to escape Mossad, was here, Mike and I are excited. We want to break into the place at night and really copy everything they have from that era. We have already mapped their security and we know they leave the door to the security monitoring station open because it has no air-conditioning of its own. This would be easy and we are willing to do it. The production crew thinks this might be above their pay grade and we call the L.A. office. They give us a hearty "Yeah . . . no, you're not breaking into a medical clinic in the middle of the night."

They are no fun.

This is not a nice place. Pinochet ran his torture camps here. Schäfer ran his rape and pedophile rings here—he was the 1960s–1970s version of Jeffrey Epstein. A lot of bad things happened here, and a lot of not nice people still work here.

They were everywhere and somehow free. The woman who greeted us when we arrived was known to have helped her husband capture and torture children. He was in prison. She was there meeting us with her black lifeless eyes and talking about the jams and sausages made on the compound. I am not scared of much, but I didn't want to be left alone with her because I kept waiting for her jaw to distend and swallow my soul. Another man, who must have been eighty-five or ninety but was still well muscled and dangerous, was the local butcher. When they introduced him as such, I couldn't help but think of "the butcher" in a different connotation. His chest was still big. His arms were leathery and powerful. Creepiest of all, he wore the front of his hat poofed up in the Nazi fashion. He weighed us with his eyes almost as a dare. He wasn't afraid of two guys most people tend to be afraid of messing with. Mike and I took one look at him and we both knew he had tortured and killed people. It bothers me that he is living out his life without penalty for the sins I know he has committed.

There are many more stories. We found bunkers. We interviewed men and women who had been prisoners here before Chile freed everyone and brought some of the perpetrators to justice. We were chased again. We were threatened again. And then we headed home. When all was said and done, for three consecutive seasons we were the top show on the History Channel.

For the next season, we wanted to examine the Nazi ties to the PLO, to Libya, to the mujahideen. We wanted to go to Israel and talk to the guy who hunted down Eichmann. We wanted to investigate the Nazis that ended up at NASA. But we went too far. You see the first three seasons were focused on places no one cared about. Jungle towns and compounds already shrouded in evil. But tying the Nazis to the terrorists of the day wouldn't sit well with the politics of many people in Hollywood. Tying Nazis to America's desire to beat the Soviets would make people uncomfortable. No one wanted that, so the show ended.

After three years of chasing Hitler, I'll tell you this: Hitler probably didn't get out, but his ideology did, and that is how he truly escaped.

I strip naked and get in the ring with Randy Couture. Three cameras are running and men and women surround the side of the ring cheering.

My good friend Brian Stann, a Marine Silver Star recipient who was in Iraq the same time I was and trained with me at Jackson's, watches us eagerly. Greg Jackson shouts at me from the sideline.

No, I'm not back in the UFC. I probably need to back up a little.

While season one of *Hunting Hitler* was kicking ass in late 2015, Nick Palmisciano had made some new friends: Jarred Taylor, Vince Vargas, and Mat Best. Vince and Mat had been Army Rangers and Jarred was a JTAC. The three of them had come together to make a clothing company called Article 15, named after nonjudicial punishment. It was clever. Technically, they were a competitor, but Nick and I didn't give a shit about that. We always operated off of one question: Are they good people? The truth is I didn't know yet.

Jarred loves attention and has a very self-deprecating sense of humor. He is great at making people laugh. Fundamentally, though, he is unhappy pretending to be happy. When he's sober, he's earnest and I believe him when he says he wants to make a difference. When he's drunk, it's entirely possible he will try to steal my car and drive it across the country because he needs to get to an alpaca farm or something equally inane. Jarred is the creative energy of this team. Nick thinks he's talented and he generally thinks everyone sucks, so there's that.

Mat is the "Blue Steel" of this group. He's a good-looking guy with a *Friday Night Lights* quarterback thing going on. He's comfortable in the limelight and loves the cameras. He's great at it. He's kind of got Sean Connery charisma with NSYNC looks. He can definitely be a star if he works at it. Like Jarred, he spends a lot of time at the bottom of a bottle. I can tell he has been through some shit, and he hasn't quite worked it out yet.

Vince is awesome. He's heart and soul, bravado and charisma, all wrapped up into one giant Mexican. Where Jarred and Mat are in relentless pursuit mode, Vince is more chill. He's sweet, sincere, and hardworking. He's not necessarily looking for the next thing as hard as the other guys. He's trying to build this thing. At first impressions, I trust him the most. He at least handles his alcohol a little better. He's also the only one that is about the same age as Nick and me, so we relate to him a little more. The other guys are about ten years younger.

There's also this little quiet guy that used to be an SF officer and a CIA guy named Evan Hafer running around. He's the CEO of Mat and Jarred's side gig—Black Rifle Coffee. He's an interesting character and I like him. He's not trying to impress anyone. He's just putting his head down and working.

Jarred called Nick with the idea to make a movie.

Nick has wanted to make a movie forever, so he was immediately interested. He came back to me and the guys and asked what we thought. I told him, "If you want to do this, then I've got your back." John, Kelly, and Tom said the same thing and we were off to the races. The process was grueling.

The idea was to make a zombie comedy with all of us as the main characters. On the Article 15 side it was Mat, Jarred, and Vince. On our side, it was Nick, Jack Mandaville, who is the weirdest Marine you will ever meet, and that's saying a lot, and me.

Nick and Jarred tried to get money from Hollywood. Everyone laughed at them, except for one guy who was interested in doing it, but he wanted to replace us as the cast with Jean-Claude Van Damme. I shit you not. They came back pissed off and we decided to crowdfund it. The guy that was going to direct the film, Ross Patterson, agreed to do it if we could get the money. He figured we needed $350,000 to throw together a fun little indie film. Nick wrote some ridiculous money-raising skit, we filmed it, and went live on Indiegogo. We raised the first $350,000 in twenty hours, surprising everyone, even us. In total, we raised about $1.2m online and then Nick and Jarred hunted down another few hundred thousand dollars doing all kinds of sponsorship deals.

Just like that, the project became bigger than two companies making a movie—it became a project for the veteran community by the veteran community. *Range 15* (a combination of Ranger Up and Article 15) became the first movie ever to be made this way. And we approached this like a military operation. Nick and Jarred had a little chart of influencer types they wanted to give cameo spots in the movie so we would get attention from YouTubers, MMA guys, and real actors in order to grow our fanbase.

It worked.

Nick convinced William Shatner to be in the film with some magical Italian charisma letter he wrote him. Then we somehow got Sean Astin. Ross knew Bryan Callen, and Nick and I knew Brendan Schaub, so they joined. We pulled in tons of MMA guys: Jorge Rivera, Brian Stann, Stephen Thompson, Phil Davis, Stephan Bonnar, Keith Jardine, Josh Thompson, Isaac Vallie-Flagg, Yves Edwards, and Julie Kedzie. Jarred brought in tons of influencers. I learned that he basically has the ability to talk to anyone and open any door, which is incredibly useful. Danny Trejo even came on as our final bad guy!

So that pretty much catches you up to where I am right now, naked and in the ring with Randy Couture. This is actually a really cool moment for a few reasons. First and foremost, nudity. Second, I am once again reacquainted with Randy Couture. Randy just knocked out *Expendables 2*. He's crushing it, but he's the same guy. I like people like that. The same guy that used to wrestle me when I was nineteen is interchangeable with this multiple-time world champion and famous actor. He doesn't have to do *Range 15*. He wants to. Because he's a veteran. Because he's my friend. Because he's a good dude. That's just cool.

Next, looking around at the hundreds of veterans that came to L.A. for two weeks to volunteer their time and be extras, or the veteran crew who are working at a reduced rate, or guys like Hollywood Heard who not only donated his equipment for the movie but is working for the minimum rate allowable by his union, is amazing. I feel like all these years with Ranger Up have paid off at this moment. We're working sixteen-to-eighteen-hour days and people are still leaving here smiling. We built a real community. We have done good work.

Lastly, I got to help Nick in a big way, and this is important to me. Friendships are a two-way street, and for the last few years he's devoted a lot of his time to helping me succeed, whether it was cornering me, helping with sponsorships, giving me business advice on my new self-defense training company, Sheepdog Response, or even just normal friend personal stuff. But because of the selfish nature of fighting, I haven't really been able to help him . . . or anyone.

Stepping away from that world has been like waking up from a dream and realizing there's a lot more to life. During most of this movie, Nick has been the guy who has had to worry about the details and the grind. For the creative stuff, everyone has been cranking. The Article 15 guys are legitimately funny, and the scriptwriting process has been a group effort. The big decisions have mostly been down to Nick and Jarred, as both teams decided they were the guys for this, but when it came down to the minutiae that makes something happen—the contracts, the lawyers, the insurance, the logistics, the props, the budget, the bullshit—it's been all Nick.

Ross, with Hollywood in his back pocket, has put in a superhuman effort to keep this complex set running on time. We can only afford sixteen days of production, but in one area we keep falling behind—stunts. The stunt coordinator is a good guy, but he is slow. He is used to a Hollywood pace, and we are at an indie film pace. For some things, he crushed it, like the scene where two zombies get lit on fire, but for others it just took too long and didn't look cool enough. To add to the challenge, he and Ross did not get along. They were oil and vinegar. Nick asked Ross if we were going to make it in sixteen days. Ross said he didn't think so with the stunt guy we had. I could see Nick dying inside as he desperately tried to find a solution. The bridges were burned between our stunt guy and Ross, Nick had no connections in Hollywood yet, and he definitely didn't know the stunt world. But I did. I had done a few small parts in various films and had been a stunt double once. So I called Greg Jackson and Keith Jardine. I asked them if they could come out. They said yes. I asked when. "We can be there in six hours," came the reply. When I think about why I came to Jackson's, nothing encapsulates it more than this moment. The best coach in MMA dropped everything, got on a plane, and came to California to support one of his fighters.

Greg and Keith came in, took over, added me to their team as a stunt coordinator, and we crushed it. We didn't sleep that night because we had to map out the final two days of production, and there was no room for error. The last forty-eight hours of the movie would have been an absolute shitshow if I hadn't gotten involved and brought these two studs out here. I directed a zombie death scene and an MMA zombie elite squad scene. That felt good. After years of taking, it was good to start getting on the giving side again. And I had a blast doing it.

The bell rings. I move forward and punch Randy in the face, but he is undeterred. I kick him in the balls. He doesn't feel it because he is a zombie. He picks me up and smashes me onto the mat and beats on me. I see my opening, and lock on a Kimura and rip his arm off and start beating him with it. Finally, I lock in a rear naked choke and rip his head completely off as blood starts pouring all over the ring. Then I punt his head into the crowd.

It's a beautiful moment.

Ten minutes later, Randy and I are still smiling ear to ear. His head is reattached (I didn't actually murder him for the movie—it was special effects), and he surprises the fuck out of me. "I envy you, man. This is what it's all about." *Envy me? You're Randy Couture.* "What do you mean?" I ask him. "When I did *The Expendables*, for about six months it's all anyone would talk about, and it was cool. When I did *Expendables 2*, it lasted for about three months. But this dumb-as-shit film is going to be a cult classic. It'll be 2049 and there will be privates in space watching this thing and giggling. This is cool, man. Thanks for letting me be a part of it." *I love Randy Couture.*

Nine months later, the movie opens in 650 theaters nationwide. It hits number one on Amazon and number two on iTunes (fuck you, *Angry Birds*) and is the first independent film ever to top the Amazon charts (they actually call us thinking it is fraud because they have no idea who we are). This crew, for all its issues, and we had several, had done something everyone not only told us was impossible, but literally laughed at the notion that it could succeed. I never doubted it. You put a bunch of military guys together and tell them they cannot do something? That's like daring the Hulk not to smash something. It's gonna happen, whether you want it to or not.

First *Hunting Hitler* and now *Range 15* are both amazing experiences. In both cases, I did something hard that carried with it tremendous purpose. Maybe this whole Hollywood thing was a good path for me after all.

Two thousand two hundred pounds of bull is hauling his testosterone-riddled bovine ass at me. His intent is clear. He is going to smash and gore the idiot standing in front of him smirking, and then he is going to carry me on his horns like a meat hat as a warning to all other humans that he is not to be fucked with.

It takes the average person ten or more years of training to make it to the point where they can stand across the arena against an elite-level bull. My dumb ass had knocked out what I could this afternoon against a wheelbarrow with horns taped to it and called it a day. My plan is to skip the intermediate 137 steps and go right from basic wheelbarrow kid's training to advanced, scary, raging death machine bull in one day. The cowboys training me originally laughed at the very idea of me even trying to get into this pen. Now they are finally realizing that this crazy sonofabitch is about to show them up on his first day.

This is my sixth bull of the day practicing as a rodeo clown. The previous five had been of increasing difficulty, but I had managed all pretty naturally, giving my new show, *Hard to Kill*, a slow start. No one wants to see a guy be good at everything. But, hey, it's not my fault I have the reflexes of a cat on cocaine.

I sense the sheer power and rage of the bull as it closes in. At this point, I have a patented move. I juke left and then cut right hard, just as I had with the five previous lower-level bulls. And that's when I get knocked stupid. I see the sky, the ground, the sky, and then the ground again with my feet, legs, and arms somewhere in the mix as this ton of hamburger sends me into orbit. The hit is so hard and the spin so fast I don't know if I am still on my way up or down when the ground greets my face, knee, and hip. I want to just lie here forever as the pain emanates through me, but unfortunately Bully McBullerson has already spun around and is on his way to kill me. I feel his breath on my neck as he snorts, and I just barely roll out of the way. I squint through the dust from his hooves as I hop up and sprint full out toward the wall, adrenaline only slightly masking the pain coming out of my rib cage and leg, and fly over the safety wall, in what might be the most athletic moment of my life thus far.

The cowboys run over to check on me. Apparently, it looked pretty bad from their perspective, but I am just pissed.

"I want to go again," I say, still panting from the exertion.

"Fuck no, you're not going again. We shouldn't have let you go in there in the first place," my one-day trainer laughs. "What's wrong with you?"

Realistically? Probably a lot.

Hard to Kill is my brainchild. It came from all the shit I took from Dana White and the UFC for making the comment about how I could make more as a trashman. I started thinking about all the tough jobs people do that are dangerous, and I wanted to show the world what those jobs look like. The more thankless the job, the more I wanted to show it. Originally, I was thinking about things like, who dives into giant New York City sewers and works on massive clogs of tissues when things go wrong? Who changes the light bulbs outside a skyscraper? Who mends power lines that head out to islands? But the show turned sharply from my original mission of highlighting the hardworking men and women of America that do crazy jobs to "How can we kill Tim Kennedy?" The experiences are cool, and the moments are fun, but unlike with *Hitler* and *Range*, there is no purpose behind it, and I'm getting restless. This is turning into Cirque du Soleil Tim, and I'm starting to wonder if the producers even see me as a human being. On the one hand, they have a lot of confidence in me. On the other hand, they do realize I can die, right?

A week later I would be crashing a helicopter into the Arctic to see if I could survive. Two weeks later, I'd be exiting a jet via parachute. The week after that, I set off an avalanche with hundreds of pounds of high explosives and was buried alive for half an hour.

For most people, any single one of these events would be something that a person would train for, devoting significant time and effort prior to even attempting. Any one of these days would be the accomplishment of the year, or even of several years. I, however, am expected to knock one death-defying event out every week or two.

It was all okay—not great mind you—but okay, until the test pilot episode. For this one, they put me in an experimental airplane, covered it with jet fuel, and set it on fire, and it was my job to find my way out. I practiced for an entire day prior to the actual event and had no issues. I could get out of the cockpit in seconds. As with all things, I didn't do it until I got it right; I did it until I couldn't get it wrong. Finally, I get in the plane. They douse it with airplane fuel. They light it on fire.

Without hesitation, I run through my drills. I create space, un-buckle myself, clear my restraints, and pull the hatch lever to release the hatch . . . and nothing happens. I push up on the hatch and I hear a "clunk!" as metal hits metal. There's something blocking it. I push up again. "Clunk!" Now, I feel the urgency. *I am not dying here.* "Clunk! Clunk!" as I push twice hard and fast. *I need to get out now!* I get my legs underneath me and drive through the hatch, ripping it right off its hinges. The air hits me. I push the broken canopy aside and get out. It had gotten hot in there and I am glad to be in the fresh air.

"What the hell happened?" I ask out loud to no one in particular.

When they finish putting out the fire, I walk over to the plane and see a screw sticking out of the cockpit.

"Did someone put a fucking screw in this hatch?"

"Yup!" came the response from one of the crew.

"Why the hell would you do that?"

The craziest thing about this moment is that the dude literally doesn't understand the problem.

"You got out so easily every other time during practice that I knew it would be bad television, so I just put in one screw. I knew you could bust out of it easy," he responds.

I look at this guy, and I cannot believe what he just said. I should be furious, but I'm more stupefied. If this had been Shane, or Nick, or Brandon, or Af, or any of the guys in my life that actually know my real capability and know that with 99.99 percent certainty, I'm going to bust through this without any problem, they still would never have done this, because they would never risk my life for that 0.01 percent chance it wouldn't work out.

Say what you want about all the dumb shows I did before *Hunting Hitler*, but none of them would have risked my life.

I have a contractual obligation to finish the show, but my heart is no longer in it, or television.

CHAPTER FOURTEEN

HUMAN TRAFFICKING

January 2010

We walk down the rubble-filled roads after the Haitian earthquake. This is devastation unlike anything I have ever seen. Over 200,000 people are dead. Three hundred thousand are injured. Entire city blocks are leveled. Sewage is running on the streets. The place smells and looks like shit. Humanitarian workers appear every now and then. The world is here to help Haiti through this biblical catastrophe.

But that's not why I am here.

I, along with three other muscles-popping-through-our-clothes, bearded, dangerous-looking dudes have a specific mission here in Haiti. We all check our gear one more time, walk up to the front of the hotel, climb the few stairs to its entrance, and flow into the front door, our weapons at the ready. The guy behind the counter looks at us for less than a half second before he puts his hands up, pushes his weapon toward us, and proceeds to lie on the ground. This garbage human being wants nothing to do with what we are offering.

"Where is the American girl?" we ask him.

"On the fourth floor," he responds in his native tongue.

We head up the creaky stairs and start opening the doors to rooms.

Every room is the same: several girls are tied down to small beds. There are heroin tracks running into every vein they could find. We find our target. She's an American girl who was here on a mission trip when the earthquake hit. These predators saw a foreigner in a chaotic situation, separated from her friends, and took advantage. She became a target of opportunity.

We untied the girls and ushered them out, but sadly we couldn't take them with us. The helicopter only had room for one. We knew most of them were just going to end up back here, either because they were so indoctrinated into this life, or later, when the drugs wore off and they needed another fix. It is really hard to stomach. They are so young. This is the worst kind of slavery.

We walk our target out of the hotel, and even though more men have arrived, no one lifts a finger to stop us. They know what type of men we are and they know how it will end. Plus, there is no reason to risk their lives for girls, when girls are so plentiful here.

I do three more of these kinds of missions. They are always gratifying and soul-crushing at the same time. It is like living out the movie *Taken*, except the bad guys are pussies and want nothing to do with fighting you, and you don't get to save everyone. You just leave knowing that in a consequence-free environment, you'd kill all of these traffickers. But there are consequences, and as you leave the other girls behind, you can't help but think if their families had money, you'd be pulling them out too.

February 2017

Regular people have a moral continuum. They think about things like selling drugs, selling guns, selling sex, and kidnapping and forcing children to have sex as progressively worse steps. And while I'd never compare the kid selling pot to his friends in college to a human trafficker, in my experience, once you get past a certain point, the moral continuum you'd expect to see disappears. Whether I was in South America, the

Caribbean, Africa, or the United States, the same assholes selling drugs
and guns were typically intertwined with selling kids as well. Assholes
are assholes, and a person willing to deal in one form of human misery
is likely willing to deal with all forms, so long as they can turn a profit.

Whether it's a rhino horn, cocaine pushed across the border, meth
being cooked in a lab, or selling eight-year-old boys or girls to pedo-
philes, these people look at their evil as "just business." As hard as it is for
us to fathom, to them selling pain is simply the sale of a product—and
their product has a shelf life. They want to sell it or use it as quickly
as possible to make the most money possible, and then do it all again
tomorrow.

This is where many of the popular anti-trafficking organizations fall
short. These organizations, though well meaning, are feel-good stories
that have little impact on the actual problem. They go in and they rescue these kids or women, and it is gratifying to give these people their
freedom, but they don't attack the underlying financial organization that
allows all of this to happen. To look at it another way, the real players
should be thought of as major corporations. Imagine that human traffickers are British Petroleum or Shell, and each individual sex house is
a gas station. If you shut down one gas station, does Shell or BP even
notice? What about five or ten or a hundred? No, of course they don't.
The major corporation is completely unaffected. The demand for the
product still exists and you've done nothing to stop or even slow the
supply of the product. It's like turning off the sprinkler when it's pouring
rain—there's still water everywhere.

But that's where people want to invest. That's what's sexy. The idea
of coming in and breaking women (and men) and kids out of these hell-
holes where they are fed meth until they die or are all used up is incredibly invigorating. It makes people feel good. But to hurt the corporation,
we need to dig a hell of a lot deeper. We need to go after the source.

And for those of you saying, "So what if they don't take the whole
organization down? They at least save those girls that were trapped!"
Not really. These organizations don't even have halfway houses built into
their programs, so when they free these girls, and they are addicted to

meth, and their families don't want them or they're orphaned to begin with, they go right back to their handlers. Hell, most of them don't even have families. Over 70 percent of the kids and women who are freed walk right back to the same life. It's the saddest thing in the world. There is no escape for them unless we provide it. Not the Band-Aid. Not the day of freedom. These victims *need a structured path* to success.

I have to put this in a cold way, because there is no other way to show how little these bastards value human life. Think about the trafficker as a grocer. He can only fit so many peaches on his shelf. If you come in and save two of his girls, he simply goes to the orchard and plucks two more peaches. His costs are virtually nothing to get two new slaves, but his return on each is in the thousands of percentage points. There almost isn't a more lucrative business, and the supply of the product is limitless. Poor and abandoned kids are always available.

So even though emotionally I want to kick in doors and save girls, logically I know it is a waste of time and resources. I have to put my efforts elsewhere. I want the big guys. I want to solve this problem.

And after years of working around this abomination all over the world, I've committed myself to attacking it two different ways: by opening my Sheepdog Response courses up to a partnership with any organization that helps survivors of trafficking, and by volunteering my time to execute stateside missions for the same organizations.

Sheepdog Response has grown a ton over the past two years. It went from an occasional shooting course I taught to a few dozen people, to an organization with elite trainers, a strong detailed curriculum, and courses all over the country. At the core of it, I want to remove the feeling of helplessness so many people have and set them up for success should a bad situation ever arise.

My instructors are amazing and share my ethos. Matt Smith is a twenty-five-year Special Forces veteran who has worked for all the elite special missions units in the United States, and spent the last ten years of his career teaching them. Kris Perkins is the winningest coach in Army Combatives history, a collegiate wrestler, and a black belt in Jiu Jitsu who lives by the saying, "Yeah, boxers get to punch people in the face, and that's cool, but wrestlers get to smash them with the earth." Travis Lloyd is a two-time Team Sergeant in Special Forces, a retired Master Sergeant, with ten years as an infantryman, and a Ranger Instructor before joining SF. Blake Hayes is a Golden Gloves boxer, a black belt in Jiu Jitsu, and a longtime self-defense instructor. Iako Kalili is an infantryman, a master combatives instructor, and a Jiu Jitsu black belt who was one of Ranger Up's earliest sponsored fighters. Justin Jones is a Recon Marine. Justin Lakin, the guy who drove down with me so many years ago when I left Fort Bragg, has the same military experience that I have. Casey Bywater is an elite grappler who excels at getting the attention of men and making them believers in combatives by smoking the dogshit out of them on the mat, and making women comfortable in an aggressive environment they may be unaccustomed to being in. I also bring Shane Steiner into the fold. His passion for working out has turned into a passion for Jiu Jitsu and shooting, and I've decided that in addition to being my trusted friend, he is now my lethal protégé.

So, when you get a group of people like this together, all of whom have seen the results of trafficking around the world, the solution is simple: Anyone who has ever lived through trafficking can come to our courses for free. We hold women-only courses specifically to facilitate that purpose. We want the women (and men) who have been in these awful situations to eliminate the fear from their lives, to learn how to be situationally aware and avoid bad situations if possible, and to defend themselves, and their loved ones, if necessary. Hearing former victims tell me how much of their mental health we have been able to return to their lives through our work is one of the few things in my life I take great pride in.

But I'm not in Houston, two days before the Super Bowl between the Atlanta Falcons and the New England Patriots, to give a Sheepdog Response course. I'm here to hem up some bad guys with the Deliver-Fund. These guys are not caught up in the idea of kicking in doors and doing the sexy stuff, but in nerding out with data, and putting people in prison. Their founder, Nic McKinley, isn't an Operator-type. He was a CIA analyst. He looked at maps, data, spreadsheets, and human intelligence and put together target packages. Well, that's exactly what we are doing here. DeliverFund is mostly made up of nerds and I mean that in the best way possible. Their CEO is like the head smart nerd guy and he has an army of smart nerd guys who will combine their nerd powers to fuck up people who want to hurt kids. Data, in the right hands, is a powerful thing—just the kind of thing, in fact, that police officers need to make arrests. That's the ultimate goal. We want to collect enough information on these traffickers to put them away for a long time or set the police up to break them and climb higher up the food chain.

I am not here to be a nerd. I'm not smart enough. I'm here to run counterintelligence operations, like I have done in South America, like I did in Trinidad and Tobago, and like I did on *Hunting Hitler*. If all goes right, I'm going to catch these guys in the act of selling kids.

If we do this right, we can hurt the big boys. We don't care about the local pimps. We want the power players who bribe politicians and serve the Harvey Weinsteins or Jeffrey Epsteins of this world, for lack of a better term. It's shocking to me our government doesn't have an organization who chases these cretins, but the more time you spend fighting trafficking, the more you realize how many wealthy and powerful people have a lot to lose by breaking the whole thing apart. The blatant manner in which power and money have been used to stop us from bringing people down is appalling. I don't generally condone vigilante behavior, but if I ever lose it and go full "Punisher" mode, these guys are at the top of my list.

I got pulled into this particular mission, Operation Game Changer, by young Matt Tiberius Phinney. Matt, who originally came to Jackson's for a camp at the same time I was training for Bisping, hit it off with Greg Jackson, and we all started shooting together. Through that relationship, Matt learned that Greg is on the board of the DeliverFund. Greg introduced Matt to Nic McKinley, and next thing you know Matt is doing undercover work on a continuous basis under the guidance of Special Operations legend and former Delta Operator George Hand IV, affectionately known as "Geo." As Matt got more and more involved with the DeliverFund, it started to dominate more of our conversations.

I wanted to get involved and let him know to hit me up if they ever needed me. That call came, and now here we are.

The structure is analyst-heavy. Geo runs the TOC and all communications. At the TOC he has ten analyst nerd types processing all of the data and building target packages, both for us and to hand off to the authorities when the operation is complete. There are two teams. Team one is Matt and me. Team two is run by a guy named Jim Perdue.

Heads up: I'm purposely omitting details about what we do, because I do not want to give traffickers the playbook. I can tell you that the search starts online. We start with Backpage and escort sites. The first thing we try to identify are markers and verbiage that are tips to potential johns that this is not consensual, but rather trafficked sex. I'm a maximum freedom kind of a guy. If you're a woman or a man and you want to peddle your wares, then by all means do so. I don't think anyone should be messing with you. But, willful prostitution and trafficking are two very different things. It's the difference between freedom and slavery, or consent and force. No one should have to live in sexual slavery.

Once we narrow it down to potential traffickers, we use a combination of reconnaissance, messaging, and phone calls to try to determine the nuance of a situation. People tend to think of this stuff as black-and-white, but there are so many different scenarios. On one end, we have obvious trafficking: Someone stole kids from their parents and is selling them for sex against their will. On the other end we have consensual prostitution. Well, what if there is a pimp that has the girls strung out, but they can leave anytime? Are they trafficked? To some extent, yes, but it's gray. What about when five prostitutes hire a pimp for 10 percent of the take for their own protection? Are they trafficked? Pretty clearly not, right? Determining all of this from afar is part art and part science. We don't always get it right.

When we do get it right, the situation almost always looks the same. Trafficking operations run out of hotels or motels. On the ground floor, there is the madame or "bottom bitch." The bottom bitch is pure evil. She's usually twenty-five-to-thirty years old and she is fucking the pimp. She used to be one of the girls, but for whatever reason, she showed loyalty or skill, and she elevated herself out of that part of the business. The bottom bitch typically runs four to six girls. She recruits them when they aren't just stolen, gets them hooked on meth or heroin, keeps them high, gets them to rest when they're off duty, interacts with the johns when they arrive, and basically runs the day-to-day operation. The reason I say she is pure evil is because she worked the job, knows how terrible it is, knows what it did to her, and still is willing to do the same thing to other girls. The girls are usually fourteen to twenty-one and the bottom bitch keeps them in a room together and releases them one at a time to rooms they have upstairs when the johns arrive. You don't usually see them older than that, because the johns that prefer nonconsensual sex prefer younger girls. Once they don't look young anymore, they are either sold into slavery elsewhere, killed, or thrown onto the street, now with a heroin habit and no way to get a fix. Or, if they're smart enough and evil enough, they become the new bottom bitch.

Back to the pimp: The pimp always locates himself close enough to get involved if a john gets violent, but always far enough away that if the police come, he isn't really involved in what is going on. The pimp may only have one bottom bitch, or he may have up to five. The structure of the relationship of the pimp to the bottom bitch and the bottom bitch to the girls, though, is always the same.

Above the pimps are the higher-end traffickers. What we do is try to hem up the pimps so their asses are on the line, and get them to turn on the traffickers. To do this effectively, we need to inject ourselves into the system they have built. To start that, you have to understand the schedule:

11:00 AM Wake up from the previous night partying
12:00 PM Pop up as available on all the sites
2:00 PM to 5:00 PM Service Mr. Lonely
5:00 PM to 8:00 PM Sleep
8:00 PM to 9:00 PM Prep to be an escort at parties
9:00 PM to 1:00 AM Escort at parties

1:00 AM to 2:30 AM Troll bars and clubs

2:30 AM to 4:00 AM Have sex with guys snagged at bars and clubs

4:00 AM to 11:00 AM Sleep

For this Houston operation, our work starts at around noon. We look for girls that fit the profile we outlined and look super young. Once we find them, we run facial recognition software and find them on social media. We quickly find one who is underage. We are off and running!

It is now time to set up the jilt. We start texting her. When you do this, you can't just text like a normal person, because they will know you're not one of the losers that come to them. You definitely cannot text like a Gen Xer like me with proper punctuation and coherent thoughts. You have to text like an idiot, with misspelled words and monosyllabic vocabulary. Believe it or not, our best texter is a white female PhD from MIT. I don't know where she picked up her ability, but she is almost undefeated in getting us "dates." Honest to God, watching her work is like watching the June Cleaver scene in *Airplane!* where she speaks jive. There's something both unnatural and impressive about it.

The biggest challenge is that we have no legal ability to set up a sting. We are not law enforcement. We can't give a prostitute money, or we have broken the law, even if no one exchanges sexual favors. So instead, we set up a surveillance point and ask the girl to meet us in a public place. In advance of the meetup, we pay off a construction site to give us access to the third floor of a building. I climb upstairs and set up a long-lensed camera. It's the same concept as being a sniper. I'm capturing everything that occurs. Matt is set up downstairs in the vehicle, also capturing photos.

At the appointed time, our girl gets dropped off. We take pictures of the guy and the car that dropped her off and we attempt to confirm that it's the same girl from Backpage. It clearly is. Now we wait. This is the worst part. As time goes on, we see the girl get more and more upset. The texts from her become frantic. She knows that if she gets a no-show, she'll get beaten for not closing. After an hour, the guy comes back to pick her up. He beats her right there on the street. The three of us—me, a Special Forces guy, George, a former CAG guy, and Matt, a professional fighter—have to sit there and watch as this giant black man beats the snot out of this little girl. We snap pictures of the entire thing, because that's all of the ammunition we are allowed in a civilized society. We'd much rather be uncivilized and permanently solve this problem.

After he's done beating her, he throws her in his vehicle and drives off. I've already positioned myself downstairs, and as soon as they head out, Matt pulls up and I hop into the car with him. We follow the vehicle at a distance and are led to the prototypical hotel—one pimp, one bottom bitch, twelve girls, and two guys as muscle.

We follow them every night and capture as much as we can. We identify which clubs they work—the ones that get kickbacks for this filth. We know which bars they do cleanup duty on. We photograph the muscle collecting the money. We video the pimp coming outside every night at 11:30 p.m. with twelve ATM cards from the girls. He takes the max daily withdrawal out of each one and then does the same again at 12:01 a.m. They will never get a way out of this on his watch. It's hard to imagine what it must be like for them—they live smack dab in the land of opportunity—the place people risk their lives to get to in the hope of attaining the American dream, and they are slaves. They have no hope. Their suffering builds the wealth of evil men.

It's hard to be a man of action and not act. Matt and Geo have a good rapport full of dark humor that lightens the mood. Again, they've done this a while, so this pain isn't new for them. As a Bostonian, Matt loves the Patriots. Everyone else on this op hates them. The radio is constantly bustling with Geo and others talking shit about the Pats, and Matt firing back with his thick accent. It's good. It's distracting. And I need that, because I know the right thing to do isn't the legal thing to do. If we were all truly moral men with no self-interest, we would walk in there and save these girls, and leave a stack of bodies in our wake. But we don't want to go to prison. We want to go back to our families. We want to have our lives—our freedom. I tell myself we need to hold back for the larger mission: we need to get the big fish. I try to cling to that.

As the girls leave to party every night, the bottom bitch drops a variety of drugs into their handbags. The whole thing is like clockwork. It is as efficient as any business you'll ever see. These assholes probably have their own Six Sigma class. When you think of it like that, it is horrifying. Once people reduce another human being to chattel, to a product, to being less than, any amount of cruelty is possible. I've seen it in Iraq and Afghanistan. I've seen it dealing with the FARC in South America. I've seen it on *Hunting Hitler*. I see it here. Terrible as it is, however, it allows us to build a huge portfolio of target packages. These are some of the best ones that Geo and Matt have ever seen, and they've been doing this a while. With the information we have gathered, there's enough clear evidence to arrest the pimp, the muscle, the bottom bitch, and even the strip club owner.

By the time we hit Super Bowl Sunday, we have put together seventy-five target packages. We did all of this with the support and knowledge of the local police, the state police, and the FBI. It is going to be a glorious takedown. This is going to be all worth it.

Geo walks over. He looks upset. "What's going on, man?" Matt asks him. "I don't know how to tell you this, so I'm going to come right out with it. Houston PD has essentially shut us down."

Matt and I cannot believe it. A high-ranking member of local law enforcement has just prohibited any federal agents from working in Houston during the Super Bowl, stating, "We don't have a trafficking problem in Houston." *The hell you don't! I've been here for less than a week and it's pretty damn obvious you have a huge problem!*

I've done all of this—this team has done all of this work. We've watched girls get beaten. We've watched girls get dragged off to be raped. And this guy is shutting it all down despite overwhelming evidence of it occurring?

I don't know what is behind this decision.

Is it a moral failure on his part?

Is it pride? Is he afraid it will reflect poorly on his ability to police his city?

Is he afraid that his city will be embarrassed?

Is it personal protection?

Is he in on it? Is he getting kickbacks?

Is he looking out for someone who got him in office? We already know he gets massive financial support from one of the strip clubs we are targeting. Is that the reason?

I can't just draw that conclusion, but it's my top pick.

Geo spends the rest of the night trying to change the decision. He calls up to headquarters at the DeliverFund. They call all the politicians they know. Everyone is on board with solving it, but it only takes one guy to slow it all down just enough so that the bite is taken out of the operation. I sit quietly, watching the pain of trafficking through a camera lens, while the guys make fun of Matt over the Falcons' lead. They've developed coping skills I do not have yet. I can deal with war, but this is more frustrating.

By the time the Patriots have staged their comeback to win the game, and Matt has come over the radio in his most professional voice possible and said, "I'd like to ask all the Patriots haters in the TOC to kindly suck a dick," and Geo has replied, "Roger, will convey," the police have only moved on two of the now eighty targets we built.

If you want to know how traffickers keep winning, this is how. This is the reason. It's no one's priority. Are the politicians shady or uncaring? It doesn't matter which. If enough people don't care about the problem, then politicians won't care about it. The girls that get taken aren't middle-class white girls with parents who adore them. They're poor black and Hispanic kids, whose parents are either dead, don't care, or have abandoned their children completely. These kids are alone. And now even when guys like us do care, and do try, we cannot even get the police to get up off their asses and do the job they are getting paid to do!

I want to scream at the top of my lungs from our current surveillance point watching a Holiday Inn Express. I cannot give up like this.

"Matt, let's go pick a fight," I say. Matt comes with me.

These guys aren't even trying to hide what they are doing. There are expensive cars parked out front, and more coming and going all the time. They have their own security—two of the biggest guys I have ever seen. I whisper to Matt, who again, is also a professional fighter, "We're going to have to shoot those two." He nods.

As we walk into the hotel, the bottom bitch's eyes go wide. She smells something off about us, and follows us. We know they have the entire fourth floor rented, but we get off on two to take her off the scent. She walks up the stairs with us, smirking, staying right behind us. My temper is at its end. "Hey, do you know where the concierge is?" she asks. Before I can say anything, Matt jumps in with a very aggressive, "Yeah, you're on the wrong fucking floor." With that, she walks away, now worried about her own safety, and I tell Matt to stay nearby, but I'm going to the pimps' room.

I see her pick up the phone and call someone as I get in the elevator. The unoriginal fucks are in room 420. I walk into the room and I see 6'4", 280-pound Jamal the Pimp, complete with a tacky gold grill. I have no authority to do anything. I am not here in any official capacity, but if I can just get him to hit me, to draw down on me, *anything*, then I can act as a private citizen.

He smiles at me and says, "What the fuck are you gonna do, faggot?" I get right up in his face and say, "I'm gonna do whatever the fuck I want to do." He pulls on a cig, accentuating the fact that he doesn't give a shit about me. "You ain't gonna do shit, cracka. Now take yo' tiny white dick and get the fuck out of my establishment."

Our surveillance wasn't as covert as we had believed. They had made us a day ago and had been waiting for this moment. He knows the rules we have to play under. He knows exactly who I am. He isn't going to touch me. We have lost. The only way left for me to solve this leaves me as the only guy who goes to prison. In a haze, I walk out of the room and get into the elevator. Matt is nearby and joins me. I walk past the bottom bitch, who has a smug smile on her face.

I had just stomached a week of watching women be abused; a week of going against my nature in order to win in a court of law; a week of building optimism that we were doing good work and that we were going to put these motherfuckers away for a long, long time; and then *poof,* that dream died. I am thirsty for a justice that will not come. I feel absolutely and completely empty. The energy inside me has evaporated into nothingness and I just want to curl up and die.

In a catatonic state, I debrief with the DeliverFund, say my goodbyes to Geo and Matt, and walk to my car. As soon as I slide behind the wheel, I start sobbing uncontrollably, and simply cannot stop, no matter how hard I try to control myself.

Two hours later, my chest hurts from crying and salt is stinging my cheeks and lies crusted against my chin. I spend the last hour of my drive in silence, collecting myself so that my daughters, my son, and my wife will not feel or see any of what dad has just gone through.

As I pull into my driveway, I make a decision. This imperfect ending will not stop me from doing more. *This is a marathon, not a sprint, and I have terrific cardio. One day, much sooner than later, I'm going to get these guys.* I've been hurt many times, but never stopped. This is just another scar.

It will heal, and I'll be stronger for it.

I stop outside my front door and take three deep breaths. In through the nose, letting my chest and stomach fill with air, out through the mouth, compressing my stomach against my spine. *Okay, here we go.* I lock a smile on my face and open the door to greet my wife and my excited three-year-old son, Rollo.

CHAPTER FIFTEEN

RESCUE

August 2021

Nick and I step off Shane Steiner's red R44 helicopter into my backyard in Austin, Texas.

It's a gorgeous, sunny Texas day. The sky is blue. There's a little breeze. We just got in a great MMA workout with Shane and Sean Apperson and then grabbed some delicious Texas BBQ at the original Salt Lick.

Shane waves and the engine of his helicopter whines as he throttles it up and takes off on his way home, blowing grass and sand and whatever else is on my lawn into our backs. Having one of my best friends also be an avid helicopter aficionado is pretty damn cool, and also saves a lot of wasted hours in traffic. Plus, he lends me his helicopter so I can take my own pilot lessons!

Now it's time to get to work. This is a crazy-busy week for me and I need to get a lot of stuff done in a very short time. First, Sheepdog Response just bought a headquarters building and we are working hard on getting that open as soon as possible so we can better serve the tens of thousands of people we are training each year now. I can only attend about 10 percent of our courses, because it has grown far beyond just me.

Second, I am opening my own school in one week. My newest project, Apogee Cedar Park, is to teach elementary school children. I've generally been unhappy with public education and decided to do something about it. Our model is similar to the Montessori model, in that it is learner driven, but it also puts a premium on physical activity. We're leasing an old church building for the school, so we have about a month's worth of construction work to get done in the next ten days.

I've also just closed the deal to buy one hundred percent of my Live Relentless supplement line. I had been the minority owner, but ultimately decided that I wanted to control the whole thing, so working through that has been a little bit of a chore.

Later today, I have a call with Evan Hafer from Black Rifle Coffee to finalize a new partnership with them. That little coffee company he started with Jarred and Mat during Range 15 is now valued at $1.7 billion. Both of those guys have grown up a lot and have legitimately become good friends of mine. The fourth member of their team, Vince Vargas, went his own way and is now a big Hollywood actor.

Oh, and Nick and I are finishing up this book for Simon & Schuster, which is why he is out here from North Carolina for the week.

Most of the stuff on that list is being handled by Justin Lakin, who is now my Chief of Staff and basically runs all of my businesses, but with so many new things happening, I need to be directly involved. I try to always put my time toward the main effort, but deciding on the main effort in this scenario is challenging. What's most important? My new headquarters, my new school, my supplement line, my new partnership, or my book (which is due soon)? The answer is they're all important, so I'm trying to make it all work.

I walk into the kitchen, give Ginger a kiss, and start to make some coffee. My phone has been blowing up all day on every platform with people talking about the dire situation in Afghanistan. Once the United States pulled most of our forces out of the country, Afghanistan quickly fell to the Taliban. The government leadership fled, which left hundreds of thousands of Afghans who worked alongside us for twenty years, as well as thousands of American citizens and Green Card holders, stranded. Now, the last bastion of hope for fleeing Afghans is Hamid Karzai International Airport (HKIA), which we almost lost control of as the Taliban surged past our limited forces on the ground and onto the airstrip. The government sent in 6,000 more troops in the form of soldiers from the 82nd Airborne Division and Marines from the 24th MEU, and they finally brought it under control.

But the images and sounds from Afghanistan on the news have been awful. The most poignant moment thus far, which was all over the news, was when a C-17 took off and Afghans were hanging on to the landing gear in sheer desperation and fell off about 1,000 feet in the air. It instantly gives me a sharp recollection of the Falling Man on 9/11.

Every veteran I know is getting the same messages that I am getting: either from Afghans begging for help or from other veterans trying to figure out what we can do.

We all want to help people get out, so we're using our connections to communicate directly with the soldiers and Marines on the ground in Kabul via WhatsApp or Signal. Many of us have interpreters that we worked with during our deployments and, as far as we're concerned, those interpreters are part of us—we cannot leave them behind.

For other veterans who didn't serve in Afghanistan, the effort to help is about making amends for the interpreters they couldn't save in Iraq or elsewhere. Even veterans who served in Vietnam, like my uncles, felt this call to duty. They do not want a repeat of the history they lived.

For others still, it's a final chance to bring some positive closure to the Global War on Terror and to just do the right thing and stick by the people who stuck by us.

Ginger heads out the door to grab our kids from school and I hand Nick a cup of coffee. He's been on the phone with another West Pointer named Adam DeMarco who started up a group called Allied Airlift 21. It's basically a bunch of West Point nerds that have taken the various data that everyone is throwing around in solo endeavors from emails or signal messages and consolidating it into a database to better communicate with the State Department and the ground forces in Kabul. He gets off the phone.

"What a fucking shitshow, man," he says, referring to our government's performance so far, while shaking his head in disgust. Nick's an idealist. He still gets genuinely surprised when people fail as badly as we are failing on this mission right now. "How do we pull out all of our forces, and then try to evacuate?" he asks. He isn't really talking to me. He's just venting. He and I have had this conversation about a thousand times in the past forty-eight hours. We sip our coffee in silence for a little while, him wrestling with being let down by America, and me wrestling with a conversation I had earlier today with Chad Robichaux.

Chad was a Ranger Up–sponsored MMA fighter who fought in Strikeforce at the same time I was there. A lifetime ago, he was a Force Recon Marine who was then assigned to JSOC and deployed multiple times to Afghanistan. Now he runs a successful nonprofit called the Mighty Oaks Foundation, which helps veterans find resilience in all aspects of their lives. I personally attended one of their resiliency programs and it was life-changing. Chad is a good friend, and he has a problem: His interpreter Aziz is trapped and is actively being hunted. Because of who Aziz is and who he helped, if he is caught they will rape and murder his wife and children while he watches—then they will kill him.

Chad isn't looking to send messages to Kabul like everyone else. He's been working with his old JSOC buddy, Santa 6, who now does contracting work in that region, putting a plan in motion to get Aziz out. Unfortunately, their timeline just got blown because no one expected the entire country to fall to the Taliban in a week.

Chad wants to know if I will go with him to Afghanistan via the United Arab Emirates. Apparently, Santa 6 rides motorcycles with another former Force Recon Marine that has some kind of connection to the UAE, and they might let us use a plane to get into Afghanistan.

This already feels like six degrees of Kevin Bacon and I'm nervous at the "friend of a friend" structure we discussed.

"Is there a plan?" I asked him when we were on the phone earlier. "If we're going to do some crazy shit, I need to know that we're doing this to make a difference, and not just go."

As I'm thinking about this, Nick gets lost in his phone for a minute, and I see that I have another text message from Chad. He's heading to UAE in forty-eight hours. The only thing he's waiting for is his Covid test to come back so he can travel. He wants me to go. "I'm with Nick right now working on the book," I text him. "Awesome. Bring him too. We could use him!" he answers.

Yeah, I really want to tell Nick's wife Suzanne that I dragged him to Afghanistan with me on another dumb adventure.

I'm waiting for Nick to be off his phone so I can tell him about the crazy thing that Chad just said to me, when he looks up from the intense text message series he appears to have been on and says, "Sarah Verardo just asked me to go to Afghanistan to help."

Well, this just got interesting.

Sarah Verardo is the CEO of the Independence Fund, which helps badly wounded veterans succeed post-injuries, but she's also a political powerhouse who has a tendency to make things happen. I met her through Nick, who met her through a charity event. Her husband Mike was badly injured in Afghanistan, which led her to become involved with and eventually run the Independence Fund. She's a force for good in a pretty gross D.C. world.

"What did you tell her?" I ask.

"I asked her if there was a plan, because I don't want to go there just to say I went, and that if there is one, I have to ask my wife," he responds. "What do you think?"

I smirk. *I don't know if we have great minds, but we do think alike.*

I started Sheepdog Response because I am awful at dealing with helplessness. I've felt it many times in my life: when my childhood friend Jared died, at the van crash as an EMT, after the grenade toss in Afghanistan, losing to Romero, and most recently having to endure human traffickers simply getting away with it. Not being able to change a devastating outcome is awful, and I do not want other people to experience that feeling. I want my students to be able to save lives—whether through self-defense or medical aid. That's my chief motivation. That's what I preach. I tell them it is their responsibility to help others. They are the sheepdogs watching their flocks.

With the crisis in Afghanistan, I am living with helplessness in the present moment.

With all the other cataclysmic events in my life, I was briefly helpless, and then I had to deal with the aftermath. I couldn't change what had happened—it was the past. But here, I am watching a real-time crisis that I know I can help with, but I simply don't have the means to do anything about it. Now, with Chad having the access, and Sarah having the ability to make this official, this equation is rapidly changing.

We get Chad and Sarah on the phone and hash out the details. The two of them have already been working together and have built a coalition between their two nonprofits called Save Our Allies. There was a third organization briefly involved in the coalition, but their board overrode their entry for fear of one of us getting killed overseas and dragging them down, or something like that—I leave the politics to Sarah. Senator Thom Tillis, out of North Carolina, is lending his support to our efforts, and Sarah is able to clear manifests directly through the Joint Chiefs of Staff. General Mark Milley, in particular, is leaning forward heavily trying to help us in this effort to complete the mission. That's a heck of a lot more than I thought we had going for us. This shit just got real.

We get off the phone and Nick and I look at each other. "Are we really going to Afghanistan?" he asks me.

"I think we're really going to Afghanistan," I answer.

We spend the rest of the afternoon working on the book, figuring out flights, visas, and Covid tests, and then Nick hops a flight back to North Carolina to spend his anniversary with his wife. I take Ginger out that night and spend the next day working with Justin to determine how fucked he would be with all of the major projects that we have going on, if I were to, say . . . I don't know . . . disappear for a couple of weeks?

"Why are you so hot?" I bark at Nick. We are in the last two seats in the last row, right next to the toilets, on our flight from Paris to UAE. We have been traveling for almost a day, and this trip has already seen me fly from Austin to Atlanta, where I linked up with Nick, then from Atlanta to Paris, and now Paris to UAE. By the time we land, the journey will be thirty hours, and Nick is basically a heat engine and it is annoying the hell out of me. He's the New England Italian dude who wears shorts in a blizzard. He doesn't get cold ever, and he has wide shoulders, so sitting next to him is like sitting next to a space heater in the summer.

"Can I move over there?" I ask the flight attendant. There's a couple of seats completely open and I want one. "Sure!" he answers. I jump over Nick like a cat and sit down in one. He gets up and sits next to me, smirking.

"I will kill you," I tell him, mostly serious. He smiles and gets up and I sprawl out and try to get as much sleep as I can. It's not the best sleep, but you take what you can get.

By the time we land, I am ready to get off this plane. We've both been here before, so we're not overwhelmed by the cultural differences, but it is always interesting to transition from the West to the East. People carry themselves differently. The smells are different. The clothes are different. You have to remind yourself that the rules are different. UAE is incredibly progressive by Arab standards, but the expectations of decorum are not Western. Luckily, we've both been pretty much everywhere. We transition from handshakes and "Nice to meet you" as the default greeting to "Salam Alaikum" with our hands over our hearts. We ensure we do not look women in the eyes too long, for fear of insulting anyone. We do not want to be seen as rude Americans.

UAE is one of the cleanest places you will ever visit. There is a lot of pride and respect for their buildings and their space. The airport is no different. There is white marble everywhere, and even when we arrive at the customs area, everything is bright white. There are stewards passing out free water to everyone and ensuring everyone is comfortable. *They do things right here.*

Everything is going smoothly until the point where we hit the customs officials. To enter the UAE, even with a negative Covid-19 test, we need to wear an ankle bracelet that is essentially a Lo-Jack, like the kind criminals on parole have to wear in the States. The problem with that is that Nick and I plan on disappearing from tracking and then reappearing from time to time and we frankly cannot have these on. We are carrying letters signed by Senator Tillis asking Emir Sheikh Khalifa bin Zayed Al Nahyan to allow us to enter without them. This letter was accepted for the guys we are linking up with: Santa 6, Joe Robert, Sean G, Seaspray, and Sean Lee, but it isn't working for us. Those guys were all able to call the embassy and the embassy allowed them in, but we arrived just shy of midnight, and the embassy is closed. The airport team won't budge.

Nick calls Sarah, who connects him with Senator Tillis, who reaches out to the embassy. There is only a lackey available at this hour, and this is not the kind of thing that you wake the ambassador for, so our options are either wait in the airport for eight hours until the ambassador is up or work some mojo. The head of security here is cool; he just has a job to do. That's a good start.

"I'm sorry, my friends. I cannot let you go without hearing from our embassy," he apologizes.

"I totally understand," Nick starts, "but here's the thing: we're here with permission from your government as an NGO to assist with refugees. There is a UAE driver waiting for us outside. We need to get going."

He thinks about it for a moment. "I cannot. Maybe I give you the anklet and then you call tomorrow and then you cut it off?" he half tells us and half asks.

"We can't do that," I answer. "We are not allowed to wear ankle bracelets to where we are going."

"Where are you going?" he asks.

"I cannot tell you," I lie.

"But we are not staying here long," Nick adds.

"Where are you heading out to after here, then?" he asks.

There is absolutely no reason not to tell him. We're operating as an NGO, as civilians, and there is nothing secret about this. But that won't get us out of here.

"I cannot tell you that," I say.

"But, let's just say there is a place that is currently being overrun and there are refugees that need to be saved. We are two of the guys that are doing that," Nick adds, picking up on what I'm doing.

Recognition comes over his face. He knows we are going to Afghanistan, but now feels like he is in on a secret. He takes us off to the side.

"Are you military?" he whispers.

"I am," I answer, "but this is not a military mission. I am here as a civilian."

"Do you have a military ID?" he asks.

I show him the ID and reiterate, "I am here as a civilian, not military."

"I understand," he says, and motions to Nick. "And you? Are you military?"

"Not anymore. I have a different job now," Nick trails off, ominously. I chuckle to myself because his different job is CEO of Diesel Jack Media, a marketing company, and President of Ranger Up. He has no government affiliation and hasn't for a long time. But he sells it, never once lying.

"I understand," he nods. "Okay, you can go. Thank you for what you're doing."

And just like that, we walk out the door, having dropped a pretty impressive bullshit game to get through customs. As the sliding doors open, the warm Emirates air hits me. It feels nice to have something other than recycled airport air wash over my skin for the first time in two days. We are immediately greeted by Sean Lee, a former infantry NCO who worked for Sarah at the Independence Fund for a while. He's a short guy, about Nick's height, with salt-and-pepper hair and a couple of extra retirement pounds, but he still looks the part of an infantryman.

"Nice to finally meet you guys in person," he says cheerfully, but through very tired eyes.

"How's it been?" I ask.

"Well, let me put it this way: I'm so happy to see you guys. We've been running nonstop. I've only slept an hour or two here and there. Sean G and Seaspray are in rough shape. They are looking forward to having you out there. Right now, it is Santa 6, Joe, me, and Leon running the JOC, but we think Joe has Covid so he's holed up in his room. Sean G and Seaspray are forward and Dave Johnson, who just got out here, flew to Kabul this morning," Sean explains.

"Is Chad out here yet?" Nick asks.

"Not yet, but he's on his way. He landed in Abu Dhabi already and is driving in."

"Awesome," I reply.

The only people I know on this trip are Chad and Nick. Everyone else, like us, is here through some connection to Chad or to someone Chad knows, and not all of those connections are ironclad. Sean G and Seaspray, for example, were trying to come over here to help but couldn't get permission to operate on their own. Because Sean G used to work with Santa 6, Santa 6 offered up the opportunity to work with us on this, and he jumped at the chance. With that, Joe cleared the way for him to arrive, and he immediately got to work.

But we're walking into a dangerous situation, and I like to have more airtight bona fides than, "Oh, hey, two guys I don't know, you worked with this guy Santa 6, who I don't know, who rides motorcycles with this guy Joe who I don't know, who got you in the country." Now, I'm sure they feel the exact same way about me with thoughts like, "Oh, great! This cocky asshole prima donna Tim Kennedy who is all over Instagram is coming in here. Can't wait for the selfies!"

This is the hand we are all dealt. We all decided to come here. Now we all have to rely on each other.

Still, at this point, the only people I'm trusting with my life are Nick and Chad, and I'm assessing everyone else as they come. As the trip goes on and we drive the couple hours to the military base, I start to think I can gamble that Sean Lee is one of those guys too. He doesn't play himself up—doesn't pretend to be a big deal. He talks earnestly about why he is here and his experience overseas. He tells us he is currently being used as the S3 Air—in civilian terms, the guy coordinating flights and manifests, and he thinks that's the perfect use for him. This is a good start. I was worried about clashing egos, because you have to be a little crazy and confident to be out here doing what these guys are out here doing.

We arrive at the JOC. The UAE has graciously given us rooms to sleep in and a quasi-secure conference room to work out of in their officer training center. I'm instantly amazed as I walk in. The one that we have in the United States is among the crappiest buildings you will ever see: Our stuff looks like they took World War II cement barracks and updated it with Holiday Inn Express–level luxury, because that's exactly what ours is. This building that I am now standing in is an absolute work of art. We are greeted at the door by gentlemen with white gloves who offer to carry our luggage. Everything is marble. There are water fountains. There are sitting areas, art, and luxury. This place is nothing short of majestic.

As we check in, they tell us that there is 24/7 room service and that they have comped us three meals a day for our entire stay, and that they are honored to have us here.

I did not expect this level of hospitality.

Sean Lee walks us to our rooms—Nick and I are right next to each other—and then takes us to the JOC. At this hour, the only other person awake is Leon Worthen, an Army Intelligence veteran who now works with the National Child Protection Task Force. I introduce myself and Nick does the same. While we chat with Leon and shoot the shit, Sean Lee is on Signal talking to Sean G. When he's done, he walks over. "Hey, our next flight is leaving here in four or five hours. Sean G would love for you to be on it. He needs the help. If you're up for it, then we need to leave here in two to three hours."

"Okay. We will see you then," I answer quickly.

Nick and I go back to our rooms and order steaks from room service while we clean up. When they arrive, we sit in my room and talk. "Where do you want me?" Nick asks. I appreciate this question significantly. Nick was an officer, so he's used to doling out orders and being in charge. What's more, he's been in charge of his own companies for fifteen years. But he hasn't been a man of action in a long time, and he knows it and isn't pretending otherwise. This is a consistent trend in my closest friends. They know who they are, and they know their capabilities. Nick can still fight well and shoot well, but he isn't tactically current, so he's asking for my judgment.

"I don't know yet," I tell him. "My gut instinct is that I want you watching my back from inside the wire, as opposed to running operations with me, but let's meet the guys on the ground first."

"Okay, man," he says, then starts again. "I'm gonna need you to promise me you're not going to do anything stupid. I'm really afraid of your wife, and if you end up dead, she is one hundred percent going to blame me for not controlling you, even though everyone knows damn well you cannot be controlled."

"I promise I will try not to do anything stupid," I say.

"That's not exactly what I asked you to promise," he replies, smiling.

"I know," I say.

We eat. The steak is great. Nick keeps me company while I check my night vision and satellite phone to ensure they have batteries and are working properly. By the time I am done, we have ninety minutes to sleep. That's enough time to at least get a few winks.

It's odd being on an entirely empty plane. There's seven crew members, Nick, and me and that's it. While the UAE government has lent us two C-17s to use for this operation, they make their runs later in the day; we were able to work with some large donors to get access to some 737s as well. This bird is from Kam Air, an Afghan outfit. As such, the entire crew is Afghan. There is no longer a ground crew working in Kabul, and the plane is only allowed to land at a military airstrip in UAE, so imagine a port-a-potty sitting on the side of the road for two weeks in the hot Georgia sun and that's what this plane smelled like. When we first got on and I sat down, Nick once again sat right next to me to fuck with me, but he's now sitting across the aisle, staring into the back of his chair.

"You good?" I ask him.

He looks up. "Yeah, man. It's just a little surreal. It's been a minute, you know? But this is fucking historic. It's awful historic, but it's historic. This is the fall of Saigon for our generation. Maybe we can make it a little better. How do you not help when you know you can? Just getting my head in the game."

I'm proud of him. My big three, Shane, Justin, and Nick, all reacted differently to this mission. Justin's known me longer than anyone and he knew I was going no matter what he or anyone else said, so he kept it simple: "Are you really going to leave me alone to open your school, open your headquarters, and relaunch your supplement line by myself? You probably planned this shit. That's lazy, Tim. That's real lazy."

Shane was more overtly worried. "What do you mean you're going to Afghanistan? You know you're not twenty-six anymore, right? The greater good and your moral compass won't matter when you're dead."

Guys have a tendency to hide love inside insults. I feel the love. I love those two guys too.

And then there's Nick. His dumb ass is on the plane next to me. All three of them would have gone if I asked them to—even Shane, who has no military service. It's a good feeling to have them in my life.

"I'm gonna go lay down and sleep," I tell Nick.

"I'll wake you up when we're on approach," he answers.

I lay myself on the ground in front of the first two seats in first class and pass out. Every once in a while, I wake up and see Nick talking to the crew. They're asking him to get their families out. He promises he will try and he means it. I know that will be a tall order. Some three hours later, he is tapping me on the shoulder. "We're on approach, buddy."

I pop up and stretch out. Then I pull out my body armor and gear and pack all of my stuff up. I see the Afghanistan landscape come into view. Gray mountains that seem to go on forever, a destitute city faded into those mountains, and dust that seems to cover everything. A piece of me is down there too, somewhere in those mountains.

It's been some years since I've stepped foot in this place. It feels like yesterday, and a lifetime ago, all at the same time. The wheels touch down and the plane bounces once or twice. It doesn't take long for the plane to come to a complete stop at this one-runway airport.

I look out the window and see a dude with a leg prosthetic pushing the staircase up to the side of the plane. A minute later, there is a loud banging on the door. The crew opens the door, and that same dude is sitting there waiting to greet us. In a gruff voice, he says, "Tim Kennedy and Nick from the internet. These are wild times, boys. Welcome to Kabul!" We grab our shit and follow him down the staircase. My eyes go wide.

If you've ever spent time on a runway or near a hangar, you know that pilots and ground crew are anal about the cleanliness of the area. If one random piece of trash gets sucked into one of the engines, it could blow the turbine; in the same way that pilots fear bird strike, they fear trash. Additionally, at any airport there are very specific pathways for ground vehicles versus aircraft, and there are generally ground guides everywhere.

Absolutely none of that is present here. The ground personnel are a couple of OGA (Other Government Agency) guys. They aren't guiding aircraft or anything. They're pushing staircases up to planes and loading people on and taking people off. If a plane needs fuel, one of the crew members has to climb out and connect everything himself. Ground vehicles are zipping in front of, underneath, and around aircraft. This is absolute chaos, and it sets the tone for what I am about to experience.

"Last time I will ask, you want me to go with you?" Nick says.

On the way over, I had told him that if he and I are both outside the wire, then I have no one I know as backup. We thought Chad was going to come with us, but he tore his quad getting one more Jiu Jitsu workout in before flying out, so he can't run around in Kabul right now. "I need you to West Point the fuck out of this. Build targets. Work the ground. Help everyone else. Make sure we get home. We can revisit this tomorrow after I get a sense of who these guys are."

"Okay, man. Sunset and sunrise, then, at a minimum," Nick says, referring to our minimum contact communications plan with my satellite phone if my normal phone craps out.

"Yup, love you, man," I say, hugging him.

"Love you too," he replies.

Three dudes walk up, all reeking of Special Operations. Operators move differently. They talk differently. They seem chill and on edge, all at the same time. They still maintain the bravado of the infantryman, but it's more relaxed—almost laissez-faire in nature.

The first guy is in his early fifties with a glorious mustache and introduces himself as "Sean G." He's our team leader. He emanates confidence. The next guy looks like he belongs more on a beach catching waves than he does in Kabul. He's got bronze skin, long, flowing locks with a bandana holding them back, and cool sunglasses. Even his clothing, which is the same kind of tactical shit we all are wearing, somehow looks more stylish. He introduces himself as Seaspray. The last guy in the crew is Dave Johnson. Dave is in his early sixties, but keeps himself fit. He's an SF guy and West Pointer from the '80s. Sean G and Seaspray will be running outside the wire with me. Dave will be working the gates from inside the wire, picking up targets we bring in so we can get back out as fast as possible, and solving whatever problems pop up for us.

"Nick, are you coming with us?" Sean G asks.

"If you need me," he replies.

"Nick's gonna run target acquisition for a while," I say forcibly. If they ask him, he'll say yes, and I feel strongly that I need someone I can trust that can keep his eye on the big picture. And, from a protective friend standpoint, until I know who these guys are in action, I sure don't want to risk his life.

"Cool," Sean G says, "come with me!" I walk off with him and Dave. Nick jumps into a Polaris MRZR with Seaspray and takes off in the other direction.

Sean G walks me over to an armored Land Cruiser that he has very obviously stolen. We get in and he asks, "What do you need?"

"I need a gun and local comms," I tell him.

"Good answer," he replies and hands me an AK-47, some basic comms gear, and a map of the airport. Then he walks me over to an area alongside the gate, but away from everyone else, and asks me to tell him how I would build a ratline from here.

This dude is testing me?

Well, I'm a little angry, but not surprised. If I was in his shoes, I'd be doing exactly the same thing, so I also respect it.

This is a very complicated situation on the ground. Politics in the United States is negatively affecting in real time what is happening here in Afghanistan. In some cases, the Department of Defense and the Department of State, and even smaller agencies, all have different, competing agendas. So, in some cases, we not only have to slip evacuees past the Taliban, past their own countrymen, and through a barricaded airbase, but also past American checkpoints. It is all dependent on whose list we were working off at any given time.

With that in mind, I assess the area. At first glance, it looks like a good place to slip people in and out of the wire, but I look at the terrain and ask myself where I would put an observation post (OP). Sure enough, under optics, I see the Taliban exactly where I would be set up. *This won't work.* I look at the map and find an alternate location that OP cannot watch. Foliage around here is overgrown; the Taliban are too lazy to come here. No one wants to push through bramble and thorns. I see a spot where we can move a barricade just enough to squeeze a person in, if that person traverses the wire just so. I check the area once again, under optics and thermals. It's all clear. "This is it," I tell Sean G. "This is where I'd run it."

"Okay, then. Run it."

I don't know how long I've been going, but it's been a while. I've had cumulatively one complete meal in the last twenty-four hours spread over maybe twelve micro meals that amount to a bite of a meal bar or some nuts or jerky that I brought from home. Seaspray has eaten less and has been on this mission several days longer than I have. He's at the point where his stomach cannot really process food properly, so he eats a saltine cracker here or there, to give him some energy without destroying his digestive system, shitting his brains out, and losing efficacy. He's a total stud and it took me no time to completely respect him. In fact, the whole team has come together well, across the board. It's almost like a dream scenario.

There are twelve dudes forward on this mission, plotted across two countries, plus Sarah back in the States. None of us know each other, and we've all been able to put ego aside and just work. Nick, Sean

Lee, Leon, and Santa 6 are working seamlessly, and we are getting excellent target packages put together, and then approved through Sarah by the Joint Chiefs of Staff. I have no idea how many people I have personally grabbed, but apparently the entire team is getting close to 10,000 people evacuated, which is insane. When I came here, I thought if we got a few dozen out, it would be a win, but this team is just clicking and the generosity of the United Arab Emirates seems to be boundless.

I wait quietly in the night and send a WhatsApp message to my target. "I'm here. Send me the signal," I command. I watch the double check marks appear and a moment later, some 100 meters away, I see a phone screen lit up green. "Stay there," I tell her. Seaspray and I move quietly to her location. We wait 50 meters away and observe. There's no movement. We inch closer.

"Have you seen the new movie about the astronaut?" I say firmly.

"I have and it was absolutely bananas," comes the reply.

She's passed the far and near recognition signals. My challenge had to include the word "astronaut." Her response had to include "bananas." We close the distance.

When we get there, she has her documents ready. Seaspray and I confirm that the passports she has with her match the ones we received digitally. Okay, this is our lady, and these are her five kids. "Let's move," Seaspray offers up.

We start to move out from the field we're currently in, toward the town proper, when we see movement that doesn't belong to us. *Taliban.* The news has shown a very calm and nonviolent Taliban, but that isn't the Taliban we're seeing out here. Another group, operating parallel to us, had rescued a woman and was about to load her into their vehicle when she got separated from them by a few feet. The Taliban merc'd her right on the hood of their vehicle—brains everywhere.

It was a dare.

Now that she was dead, that team had no legal cause to fire on the Taliban, as they were no longer a threat. So they left. We didn't want that situation, but we also didn't want a two against lots of bad guys gunfight with a woman and five kids in tow. In fight-or-flight, sometimes flight is the right response. We grab them and start running.

There's no way we are going to outrun adults while dragging kids in a straight line, so we cut tons of angles, running through alleyways, houses, and gardens, and take whatever turns we can to slow them down by forcing them to make a directional decision.

My heart is pounding, and I keep looking over my shoulder as we move through the city. Finally, I see the crowds in front of me. They go for blocks and blocks, but the crowds mean that we are close to the airport, and that means there are cameras everywhere. At some point, they stop following us, and we arrive at Abbey Gate. Dave Johnson is waiting there for us to escort these six inside. Even still, it takes an hour to get them through the wire.

I look around at the thousands of people pressing against the walls and the wire. I have never seen such desperation in my entire life. They want so badly to be on the other side of this wall—it's the real difference between life and death for many of them. They all know the clock is ticking and that come August 30, in six days, their chance to get to safety will be gone.

I feel incredible pain for the soldiers and Marines guarding these walls. They're playing God right now—deciding who lives and who dies—and I know that will weigh on them for the rest of their years. Every once in a while, as the Taliban beat people away from the cameras, or fire AK rounds into the occasional person they can separate from the crowd, the entire body of humanity comes to life and surges toward the walls. I see people ripped up by the concertina wire as they get pushed forward and they have nowhere to go. I see babies crowd-surfed to the front of the wall the way the rest of the world would crowd-surf a beach ball at a rock concert. Imagine being so afraid that you just trust your infant to a sea of strangers because you legitimately think that it is their best chance at survival? In the worst cases, mothers throw their babies over the wall, hoping someone will catch them on the other side. Instead, those children hit the concertina wire on the inside of the wall and bleed out.

I've only seen moments of this pain because I'm trying to keep up with the Adonis that is Seaspray, and I don't have time to think about it. But these guys are just sitting on this wall, doing the best they can doing their jobs and giving comfort to these poor people.

God bless them.

———————

Anticipation reaches its apex as the buses Sean G acquired come to a complete stop in front of Black Gate. "We're at the gate," I tell Nick over the sat phone. It's the middle of the night, and I'm reporting back to the guys. Nick flew back to the UAE with some high-value personnel that we recovered and is flying back here tomorrow, possibly with Joe Robert, who doesn't have Covid after all. Nick and Sean Lee are manning the JOC. They're excited. We're excited. Tonight has been incredible.

Sean G crafted a master plan to rescue several high-risk populations in a single night. It was daring and we are smoked, but in our convoy of buses, we have 300 orphan children, just under 100 Nazarenes— Christians who will likely be killed or tortured under the Taliban— several families of the Afghan pilots who have been flying us in and out of Afghanistan, several personnel the government asked us to rescue, and best of all, more than seventy United States citizens. All we have to do is get through the gate.

Dave Johnson is waiting for us there. He's greased the skids and sure enough, the buses get escorted through the gates and into a holding area.

We did it! This is a huge moment. I'm almost brought to tears.

The amount of planning, work, and frankly, luck that went into making this mission successful is impossible to understand. Seaspray smells like ammonia—that Ranger School your-body-is-eating-all-your-muscle smell. No one has gone harder in the paint than he has this week. Sean G looks worn as hell, but the ever so slight smile creased only at the corners of his lips tell me otherwise. He's energized by this moment. It's the reason he came here. It's the reason that, in his fifties, he walked away from a huge D.C. job to prioritize saving human lives. Five hundred people in one night. And we still have time to work.

"Who the fuck is bringing buses onto my base?" comes a voice I don't recognize.

I squint into the night and see a figure walking over. I pop out of the bus and walk in that direction. From the tone, this is either a Field Grade Officer or a Command Sergeant Major. I put my nicest face on.

By the time I get to him, Seaspray, Dave, and Sean G are here as well. It's a Colonel from the 82nd Airborne.

"Hey, sir. How are you tonight?" I ask.

"What the fuck are you guys doing, driving buses onto my base?" he asks again.

I immediately realize that we need to defuse the situation quickly or it is going to go bad.

"My apologies, sir. These buses have a bunch of U.S. citizens, children, Christians, and folks that State asked us to pick up. I thought this was fully coordinated with you, but clearly it wasn't. We'll follow any protocol you want to get them cleared."

"Let me tell you something. This isn't the Tim Kennedy show! This is my show! You hear me," he snaps.

"Yes, sir," I answer.

Seaspray stares him right in the eyes, then shakes his head in disgust and walks away.

Dave figures out that the Colonel is a West Pointer somehow. Maybe he had his ring on, maybe they have some lame secret signal, or maybe they can smell each other's West Point pheromones, but once he realized it, he tried that approach.

"Hey, brother, I graduated from the same place you did. I promise that we did this right. We cleared all of these folks. Tell us what we need to do to make this right. We will walk them right to our plane and fly them out," he offers.

"I don't care where you went to undergrad. These people aren't coming on my base, period. Turn these buses around," he says as he starts turning from us.

Sean G has had enough.

"Are you fucking kidding me? You're good with throwing American citizens and kids out the fucking gates because it wasn't your idea? You do this, I will call every general I know, every politician I know. I will commit myself to making sure you regret ever meeting me."

At this moment, I am legitimately afraid of my mustachioed team leader. He is not joking. The Colonel just sees this as a threat to his masculinity and power. "Get all of them off of my fucking base," he growls.

"This isn't your base. This is an Afghan airport," Sean growls back.

I try to negotiate this to a reasonable level. "Sir, can we at least go through the bus and pull out all the blue passports. We can't kick out American citizens, right?" I almost beg.

"Turn these buses the fuck around, now," he says and walks away to some of his guys a few meters away. They look uncomfortable and ashamed.

Dave and Sean G are not giving up and they walk over to him and keep the argument going. I call Nick.

"They're kicking the bus out, man," I tell him on the sat phone.

"What!" he exclaims. "How can they possibly do that."

"There's some fucking West Point Brigade Commander here that thinks I'm trying to challenge his authority, and he's willing to kick 300 kids to the curb to show he's in charge."

"Are you fucking kidding me? Can you reason with him? Did Dave try the West Point card?" Nick asks as a West Pointer who knows that shit has worked every time in the history of the world.

"Yes. The Colonel doesn't give a shit," I tell him.

"What's his name?" Nick asks.

I tell him.

"I know him. He's a class ahead of me. If you cannot solve this on the ground, I'm calling Senator Tillis. We cannot let this happen," Nick proclaims.

"This guy isn't listening to us, man. There's nothing I can say to him," I tell him.

"Stand by," Nick answers. The last decade and a half of civilian life are gone and he is back in officer mode.

I hear him switch to his cell phone while my line stays open. He calls Sarah, who connects him to Kim Barnes from Senator Tillis's office. Senator Tillis drops everything and tries to solve the problem. He's making calls to DOD and DOS as Nick is on hold. While Nick is on with Tillis, Sarah calls the Joint Chiefs of Staff and numerous congressmen. As a result, multiple powerful people begin calling down to Kabul.

In a matter of about twenty minutes, our ragtag group has managed to mobilize the handful of people of character at the highest levels of government who actually care about this mission.

We needed twenty-five minutes.

By the time the runner gets to the Colonel to stop him, he has already kicked our buses out. All of the U.S. citizens. All of the kids. All of the Christians. And all of the people our government asked us to save. In my entire life, I have never seen a more pointless display of authority. I don't know how guys like my Special Forces boss, Colonel Theo Unbehagen, and Nick come from the same place as this guy.

By now, Sean Lee and Nick are not the only ones on the other end of the phone. Santa 6 just arrived in the JOC, as did Leon. I can hear Sean Lee explaining what happened. I can hear Santa 6, an absolute bear of a man, who has seen and done everything there is to do in and around the military, ask how he could do that, his voice cracking like a child's. I hear Nick swearing like a sailor. Then a long pause.

"I'm so sorry, man," he finally says.

"Yeah," I answer. "Me too."

"What are you guys going to do?" he asks.

I look at Sean G, dejected, rage fueling him. I look at Seaspray, checking all his gear, stoic. I look at Dave, embarrassed by his fellow West Pointer, but resolute.

"We're going back to work," I say.

After the bus incident, things get a lot tighter. The ratlines we were using before are now being watched by the Taliban. We cannot move in big formations, so we have to work solo. The guys at the JOC tried to convince us to stop for the night, but we couldn't do that. Once again, I am faced with the thing I hate most—a lack of control over an outcome I desperately want to go another way. But I had to—we had to—accept that outcome as the past and focus on the present. We cannot control the bus decision. It's over and done with. What we can control is to get more people out.

So we do. All night. All morning. All afternoon. Seaspray and Sean G run off and find their own fresh ratlines, and I choose one where I know no one will follow: the sewer line. It takes a special person to walk calf-deep in piss and shit, and I am that person. The families I took back through here weren't necessarily happy to be wading in muck, but they were safe. Twelve hours and no sleep after the bus incident, I smelled like literal shit, but our little crew had managed to move another couple hundred people to safety.

Now we had yet another problem: The aircrews for Kam Air were no longer willing to fly. There had been numerous incidents this entire time. One of the engineers on the flight that Nick and I flew in quit when we landed in Afghanistan and said he would not come back until we got his family out. Another set of pilots shut down the plane in the middle of the runway, essentially taking the entire airport hostage for a period of time. They too wanted their families' safety guaranteed. This was a tough pathway to walk. We tried our asses off, but getting them manifested legally, finding them, and getting them on base was a huge task. At this point we probably had gotten 8 to 10 percent of them to safety. That wasn't enough for this group, so they got off the plane and huddled nearby, waiting to get their way.

At first, we just step up: The planes have to move and we are the only ones here to move them. We all start figuring things out like how to open the cargo bay doors and load luggage, or move the staircase to the plane, and other random airline stuff the crew would normally do. One of the engineers who didn't quit told us we needed a new battery, so Sean G starts rummaging through the other grounded aircraft and finds a battery that will fit. We somehow cobble enough parts and effort together to get the plane ready to fly again.

Right when we feel we've succeeded, the pilot walks over and tells us if we don't get his family out, then he will not fly. *Damnit.*

I feel rage and am about to lay into him, but Seaspray goes down a different path and I follow. "I know you're scared," he starts. "I would be too. You have to understand I want to get them out too, but I cannot promise that I will. I can only promise I will keep trying." Our pilot friend is surprised by this honesty.

I jump in. "We're a team. There's a ground component and an air component. We're the ground. You're the air. Look, man, if we were only worried about our own families, we'd be home. We're volunteers!" He is very surprised to hear this statement. He thought we were in the State Department or military.

Seaspray continues, "Set aside your personal feelings for a minute, and look at the big picture. You're part of a rescue operation and you're saving Afghans. Every single time you decide to put your uniform on and fly, you're saving 400 people. It's not just you and yours, but a larger responsibility."

The pilot starts crying. I tear up a little. Seaspray is not only right, but he means it. This isn't psychological warfare for him. His emotions are on his sleeve. He's all in. This is a dude who graduated from two of the best institutions in the world, who could be making bank in the business world, and instead is running around with me risking his life.

"I will fly," the pilot says. He then calls all of his fellow Kam Air pilots and asks them to fly as well. It is an incredibly brave moment. We start loading people onto the plane.

———

The earth shakes and the explosion echoes through the airport. *That was a bomb.* Sean G, Seaspray, and I look at each other. We're simultaneously hoping no one got hurt and that our trip isn't coming to a premature end.

The internet moves at the speed of light. At the same time that some of our partners from DOD and DOS are letting us know there are casualties at Abbey Gate, a gate we have frequented many times over the past week, Nick and Santa 6 are hitting up Sean G and me, asking if we are okay.

A suicide bomber got inside the wire and detonated, killing thirteen U.S. service members, all twenty-five years old or younger. One of them, I would find out later, is Sergeant Nicole Gee, a young leader who grew up a few hours from where I did, in Sacramento. She helped us earlier that day when we had to search the women we rescued before bringing them on base. She was really sweet, and high energy. She wasn't going through the motions—she greeted every Afghan with a smile. She loved her job and her service.

This is absolutely the worst possible situation. I joined the military in my early twenties. I felt old then. I felt knowledgeable. I felt like I had experienced life. I had no idea. These brave troops—eleven Marines, one Corpsman, and one Soldier—gave their lives to help those in need.

There is nothing more honorable.

As I stand on this tarmac and think about them—people I had stood next to hours before—I cannot help but be reminded of my children. My daughters are this age. Sean G and Nick have kids this age. When I was young and my friends died, it was personally painful. This feels worse even though I don't know them, because now I understand what they have traded. I know the years they will never have, the families they will never grow, and the laughs they will never enjoy. We take a moment of silence for them as the sun goes down.

An hour later, Sean G and I are sitting in a Razor four-wheeler eating a snack. The whole world is locked down now. Santa 6 has confirmed that, at least for now, he will not be able to land an aircraft in HKIA. The military is blocking all civilian aircraft and UAE is not super excited to send their C-17s into a place that just got bombed. Suddenly, our Signal lights up. It's Seaspray. He had been off visiting some of his buddies that he used to work with. "Hey, guys, get everyone you know, grab your guns, and come here now. Things are bad and need immediate QRF."

Seaspray is not a drama queen. He's the kind of guy who could be in a firefight against an entire platoon of enemies and say something like,

"Hey, if you get a chance could you come and help out?" Sean G and I know this is a big deal. We call every Special Operations or State Department guy we know in this airport, then go lights out on the vehicle and race to his location.

When we arrive, we are shocked to see that right outside of a top secret hangar is a foreign military plane. We park, drop our night vision down, and maneuver to where Seaspray is waiting with one of his buddies from a former life. He believes there's twenty guys who look like Special Operations types. We creep into the entrance of the building, and under night vision we see sparks flying everywhere. These guys are cutting pieces off vehicles and equipment and trying to use the fact that HKIA is chaotic after the bombing to extract intelligence information. *Motherfuckers.*

A couple of them start to move toward the plane with gear. *Fuck.* Four against twenty is not my idea of a good time. Seaspray's friend moves away from us and then identifies himself. The bad guys stop and face him, and then more show up, and then more. They all speak perfect English, but their accents accentuate the fact that they are not Americans. At least another dozen dudes with guns filter out of every crevice of this hangar. There's now definitely more than thirty guys against four of us and I like nothing about this situation. What's worse is that these guys act like us and they move like us. They might not wear the same uniform, and they might not be quite as good, but they're going to be close. If anyone gets an itchy trigger finger, there is a good chance we're going to die in place here.

The room is completely silent. You can hear everyone's breathing.

Then something miraculous happens. You know how in movies when the heroes are trapped by a larger army of bad guys and are seemingly defeated, and all of a sudden the reinforcements show up over the horizon, and the bad guys have no choice but to stand down? That happens, except instead of some medieval army or cavalry unit riding up, it's a who's-who of Special Operators pouring into the building. I am instantly significantly more happy that these thirty-some-odd dudes wearing the other uniforms are instantly significantly less happy.

However, we are still in a Mexican standoff with another Special Operations force. The tension is palpable.

Our guys bark orders at our guests. Tense shouting comes back our way. I'm less interested in the words and more interested in trying to gauge facial expressions and body language. Finally, after several back-and-forth exchanges, our guests lower their weapons.

"Do you need us anymore?" Sean G asks Seaspray's friend. "Nope, you guys should bail now," comes the response. We do.

Seaspray, Sean G, and I get back in the Razor. "Did that just fucking happen?" I ask. "I think so," Seaspray answers, "but I'm really fucking tired, so maybe we imagined it." "All I know is that foreign militaries weren't landing in HKIA to steal our stuff before Tim Kennedy showed up. I think you're bad luck, man," Sean G says, smiling, and then adds, "We need to find a ride out of here, because after all this shit, no one that isn't the U.S. military is landing here."

He was right. Santa 6 definitively let us know that nothing from the UAE was going to land in Afghanistan, so he and the boys were going to work on an alternative option. We, however, need to be doing the same, because nothing is definite out here for guys who are here in a quasi-official capacity.

In the midst of all this bad news, we get a little bit of good news: Chad's interpreter Aziz has made it to the UAE safely. While he flew there on our plane, we weren't the team that grabbed him and saved his life. We owe those guys a huge debt of gratitude and I wish I could thank them by name.

We link back up with Dave to discuss our best options for getting out, and then go to every contact we have worked with or knew from our past (or current lives) to see if we can hitch a ride with anyone. After a couple of hours of this, we find some folks from the State Department that have four seats on a plane arriving here in a couple hours. I hit Santa 6, Sean Lee, and Nick up via Signal and let them know. Internet access is in and out now because they've jammed all the cell phone towers in the area since the bombing in case there are any phone bombs or terrorist cells coordinating in the area, but there are a couple of organizations still here on the ground that let me bounce off their signal. We'd be flying into Uzbekistan and then we'd have to fly commercial out of there. Not ideal, but it should work!

Except the plane crashed. Mechanical issues began in mid-flight, and they couldn't make it to the airport, so they had to hard land in the best place they could. The Hail Mary chance we had at getting out of here crashed into Pakistan. Everyone ended up okay, but we are now once again planeless. I call Nick and give him the update. "Okay, man, we'll find a way out."

Every lead we run down comes up short. The military birds are full, as are the Department of State birds. I begin to wonder if we're going to have to walk out of this place. If we have to, at least I know this is the team to do it with. Still . . . I'd rather not.

Finally, I find an Airman that recognizes me. "Oh, shit, are you Tim Kennedy?" he asks.

"He is Tim Kennedy," Seaspray answers with a smirk.

"Awesome, man! I'm a huge fan," my new Airman friend says.

"Me too," Seaspray chimes in.

Ignoring him, I ask, "Is there any chance you have some room for us? Our ride crashed in Pakistan."

"No shit? How many of you are there? Four?" he asks.

"Yeah, just the four of us," I answer.

"Hey, did you know he's Tim Kennedy?" Seaspray chimes in again.

"He is, in fact, Tim Kennedy," Sean G says, joining the game.

Dave, at least, just smiles.

"I can put you on the ramp, man. No problem," my Airman buddy tells us.

"You're the shit. I really appreciate it!" I say, and then add, "So, where are we going?"

"Qatar," he tells us.

Looks like we're going to Qatar. I jump on the Signal app and type, "Found a ride to Qatar. Will touch base when we land." Communications now complete, I shut my phone off to save battery life and walk to the edge of the ramp. I turn to look one last time at the vastness of the

Afghanistan landscape. I have left so much of my life in this place. A lot of Americans died here. Hell, I almost died here. *Was it worth it?* It's dark now, but I can still see the edges of the mountains against the night sky. A feeling of sadness and failure encompasses me. *I might never be here again.* I walk up the ramp.

———

This is the worst flight I have ever been on. It only takes about two and a half hours to fly from Kabul to Doha, Qatar. We have now been in the air for almost fourteen hours. This is what happens when everyone is fleeing a country, you're flying to the last place still accepting Afghan refugees, and there's only one ground crew working the whole airport. We have been literally circling the airport for twelve hours.

Most of the people on this airplane have never been on a plane before. Prior to getting on, they were hungry and dehydrated. At best they have a bag each. They left the crushing heat of Afghanistan. Now they're in a barely climate-controlled freezing C-17 with leaky hydraulic lines and occasional hissing coming from one component or another. They're all rammed together sitting on hard metal floors and people are getting claustrophobic and irritated.

The shouts come more quickly from the men now.

"Where are we?"

"When do we land?"

Women start passing out from exhaustion and dehydration and that sends some of the men into more of a fury. "We want to land now!" a few demand.

It's not their fault. For over a week these people have tried desperately to get on base and to get a flight out. Now that they have one, and we have been circling for over half a day, the excitement has worn off. They left everything that they know behind—their homes, jobs, families, possessions. Now they're wondering where they are going, how they will eat, and whether they will be able to find work. The anxiety is building, made worse by the conditions.

For our part, we actually lucked out sitting on the ramp. We're the only four guys up here, so after we moved things around to get comfortable, it has been pretty good. For me, the only negative is how much enjoyment Seaspray, Sean G, and Dave are having at my expense. The aircrew, the security forces guys, and even a couple of the Afghans have recognized me and asked for selfies. Seaspray keeps offering to take them and is adding his own commentary now, in the same way that Af provided his during Ranger School.

As much as the ribbing is annoying, them knowing me did work out for us. When four dudes dressed in Operator gear with no papers get on a plane with no questions asked, everyone assumes you are operating deep in the black. When they realize I'm one of them, they extrapolate a lot more that isn't actually there. Not once do any of us lie. We all tell them the absolute truth. "We're here on a volunteer mission as civilians, not as military." But no one believes us because it is just too absurd. Who the fuck just flies to Afghanistan and runs a ten-day evacuation effort and gets their own hangar, ramp, weapons, and call sign at the JOC if they were just dudes who showed up here on a whim?

Actually, when you say it like that it sounds absolutely ridiculous.

After seven women pass out, we get permission to cut to the front of the line ahead of fourteen other birds and land. It is a welcome relief to feel the tires hit the ground . . . for about thirty minutes. We've landed, but there is still only one ground crew, so we are still stuck here, except now it isn't cold, it's smoldering hot because we're on the ground in Qatar and the A/C is off.

The Afghans lose it. The men are yelling at people. One guy starts throwing shit at the guards, who are now holding their weapons instead of slinging them. Another woman starts having issues breathing and the guards cannot get to her because the men on the plane are too aggressive, so they have to crowd-surf an oxygen bottle to her husband and pantomime how to use it. I have had enough.

The four of us work our way off the ramp and to the security forces guys by the door they are using to offload women who need ambulances. Both guys are really cool and I took photos with them earlier and shot the shit for a while. "Hey, man, can we get off?" I ask.

"Yeah, no problem, Tim. I'm gonna call my buddy to pick you guys up so you don't have to walk. It's a couple miles, man," he says.

I did not expect that.

So we hop out of the plane, and a few minutes later a truck shows up with an E3 driving it, and we all hop in. "Is this what it's like to be Tim Kennedy?" Seaspray asks, mockingly.

"Tim's the kind of guy that only uses Uber Black," Dave chimes in.

"Little known fact: Tim doesn't pay Uber; Uber pays him," Sean G adds.

I'm happy they are enjoying this.

This Airman is awesome, and he's absolutely looking out for us. I turn on my phone. There are several messages in my Signal app from Nick. "Dude, I don't know if you're getting any of these, but we're working on exfil." Then, "Bro, if you have any comms, now is the time to tell us if you have a ride. If I don't hear from you, we are coming for you. Santa 6 is working on options." Then, "Man, I hope you guys are okay. Transportation is almost locked up. We're working on getting the money together."

What the fuck? I sent him a message letting him know that we were flying out. I look for that message. There it is. With one checkmark . . . and there's the second one. It just sent. *Oops!*

When you send a message in Signal, it shows one check mark when you send, a second when it has gone all the way through and been received, and then both check marks turn white when the recipient has read them. I had only waited for one check mark before shutting off my phone. Nick and Santa 6 never received anything from me. I call Nick.

"Oh, dude! Just got your message! I'm so glad you're okay and you have a ride to Qatar! When do you land?" he asks, clearly relieved we're actually safe.

"I'm here, man," I say.

"What do you mean, you're there? We've been working on transpo for twelve hours. Santa 6 did a drug deal to get a Black Hawk to fly you into Uzbekistan. We're sitting here freaking out and we are about to wire $500,000 to a contractor to get this done, and that's because Santa 6 negotiated him down from $1,000,000! Why didn't you say anything?" he asks, his voice getting somewhat agitated.

"I sent you a message," I say blandly.

"No, you didn't . . ." he trails off. "Okay, I just got it. Did you just send this to mess with me?"

"I sent it from Kabul . . . it may have not gone through," I respond.

"Did you not wait for it to go through?" he half yells.

"Hey, you're breaking up," I say as I make fake static noises with my mouth. "I have to go!"

"I'm happy you're safe and I hate you!" Nick says as I hang up.

After talking to our E3 buddy, we realize we will need another Covid test before getting on our next plane, wherever that will be taking us. The way all of these countries work is that you need to take a fresh test every time you enter the country, and you have to have a PCR test (the one where they tickle your brain by sending the swab way up your nose) within seventy-two hours of taking off. So our E3 grabs another one of his E3 buddies, and that guy watches our gear while our guy takes us to the Air Force clinic.

These guys knock out these tests like a mass production factory, so as we walk in they get right to it. "Where are you guys coming from?"

"Kabul," I answer.

"You have your orders?" he asks.

"We do not," I say.

"Any paperwork at all?" he asks.

"Nothing, man," I say, shaking my head.

"Ah fuck it. You guys are all American and you're Tim Kennedy, so you're probably not terrorists," he says matter-of-factly. I had not introduced myself yet, so Seaspray is really enjoying this.

We wait a little while for our test results and are ready to head out. "Can you drive us to Doha proper?" I ask him. The city is actually twenty or so miles away from the military base.

"I wish, man, but we're not allowed to leave the base. The best I can do is get you to the gate, and then you could try to get a taxi," he says, clearly bummed out by not being able to come through for us.

"That's perfect, man. Thank you!" We reload on water, hit the bathroom, and drive to the gate.

And there we sit. No taxi will come get us. It gets dark. There are no cars. We are in the middle of nowhere. I take off my shoes and socks to let my feet air out and make a pillow out of my backpack. "We're not going to solve this problem right now. I'm going to sleep."

Seaspray, Sean G, and Dave, after considering for a moment, join me in grabbing some well-deserved, side-of-the-road shut-eye. Before nodding off, Dave gives us the Danny Glover classic line, "I'm getting too old for this shit."

I hear something. My eyes pop open. I see light. *A car!* I jump up and as it rolls toward us, I run out into the street and try to flag it down. The driver, apparently not impressed with a chimp-shaped man with no shoes running at his vehicle, swerves out of the way and keeps driving.

"Maybe he doesn't watch *Hunting Hitler*," a sleepy Seaspray chimes in from out of nowhere. I do not give him the satisfaction of acknowledging his comment. I still feel exhausted, but the edge is off. I scan the horizon. I see more lights! There's another car coming.

Once again, I try to flag the vehicle down. This guy stops. I explain our situation. He waves us in and we cram ourselves into his vehicle.

When we get into the city, we grab a couple of hotel rooms and share them for the couple of hours we have left before we catch our morning flight back to UAE.

———

Nick and I were planning on staying here longer, but once the U.S. government pulled out of Afghanistan completely, there was no longer an easy way into the country from the Emirates, so after a day of recovery, Sean G and Santa 6 have a new mission for us: We need to help get some of these refugees out of here.

After ten days of constant operations, this amazing twelve-man team evacuated over 12,000 American citizens, permanent residents, and Afghan refugees, including 8,911 personnel we moved to the UAE, and another 3,200 we moved elsewhere at the request of the State Department. Our evacuations represented 10.2 percent of every soul that left Kabul. Only the U.S. government did more, and no other private entity came close.

I don't know if it was divine intervention, cosmic luck, or unbridled determination, but I strongly believe the right twelve guys (and the right woman back stateside) came together to make this happen. Chad was the spark. Santa 6 was the structure. Joe was the mechanism. Sean G and Seaspray were the scalpel. The rest of us fell into place and worked. Twelve other dudes with our résumés might have spent a lot of time getting into pissing contests for dominance. It never happened and that's why we were so good. No matter where life takes us, I will always be thankful for this team. It was magic.

But now we have to get working on the next phase, and for that, Nick and I, with permission and approval from the State Department, are heading to Albania with 300 Afghans. A nonprofit by the name of the Open Society Foundations, which is funded by George Soros, and another—SolidarityNow, which also has ties to Soros—are paying for their resettlement in Albania, either with the intention of eventually coming to America or staying there if they choose.

While Soros is substantially left of my political comfort zone, this is good, solid work, and we're thankful for the assistance. So, less than twenty-four hours after I stepped foot back in the Emirates, I am leaving their incredible hospitality and generosity (and delicious lamb meatballs and hummus), and I, along with Nick, Chad, and Joe, are heading to Albania.

As a parting gift, Santa 6 lent me a book: *The USAID Humanitarian Guide to Crisis and Disaster Response.* "That'll help," he says.

"I'll read it on the plane, man. Thanks!"

We arrive after midnight in Albania and there are press everywhere, as well as representatives from SolidarityNow and the U.S. Embassy. The Lieutenant Colonel from the consulate helps us pull our bags off the plane and skip the line and walk right up to the gate to leave the airport.

We walk up to get our passports stamped by the customs agent, but he just waves us through.

"Man, I know it is convenient now, but I wonder if this will bite us in the ass in Greece," Nick wonders aloud. Joe and Chad are on the ground for a meeting in the morning, and then a quick turn back to UAE, but Nick and I are spending the morning with the U.S. Consulate to Albania, and then the day with Lauren Silber of the Open Society Project, before driving to Athens the next day to catch a flight back to the U.S. We're hoping the consulate, the Open Society Project, and SolidarityNow have an appetite to take on more refugees.

It's late enough that there aren't really any restaurants open, but we manage to find some pizza. The four of us scarf it down and say our goodbyes. We hit the hay, planning on meeting LTC Erol Munir in the morning for breakfast. It's already 3:00 a.m.

After about four hours of sleep, we wake up at 7:00 a.m. to meet him at 8:00 a.m., but happily there is a WhatsApp message from him saying he is running late and that he will meet us closer to nine instead. This gives us an extra ninety minutes to sleep, which at this point is a gift. When he arrives, Erol gives us the lay of the land: who to talk to, the cost to house people here, the concerns of the government toward refugees. He has his shit together and it's great information to have going into the day.

Next up is our meeting with Laura Silber. She is staying at the same hotel that we're staying in and her car is picking us up and bringing us to the seaside resort where the refugees have been brought. The car ride is interesting. Laura is a whip-smart New Yorker with a lot of probing questions. I don't think there's anything that she would be surprised by or that she couldn't handle, but I also have this feeling she is looking at Nick and me like lions or gorillas on the other side of a cage.

Her questions to us are all political ones, giving us the litmus test to determine if we are good guys or bad guys or what based on her worldview. She covers everything from guns to Trump to vaccines to you name it. Sometimes she nods along with a smile. Other times I see her almost grimace when I answer, not so much in pain, but more of a "How can he be so misguided?" sort of way.

Nick and I, being us, ask her how bad we failed the test, and whether she's going to try to kill us. She laughs. "There's no test!"

"Yes, there is," I reply.

"We definitely just got tested," Nick adds.

"Okay, there's a test," she admits. "You guys didn't quite pass, but you're smart and I like you, so I can work with it!" She's very smart and very good at what she does. This might be an interesting day.

We finally arrive at the resort. It's gorgeous. It's truly beautiful and they have spared no expense. It's surreal. The Mediterranean is lapping up against the beach, and there's a tiki-style bar and a real Italian pizza place sitting right on it. The buildings where the Afghans are staying are gorgeous. There's a huge courtyard filled with soft grass and trees and there are tons of children playing inside. Lauren introduces us to Domniki Georgopoulou, a member of her sister nonprofit, SolidarityNow. Domniki is from Greece and is the Project Coordinator for SolidarityNow in this region. She's a Harvard graduate with a Globed Erasmus Mundus Master's Degree. We have now established once again that we are the dumb ones.

Laura lets us know she has to go meet Alex, whoever that is, and Domniki is going to give us the tour. She walks us over to the courtyard and we see the kids that we brought in last night—the kids that we put on our planes in Kabul. The same kids that lived in fear outside the gates and slept on the hot tarmac hoping we'd find a plane for them. The same kids who had likely seen several people killed or beaten on the journey that brought them here. These same kids were now playing, running, and laughing at a resort!

SolidarityNow had already hired teachers who spoke their language. These kids were already learning. The exercise for the day had been to "draw the ideal village." Domniki explains that the teachers do this to see if any of the kids are potentially suffering from post-traumatic stress or other traumas. All of the villages were beautiful and colorful, like the stuff you'd see happy American kindergartners draw.

I feel tears hit the corners of my eyes and I keep my composure. Nick and I film them playing for a minute and then just sit down on a picnic table and watch them for a while. We upload the pictures to the other ten guys so they can see the fruits of their labor in action. It's an awesome moment.

After a while of chatting with Domniki, Laura comes back and tells us she wants to introduce us to Alex and the Mayor of Tirana, Albania's capital, Erion Veliaj. *Wow, pretty cool that the Mayor wants to meet us.*

We walk over to a table near the beach. The Mayor is a tall, good-looking dude, with a lot of charisma. He's warm and kind to us, but he's not here to see us. He's here to see this Alex dude. I case him quickly. Alex's watch is nicer than most cars. He is not moved by people easily. *This guy comes from money—lots of money.* He's got two security personnel. One's armed. One isn't. One's pretty good. One isn't.

"Hi, I'm Tim Kennedy," I say.

"Nick Palmisciano, nice to meet you," Nick adds.

He makes eye contact for a second and says, "Hey, guys, I'm Alex," and goes back to talking to the Mayor.

At some point, I realize this is Alex Soros, George Soros's kid. Nick does as well. *Well, this is interesting.* They excuse themselves to another table for a private conversation, while Domniki keeps us company. She's good company: genuine—a "change the world" idealist like we were fifteen-to-twenty years ago. These guys are lucky to have her. We kill a pizza from the pizza place together while they have their meeting.

Finally, Laura returns and asks if we want to ride back with Alex so we can get some time with him. "Whatever works for you," I answer. I'm realizing this guy must live a life where everyone wants something from him. I don't want anything at all unless he wants to fund some more refugees. *Hell, I kind of want to be a refugee if these are the digs.*

We get into the van with Alex, his friend Zac, who is sporting a tracksuit of sorts, Laura, and the security guy with the gun. The other security guy drives. I decide to break the ice. "This guy's pretty good. You should keep him on as your security guy."

That makes everyone look at me.

"But you should know we'd kill all of you if we wanted to. I'd grab him and get his gun. Nick would watch my back until I had it, and probably take Zac because he's closest. No one else is armed, and none of you are fighters. And then . . . boom! This is over."

"Jesus, Tim!" Nick starts laughing and can't stop.

Alex smiles. "Are you going to kill us?" he asks.

"No! You're super nice! I'm just saying. We could kill you if we wanted to. You need two or three of him," I reply, pointing at the security guard who doesn't suck. The guy, who is very cool and used to be a British cop, agrees with us, but adds, "I know who you guys are, and I know you're safe. Otherwise, you wouldn't be back here."

After that, the conversation is more relaxed. We talk about Afghanistan, tell some stories, and bring up the refugee issues. We arrive at the airport. Apparently, it's time for them to fly somewhere—Argentina, maybe? We shake Alex's and Zac's hands. Laura gets out of the vehicle to see them off.

"Just to be clear, did you just sort of threaten to kill Alex Soros?" Nick asks, as he starts laughing again.

"No! I was just trying to tell him his security sucks and he needs better staff! You can't be a target like him and roll like that! But also, we could have," I say, smiling like an asshole.

"We could have," Nick agrees.

That night we grab drinks with Laura and Domniki and then Nick and I have a stellar dinner that Laura reserved for us in the Mayor's name. After ten days of running hard, enjoying a Wagyu Tomahawk steak was an extra nice touch. I allow myself one glass of wine with the meal (a rare treat, as I do not really drink anymore).

The next day we hire a car to drive us to Athens. Naturally, when we get to the border of Albania and Greece, they are super happy that two American dudes with body armor are in a car driven by two sketchy Albanian guys, and *we don't have passport stamps for entering Albania.* After a fun hour sorting that out, we get through and check into a Hilton overlooking the Acropolis. It's 1:00 a.m. when we check in and I am absolutely done.

"You want to walk out to the Acropolis?" Nick asks.

"Nah, man. I'm crashing. We have that meeting in the morning."

I crash. Nick goes for a walk around Greece.

Once again, morning comes fast. The meeting is with Domniki's direct boss, Antigone Lyberaki. Domniki recommended her as a woman we needed to meet to talk about the possibility of doing more work in Greece, and she was absolutely correct. On a trip full of impressive women with gravitas, Antigone takes the cake. She's no-nonsense, charming, and smart. She spent years in the Greek Parliament. Her uncle is the Prime Minister of Greece. She's a force to be reckoned with.

She cuts right to it. The Greek people have a tremendous appetite to help people, but they got burned with the Syrian refugee situation, were promised family units, and instead were given a lot of high-risk single males, who have caused problems. If we can send women and children or full families, she believes Greece will support a group of up to 1,000 refugees. We report this information back to Sean G and Santa 6.

With our final mission complete, Nick and I race to the airport and get on our flight to Atlanta, Georgia. Within thirty minutes of being on the plane, Nick passes out, and for once, I cannot fall asleep.

Ideas are racing around my head. In the last ten days, I've experienced loss, death, fear, suffering, success, failure, sadness, and joy. I've saved women and children. I've saved our allies. I also left thousands more behind, including 300 orphans, 100 Christians, and almost 70 American citizens. I've pushed my body and mind to the limit. I've also met with NGOs and politicians in three countries and been asked to negotiate to improve the lives of thousands of people. I've bonded with amazing veterans in Seaspray, Sean G, Santa 6, Joe Robert, and Sean Lee. I came through for my friend Chad, who is so fundamentally happy Aziz is safe. I've met global power players and let them know they could die at my hand. This has been a wild ride.

I look over at Nick. He looks battered. He's the same good-natured idealist I met fifteen years ago, but he's earned some scars. Divorce from his first wife hurt him badly. Being a single dad changed him. Ranger Up almost died, not once, but twice. He's emptied his 401(k) to save it. He's been screwed over. He's had money stolen from him. He's had people he devoted time and effort to turn on him in the worst ways possible. But there he is. Still positive. Still fighting the fight.

Come to think of it, all my friends are scarred. Shane, Justin, Af—they have not been aged by time as much as they have been by experience, risk, bad decisions, and good decisions gone bad. They've overcome so much adversity that to me sometimes, their lives don't even seem real. They've been forged by hard experiences—most they sought, some that were foisted upon them.

And then I come back to my life. I think about my own trials, and the scars that came with them. My thoughts finally land on that moment all those years ago standing on that beach. I had failures stacked against me: two women pregnant, possible HIV, kicked off the police force, and a host of other problems. It seemed like the end of the world. Those challenges seemed impossible to overcome.

Now, that night in the ocean is a blip on the radar; it doesn't matter except as the impetus to finally get off my ass and attack life. Those two pregnant women gave me Sabrina and Julia, my first two reasons to be a better man. Those girls have given me nothing but joy and pride. Being kicked off the force created a situation where I had to come to terms with my shortcomings: I didn't fail because life was unfair. I failed because I was a cocky asshole who made poor decisions. Without that failure, I would never be a Green Beret. I would never have found my calling. I would never have reached my potential.

Thank God for those failures and that night.

The guy standing on that beach looked at life as a scorecard that you win or lose. He thought failure was the end.

He was an idiot.

The guy in Iraq who got beaten up for not being a team player couldn't have succeeded in the rescue effort I just undertook with this amazing team. He would have wanted to lead it—to show everyone how good *he* was instead of contributing to the group effort.

He was an idiot.

But it's okay that he was an idiot.

In the Army, when you graduate from being a soldier to a noncommissioned officer, you earn the title of "Sergeant." In that moment, you earn your stripes, the upward-facing rockers that affix to your uniform. Those stripes are the symbol that shows you are a leader—that you assume responsibility for yourself and those around you.

It took me a lot to get there. It's been a hard road. And every step of the way—every additional rank, every additional accomplishment, every great success—has required more of me. I have had to sacrifice more, suffer more, and yes, fail more.

Failure isn't final. It's necessary. It's the fuel that allows you to advance, to succeed.

To earn those stripes, you need to earn those scars first.

I take a deep breath. In through the nose and out through the mouth, pulling my stomach to the back of my spine. My mind is now calm.

My eyes feel heavy, and I lean back into my seat. When I wake up in Atlanta, it will be my birthday and I will be forty-two years old. I'm excited. This is the beginning of a whole new amazing year of failure and suffering.

I can't wait to get started.

AFTERWORD

May 2022

The air, warm this time of year in most of the country, had an extra chill from the lack of vegetation. Months of shelling had turned what was previously a beautiful Ukrainian valley into a desolate and sad place.

The whine of the drone ignited my fight or flight response, kicking off a daisy chain of electrical explosions in my nervous system. My body tingled with adrenaline. *Is it ours? Is it theirs? Even if it is ours, do they know who we are?*

Drones are not new to the battlefield, but these aren't Predators or Reapers. These are the kind regular people can buy at the store—the ones kids buy for fun and videographers buy to film. Except now when you hit the camera record button, instead of capturing video, these have been fashioned to drop grenades or explosives.

These drone attacks had become more and more of a problem for both sides. If a drone was in the air, the pucker factor immediately went from a normal "I'm at war and people want to kill me" seven out of ten to an eleven. This was true not only because they had become more successful as of late, but because you had no way of telling whose side they were on or what their intentions were until it was essentially too late.

A few days ago, while delivering medical supplies to the front with Sea-spray, a Ukrainian Special Forces Unit showed me how they made them so effective. The problem they had been having is that if a drone was high enough when it dropped its charge, the charge, be it a grenade or something else, tumbled. That tumbling led to missed targets. So the guys decided they needed to stabilize the charge. They tried a lot of different things, but in the end, they found that a Red Bull can was the exact right size to clamp on to their cylindrical grenades. Then they'd cut the back size of the can into fins to stabilize the grenade. They joked with us that Red Bull "gives you wings." I laughed. Dark humor rules the battlefield. But I knew it wouldn't be funny to the Russian on the other side of the charge who would be screaming in agony if he was lucky, and would never scream again if he wasn't. Nor would it be funny to his mother and father, who would never see him again, at least not whole.

I didn't think about things like this as a young man, but I do all the time now. I've been in enough war zones to know that it's never the bill of goods that you're sold on television. It's never what the politicians are telling you. It's always young men dying to give old men something they want: money, power, or pride. And in the case of Ukraine, it's far worse.

These people considered each other blood not long ago. Even after Ukraine became its own nation, ties were close. Intermarriage was common. Both Russian and Ukrainian were spoken freely on both sides of the border. Not now. Vladimir Putin and the evil cowards who serve him have ruined that for generations—maybe forever. People don't forget the loss of a son, of a daughter, of a parent, of a friend. Those wounds don't heal. What's left is a need for Vengeance.

As I'm writing this, the official number of casualties in Ukraine is just over 500,000, with 300,000 of those belonging to Russia and the rest to Ukraine. Based on what I've heard from those close to the issue, and what I have seen, I believe it's closer to double that. But even if we take those numbers at face value, there are ten times more casualties than the United States took in Vietnam, and we're halfway to the number of casualties the U.S. took in World War II. Ukraine's population is just north of 40 million. They've already lost 1.4% of their male population.

Death is everywhere.

The Special Operators continued their explanation as my mind drifted back to the present. Instead of tumbling, it would now stay level. However, if the drone was at even a slight angle, it would still fall off target. Their solution? To place the Red Bull finned munition in a toilet paper roll to act as a launch tube.

It was an ingenious idea and an impressive design. I wished they were using their brains for anything else.

Right now though, there was nary a reflective thought in my mind about war and sadness. My only wish is primal: for that drone to fly anywhere but toward us. It isn't quite close enough to shoot yet, but Vitaly and Maks, our Ukrainian guides, train their rifles on it, just in case.

Thankfully, after what seems like an eternity, it banks to the left in a slow arc. As it changes course, we breathe a collective sigh of relief.

The drone anxiety is a new wrinkle on the battlefield for me, as are the World War I–style trenches that I have encountered on this mission, but everything else is the same. The smells of burning fuel and rot and the thousand-yard-stares of the men in the trenches are old friends I wish I didn't know, but are so much a part of me that I will never be able to shake them.

We are between Kharkiv and Donetsk. The city of Neebro and the Neebro River are the beginning of the Eastern front, and we are about six hours past that in the area between the trenches that can receive artillery fire. In civilian parlance, we are in no-man's-land.

I'm out here under the banner of Save Our Allies, a nonprofit organization that Sarah Verardo, Chad Robichaux, Nick, and I stood up after our Afghanistan mission in order to be able to continue providing aid to our Afghan allies and any other people who needed help. Seaspray has been out here since before the war started, and we hired him to be our ground force commander.

Two months ago, our incredible Save Our Allies ground team, led tactically by Seaspray and medically by Dr. Rich Jadick, rescued Fox News reporter Benjamin Hall and recovered the bodies of Oleksandra 'Sasha' Kuvshynova and Pierre Zakrzewski. Their efforts were so heroic

escort us from the front trench (the fighting trench) to the second trench, where the support personnel are operating. Here we finally meet up with the medic we've come to see, whom I will call Anna. In any other situation, your average guy would call Anna adorable. She's a tiny, fit, blond girl with all of the delicate angled features that every Ukrainian woman seems to come with. But here, in this world, she is as hard as any man I have ever met. Her blue eyes seem gray, almost haunting. The bags under them are dark and sullen, but I can't shake the hollow look in her eyes—like looking in the eyes of a shark. There's no emotion left—just the mission. She's exhausted, but doesn't have the time to rest or recover, and even if she could, her dreams would likely be worse than her horrific reality.

"What do you need?" I ask.

"What do I need?" she responds. "I have no medical supplies. I have no food. Even if I somehow can keep people alive with the scraps of supplies I have remaining, I have no way of getting them out to a hospital. The few vehicles we have are always breaking, and when they are running, we can only fit so many people in them. Every day, I have to choose who lives and who dies. Every. Single. Day. So what do I need? Everything. What will I take? Anything you can give me. Anything."

As I stared into those eyes that seemed to turn grayer and grayer with every second I stared into them, almost like they were attempting to match their dismal surroundings, I knew that while we would do all we could to help her, it wouldn't be enough.

I was going to fail her, and there was nothing I could do about it. And even if by some miracle, Save Our Allies was able to help provide her with every single thing she needed, I knew there were hundreds, if not thousands, of Annas sitting all across the front lines in this exact same situation.

And try as I might—try as we might—we did fail her. We couldn't do enough. I couldn't do enough.

A year has passed since *Scars and Stripes* came out, and two years have passed since the events in the last chapter. First and foremost, I want to thank you for the profound support you have given me. I very much hoped that you would like the book. When you're putting your life out there for the world to see, unvarnished, it's scary as fuck. I knew for the book to be meaningful, I had to be honest, but it hurt to relive, and it was often embarrassing and painful to recount. Sometimes it downright sucked.

So thank you for making it feel worthwhile.

But as I have so often said, the journey is more valuable than the destination, and what I found was that I needed to write the book for me, perhaps more than I needed to write it for you. I needed to come clean about my failure, apologize to those I have hurt, and take a moment to appreciate all the good people I have had, and still have in my life. So thank you for that gift as well.

To that end, please know how much I really appreciate my longtime supporters. Some of you have had my back for over twenty years, and I cannot thank you enough. But I also want to thank those of you who hated me and decided to read the book just to hate me more, but begrudgingly acknowledged that while you still thought I had some work to do as a human being, maybe I wasn't a total piece of shit. I'm not even joking when I say that. It's really hard to unhate someone, so I know you had to dig deep. Thanks for giving me the benefit of the doubt.

But thanking you guys is only a small part of why I'm writing this afterword, and specifically sharing the story above. *Scars and Stripes* is a book I'm very much proud of—it shows how failure forced me to improve or die, literally and figuratively. And as all good books do, it wraps up a lot of challenging topics into a neat and tidy bow at the end. Many of you understood that even though the book ends with what most people would consider a success, it doesn't mean that the "Happy Ending" started there and I now have everything figured out.

I don't.

The last two years have been both awesome and horrible.

Awesome because I'm a *New York Times* bestselling author! You guys kept me on the list for almost three months. How cool is that?

Horrible, because immediately after I returned from Afghanistan, I was deployed to the Texas border as part of the Texas National Guard Operation Lonestar. I spent six months there fighting cartels, coyotes, drug smugglers, and human traffickers. We worked hard and did a lot of good to try to keep our border secure, but when the enemy is willing to throw babies into the river in front of you as a diversion, knowing you'll jump in the water to try to save them, so that they could cross their product two hundred meters upriver, it's hard to feel good about the work you do, or about humanity for that matter. Especially when one of your own drowns trying to save a child's life.

Awesome, because as I'm writing this, I just graduated the second class from my Apogee Cedar Park school and it's one of the proudest moments of my life. I loved every teacher, every student, and every parent that spent time with us this year. It was so incredible to see them grow and thrive in the exact kind of environment I have always wanted to build.

Horrible, because after the first year of Apogee Cedar Park, I had to replace my entire staff and almost hung up on the idea of owning a school entirely. I got everything wrong. I built the wrong team. I focused on the wrong things. And I failed my students in the process.

Awesome, because in the months directly after HKIA, our team, working with a lot of other great teams, was able to facilitate thousands more Afghans getting safely out of Afghanistan.

Horrible, because in the months after that, everything has ground to a halt as the politicians show little interest in upholding our oath to these Afghan allies, other than grandstanding about doing "everything they can" to help. Their inaction has led to all kinds of bottom feeders preying on the desperation of Afghans and the kindness of strangers.

Awesome, because the movie we produced about Afghanistan, *Send Me*, did extremely well and qualified for Academy Award voting.

Horrible, because the intent of the film was to show the moral injury the events covered in that film have left on our nation and our troops, especially those who stood post in HKIA, and spur our soulless politicians to action. Action they have not taken.

What I'm explicitly trying to tell you is that I haven't "made it" and I absolutely don't have it all figured out. In the last two years, I have split my time pretty evenly between brutal failure and fulfilling success.

Failure isn't the end, but nor is success. When you fail, you have to use it as a springboard to move on to the next challenge. The failures in Ukraine and our border were beyond my control, but I felt them personally. I witnessed the pain inflicted by the evil, and I could only help in the smallest of ways. One man cannot solve multinational problems. I don't care who you are. So I had to focus on what I could do.

I could help veterans reconnect in a meaningful way by founding the Heroes Jiu Jitsu program, where once a week veterans can train for free. I could open up my own jiu jitsu school at Sheepdog Response, something I've wanted to do since the first time I stepped on the mat. I could build a new Sheepdog Response Headquarters, where I could train people in an environment conducive to learning. I could spend more time with my kids, and plan more robust activities and enjoy my time with them, knowing that my time away from them is often fraught with danger.

Are these victories comparable to the other catastrophic losses? Maybe not. But I've helped hundreds of veterans and I'm on my way to helping thousands. My kids love our new adventures, where I've doubled down on being present for them. And selfishly, it rejuvenates my soul to see their happy faces. So, I'll take the wins when I can get them.

I ended the book telling you that failure isn't final. It isn't. But the converse of that is also true. Success isn't permanent. They are a yin and yang that complement each other. Failure breaks you down, and if you're strong enough and resilient enough to stand up, success builds you back up.

So if you're sitting around at a low point right now, and maybe looking around thinking other people are farther along on their journey, or that maybe things haven't gone your way, that's okay. This moment— the one you're living right now, the one that hurts, the one that is embarrassing—is the fuel that will lead you to your next great achievement.

But only if you let it.

No, that's wrong, actually.

Only if you take that fuel and make it happen.

TIM'S ACKNOWLEDGMENTS

While I hope I imparted something of value to you in my memoir, I also learned a lot—namely that it's really damn hard to write a book. So, there's some people I want to thank. I do not want to thank Nick. My gift to him is all the time he got to spend with me during the past year working on this thing.

First, I want to thank my wife, Ginger. It's very easy to be me: the person living all of these crazy adventures. It's very hard to be her: the person cleaning up the mess from those adventures, providing emotional support, keeping our businesses on track, and ensuring our kids are happy. She does all of that with tremendous grace. I love her very much for it.

Next, I want to thank what we call the Council of Dads. After Nick and I finished every chapter, our process was to send it off to my dad, Mike Kennedy, and his dad, the senior Nick Palmisciano, for editing and fact-checking. When we turned in our chapters to our Simon & Schuster editor, Amar Deol, he asked us if we used a professional editing service. We told him, "No, we used our dads." He then asked if they were editors or writers, and I told him, "No, my dad's a cop and Nick's dad is Italian." That didn't make sense to him, but it made perfect sense to us. So thanks to Mike Kennedy and the original Nick Palmisciano for keeping us on track.

I also want to thank Suzanne Palmisciano, Nick's wife. She's responsible for the name of our book, *Scars and Stripes*, for the cover artwork, and for getting us out of a few tight spots over the years earning her the title of "M" à la James Bond. I can't share all the details, but she could easily work for an intelligence agency, and I appreciate the help!

This brings me to thanking Amar Deol. When we pitched this book in late 2020, we were fortunate to receive seven amazing offers from seven amazing companies. We chose Simon & Schuster's Atria Books specifically so we could work with Amar. His guidance, attention to detail, and calm under pressure, especially when we told him, "Hey, man, we are going to blow your deadline, because we have to go to Afghanistan to do . . . something," was invaluable and exactly what we needed out of a member of our team. So thank you, Amar, for joining the team and remaining steadfast and unflappable, despite our best efforts. (Plus we made our deadline, anyway!)

Which brings me to how we landed so many offers in the first place. While Nick's good with fancy words, it took another man to make our book pitch fancy—that guy is Diesel Jack Media's Alex Pokki. Pokki built such a good visual presentation that the majority of the publishers we sent it to told us it was the best pitch they had ever seen. A tip of the cap to you, sir. You really go for it.

Thank you to my managers and agents. Leo Khorolinsky, you're the most honest Russian on the planet and I love you. Mike Fonseca, Jennifer Brasile, and David Larabell, you opened doors for me that I could have never imagined. You're the best in the world at what you do, and I will always appreciate you.

I'd like to add a major thank-you to my military leaders over the years. I've been very fortunate to have a lot of good ones that supported me. While I've been blessed in this regard, I want to especially thank Alex Ortiz and Theo Unbehagen. Good leadership is rare. Positional leadership is a construct that is only real on paper and not in the minds of those they lead. The two of you showed such profound genuine leadership and caring for those around you that I want to let you know I'm thankful for your rare quality of leadership.

On to the people who helped me live my life well so that I would even have the ability to have a life worth writing about! Thank you to my mom, for teaching me art, dance, cooking, and critical thinking, and for giving me a home I was always excited to return to. You are always with me, and I love you. Dad, I thanked you as an editor, but now I want to thank you as an example. Not every kid gets to grow up with a hero for a dad, but I did. Thank you to my brother, Nick Kennedy, and my sister, Katie Koenig, the first for taking me on adventures, the latter for tolerating all of the torments I put you through. I'm proud of both of you, and the nieces and nephews you've blessed me with. To my kids, Julia, Sabrina, Rollo, and Toren: I know it might not seem easy having Tim Kennedy for a dad, but the truth of the matter is that it's even harder trying to keep up with the four of you and all that you accomplish. I'm so very proud of each of you.

To Justin Lakin, thank you for having my six for longer than anyone without the last name Kennedy. I trust you with my family, with my businesses, with my life. To Shane Steiner, who would have thought that one of the best friends on the planet could come in the form of a dude who can go shirtless while sporting a floor-length fur coat, a blond ponytail, and a fedora, but damn, man, if you don't pull it off. Thanks for the workouts, the rolls, the long conversations, the loyalty, trust, and guidance. I don't deserve you.

Thanks to Joe Rogan, for your friendship and support. After our first conversation, I changed a lot of things about how I approached life, and I've never looked back. I appreciate your wisdom more than you will ever know.

To Chuck Liddell, thanks for taking in a kid who really didn't deserve to be around you, and for beating the absolute shit out of him. No beating ever hurt as bad as the ones you gave me, and it made all my future suffering a lot easier.

And finally, thanks to you. To those who have supported me, doubted me, defended me, fought by my side, or fought against me. To those who gave me scars or dragged my bloody body through the dirt. But especially those of you who have had my back over the years, whether it was from the early Ranger Up days, to the Strikeforce days, the UFC, or *Hunting Hitler*, I sincerely appreciate you.

NICK'S ACKNOWLEDGMENTS

When Tim asked me to help him write his book a few years ago, it was the rare moment when I was taken off guard. I've never written a book until this one and Tim can, quite literally, get any author he wants to work with him. I wanted to say yes because my friend asked me to do it, but I also had a lot of trepidation. You see, Tim Kennedy is a tough person to cover. He isn't one-dimensional. I've seen him quietly do some of the kindest and most generous things I've ever seen a human do. I've seen him fight some of the best fighters on the planet and come out on top . . . and on bottom. I've seen him coming home from war, and I've stood next to him as we pulled people out of Afghanistan. But I've also been more pissed at him than you can imagine. I've wanted to punch him. I've wanted to scream at him. I've wanted to shake sense into him. He's a very complex story, and as a neophyte writer I wasn't quite sure I was up to it.

There are two reasons I ultimately committed completely to this project. First and foremost, he made it very clear that he didn't want to write a book glorifying himself. He wanted to write the true story of his life, with all the incredible lows and failures that entailed. That was

ABOUT THE AUTHORS

Tim Kennedy is a Green Beret, sniper, and former MMA fighter. He's starred on the History Channel's *Hunting Hitler* and Discovery's *Hard to Kill*. Tim owns Apogee Cedar Park, a private school in Texas, and Sheepdog Response, a tactical training company. He lives with his wife and children in Texas. Follow Tim on Instagram and Twitter @TimKennedyMMA.

Nick Palmisciano is a graduate of the United States Military Academy at West Point and Duke University's Fuqua School of Business MBA Program. He served for six years as an infantry officer before moving into the world of business, creating the successful marketing firm Diesel Jack Media, and Ranger Up, which grew to prominence as the first military lifestyle brand. He lives with his wife and children in Chapel Hill, North Carolina. Find out more at NickPalmisciano.com, and follow him on Instagram @NickPalmisciano and on Twitter @Ranger_Up.